MANDELA

THE AUTHORIZED PORTRAIT

Editorial Consultants
Mac Maharaj and Ahmed Kathrada

Narrative: Mike Nicol; Interviews: Tim Couzens, Rosalind Coward and Amina Frense
Editor: Kate Parkin; Picture Research: Gail Behrmann

—————— ⟩⋆⟨ ——————

**Andrews McMeel
Publishing, LLC**
Kansas City

in association with PQ BLACKWELL

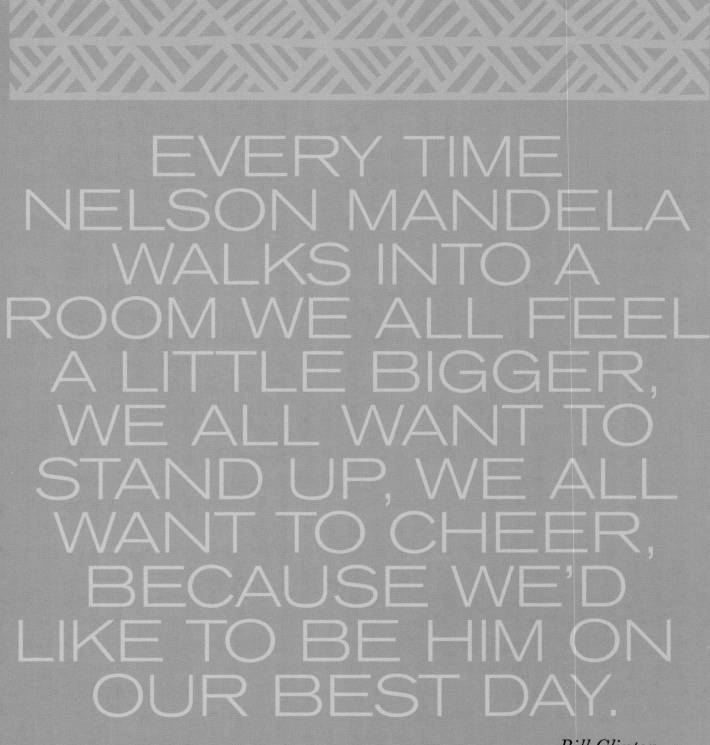

EVERY TIME NELSON MANDELA WALKS INTO A ROOM WE ALL FEEL A LITTLE BIGGER, WE ALL WANT TO STAND UP, WE ALL WANT TO CHEER, BECAUSE WE'D LIKE TO BE HIM ON OUR BEST DAY.

Bill Clinton

Early on the morning of February 11, 1990, I woke my daughter, Chelsea, and took her down into the kitchen of the governor's mansion in Little Rock, Arkansas.

I wanted Chelsea, who was then ten years old and knew who Nelson Mandela was and what he stood for, to watch his release. I felt it would be one of the most important political events in her lifetime, just as Martin Luther King Jr.'s speech at the Lincoln Memorial in 1963 was one of the most important in mine. So I sat her up on the kitchen counter and turned on the television. I still remember it like it was yesterday – Mandela walking slowly toward that gate and then waiting; the car; Chelsea, like so many millions of others, moved by the power of his unbreakable dignity and strength. As I watched him walking down that dusty road, I wondered what he was thinking about the last twenty-seven years and whether he was angry all over again.

Many years later, when we were both Presidents of our nations, I had a chance to ask him. I said, "I know you are a great man. You invited your jailers to your inauguration. You put your persecutors in the government. But tell me the truth. Weren't you really angry all over again?" And he said, "Yes, I was angry. And I was a little afraid. After all, I'd not been free in so long. But," he said, "when I felt the anger well up inside of me, I realized that if I hated them after I got outside that gate then they would still have me." Then he smiled and said, "But I wanted to be free, and so I let it go." It was an astonishing moment in my life. Not long afterward, in a moment of difficulty for me, Mandela sent me a message through now President Thabo Mbeki: "Mandela said I should remind you to let it go."

I am honored to be a part of this magnificent tribute to Nelson Mandela and his service. What makes his story so special is that he's a real human being. He laughs, he cries, he gets mad. He's got a real life. He cares deeply about his family and friends. His common touch and common sense make his greatness and his infectious optimism in the face of all that has happened to him all the more remarkable.

Bill Clinton
42nd President of the United States

INTRODUCTION

In 1988 Archbishop Trevor Huddleston, then president of the Anti-Apartheid Movement and a lifelong friend of Nelson Mandela, suggested that the world should celebrate Mandela's seventy-fifth birthday spectacularly and that it should be his last birthday in prison. Not bad when you think that two years later in 1990 Mandela would walk out of prison a free man.

Archbishop Trevor proposed that young people from all over the United Kingdom should go on a kind of pilgrimage culminating in what would be a mammoth rally at London's Hyde Park Corner in July, the month of Mandela's birthday. The response from the young people was phenomenal. Hundreds, no, thousands began marching from all corners of Britain and most of those who responded so enthusiastically had not even been born when Nelson went to prison in 1964 to serve his life sentence on Robben Island, the notorious maximum-security island prison across from Cape Town. For a quarter of a century he had been incarcerated. The world had not seen him, had not heard him speak for all those many years, yet he could have this extraordinary effect on people. He was already a moral giant bestriding our globe as a colossus. I was privileged to be at Hyde Park Corner on that memorable July day in 1988 when the pilgrims converged at that famous rendezvous. There were two hundred and fifty thousand people gathered there and we shouted out to Madiba across the ocean very warm greetings for his birthday and shouted to Maggie Thatcher and other Western leaders who colluded with the apartheid government that we in South Africa would be free, all of us, black and white together.

Mandela's stature in the world was already phenomenal. In fact many feared that he could not live up to what the world had come to believe about him; that he would disillusion us because he would be found to have feet of clay, to be all too human with his foibles and weaknesses. It was whispered in some circles that it might be better to assassinate him before he could be freed because he was so much more valuable as an icon in prison than he would be if it turned out that he was too human.

We need not have feared. When he emerged from prison people discovered that he was all the things they had hoped for and more. He had already whilst in prison begun the negotiations with the apartheid government that would lead to the demise of that ghastly system of racial oppression. His enormous moral stature was used to good effect in persuading his organization and many in the black community, especially the youth, that negotiations, accommodation and the willingness to compromise were the way to go for achieving the goal of our noble struggle: freedom and justice and democracy for all.

Many have sometimes decried the long years he spent in prison as wantonly wasted years. But they forget that when he went to prison he was an angry young man appalled at the miscarriage of justice that had happened in his trial and many other such trials before, penalizing people for wanting to claim their God-given inalienable rights to freedom and true citizenship in the land of their birth. After all, he had been the head of Umkhonto we Sizwe, the armed wing of the ANC, because he believed firmly that you should return force with force and use all available means to overthrow a despotic dispensation which had spurned nonviolent overtures to change. Those years in prison were quite crucial. Suffering can of course embitter the one who suffers. But in many other circumstances it can ennoble the sufferer. We were richly blessed that the latter happened with Mandela. The crucible of excruciating suffering through the rigors and tribulations of incarceration, the forced separation from his beloved Winnie and their young children purified the dross and he deepened his spiritual resources. He began to be one who could understand the fears and anxieties of his adversary and he grew in that time in magnanimity and generosity of spirit.

What a remarkable man he proved to be. He threw himself with passion and dedication into the negotiation fray, ready to concede this and that position, ready to parley even with those who might have been thought to be beyond the pale. He was deeply distressed by the bloody internecine strife between the ANC and the Inkatha Freedom Party, especially in what turned out to be the killing fields of KwaZulu-Natal. He was appalled at what appeared to be the collusion of the de Klerk government with a sinister 'third force' that seemed intent on stoking so-called black on black violence with the awful massacres on trains and drive-by shootings at taxi stands and bus stops. He showed he could get quite livid with indignation at the apparent indifference of President de Klerk when blacks were being killed, as if for him black lives were cheap and expendable, and he pulled the ANC out of the CODESA talks after the Boipatong massacre.

I saw how deeply he wanted a resolution to our crisis and a new democratic dispensation when Inkatha balked at participating in the elections, threatening to boycott them and refusing to go along with the majority at CODESA who had agreed to a date for what would be our first democratic elections. As archbishop of Cape Town, together with the then presiding bishop of the Methodist church, Dr. Stanley Mogoba, I managed to convene a meeting between the two leaders of the ANC and Inkatha, Nelson Mandela and Dr. Mangosuthu Buthelezi at Kempton Park. Mandela gave in on all the demands that Dr. Buthelezi made and even went beyond his mandate, as he confessed, to say he would if the ANC won the election appoint Dr. Buthelezi to a senior position, even make him minister of foreign affairs. All he wished for in return was Dr. Buthelezi's acceptance of the proposed election date. Sadly he left empty-handed.

How blessed we have been that he should have been at the helm at what was without doubt the trickiest and most delicate transition process, and he took our breath away with his magnanimity. Didn't he invite his former white jailer to attend his presidential inauguration as a VIP guest and didn't he amaze us all by inviting Dr. Percy Yutar to lunch at the Presidency, the Dr. Yutar who had been the prosecutor in the Rivonia Trial? As if this were not enough he then had a tea party in the Presidency for the former political leaders' wives and most of these were the wives of Afrikaner politicians. While we were getting our breath back he carried out a remarkable gesture. Mrs. Verwoerd could not attend the said party in Pretoria. What did Mandela do? He flew to Orania and had tea with the widow of the high priest of apartheid. Those who had dismissed and defined him as a communist stooge and terrorist began to have second thoughts.

He had the extraordinary knack of pulling off gestures that could, done by somebody else without his panache, have been awkward embarrassments. When the Springboks played the All Blacks in the World Cup rugby final at Ellis Park in 1995, Mandela strode onto the turf wearing a Springbok jersey with Francois Pienaar's number on the back, the captain's number, and the whole stadium erupted with ecstatic shouts of "Nelson, Nelson" and most of the spectators were Afrikaners. The Springbok emblem was controversial, with many blacks rejecting it as a symbol of the apartheid past when blacks could not represent their country on the same team as their white compatriots. With this magnanimous gesture, in one stroke he had rehabilitated the Springbok much loved and revered by white enthusiasts. He realized that the Afrikaners were feeling rather sore, having lost political power and thinking that they would lose even their cherished symbols. He had in that masterly stroke begun to get many who had rejected him previously eating out of his hand and after that famous victory blacks were dancing in the townships to celebrate a victory in a sport that was largely the white man's, indeed the Afrikaner's game.

He has a remarkable gift of making us South Africans feel good about ourselves. During his presidency this feel-good factor was at its peak. Almost all of us would look at a glass with some water in it and say, "It is half full." Hardly ever did we get to say then, "It is half empty."

One of his lasting gifts to South Africa and the world will surely be the Truth and Reconciliation Commission where the victors demonstrated a graciousness and magnanimity in their victory, where they did not rub salt into the wounds of their vanquished foe, where they did not engage in an orgy of retribution and revenge but decided to walk the path of forgiveness and reconciliation. We saw deeply moving moments when victims of some horrendous atrocities instead of baying for the blood of their tormentors showed an amazing generosity of spirit, often even embracing the perpetrators.

The world turned South Africa into the flavor of the month and we saw heads of state and other distinguished and famous persons flocking to South Africa, the former pariah state, the repulsive caterpillar now turned into a gorgeous butterfly. They all wanted a piece of this former terrorist who presided over a government of national unity and a national assembly in which virtually all the parties, big and small, were represented. One of his deputy presidents was the last apartheid state president.

Nelson's many conciliatory gestures had the longed-for result of making all kinds of people feel they belonged. Yes, he was the inclusive man.

He has been amazing in his selfless altruism and recognition that a true leader exists for the sake of the led. He has been a spendthrift of himself on behalf of others, rushing about to raise funds for schools and clinics in the deprived rural areas. Once when I had lunch with him in Houghton he opened the door to call out, "Driver!" thinking that I was chauffeur-driven. I told him, "Oh, no, I have driven myself from Soweto." He said nothing in response. A few days later he called to say he had been very concerned that I was driving myself. He apologized that he had not consulted me but he had gone ahead to ask one or two of his corporate friends whether they could do something about this unsatisfactory, in his view, situation. The result is that one company now gives a substantial monthly grant enabling me to use chauffeured rental cars. His concern for others is genuine and almost second nature.

His one weakness has been his unshakable loyalty to his comrades so that he allowed poorly performing ministers to continue in his cabinet. He has suffered grievously in his loss of Winnie. He loved her deeply and it was a very traumatic experience for him to have to divorce her. He aged visibly. Thanks be to God that he has found such solace, caring, and love from Graça who lives out her name as a gracious and devoted and beautiful person. I am glad that he accepted my admonition and made a respectable woman of her by marrying her. They are so obviously in love and happy. He deserves no less.

The world marvels at South Africa for three things especially – our peaceful transition in 1994, the TRC and Nelson Mandela, and he is by far the most admired and revered statesperson in the world and one of the greatest human beings to walk this earth.

God be praised.

The Most Reverend Desmond M. Tutu, OMSG DD FKC
Anglican Archbishop Emeritus of Cape Town

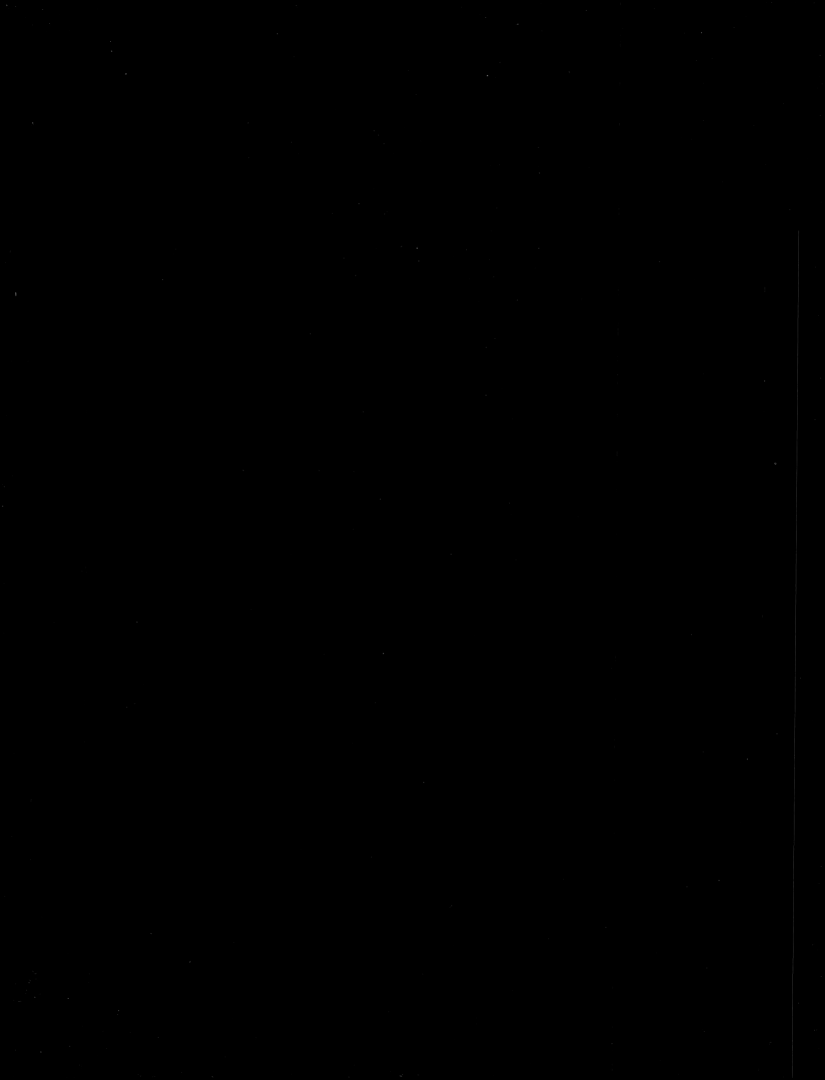

PART ONE

The Call of Freedom, 1918–1964

At the age of fifty-seven, as he sat in his tiny cell on Robben Island, Nelson Mandela was to write of the beautiful country of rolling hills where he was born. He remembered the rivers and the myriad streams which kept the valleys green even in winter. He thought of the majestic Drakensberg mountains to the north and the wild rugged coastline of the Indian Ocean to the south. He could smell the musty aroma of the *veld*. He was serving a sentence of life imprisonment; he must have wondered if he would ever see that haunting landscape again.

While he wrote, a guard paced the corridor, every now and then looking in. Mandela often lent him a copy of the Afrikaner weekly *Die Huisgenoot,* which ensured good relations and deflected attention from what he was doing. As the guard returned to his pacing, Mandela would return to Mvezo, a tiny village on the banks of the Mbashe River in the district of Umtata in what was then called Transkei.

Here his mother, Nosekeni Fanny, the third wife of Gadla Hendry Mandela, had her *kraal* of thatched *rondavels*, her land that she farmed and her livestock that grazed on the communal pastures. "Mvezo," wrote Mandela in his autobiography, *Long Walk to Freedom,* "was a place apart, a tiny precinct removed from the world of great events, where life was lived much as it had been for hundreds of years." Here he was born on July 18, 1918. In celebration, his father slaughtered a goat and mounted the horns in the house. He named his son Rolihlahla: literally, "pulling the branch of a tree," or colloquially, "troublemaker." Although Mandela never believed that a name conveyed destiny or that his father glimpsed the future, there would always be a poetic tension between his name and his life.

This "place apart," Mvezo, was deep in the heartland of Transkei, a vast land between the Cape and Natal, and the home of the Xhosa nation. In the nineteenth century it had been designated a "native reserve" after bitter wars between the British settlers and the indigenous people had ended in a brooding truce. In 1910 the land was absorbed into the Union of South Africa, but the memories of the battles and the kings who had stood against the invading forces remained alive whenever the elders sat down to tell stories of the past. For Mandela, it was a land as rich in beauty as it was in myth and history.

Left: Mandela spent his childhood amongst the thatched rondavels *of rural Transkei, the vast land between the Cape and Natal which is home of the Xhosa nation.*

His ancestral roots were buried in the Thembu people and the Madiba clan. According to custom, the line of succession to the Thembu throne passed through the Right Hand House while those in the Left Hand House – or Ixhiba – acted as counselors to the rulers of the tribe. Although he was a member of the royal household, Mandela was a descendant of the Ixhiba house on his father's side, while his mother belonged to the Right Hand House. His father was a respected chief, renowned for his strictness and stubbornness, but he was also valued as a counselor and adviser – an unofficial prime minister of Thembuland, a custodian of Xhosa history. He could be outspoken and rebellious when faced with situations he considered unfair and was not cowed by white authority. These were characteristics Mandela would later come to acknowledge in himself.

About a year after Mandela's birth, his father had a dispute with the local white magistrate and was found guilty of insubordination. He was deprived of his chieftainship, losing most of his cattle, land, and income. The family moved to a *kraal* of three *rondavels* in the nearby village of Qunu where they had the support of relatives and friends. It was here that Mandela grew up surrounded by family, running in the *veld* with his friends, herding cattle, moving between his father's wives who were all "mothers" to him, as the Xhosa language has no words for stepmother or half-brothers and -sisters. To the man writing in his cell, his childhood years must have seemed idyllic.

Although Mandela's father never wavered from his traditional religious beliefs, his mother became a Christian and had their son baptized a Methodist. The men who officiated at the local Wesleyan church saw promise in the young Mandela and suggested that he be educated. As no one in the family had received formal education, the day that the seven-year-old Mandela walked to the single-roomed school on the hill was auspicious. He was wearing a pair of his father's trousers that had been cut off at the knee and were tied at the waist with string. "I must have been a comical sight, but I have never owned a suit I was prouder to wear than my father's cut-off trousers," Mandela would write years later in his island cell.[1] That first day at school Mandela was given the name Nelson by his teacher. Her choice of name was probably arbitrary, although at the time mission-educated children were often named after British imperial heroes. That an English name was necessary at all had as much to do with the English bias in the education system as with the then reluctance or inability of most whites to pronounce African names.

Two years after he started school, in 1927, Mandela's father died of a lung disease that was undiagnosed but might have been tuberculosis. He had been ill for some time and, with prescience, had asked his friend Chief Jongintaba, the regent of the Thembu people, to take care of his son. A few days after the funeral, Nosekeni Fanny packed a small tin trunk for Mandela and the two of them set out for Mqhekezweni, the regent's Great Place. The quiet, shy boy was taken to the small whitewashed *rondavel* he was to share with Jongintaba's son Justice. Four years his elder, Justice was in every way Mandela's opposite: cheerful, outgoing, a sportsman, but also already something of a dandy and a playboy. All the same, they were soon firm friends. Equally quickly, the family "adopted" Mandela, calling him Tatomkhulu – grandpa – partly because of his serious disposition and partly because they thought he looked like an old man.

Jongintaba was renowned as a powerful and just leader, and a committed Methodist, yet he was also steeped in history and tradition. Mqhekezweni was regularly visited by old chiefs and headmen, and the stories of the great heroes of Xhosa history, and those of other African nations were constantly in the air. This sense of history as a living force and the pervading philosophy of *ubuntu*, that is "humanness," the idea that one's humanity derives from the way in which one interacts with others, entrenched themselves in the boy's forming personality. At Mqhekezweni, too, he learned about the coming of the white people and the battles that had led to the subjugation of the indigenous peoples they encountered. Jongintaba's Great Place was also the judicial center for the region, and it was here that the tribesmen came to express their grievances. On many occasions Mandela heard complainants being highly critical of the regent, yet always Jongintaba listened without interruption, and, in the end, sought consensus. This was democracy, a form of leadership that insisted on everyone's right to be heard, and the regent's self-control and fairness greatly impressed his young ward. Many decades later, as president, Mandela would adopt the same technique to seek consensus in his cabinet.

Of equal impact, if lesser importance, to the young boy was the regent's attention to his image. In his wardrobes hung a number of suits, and Mandela spent many happy hours pressing creases into the trousers. This attention to clothing, however, was not simply one of vanity; it was about dignity and self-worth and became a theme that was to resonate throughout Mandela's life: during his penurious days as a young lawyer, on Robben Island, finally manifesting itself in the celebratory Madiba shirts that became a hallmark of his presidency and retirement.

When Mandela turned sixteen, the regent decided it was time for him to undergo the circumcision ritual. It was a sacred rite of passage that marked the end of youth and the beginning of manhood, in short, acceptance into Xhosa society. Together with twenty-five boys led by Justice, he went to a secluded lodge in an isolated valley through which the Mbashe River flowed. In the preparatory days, the boys talked, played at stick fighting, and, in a symbolic act of daring that in earlier times might have involved a battle or a cattle raid, stole and slaughtered a pig. On the night before the ceremony, women from the nearby villages came to sing and clap while the initiates danced. The next morning the boys washed in the river's cold waters, wrapped themselves in blankets and paraded before the elders and the

Jongintaba, Chief Regent of the Thembu people, was appointed guardian of the young Mandela by his dying father.

Young Thembu initiates in 1930.

regent. At midday the old *incibi* appeared with his *assegai* to perform the circumcision. Mandela waited in line, tense and anxious. The old man approached and knelt, looking into Mandela's eyes. Then, with a single pass of the spear's blade, the *incibi* severed the foreskin. Pain burnt through Mandela's veins like fire. For a moment he closed his eyes, his head bowed, then he cried out, *"Ndiyindoda"* – "I am a man."[2] There followed a time of seclusion in the lodges while the wound healed. The initiates painted their bodies with white ochre, symbolizing purity. At midnight they buried their foreskins. According to custom this was to hide them from wizards who might use the flesh for evil purposes. On a sacred level, they were burying their youth. Similarly, when the seclusion was ended, the lodges were burnt to destroy the young men's last links to childhood.

At the ceremony welcoming them as men, Mandela received two heifers and four sheep to honor his new status. "I remember walking differently on that day, straighter, taller, firmer. I was hopeful, and thinking that I might some day have wealth, property and status," he wrote in his autobiography.[3] He had a new name too: Dalibunga, meaning founder of the council, the *bunga* being the traditional ruling body of the Xhosa.

Yet on this day of celebration, the main speaker, Chief Meligqili, cast a shadow. For the chief reminded them that although they might now be men, they had neither freedom nor independence while they remained a conquered people. At first Mandela felt the chief's remarks were wrong and ignorant. Years later he was to fight for their truth.

THERE SIT OUR SONS, YOUNG, HEALTHY AND HANDSOME, THE FLOWER OF THE XHOSA TRIBE, THE PRIDE OF OUR NATION. WE HAVE JUST CIRCUMCISED THEM IN A RITUAL THAT PROMISES THEM MANHOOD, BUT I AM HERE TO TELL YOU THAT IT IS AN EMPTY, ILLUSORY PROMISE, A PROMISE THAT CAN NEVER BE FULFILLED. FOR WE XHOSAS, AND ALL BLACK SOUTH AFRICANS, ARE A CONQUERED PEOPLE. WE ARE SLAVES IN OUR OWN COUNTRY. WE ARE TENANTS ON OUR OWN SOIL. WE HAVE NO STRENGTH, NO POWER, NO CONTROL OVER OUR OWN DESTINY IN THE LAND OF OUR BIRTH.

Chief Meligqili's speech to Mandela and his fellow initiates at their circumcision ceremony was to ring true for the young man in the years to come.

BASIL DAVIDSON:

Mandela came from a chiefly family and gained enormously from his family origins. Chiefs were persons of genuine authority and expertise who drew their prestige from a long pre-colonial history and that attitude is manifested in every possible way in Mandela. African culture came from consensus and consensus comes from listening to people, from understanding, sympathizing with and respecting them. Imperialism tried to destroy African culture. It didn't succeed, but for a long time the West's knowledge of Africa and its culture was zero. Now we know that in spite of their many cultural differences, most pre-imperialist African societies were participatory societies where there was accountability of rulers to the ruled.

All this emerges in Mandela's attitudes. Deeply immersed in the culture of self-governance and in the idea of consensus, he understands that you have to get agreement and that that has to come from discussion. Even his enemies recognized that Mandela had the power to exercise authority, which is very rare. Mandela believed he knew better but he was very wise and never threw his personality around. Nothing spoils him. He never gets above himself. He never puts a foot wrong, because he's instinctively a good man, a remarkable man. Humanity does from time to time produce remarkable human beings.

PALLO JORDAN:

In a sense Mandela is part of a continuum of Xhosa history. The earliest modern political leaders came from the Eastern Cape, and although most of them were commoners there were one or two, such as Dyani Tshatshu, who had minor royal backgrounds. It was Tshatshu who led the deputation to London in 1836 after the frontier war and persuaded the colonial secretary to reverse the frontier treaty which had been imposed on the Xhosa. Dyani Tshatshu could be called the first modern African political leader in that he was trying to act within the colonial framework, rather than outside it. So I think Mandela is part of that sort of continuum.

Nelson Mandela was certainly targeted by Walter Sisulu in Johannesburg because of his chiefly status. It was felt to be important to draw personalities like that into liberation politics. Mandela later told me he was also courted by the Unity Movement when he visited Cape Town. The early ANC had founded and established a House of Chiefs until Xuma, who was president of the ANC in the 1940s, abolished it with the new constitution of 1943.

Mandela is very much in that tradition of leaders from the Eastern Cape. The narrative is very much the same: herd boys, mission school, boarding school, and then Fort Hare and professional life after that. According to all accounts, Mandela's guardian had other plans for him – marriage and chieftainship – and he rebelled. Many young men in his position – especially in the 1940s before the 1951 Bantu Authorities Act, which gave traditional leaders more powers, higher status, and made it an attractive "career" – would have reacted in the same way, so there is nothing very unusual about the option he chose.

What I think is significant about Mandela is that he always sets great store by what he had learned and absorbed in the rural setting. It was a society in transition, but one which observed many of the old ways, the old traditions and which also instilled certain disciplines. He talks a lot, especially when he is talking to very young people, about

cultivating a strong sense of responsibility a
that age. He tells the story of being given t
must have been quite a chore with that old
t, making sure the pleats were exactly right.
the political movement and I suppose it's
think he started out very much as a Trar
strongly influenced by his nephew, K. D. M
time he got to Johannesburg it was more a

A Thembu initiate strikes a chiefly pose.

where you fell. If you are an old man and h
to do is to be buried with your ancestors a
ooking forward to joining them. He lays gre
a man of his status and I think he would wa
a family burial plot. First and foremost I thi
He's Thembu, then he's Xhosa, then he's S

f good. For most of the time such thoughts give me plenty
idents of my teenager days.

edroom dragging a formidable stick to punish Justice for
. Cenge, beside whose car we stood, jumped to the wheel
ok to his feet and vanished into the dark night. I was not
ig where I was. But as the Chief approached I suddenly
by. "I am not Justice!" I loudly protested. Came back the
t of the story.

en you scolded me for stealing green mealies [maize] from
was indisposed and you conducted the family prayers. We
ne and boomed: "Why do you disgrace us by stealing from
swer], namely, that stolen food was to me far sweeter than
But the way you timed your unexpected rebuke made me
vere listening, horrified by my infernal crime. Never again
but mealies from the gardens still continued to tempt me.
ke to recall in the solitude of my cell.

ere are times when my heart almost stops beating, slowed
Umqekezo and its people. I miss Mvezo where I was born
ny childhood. I long to see Iyalara where Justice, Mantusi,
of manhood. I would love to bathe once more in the waters
'35 when we washed off ingceke. When will I again see
institution which enabled me to see the distant and dim
Above all I miss Ma with her kindness and modesty. I
only now that she is gone that I think I could have spent
by. You know what I owe to her and the Chief. But how
owed to the deceased?

t from a letter written to his sister from Robben Island.

My dear Sisi,   April 1, 1971

Thinking about you and home does me lots of good. For most of the time such thoughts give me plenty of fun. I am able to recall many amusing incidents of my teenager days.

One evening the Chief stormed out of his bedroom dragging a formidable stick to punish Justice for having forgotten his portmanteau at Umtata. Cenge, besides whose ear we stood, jumped to the wheel and raced away at top speed, whilst Justice took to his feet and vanished into the dark night. I was not involved, so I thought, and remained standing where I was. But as the Chief approached I suddenly realised that I had been left to handle the baby. "I am not Justice!" I loudly protested. Came back the terrifying retort: "you are!" You know the rest of the story.

Then there was the unforgettable occasion, when you scolded me for stealing green mealies from Rev Matyolo's garden. That evening the Chief was indisposed and you conducted the family prayers. We had hardly said "amen" when you turned to me and boomed: "Why do you disgrace us by stealing from a priest?" I had a perfectly straightforward, namely, that stolen food was to me far sweeter than all the lovely dishes I got effortlessly from you. But the way you timed your unexpected rebuke made me speechless. I felt that all the angels of heaven were listening, horrified by my infernal crime. Never again did I tamper with the property of clergymen, but mealies from other gardens still continued to tempt me. There are dozens of such incidents which I like to recall in the solitude of my cell.

But why should I yearn so much for you? There are times when my heart almost stops beating, slowed down by heavy loads of longing. I miss you, Umgekezo and its people. I miss Mvezo where I was born and Qunu where I spent the first 10 years of my childhood. I long to see Tyalara where Justice, Mantusi, Kaizer and I underwent the traditional rites of manhood. I would love to bathe once more in the waters of Umbashe, as I did at the beginning of 1935 when we washed off ingceke. When will I again see Qokolweni and Clarkebury, the school and institution which enabled me to see the distant and dim outlines of the world in which we live. I often wonder whether Miss Mdingane, who taught me the alphabet, is still alive. I miss Bawo Mdazuka, Menye, Pahla, Njimbana, Mbanywa, the Moulanes and all the other wise and eloquent counsellors of the Mqhekezweni court. I think of Chief Jongintaba who made it possible for me to be where I am. He inspired me to set goals for myself which I hope will be judged to be in accord with the interests of the community as a whole. ~~My~~ our hopes and aims centre around this ideal. Above all I

Not long after his initiation, Mandela was admitted to a highly regarded school, Clarkebury, the oldest Wesleyan mission and the biggest educational center in Thembuland. A sheep was slaughtered at the Great Place to mark the occasion and Mandela took great delight in a celebration of singing and dancing that was solely for his benefit. The next day the regent drove him to the boarding school, cautioning his ward that the governor, Reverend Cecil Harris, was closely involved with the local communities and their chiefs and should be treated with respect. Intimidated, Mandela was ushered by his patron into the governor's study. Harris warmly shook the young man's hand and said he would make arrangements for Mandela to work in his garden, as some manual labor after school hours was mandatory. Somewhat in awe, Mandela nodded and released the first white hand he had ever shaken.

He adapted quickly to life at Clarkebury, performing so well in class that he completed the junior certificate in two years instead of three. On the playing fields his performance was, by his own admission, mediocre, but the hours he spent with Harris and his wife in their garden were happy and memorable. Most importantly, he came to love gardening and growing vegetables, a pastime that would distract him and comfort him during his long years of imprisonment.

Clarkebury, too, opened Mandela to a wider world. Among his contemporaries were young people from the distant metropolis of Johannesburg, and from other parts of the country and the neighboring British protectorate of Basutoland (Lesotho). Many of them he found sophisticated and cosmopolitan, which made him feel every bit a country boy, despite the new boots the regent had given him. Yet he was content with his lot. He believed his roots were his destiny and his ambition was to fulfill the regent's plans for him and become a counselor to the Thembu king. All this was soon to change.

Clarkebury, where Mandela received an "English" education.

After Clarkebury, Mandela was enrolled at Healdtown, a Wesleyan college in Fort Beaufort, some two hundred and fifty kilometers from the regent's Great Place. The town's name resonated with the battles that had been fought between the British settlers and the Xhosa in the previous century, and the Victorian college buildings covered in ivy spoke of a "privileged academic oasis"[4] to the young man. Once again the education was uncompromisingly British and flavored with a Methodist bias. However, while the religious tenets did not move Mandela, he was influenced by the strict ethical standards of the Wesleyans and their mental discipline of honing an idea to its essential ingredients. Both these elements, and the self-reliance demanded by life at a boarding school, went to fortify a character that was already principled and stubborn.

Healdtown further broadened Mandela's horizons. He became friendly with Zachariah Molete, a Sotho, which struck him as "quite bold" as he was venturing beyond the tribe. He witnessed a black housemaster stand up to the white principal and realized that white authority could be challenged. In his final year, Krune Mqhayi, a Xhosa praise singer resplendent in a leopard-skin kaross, matching hat, and wielding *assegais* in each hand, came to recount a poem that eulogized the Xhosa as a proud and powerful people. The poet's performance was electrifying: the themes of African unity excited Mandela, but, equally, so did the strident nationalism.

After graduating from Healdtown in 1938, Mandela went on to Fort Hare, the only black university in South Africa, and the alma mater of the revolution to come. He was twenty-one years old and dapper and confident in a grey double-breasted suit bought for him by the regent. For Mandela and his

RICHARD STENGEL:

When I was in the Transkei working on *Long Walk to Freedom* with Mandela, I would accompany him on his early morning walks. Each day he would set off in a different direction from the house, basically going back to places he remembered. Some of the villages were literally an hour and a half's walk away and we would walk into them and four out of five times the people didn't know who he was. These villages were so remote, the people were living in *rondavels*, they didn't have electricity or plumbing and I remember one woman saw him and thought he was a visiting headman, like his father was. Sometimes they might say, "I saw your photos in the paper."

Nelson Mandela speaking in Xhosa is a very different person to Mandela speaking in English. He has a very good sense of humor in English, but when he spoke in Xhosa in these villages near his home in Qunu, people were laughing so much you would have thought it was a comedian talking. Sometimes we'd go to the villages and a hundred or so people would come out. When I started working with him I taught him the term "ghost writer". He always introduced me when we went to these villages and one day he used the Xhosa word for "ghost" and did this sort of mystical ghost act and everyone was going "Whoo hoo!" and laughing and it was very funny, very playful, and ironic.

I remember once walking with him in the undulating hills near his house in the countryside. The building which was his school still exists and he remembered sliding down the hills on cardboard. There was a little stream there he remembered playing in. When he talks about being a country boy, that's not propaganda: he has a strong feeling for the landscape. He had a real African country childhood. They didn't have running water or electricity. It was very simple. There were no toys, except what they made, and the kids had to work; he worked as a shepherd from a very early age.

I think he was a quiet boy, a little in awe of his surroundings, and learned from his friend Justice because he was more outgoing. Nelson was more of an introvert. His real name is Rolihlahla, but he was in this little Methodist school and the teachers couldn't or wouldn't pronounce the African names and gave them all Christian names. They just told him, "Your name is Nelson" and he just said, "Sure."

Mandela's a real Anglophile. He loves England and loves English style. Growing up and going to school in the Transkei in the 1930s was probably like going to school in England in the 1870s: they were half a century behind. He had in essence an English education: he read Dickens, he loves all the pomp and ceremony, and he loves cricket and rugby. That was the model he had.

But his chiefly background shows in his style of leadership and in the way he carries himself. I think he watched how Chief Jongintaba Dalindyebo ruled with both power and respect and the kind of dignity with which he carried himself. Mandela tells how as a shepherd you lead the sheep from the back not the front, meaning that you have to listen to people and coax them in the direction you want them to go. It's a princely style of leadership, courtly. People always mistakenly say he's royalty – he's not, but part of the contemporaries, the university was at once Oxford and Cambridge, Harvard and Yale. It had been established in 1916 by white missionaries and black educationalists and was the focal point of the black intelligentsia. Nevertheless, it remained a small college of one hundred and fifty students, only a handful of whom were women. In his first year Mandela studied English, anthropology, politics, native administration, and Roman Dutch law. He took to the sports fields, excelling in the long-distance running and boxing he had taken up at Healdtown. Team sports were not Mandela's forte: he was a loner, in many ways self-dependent.

Among the first people he befriended was Kaiser (K. D.) Matanzima, actually his nephew from the Thembu royal family although K. D. was four years older. Unlike Mandela, his line descended through the Right Hand House and he was destined to be a king or paramount chief. Mandela hero-worshiped him and the two became inseparable. In fact, K. D. even shared his allowance with the younger man as the regent did not believe in sending his ward pocket money. Despite their friendship and Mandela's admiration for K. D., politics would drive them apart as Matanzima's later alliances with the apartheid government drew him into the Bantustan policy of separate homelands for blacks. When Transkei was declared self-governing in 1963, Matanzima became its chief minister. However, Mandela would always acknowledge that K. D. had once been his idol.

Many of Mandela's friends at Fort Hare were already politically active and, in some cases, members of the African National Congress (ANC). Invariably they were far more politically astute than the self-styled country boy. It was at Fort Hare that he first encountered Oliver Tambo with whom he was to form his legendary friendship. They met while teaching Bible classes in neighboring villages and the somewhat reserved young man impressed Mandela with his intelligence, his scholarship, and his expertise as a political debater.

Right: Mandela in his first suit given to him by the regent when he went to Clarkebury. After Clarkebury, he went on to Healdtown College and then to Fort Hare, the only black university in South Africa and the alma mater of the revolution to come.

Perhaps unsurprisingly given Mandela's ideas about fairness and democracy, the first incident that moved him into the political arena concerned his house committee. As there were no freshmen represented on the body, Mandela led a referendum to reconstitute the committee along more equitable lines. He and his cohorts were duly elected, much to the chagrin of one of the seniors who laid an official complaint. The warden of the college was called in to mediate but decided against intervening. "This was one of my first battles with authority, and I felt the sense of power that comes from having right and justice on one's side," the prisoner would write many years later on Robben Island.[5]

But the event that was radically to alter the course of his academic career occurred during his second year when he was nominated to stand for the Student Representative Council. A student meeting held prior to the elections agitated for a greater say in the administration of the university, particularly regarding their diet. The poor quality of the bland and unvaried food had been the bane of Mandela's life at boarding school. At the meeting it was agreed that unless the administration conceded to their demands, the student body would boycott the elections. Mandela wholeheartedly supported these motions.

When voting took place a few days later, in the wake of a silence from the administration regarding their concerns, only twenty-five students participated. To his dismay, Mandela found himself elected to the six-member SRC. The six responded by tendering a letter of resignation to the principal, Dr. Alexander Kerr. Kerr accepted their resignation and immediately announced that a second ballot would be taken in the dining hall at supper. The result was the same, except this time Mandela's five colleagues decided to accept office. Again, he refused. Kerr warned that if he insisted on resigning he would be expelled. He gave the principled student a night to reconsider.

Mandela badly wanted a degree. He felt it would open a career whereby he could restore to his mother some of the prestige and wealth that she had lost when his father was deprived of his chieftaincy, and he

also believed he owed it to the regent. Yet he had taken a stand on what he considered moral grounds. The next morning he informed Kerr that he would not serve. Kerr offered to accept him for his final year on condition he took up a position on the SRC. Confused, Mandela sat his exams, then went home to tell the regent he had been expelled.

Predictably, Jongintaba was incensed by what he regarded as Mandela's senseless act of high-mindedness, and instructed him to return to Fort Hare at the start of the new term and apologize to the principal. Mandela decided to bide his time. Meanwhile he was reunited with Justice. A few weeks later, however, the regent summoned his son and his ward to say that he believed he would not live much longer and wished to see them married before he died. Consequently, he had selected two women from respected families and paid *lobola,* the bride price. The regent was acting according to custom, but Mandela was appalled. For a young man who had been surrounded by strong-minded women all his life, and had had his first meaningful friendship with a girl while at Clarkebury, women were to be respected as individuals with their own ideas and hopes. He had enjoyed a few love affairs at college and university and was not prepared to let anyone select a bride for him. Furthermore, the young woman chosen for Mandela was in love with Justice. Mandela was a romantic; love could not be bought. Justice was of like mind. Fleeing to Johannesburg seemed the only option, although it galled Mandela to abandon his ailing benefactor.

Travel was difficult for black people in the 1940s. Adults required a "native pass" to leave a magisterial district, and a letter from an employer or guardian. They were missing the two latter documents but had to run the risk of being stopped by the police. Early one morning they left Mqhekezweni and made their way to Queenstown, a small town outside the Transkei where Justice had a friend who worked for a white attorney. The attorney's mother was driving to Johannesburg and, most unusually for a white, agreed to give the young men a lift. The journey took a day and they arrived late in the evening, much to Mandela's excitement at the dazzle of the big city lights. The woman drove to her destination in the leafy northern suburbs, eventually entering the grounds of a mansion through stately gates. The two black men were taken around the back to spend the night in the servants' quarters. It was a stark reminder of their place in a white world.

Right: The rush of black people arriving in Johannesburg looking for work in the 1940s spent hours in "pass" queues acquiring paperwork that would allow them to stay in the city legally. Once the necessary pass was obtained many ended up working in the underground gold mines (below) where conditions were dangerous and the pay low.

In April 1941 when Mandela arrived, Johannesburg was a mere fifty-five years old but it was the economic heart of the country and experiencing boom times thanks to World War II. To meet the increased demand for labor, the South African government relaxed some of the regulations that had restricted the movement of black people. In addition, two years of drought had devastated large swathes of the country, and ever-increasing numbers of black people were seeking refuge in the cities. But this migration was being closely monitored by Afrikaner nationalists who began to talk of the "black peril," and the need to keep the native in his place.

One of those places was the gold mine. The work underground was hard and dangerous but in high demand although the wages were meagre. As the mines operated around the clock, the men worked shifts and were housed on site in crowded single-sex hostels, bleak and prison-like.

It was at the dilapidated offices of Crown Mines that Mandela and Justice sought work. Some months earlier the regent had secured a clerical job at the mine for his son, and Justice now persuaded the local headman to give Mandela a job as a night watchman. The mine hostels were organized to retain the tribal hierarchies and links to the rural chiefs which greatly eased the recruitment of labor. Mandela, duly equipped with a uniform, had to patrol the grounds of the compound and check the credentials of those entering and leaving. On his first night he stationed himself at the entrance next to a notice that read: "Natives cross here." In the fifties, some wag amended it to: "Natives very cross here."

JOHANNESBURG WAS THE CITY OF GOLD. TO THE POVERTY STRICKEN IN THE RURAL AREAS IT PROMISED MONEY AND THE GLITTER OF AN URBAN LIFESTYLE. EVERY YEAR THOUSANDS OF BLACK PEOPLE ARRIVED AT THE CITY SEEKING WORK IN THE GOLD MINES OR AS DOMESTIC SERVANTS IN WHITE HOUSEHOLDS. BUT THE PROMISE OFTEN REMAINED JUST THAT, A PROMISE. THE CITY WAS DIVIDED: THE BOOMING DOWNTOWN AND THE SUBURBS WERE WHITE AND PROSPEROUS, EVEN THE WHITE WORKING CLASS AREAS WERE AFFLUENT COMPARED TO THE BLACK TOWNSHIPS AND SQUATTER SETTLEMENTS THAT BY THE MID FORTIES WERE RISING ON THE CITY LIMITS.

Left: The two faces of Johannesburg that greeted the young Mandela and his cousin Justice when they fled there in 1941 to escape the arranged marriages that Chief Jongintaba had planned for them.

Following page: Mandela spent several nights in one of these crowded mine hostels during his early days in Johannesburg.

Mandela and Justice had not been at Crown Mines for more than a few days before they received instructions from the regent to return home immediately. They had boasted of their exploits, never imagining how quickly word would get out. Faced with the regent's wrath, the headman fired them. Out of work but with no intention of going home, they decided to make their own arrangements. Mandela's were to lead him, via a relative, to an office in the city center where a man called Walter Sisulu ran an estate agency.

Sisulu was also a Xhosa although his father was white. At the age of sixteen he had left school in the Transkei and worked for four months in a Johannesburg gold mine. But the brutality of the system outraged him. After a series of odd jobs in various cities, he found employment at a Johannesburg bakery before setting up an estate agency with five friends. Mandela quickly warmed to the fast-talking, astute businessman who was well-regarded in the black community. When Mandela confessed his ambition to be a lawyer, Sisulu took him to see a white lawyer he dealt with for property transactions. Lazar Sidelsky, a partner in the firm of Witkin, Sidelsky & Eidelman, had no interest in politics, but he believed that blacks should be given a fair deal and agreed to employ Mandela as an articled clerk at no charge. The offer was

Left: Alexandra, "Dark City," one of the crowded slums on the outskirts of Johannesburg where Mandela lived.

Below: Mandela met Walter Sisulu soon after arriving in Johannesburg. In this photograph of Walter and Albertina's wedding in 1944, Mandela is on the far left while Evelyn Mase, his future wife, stands next to him.

exceptional: a black articled clerk in a white legal firm was rare. Sidelsky's generosity also extended to a £50 loan and an old suit which Mandela wore for five years until it was threadbare. With a job secured, he enrolled at the University of South Africa to complete his undergraduate degree by correspondence course.

Sidelsky advised him to keep out of politics, but Mandela shared an office with Nat Bregman, a white articled clerk who took him to communist lectures and multiracial parties. Another of his colleagues, Gaur Radebe, ten years older, flamboyant, outspoken, and a committed communist, was keen to have the newcomer join the Communist Party but Mandela was focused on completing his legal degree and devoted long evening hours to studying. However, he was struck by Radebe's no-nonsense attitude toward the white staff, particularly the way he chided them for sitting around like lords while "his chief" ran their errands. One day, Radebe would warn them, they would be rounded up and dumped in the sea.

Mandela had found accommodation in Alexandra, a township without electricity about nine kilometers north of the downtown center. Known as "Dark City," it was a crowded slum of small brick houses and shanties, noisy and often unsanitary. At night it was dangerous, the territory of gangsters. But it was also a vibrant cosmopolitan "village" made up of Sothos, Zulus, Xhosas, and Swazis. Mandela's room was a corrugated iron shack tacked on at the back of a little house. The floor was dirt, there was no running water; he had to study by candlelight.

His days here were hard. Often he walked to work to save on bus fares and sometimes went to bed hungry. He was embarrassed by his much-patched suit but had no spare cash to buy a change of clothing. Yet he was not weighed down by his poverty and he was constantly on the search for love, first meeting up with an old flame from Healdtown and then switching his advances – which were to be spurned – to his landlord's daughter.

Toward the end of 1941, the regent visited Mandela and the two were reconciled. When six months later the regent died, Mandela went home for the funeral. He spent a week at Mqhekezweni mulling over a personal conflict: Did his future lie in the Transkei or in the city? As much as his heart told him he was a Thembu, his head argued for his right to determine the course of his life. *"Ndiwelimilambo enamagama,"*[6] he decided, "I have crossed famous rivers" – and there was no going back.

High on the veld upon that plain

And far from streets and lights and cars

And bare of trees, and bare of grass,

Jabavu sleeps beneath the stars.

Jabavu sleeps.

The children cough.

Cold creeps up, the hard night cold,

The earth is tight within its grasp,

The highveld cold without soft rain,

Dry as the sand, rough as a rasp.

The frost-rimmed night invades the shacks.

Through dusty ground,

Through rocky ground,

Through freezing ground the night cold creeps.

In cotton blankets, rags, and sacks

Beneath the stars Jabavu sleeps.

One day Jabavu will awake

To greet a new and shining day;

The sound of coughing will become

The children's laughter as they play

In parks with flowers where no dust swirls

In strong-walled homes with warmth and light.

But for tonight Jabavu sleeps.

Jabavu sleeps. The stars are bright.

Shanty Town, Anonymous

*Right: A street scene in the township of Orlando.
The spirit of shanty living is captured in the poem
above about the nearby area of Jabavu.*

During 1942 Mandela moved from Alexandra, staying briefly at a mine compound before finding a succession of rooms in Orlando, an area of "matchbox" houses in what later came to be known as part of Soweto, a township some fifteen kilometers from the city center. Conditions were more hygienic than in Alexandra but Mandela missed the chaotic intimacy of Dark City. However, he was now near the house Walter Sisulu shared with his mother, a magnet for activists and ANC members who thrived on the political debate flavored with Ma-Sisulu's cooking.

Despite this attraction, Mandela's priority remained his studies. At the end of the year he passed his final examinations: he now held what he had most wanted, a BA, but it still did not seem enough. He enrolled at the University of the Witwatersrand for a law degree. Wits admitted a small number of black students each year, but they were barred from the residences and the sports facilities. Nor were conditions in class necessarily any less racially fractious. Some of the lecturers were liberals, as were some of the students, but Mandela also bumped up against overt prejudice. On one occasion when he sat next to a white student, the man ostentatiously moved away. In a similar vein, a senior professor, H. R. Hahlo, who believed blacks and women did not have the mental agility to master law, told Mandela he should not be studying at Wits.

Perhaps because of the ever-present threat of abuse, Mandela kept himself at one remove from his fellow students and campus politics, and was remembered as being unsure, cautious, and sensitive. Others found him arrogant and proud. Among his classmates were Ismail Meer and J. N. Singh, active in the Indian Congress and Communist Party circles, men whose names would be written in the annals of the struggle for freedom. He also came to meet other students such as Joe Slovo and his future wife Ruth First, both communists and virulently anti-racist, who were given to throwing lively parties. Through them he met other members of the Communist Party, and the lawyers George Bizos and Bram Fischer, who would come to play significant roles in his life and in the legal history of the country.

Right: These portraits show a more mature and confident Mandela. His time at Wits had introduced him to a new world of political and social ideas.

But if his six years at Wits were to open him up to a new world of ideas and political ideologies, they ended in disappointment when he failed some of his final exams. Mandela applied to resit the subjects arguing that had it not been for fatigue, hunger, and poor studying conditions he might have done better. But the pedantic Professor Hahlo dismissed the appeal. Smarting at his academic failure, Mandela left Wits without a law degree.

If anything, Mandela's life during the six years he was registered at Wits became increasingly hectic. He was holding down a job, attending part-time lectures, studying, being drawn more and more into political activities, and he had met and married the attractive, quiet Evelyn Mase. The two were introduced in the always bustling Sisulu household in 1944, around the time of the marriage of Walter and Albertina. Evelyn was Sisulu's cousin, and, with Albertina, was serving an internship as a trainee nurse at the Johannesburg Non-European General Hospital. A Transkei girl from Engcobo, an area to the west of Mandela's home ground, her lazy eyes soon captivated the tall, romantically inclined man who had already acquired somewhat of a reputation as a ladies' man. Within months they were married in a civil service. Their first home was a room in her brother's small Orlando house, then they moved in with her brother-in-law before acquiring one of the "matchbox" houses for themselves. They had no electricity and the toilet was outside, but Evelyn was house-proud and soon created a warm home with a garden.

A year later she gave birth to a son, Thembi, and the following year to a daughter, Makaziwe. The baby was sickly but Mandela kept his worries about her health to himself, enjoying his new position as husband, father, and host. A string of guests came to visit, yet in the tiny house, if they stayed overnight, the only sleeping space was on the floor. Not that anyone was deterred. Among his visitors were K. D. Matanzima (still keen to have his relation return to Transkei, a prospect that remained an option for Mandela throughout the 1940s), his sister, and his mother who came to help with the babies. Mandela thrived in the family atmosphere, enjoying the domesticity of helping with the shopping, cooking, and bathing the babies. Nothing gave him greater inner peace than playing with his children or putting his son to bed with a story. Yet these moments of family life were few and far between. Mandela the politician was emerging.

GILLIAN SLOVO:

My father left school at thirteen, but after the war South Africa passed a law allowing soldiers to go to university without the usual qualifications. So he got into Wits University, which at the time was a very radical environment, especially doing law. That's where people like Mandela had studied and they were part of a new, more radical breed of ANC members. There was a real feeling of excitement; that they could begin to change the world.

Joe and Mandela shared a friendship as well as a history of political and intellectual involvement. Because much of what they did then was illegal, including just partying – blacks and whites were not allowed to drink alcohol together – it threw all of them very closely together. They were beleaguered in a sea of hostility. I remember my father talking about how once, after they had both qualified as lawyers, Joe met Mandela in the street. Without thinking he went up, shook hands and greeted him very friendly and then suddenly stopped and looked around this Johannesburg street. Every white person had absolutely frozen because of this uncharacteristic sight of a white man and a black man shaking hands and expressing obvious friendship. Joe said it made him understand what people like Mandela lived through every minute of their day.

Although my father had the most tremendous respect for Mandela, I don't think he particularly picked him out as the prime leader in those early years. He saw him very much in the context of that whole generation who had broken with the past and understood what was needed to move South Africa on. In later years my father always said Mandela had exceptional characteristics – but so, in different ways, did Sisulu, Tambo, and Mbeki. They were a group of giants. They were the first generation to make the transition from the country into the cities and therefore had a much more modern take on life than the previous ANC leaders. Theirs was very much an urban sensibility. So Mandela was one amongst an exceptional group.

One of the things that does slightly separate Mandela is his tremendous charisma. Walter Sisulu was always very happy to be in a supporting role; Oliver Tambo's great achievement was to keep the ANC together during exile. But Mandela always had the ability to be a star. Perhaps also he stood out because in many ways he's an aristocrat and has that understanding of how chiefs worked with the people. He was a boxer and he married the beautiful Winnie and it was very romantic when he was in hiding and they called him the "Black Pimpernel." Part of the romanticism was forced on him, but he is quite a flamboyant character. He's got a fantastic physique. He looks like the sportsman he was.

Unusually for a leader, Mandela, like Tambo and Sisulu, has this exceptional ability to make ordinary people feel important. It's something to do with the nature of the South African struggle. No matter how highly educated any of that generation was they were still regarded as second class – fourth class – citizens. They understood what it was like to be looked at just for the color of your skin and not for what you can do. They understood what it was to be treated as less than human so they knew that the fight was for justice for all human beings. The reason South Africa didn't have a civil war has much to do with that generation.

Mandela had befriended K. D. Matanzima at Fort Hare. The friendship was very important to Mandela who had a great deal of admiration for K. D. The relationship suffered, however, when Mandela went to Wits, and, through meeting fellow students Ismail Meer, J. N. Singh, Ruth First, Joe Slovo, and George Bizos among others, changed his political thinking. Politics would eventually drive the two apart as Matanzima's later alliances with the apartheid government drew him into the Bantustan policy of separate homelands for blacks while Mandela and his Wits friends were working

In 1940 Dr. Alfred Xuma became president of the ANC, reviving a flagging organization and forging unity between Indians and Africans.

Life in the city constantly brought Mandela up against the harshness of racial discrimination. Even in the benign atmosphere of Witkin, Sidelsky & Eidelman he had experienced prejudice when the secretary informed him that new tea cups had been bought for him and for Gaur Radebe. The implication was clear: don't use the existing crockery. But it was not until the Alexandra bus boycott of August 1943, organized by Radebe, that Mandela first committed himself to political action by marching with ten thousand others protesting against the rise in fares. The effectiveness of the boycott, which lasted nine days until the old ticket price was reinstituted, greatly impressed Mandela. "I found that to march with one's people was exhilarating and inspiring," he wrote many years later.[7]

Sisulu, too, played an important role in shaping Mandela's political ideals. As a staunch ANC supporter, he believed that the movement was the only hope of realizing black aspirations, but it needed considerable rejuvenation. Founded in 1912 by a black lawyer, Dr. Pixley ka Seme, the ANC had adopted a policy of sending delegations or politely worded letters to the government whenever it wished to protest against racist legislation. As an extreme measure it would organize demonstrations but only reluctantly. Among its members were various paramount chiefs who believed that persistence and patience would eventually convince the authorities that blacks should have representation, say, in a House of Chiefs. These formal approaches were easily brushed aside by the government with promises that were no sooner made than broken. By the late 1930s the organization was effectively dormant, even discredited by its inefficacy.

Walter Sisulu, a staunch ANC member, played an important role in shaping Mandela's political ideals. He, Oliver Tambo, and Mandela became executive committee members of the new ANC Youth League, launched to counteract what they saw as an ineffective old guard.

In 1940, a doctor, Alfred Xuma, became president. He toured the country, reconstituting the branches and recruiting new members, but despite increasing urban support, the ANC remained conservative in outlook. It left those such as Sisulu, Mandela, and a firebrand named Anton Lembede, who recently had entered Sisulu's circle, frustrated at the lack of action.

Lembede wanted to form a Youth League within the ANC. As far as he was concerned, unless blacks mobilized, the only change in their lot would be for the worse. Mandela (and a number of others including Sisulu and Oliver Tambo) had much sympathy with this point of view. Xuma, however, neither agreed with the Youth League's Constitution nor with the strategy of mass action. Undeterred, the young men launched the Youth League in April 1944 at the Bantu Men's Social Center in Johannesburg, with Lembede as president and Mandela, Sisulu, and Tambo on the executive committee. The league's manifesto, while conforming to the ANC's Constitution, was forceful: it would be the movement's powerhouse on the march for political freedom. On the one hand, the manifesto challenged the ANC old guard; on the other, its rallying cry was African nationalism. In this, it expressed wariness of the communists, then seen as being dominated by whites. Although at the time Mandela considered himself a nationalist, in the coming years he would be torn between this and the non-racialism being propounded by the Communist Party.

Toward the end of World War II there were hopes that a more tolerant government might emerge. After all, the prime minister, Jan Smuts, had been a co-signatory with the British prime minister, Winston Churchill, and the United States president, Franklin Roosevelt, of the Atlantic Charter which advocated freedom, democracy, and the right of people to self-determination. The ANC old guard wrote a respectful letter to Smuts requesting a meeting and stating that they believed the charter promised them universal suffrage. Smuts refused to see the delegation. If this was not unusual, neither was the way Smuts dealt with the next political challenge. Seventy thousand miners – the biggest strike the country had yet experienced – went out on strike for better working conditions and more pay in August 1946. They were forced to capitulate at bayonet point and nine died and hundreds were wounded when police opened fire. Two weeks later the strike leaders were arrested. A number were found guilty of organizing the strike and fined or imprisoned.

Mandela and his comrades in the Youth League criticized Xuma for not calling a supportive general strike, feeling that Smuts had made fools of the old guard. For his part, Mandela marvelled at the bravery and dedication of the strikers, and began a friendship with J. B. Marks, a member of the ANC and the

Communist Party and president of the African Mineworkers' Union, which had organized the strike. One of their perennial debates was Mandela's opposition to communism which Marks attributed to his youthful ardent nationalism. If the strike impressed Mandela because of its spirit, the passive resistance campaign organized by the Natal Indian Congress was to influence his political thinking. In 1946, the Smuts government passed the Asiatic Land Tenure Act, which further restricted Indians from owning and occupying land, and specified their trading areas. The South African Indian Congress organized a resistance campaign that lasted for two years and saw more than two thousand people jailed. Because the action involved stay-at-homes, and voluntary imprisonment, Smuts could not send in the big guns. Mandela saw this as a model for future action. He realized, too, that suffering and sacrifice were a necessary part of the struggle. Although the campaign was restricted to Indians, the ANC supported them and eventually the two groups formed a pact. Personally, while Mandela moved closer to his Indian friends during the campaign, he remained convinced that Africans had a unique identity and political future. Years later, however, he would look back on the strike and the campaign as the beginning of a multiracial strategy to defeat what would soon become known as apartheid.

Early in 1947, Mandela decided to resign from the legal firm in an attempt to finish his degree. He reasoned that the sooner he qualified, the sooner he could practice, although it cost him an income. He was able to raise a loan from the Institute of Race Relations, but it fell considerably short of his budget. Evelyn was also pregnant with Makaziwe and about to take maternity leave, and would lose her salary. The hard times were just beginning. Makaziwe needed constant attention and the parents took turns to watch her through the nights. Nine months later she was dead, leaving her parents distraught and exhausted.

In the interim his comrade Lembede had died unexpectedly. Mandela was devastated. The position of president of the Youth League was taken by Peter Mda, a clear-headed thinker whose nationalism was not as strident as Lembede's. Also, his attitude to the communists was easygoing; he didn't see them as a threat, contrary to Mandela who had even gone so far as to break up meetings.

The changes saw Mandela become secretary, responsible for establishing branches and the political organization of the league. At much the same time he was elected to the Transvaal national executive of the ANC. He developed a loyalty to the movement (and through it, the cause) which would influence his political decisions and seriously affect his private life. In demonstration of this conviction, when his friend, Constantine S. Ramohanoe, the president of the ANC for the Transvaal province, defied a majority decision, Mandela moved to depose him. Although the call of no-confidence cut him to the quick, for Mandela the party was more than the sum of its parts. Similarly, he had adhered to the party's decision to boycott the British royal visit. When the Youth League met at his house to discuss their strategy, Mandela, constantly aware of his own regal roots, took another tack. He suggested that the monarchy should be respected as an institution, but his opinion was outvoted.

The following year the Smuts government lost the election by a narrow margin and the National Party came to power. White fears of the "black peril" now had a champion. The National Party's intention was clear and quickly expressed: the races would be rigidly segregated, every aspect of African lives would be controlled, and an Afrikaner state built on Afrikaner nationalism would be established. The racist laws that had shaped the country since 1910 were refined and compounded in ways that drew comparisons with Nazi Germany.

The Youth League replied to the government's hardline approach with a program centered on mass action. Mda, together with Mandela, Sisulu, and Tambo, tried to gain the president's support for their initiative but Xuma angrily showed them the door. At the 1949 ANC conference, Xuma was dismissed in a vote of no-confidence and Dr. James Moroka was installed in his stead. A strange choice, Moroka was a wealthy doctor in the conservative Xuma tradition, but he endorsed their Program of Action. On to the national executive went the Youth League hierarchy of Mda, Sisulu, and Tambo, with Mandela being co-opted some months later. Effectively, the Youth League now had control of the larger organization. Mandela, much to his annoyance, was unable to attend the conference. Facing the reality of his LLB failure, and the prospect of losing his recently acquired job at another legal firm, he had to celebrate at a distance.

In the new year, the government opened the offensive by preparing a bill that would become the Suppression of Communism Act. In protest the Communist Party, the Transvaal Indian Congress, and the Transvaal ANC first organized a successful "Defend Free Speech Convention," which then called for a one-day general strike on May 1. Convinced that the ANC should instigate and lead any united mass action, Mandela and the other Youth Leaguers initially feared it risked losing its identity in such joint action. However, the 1949 Afro-Indian riots in Durban and disturbances elsewhere in the Transvaal shook the leaderships of the ANC and the Indian Congress who saw this display of hatred as being inspired by the government's divisive policies, and joint leadership teams went into the strife-torn areas to restore calm.

The May 1, 1950, strike was supported by at least half the black workers in Johannesburg. That evening, under a full moon, Mandela and Sisulu were on the fringes of a march through Orlando when police opened fire and charged into the crowd on horseback. The two men managed to find shelter in a nearby nurses' dormitory, while bullets smashed into the walls about them. The police opened fire on strikers in Orlando, Sophiatown, and Alexandra. When calm was restored, eighteen were dead and many injured. The incident brought a new tone into Mandela's attitude toward joint action. A threat to one liberation group was a threat to all, he told a joint meeting of the executives of the ANC, the Indian Congress and the soon-to-disband CPSA. Together they planned a National Day of Protest on June 26 against the shootings and the act.

Ahead of the promulgation of the Suppression of Communism Act, the Communist Party disbanded, and reorganized itself in the underground in 1953 as the SACP. This move also propelled some of its members closer to the ANC and closer to Mandela. His Wits friend, Joe Slovo, would watch Mandela mentally wrestling with the legacy of racism that determined his attitudes as opposed to the "cold grey tactics of politics."[8] Yet he would not deviate from his beliefs.

He's Waking Up, Little Men, What Now?

Cartoon in the Guardian *(a left-wing South African paper), March 9, 1950, as Mandela and the ANC were preparing for mass action in protest against the National Party's increasingly hardline approach toward non-whites.*

Mandela was a key figure in the Johannesburg ANC office as it organized the 1950 stay-at-home protest. The pace was frenetic, complicated by his need to convince his employers that he was not indulging in political actions, and by the demands of his family. Evelyn gave birth to their second son, Makgatho, during this period, and Mandela had to juggle visits to the hospital with the demands of the planning office. It wasn't easy, especially when Evelyn told him that Thembi, then five years old, had asked her, "Where does Daddy live?"[9] The lack of time he had for his family troubled him, but was this not part of the sacrifice? The question would plague Mandela all his life.

In an attempt to relieve stress, Mandela went back to the boxing ring. This was a makeshift gym in Orlando where the tall, physically imposing heavyweight would spar for ninety minutes on most weekday evenings, not to fight tournaments but to keep fit. Boxing intrigued him: he viewed it as more about strategy than a display of violent strength. He improved his skills of attack and retreat, learned to keep light on his feet to protect his body, and paced himself to stay the match. "It was a way of losing myself in something that was not the struggle," Mandela would write in his autobiography,[10] yet he would come to use boxing as a political metaphor.

Although the National Day of Protest stay-at-home was not entirely successful, in working alongside Indian and white activists Mandela found his long-standing opposition to communism becoming more muted. This was probably less about a softening attitude toward the dogma and more about strength in numbers, but either way, the recently elected president of the Youth League was thinking differently. Evidence of this came at the ANC's national conference in December 1951.

It was a buoyant Mandela who attended the conference. He had a second son, and he had been working as a candidate attorney at the firm Terblanche & Briggish for a year which had eased his financial position. More importantly, he had received his driver's license and acquired a car, both of which carried status. For a man who had long been self-consciously aware of the figure he cut, the accessories were important. Given, too, his increasing political confidence and his chiefly attitudes, he was a man on the move.

Right: Mandela and Ruth First at the ANC conference in 1951.

Below: The 1951 conference demanded the government repeal six "unjust" laws, a resolution which was rejected outright by the prime minister.

Mandela headed into the conference discussions with vigor, proposing his usual go-it-alone stance, then, sensing that he did not have the support of the majority, did an about-face and argued for a united front. He received a resounding ovation. Never again would he deviate from this inclusive position, adopting it as if he had never held contrary views. His fancy footwork – not far removed from his adroitness in the boxing ring – showed an astute ability to read the prevailing mood.

The conference concluded with a resolution demanding that the Nationalist government repeal six "unjust laws". Those they singled out from the considerable body of racist legislation that had been written into the statute books since 1948 concerned the pass laws, the Population Registration Act (which listed the entire population in racial categories), the Group Areas Act (enforcing residential separation), the Voters Representation Act and the Suppression of Communism Act (affecting political rights), the Bantu Authorities Act (seeking to realign political and economic relations in the "reserves"), and a law on stock limitation. Disguised as an attempt to prevent overgrazing, this law would have further limited black property rights.

Once the letter was written, Mandela was deputized to drive the five-hundred-kilometer round trip to Dr. Moroka for his signature. Mandela enjoyed being out on the open road but his trip was far from uneventful. At one point he was involved in a minor accident with two white boys on bicycles. In the ensuing altercation with the police, Mandela upbraided a sergeant for swearing at him and almost ended up in jail. Late that night he was allowed to continue his journey but toward dawn ran out of gas. In the middle of the Free State's vast plains, his only recourse was to beg fuel from a white farmer. The first farmer he approached refused to help him. With the second he adopted a subservient tone, "My *baas* [car] has run out of petrol [gasoline]."[11] The ruse worked. The ANC's petition, however, received short shrift from the prime minister. He replied, in a letter signed by his private secretary, that whites had a right to preserve their identity and any threat would be forcibly suppressed. The ANC began preparing for mass action.

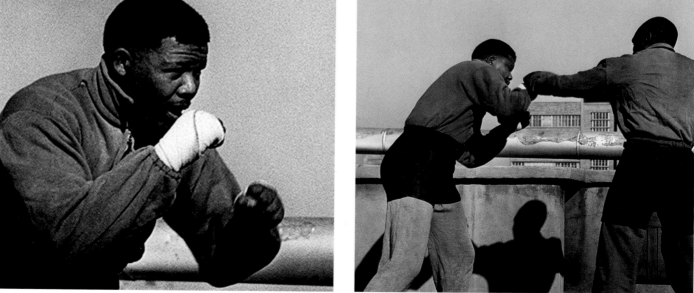

Torn between work, politics, and family demands, Mandela attempted to relieve stress by going back to the boxing ring. He was intrigued by the sport, viewing it as more about strategy than a display of violent strength, and the fancy footwork he learned in the ring was to stand him in good stead in the political arena.

remember being awestruck when I first met Nelson Mandela, superstar or a celebrity, but because he is truly awesome. What makes him so exceptional, what sets me in awe of him, is his tremendous energy and courage. He is uncompromising in his efforts to combat adversity and injustice, not just in South Africa but everywhere.

Our children and future generations need to understand that Mandela is not just another person learned about in history books. They need to know that his actions, his perseverance, his courage changed the course of an entire nation. He boldly, and quite literally, changed history. He is living proof that one person has the power to effect positive change in our world.

Nelson Mandela has always inspired me to think beyond myself, to think of people in the wider world as part of a common humanity. I am blessed by his friendship. I love him for what he has accomplished, for what he has been through, for his journey forward. He remains a hallmark of what it really means to give selflessly of oneself, which is indeed a gift for us all.

Above and top right: The Defiance Campaign – a mass protest at the government's racist laws – was launched with a meeting at Red Square, Johannesburg (also called Freedom Square) which was addressed by the South African Indian

The Defiance Campaign, as it became known, was to follow the Gandhian strategy of nonviolence. Mandela supported this as a tactic as long as it was effective – a stance that would allow him to advocate armed resistance a year or two later. The campaign had two phases: initially, selected groups would break various racist laws by for example entering Whites Only toilets, travelling in Whites Only railway carriages, queuing in Whites Only sections of post offices. In each instance the police were notified in advance. The second stage envisaged protest marches, strikes and industrial action across the country. The campaign was to begin on the anniversary of the first National Day of Protest, June 26, 1952. A few days prior to this, Mandela, who had been appointed National Volunteer-in-Chief with Maulvi Cachalia of the Indian Congress as his deputy, drove down to a rally of ten thousand people in Durban. After the Natal president of the ANC, Albert Luthuli, had spoken, Mandela told the crowd that the campaign would make history and stressed the importance of black unity, a united front of Africans, Indians, and coloreds in a display of mass action never before experienced in the country.

Back in Johannesburg and on the first night of the campaign, Mandela and Yusuf Cachalia, secretary of the SAIC, were unexpectedly arrested while seeing off a batch of fifty defyers who were breaking the curfew laws, and taken to the holding cells at Marshall Square, a severe red-bricked police station. The police hustled their captives so roughly that one man fell, breaking his ankle. Mandela's protests that the man needed medical attention were met with a boot to his shin, and the jail door slammed shut. For two days they were held in the squalid, dingy jail and then released without charge. It was Mandela's first experience of incarceration and he was appalled.

On day one of the campaign, more than two hundred and fifty people were arrested. Over the next five months almost nine thousand protesters defied the laws and ended up spending anything from a few nights to a few weeks in jail. Mandela drove around the country, encouraging people, recruiting new members, and sorting out parochial disagreements in the various ANC offices. In this he was encouraged by his new employer, H. M. Basner. During the first few months of the year, Mandela had worked at the firm of Helman and Michel while he studied for the exams which would qualify him as an attorney. Once he had obtained the qualification he joined Basner. Here he gained his first court experience, a stage Mandela found as compelling as the boxing ring and the mass rally. The irrepressible Mandela was also inundated with legal work, yet he seemed ahead of the game, even when the police arrived at the firm with a warrant for his arrest on July 30. His arrest was part of a national police operation that took twenty of the senior ANC and Indian Congress people into custody. The accused were given bail, and a court hearing set for September.

Right: Yusuf Cachalia, secretary of the Indian Congress, was arrested along with Mandela on the first night of the Defiance Campaign and held in custody in appalling conditions for two days. Standing on Cachalia's right is Babla Saloojee, murdered by security police in September 1964. He was thrown out of a seventh-floor window. Immediately behind Cachalia's left shoulder is Moosa Moola who would become South Africa's ambassador to Pakistan.

In August Mandela set up his own legal practice, a decision he must have carefully considered during the initial hectic days of the Defiance Campaign. And a decision he was prepared to keep even though he was headed for a court case that was going to demand time and attention. It took a certain vigor to go it alone, although such hard-headedness was part of his temperament.

The trial, which Mandela had hoped would reflect solidarity among the leadership, was marred by Moroka's intransigence. When, three months later, it came to mitigation of sentence, the ANC president complained to the judge that he did not wish to be associated with communists, nor did he believe in equality between black and white. To dissociate himself further he employed his own advocate. Mandela tried to dissuade him but to no avail. Nor did it lessen the president's sentence. All the accused were found guilty of statutory communism and sentenced to nine months hard labor, suspended for five years.

Any jubilation was ended by a six-month banning order, the first of a series of ever more stringent banning orders, imposed on Mandela and fifty other ANC leaders a few days later. He was restricted to the magisterial district of Johannesburg and unable to attend the party's annual conference later that month. In fact, the banning order prohibited him from attending any gatherings, political or otherwise. Technically, being at his son's birthday party was a violation. Nor could he be in the company of more than one person at a time; strictly speaking even sitting with his family was breaking the order.

The psychological impact of the ban was as trying to Mandela as the physical. The bars of this prison were regulations that could easily be broken. To do so gave a temporary illusion of freedom but after each "break" the invisible door clanged shut reminding him that he was not free. The more pernicious effect of a banning order was a sense that he was not only a prisoner of the authorities, but his own jailer. They had forced him to collaborate in their draconian measures.

At court during the Defiance Campaign Trial in 1952. From top: Mandela, with Walter Sisulu on his right; (left to right) James Philips, David Bopape, J. B. Marks, and Sisulu chat outside the courthouse while Bram Fischer speaks to Yusuf Dadoo and Ruth First in the background; Dadoo greets supporters.

Right: Fourteen of the twenty defendants at the Defiance Campaign Trial, 1952. Front row, left to right: James Philips, M. Thandray, Dan Tloome, Nana Sita, Maulvi Cachalia. Back row, left to right: Barney Desai, Yusuf Cachalia (wearing glasses), Moses Kotane, David Bopape, Nthato Motlana, Yusuf Dadoo, J. B. Marks, Ahmed Kathrada, Dr. Moroka. Those missing from the picture include Walter Sisulu and Diliza Mji. Nelson Mandela can be seen on the extreme left, reading

FATIMA MEER:

I first met Nelson Mandela in the early 1950s when I had just become engaged to Ismail Meer. Nelson was in Durban at the time because the ANC had called for a mass stay-away against a battery of laws that the Nationalists had passed and they came to organize it in Natal.

Ismail and Nelson were very close friends and Ismail brought him to my parents' house in Pinetown to introduce him to me. Nelson and Ismail always joked together about it. Ismail would boast that he beat Nelson to marrying me and Nelson never stopped joking that he had wanted to marry me but I preferred to marry a Muslim.

My impression was of this physical man, very handsome, but he didn't take me seriously. He and Ismail were always teasing me – you know, these patronizing attitudes you get as a young girl – and it rather irritated me that these two men were treating me like a child when I was a grown woman.

After we were married, Nelson visited us at our house in Umgeni Road during the Defiance Campaign. At that time his wife, Evelyn, was doing a midwifery course at King Edward so he would visit her whenever he came to campaign and they would stay in our bedroom. Evelyn was a very subdued person, a very private person. She didn't speak much; she didn't think it was her place to do so. She was a very gracious person. They were a regular married couple getting on with their lives and there was absolutely no sign of any friction.

The trouble started after Nelson went into practice with Oliver Tambo. I gather that Evelyn suspected something was going on between Nelson and someone in the office there. She really protested when the woman came to her house, and would follow Nelson around – even to the bathroom to shave. Then Evelyn blew her top and Nelson felt she had no business to object to anything he did and moved out of their bedroom.

He would believe and feel differently now. I went to see him recently and he was talking in a very derogatory way about the male chauvinism of the chiefs. And he once told me a story, which was self-criticism, of how he was waiting for a plane in the Caribbean. He said that he asked one of the air hostesses when the pilot was coming and she said, "Didn't you see the pilot? She'll be starting the plane just now." And he said, "Much to my shame I must admit that I suddenly had a fear of this woman pilot being able to pilot the plane at all." So obviously some time ago he changed his attitude.

Evelyn had resigned herself to the break-up of the marriage. She never expressed any bitterness. I think she accepted also the tribal definition of a woman's place and a man's place.

Despite the banning order, Mandela took stock of the year's events with his usual optimism. The Defiance Campaign had petered out toward the end of the year but he felt it had been a display of strength and determination and freed him and many others from feelings of inferiority when faced with the might of the apartheid state. Equally importantly, the only violence had been perpetrated by the police when rioting, unrelated to the campaign, broke out in a number of cities and more than forty people were killed.

Within the ANC he had taken over the presidency of the Transvaal province when the incumbent, his ebullient communist friend J. B. Marks, was banned. In the October election he stood against a popular opponent but won by an overwhelming majority, a victory he viewed with undisguised pleasure.

The outcome of the ANC's annual conference he had been unable to attend also heartened Mandela. The irresolute Moroka had been replaced by the more energetic and forceful Chief Albert Luthuli. Mandela supported the new president, regarding him as a man of patience and fortitude. He was also pleased that the leadership had decided to make contingency plans in case the organization was banned; he and the leadership sensed that the government was moving in this direction. Without a capacity to function underground, the new spirit of protest that had been engendered by the Defiance Campaign would be lost. To prevent this, Mandela was asked to draw up what became known as the Mandela-Plan, or, more simply, the M-Plan. His system of street cells in the townships reporting to area stewards and then to the local branch of the ANC was instituted with only modest success and its adoption was never widespread even when it did become necessary.

In November, Oliver Tambo, who had escaped the state's attention, went into legal practice with Mandela under the style Mandela & Tambo. Their offices were situated in Chancellor House, a small building opposite the magistrates' court in Johannesburg. The building was owned by an Indian businessman and was one of the few places Africans could rent space in the city center. Partly to advertise their services and partly to snub the authorities they emblazoned their name across the window. As the first and only legal firm made up of African lawyers in the country, they hardly needed to advertise: they were, as Mandela drily noted, the firm of "first choice and last resort" for black people. "To reach our offices each morning, we had to move through a crowd of people in the corridors, on the stairs and in our small waiting room," he recorded.[12]

Mandela and Tambo made an ideal partnership. Where Mandela was theatrical, the essential courtroom attorney, Tambo was quiet and calm, depending on his legal knowledge to carry the case. They were inundated with work. Musicians arrested for giving a concert in town without passes came to them, as did grey-haired men from the country whose families had farmed the land for generations but were now being evicted by white farmers. They saw women accused of brewing liquor in their backyards to supplement their meagre incomes; people who had to give up homes that now fell into white areas; those arrested for breaking the 11 P.M. curfew. Every instance was an example of the all-pervading injustices of white domination. Every case reminded Mandela of why he had chosen law: to fight for basic rights.

Mandela's renown in the courtroom became such that people arrived at the courts simply to watch him in action. His reputation even preceded him into the rural districts where people would walk for miles to admire this now legendary black lawyer. With his florid language, his quirky sense of humor and his ability to exploit racial sensitivities, Mandela had a way of winning cases and scoring points.

While defending an African woman accused of stealing clothes belonging to the white "madam" who employed her, he began his cross-examination by poring over the allegedly stolen clothes displayed on a table. The court was quiet while he studied the evidence, then, with his pencil he lifted out a pair of panties. Slowly he turned to the complainant. "Madam," he asked, "are these . . . yours?"[13] Embarrassed, the woman flushed and stammered a denial. The case was dismissed.

Despite these quiet victories, Mandela was ever aware of being a black man in a white man's court. He was equally likely to be treated with courtesy as with prejudice, even hostility. In one instance, a magistrate evicted him for not producing his legal qualifications, a demand that was never made of white attorneys. Mandela, with the help of his friend, the advocate George Bizos, took the matter to the Supreme Court. The magistrate received the sharp end of the judge's tongue, which was small compensation, but these were battles Mandela thought worth fighting. In prison, he would fight similar issues with as much tenacity.

Left: Inside the offices of Mandela & Tambo, the first all-African legal firm in the country.

Right: Oliver Tambo, with his quiet, calm demeanor, made an ideal partner to Mandela's charismatic courtroom personality.

The legal work brought Mandela a measure of professional fame and eased his financial situation. He and Tambo hardly charged high fees but with the sheer number of cases they were handling had improved their lot. Mandela, always the snappy dresser when he could afford it, bought smart new suits and replaced his old Volkswagen with a big Oldsmobile. In his own estimation he had become "a man of the city."[14] But he didn't forget those who once had helped him. When he came across Lazar Sidelsky waiting at a bus stop, he immediately offered him a lift home. The lawyer was struggling financially and the next day Mandela sent him a check for £50 in repayment of a long outstanding loan.

If from the outside Mandela appeared reasonably prosperous and content, then appearances were deceptive. His friends might see a dashing man about town, but the man about town was not emotionally happy. He had a loving wife – now pregnant and soon to give birth to a daughter – who ensured that he and their family were well cared for and the home was neat and comfortable. But Evelyn was finding it increasingly difficult supporting her husband's political ambitions. Ironically, however, his banning gave them time together which Evelyn welcomed. Her husband wasn't forever disappearing to political meetings and the days were structured around his working life. He had time for the two boys. When their fourth child was born, they named her Makaziwe, a customary way of honoring the baby daughter they had lost. As Mandela was slapped with a second banning order three months after the first expired, most of 1953 was spent in closer contact with his family. And because the fissures in the marriage were at an early stage, they could still be papered over, although it was obvious the relationship was under strain.

By now, Mandela's thoughts were increasingly focused on the inevitability of armed resistance. At the first public meeting he attended after his banning order expired in June, the Indian leader, Yusuf Cachalia, was arrested on the platform and dragged away by police. Mandela had to calm the audience, fearing that at any moment the police might open fire. He sensed a growing impatience among his supporters that resonated with his own thoughts. Shortly afterwards, while addressing a gathering in "Freedom Square," Sophiatown, he breached the ANC's policy of nonviolence.

RUTH MOMPATI:

I joined Mandela & Tambo as Nelson Mandela's secretary and typist at the beginning of 1953, just after the Defiance Campaign. Nelson was very busy so he was very demanding, but both he and Oliver Tambo were good people to work for, very considerate and respectful. They expected us to look after the clients because our job was to do what the clients wanted. Nelson was a very popular lawyer, not only because he was good and he knew his law – in most cases he won, and often in very difficult political cases – but also because he respected his clients. He made them feel they were very important and that he was there for them. He listened very well; he gave people time to speak.

Mandela, the dapper and confident young lawyer.

Many of his clients came from the villages. Chiefs would come because they had been removed by the so-called native commissioners for not agreeing with them or resisting being pushed around. They were proud men, confident in their chieftainship, and didn't feel obliged to the native commissioner and this meant they got into trouble with the law.

The case of the chief in Ganyesa, Kagakile Letlhogile, for instance, was a very interesting trial. In the years of apartheid people were so cowed down that some got to believe they really were below everybody else. But Letlhogile clearly felt that he was a chief or a king in his own country and he got that country from his forefathers and nobody was going to push him around. And he was successful. He won his case.

This was the type of person Mandela appeared for, and they were attracted to him because he respected them despite the fact that some of them had very little schooling. Mandela made them realize they were right to defend themselves, that it was their right as human beings not to allow anyone to disrespect them. And I think this made people realize that he listened, that he was a man who respected people irrespective of their standing in life or in society.

I had utter respect for him because he had respect for the three of us secretaries, and for the articled clerks, and the messenger, who was a friend because he belonged to his

sometimes shout. If you made a mistake and he had to correct you, or
ught would be ready wasn't, he made no bones about letting you know.

dictated a letter to me and used certain phrases that were unfamiliar.
d gave it back to him. He said to me dismissively, "What is this?" And
your dictation." He said, "You'd better look at your notes and type i
called me and said, "I've just seen the notes that I made and I find these
yped in my notes. That was my mistake." This was the type of person he

office when Nelson was arrested and as I was the only one left in the
close the office and send the files to other attorneys. I got a job with
lost it because all the Mandela & Tambo clients followed me there to ask
ses and it became impossible.

ogant; he was more a man with a big heart. I'm not quite sure that I know
nd him attractive although he was an attractive man and he had
t be because he listened. He didn't talk down to women; he treated them
d. Anybody, women in particular because they're always dismissed, wil
ted to a man who treats them with respect.

lmed when Nelson was released. It was amazing that a man who had
-seven years in prison still had this big smile and that on his route from
ld pick up a white child and speak to those white people as if they were
ghbors. He saw himself as part of the people who had gathered to see
er but also as relating to them.

e of us on the outside had many difficulties and a number of us were
d to those leaders who were in jail, we lived in relative freedom. And fo
out waving and smiling to everybody, to the world . . . you just respected
ecause you felt that his spirit was the same, even stronger. Here was a
to have been made an even stronger and better revolutionary by his
Robben Island.

o my mind usually when I think of Nelson is that he is a unique person
d yet he's got humility. I am sometimes surprised that a man who could
ch gave it away because he wanted freedom for himself and his people
g. He's one of those people who will not worry about death; he'll accep
has lived a good life in that he's done his utmost in relation to his
ng change to South Africa.

I look at Nelson today, I see a contented man who feels that he has done

first met Nelson Mandela shortly after he came from the Eastern Cap
at the Jan Hofmeyr School of Social Work, which was housed in the B
Centre in town. We students used to be fed lunch there every day and
noticed him. I was reminded of this when I was watching television in Lor
released and he walked out of prison with Winnie and people were sayin
he's got such stiff legs." And I said, "He's always had stiff legs!" These
anky legs often walk in a stiff manner, so even in his forties he had stif
always beautifully dressed, always wearing a suit and tie, very polite.

The Bantu Men's Social Centre was very much the meeting place
n Johannesburg in the 1940s and 50s. It was a natural place for
Nelson to come to – it was where he and others launched the ANC
Youth League. Everybody used to go there. I remember a wedding
reception at night when I was about six or seven and walking home at
about eleven to Robinson Deep Mine where we lived with no trouble. It
never occurred to me to be scared. People talk now about
Sophiatown, but it wasn't just Sophiatown, it was the vibrancy of the
whole of Johannesburg then. Sophiatown was simply part of the life,
and the BMSC was really its center. The main hall was used as a
concert and dancing facility but you also used to be able to play
volleyball and other games. My parents played tennis at the BMSC.
Sometimes I think we were living such a good life that nobody now
knows about.

In a way the BMSC was quite formal then, although you did have
the jitterbug and music from America post-1945. We had very formal
dances with the Merry Blackbirds band with their bow ties. Zulu Boy
Cele's Jazz Maniacs were less formal, more like people's music – and
then came the cheeky college boys of the Harlem Swingsters, who
formally, musically, at Adams College and they took it in completely diffe.
a small child I used to go to these functions with my mother and watc
the Charleston to the Merry Blackbirds. I went to one or two dances wit
with Zulu Boy Cele, but the Harlem Swingsters era was really where I ca

About three years after I graduated, Winnie joined the Jan Hofmeyr
very, very beautiful – as she still is. She was rather stiff and very se
Jo'burger. I remember seeing her at the BMSC dancing with a Zimb
hopping around, delighted to be dancing with the most beautiful person i
was so stiff, not smiling

WE CHERISHED SOPHIATOWN BECAUSE IT BROUGHT TOGETHER SUCH A GREAT CONCENTRATION OF PEOPLE, WE DID NOT LIVE IN IT, WE WERE SOPHIATOWN. IT WAS A COMPLEX PARADOX WHICH ATTRACTED OPPOSITES; THE RING OF JOY, THE SOUND OF LAUGH-TER, WAS INTERPOSED WITH THE GROWL AND THE SMELL OF INSULT; WE SANG OUR SAD HAPPY SONGS, WERE CARRIED AWAY BY OUR EROTIC DANCES, WE WHIS-TLED AND SHOUTED, GOT DRUNK AND KILLED EACH OTHER . . .

Bloke Modisane, *Blame Me on History*

Sophiatown was the center of the creative and political renaissance of the 1950s. It was the home of speakeasies, jazz, and gangsters, inspired by such movies as Street with No Name *and actors like Richard Widmark, Humphrey Bogart, and James Cagney. Gangs like the "Americans" favored big cars, borsalinos, and two-toned shoes. Sophiatown was the locale of the great Drum writers and photographers who captured the essence of a decade.*

Sophiatown was a multiracial slum not far from the center of Johannesburg. Overcrowded, gang-ridden, awash with shebeens [speakeasies] and illegal homebrewed beer and liquor, it was also Johannesburg's bohemia, made famous by the stories, journalism, and photographs appearing monthly in the popular *Drum* magazine. But more significantly, politically, it was an area where black people could own property freehold. This was anathema to the state. Sophiatown was declared a "black spot" from which everyone would be evicted. The homeowners, supported by the ANC, gathered weekly to demonstrate against the forced removal. They were vociferous in their protests, but they remained passive and the leaders were careful to avoid making inflammatory speeches: until Mandela's outburst.

As he stood in Freedom Square, a crowd of young angry people before him, armed police bristling on the edges of the gathering, Mandela's rhetoric became increasingly militant. To cheers and clapping he said that the time for passive resistance had ended; that nonviolence was a useless strategy; that the only weapon which could destroy apartheid was violence; and that they would have to prepare to use this weapon one day. For his hot-headedness, Mandela was censured by the ANC. He accepted the rebuke and adopted the party line at subsequent public events. "But," he wrote years later, "in my heart, I knew that nonviolence was not the answer."[15]

In September he took on a case in the small Free State town of Villiers, keen for a respite from the city. He drove down in his Oldsmobile, leaving Orlando before it was light so that dawn found him on the endless plains with the limitless blue sky overhead. For Mandela, trips into the country were not simply about crossing the landscape, they were also journeys into the past. As he drove he thought of the wily Boer general, Christiaan de Wet, who, so bravely and courageously, had fought the British on this terrain. One day, he wondered, would African rebels do the same against the white government? At Villiers, relaxed by his daydreams and the open road, he strode cheerfully into the court. Waiting for him was a knot of policemen. Without a word they served on him a two-year banning order that restricted him to the Johannesburg magisterial district.

The order forced him to resign from the ANC which meant being wiped from the political stage. The ANC would have to replace him. As much as these realizations annoyed him, he still felt it wiser to obey the banning than risk imprisonment. Consequently, his first presidential speech to the Transvaal ANC conference was read on his behalf. Known as the "No Easy Walk to Freedom" speech, a quote from Jawaharlal Nehru, its tenor was about adopting new methods of protest and the inevitability that justice would prevail. He ended by saying that destroying tyranny was the "highest aspiration of every free man."[16]

Two months later, during a brief lifting of his ban and before fresh and more stringent bans were served on him, and galled by the recently instituted Bantu Education Act which further downgraded black education and placed it firmly under the government's authority, Mandela addressed a large gathering in Soweto. He spoke for ninety minutes, every word inaccurately recorded by a policeman, and, although the tone was militant, evoking warrior memories of Shaka, he suffered no official repercussions. But years later, when he stood accused of treason, the policeman's notes would be used in evidence against him.

In the new year Mandela spent time behind the scenes organizing protests in Sophiatown, and time in court defending people who were about to lose their houses. Both efforts proved hopeless. Early in February, the removal trucks and two thousand police and army troops entered the township. The houses were razed; the people dumped in a designated area in Soweto known as Meadowlands. Again Mandela realized how tame were their efforts at nonviolent protest when the state simply lashed out its iron fist.

At its 1953 conference the ANC had agreed to convene a multi-party Congress of the People and sponsor the drafting of a Freedom Charter. A joint meeting of the ANC and its allied congresses held a meeting at Tongaat, near Durban, to set the process in motion. Out of that meeting came a call for public submissions to the charter. The response was overwhelming. People sent in their ideas on scraps of paper, on serviettes, on the backs of ANC leaflets. Predominantly the call was for the vote. It was clear to Mandela, who was closely involved in the drafting of the charter, that this was the voice of the people, and not a communist inspired manifesto as its critics proclaimed.

"We Won't Move" — but the game goes on. The campaign against the government's forced removals from Sophiatown failed in the face of overwhelming brutality by the state and because of an acute housing shortage and corrupt landlords.

IN THE NAME OF SLUM CLEAR-
ANCE THEY HAD BROUGHT THE
BULLDOZERS AND GORED INTO
HER BODY, AND FOR A BRIEF
MOMENT, LOOKING DOWN GOOD
STREET, SOPHIATOWN WAS LIKE
ONE OF ITS OWN MANY VICTIMS;
A MAN GORED BY THE KNIVES
OF SOPHIATOWN, LYING IN THE
OPEN GUTTERS, A RAISIN IN THE
SMELLING DRAINS, DYING OF
MULTIPLE STAB WOUNDS, GAPING
WELLS GUSHING FORTH BLOOD;
THE LOOK OF SHOCK AND BE-
WILDERMENT, OF HORROR AND
INCREDULITY, ON THE FACE OF
THE DYING MAN.

Bloke Modisane, *Blame Me on History*

The destruction of Sophiatown happened over five years. The scheduled date to begin removals was February 12, 1955, but two days earlier two thousand armed police invaded the area and forced families out of their homes. Thus began the eviction process. These photographs tell the story from 1955 to 1959, when all that remained of the once-thriving suburb was rubble.

"My womb is shaken when they speak of 'Bantu Education.'"
Lilian Ngoyi

The annihilation of Sophiatown was an attempt to imprison blacks physically by moving them into a ghetto. The Bantu Education Act of 1955 was an attempt to imprison their minds. Left: Mandela addresses a group of women charged with public disturbance for their part in a boycott of the Education Act. Women were protesting not only against the education laws. In Pretoria, women of all races took part in a historic march against the pass laws at the Union Building (opposite and above). Above, from left to right: Radima Moosa, Lilian Ngoyi, Helen Joseph, and Sophie Williams were the delegates selected to deliver the anti-pass protest petition to Prime Minister J. G. Strijdom.

Following page: The women of Cato Manor in Durban were among the most mobilized in the country. In 1959, during a protest at the liquor laws, they were baton-charged by police as they tried to run away.

While Mandela was absorbed in the Freedom Charter, he was fighting fires in two other areas of his life. On the legal front, the Law Society of the Transvaal applied to the Supreme Court to have him struck from the roll of accredited attorneys. The reason: unprofessional conduct, given his political activities and his suspended sentence in the Defiance Campaign case. At the time the firm of Mandela & Tambo was flourishing, and the motivation behind the action was clearly an attempt to hobble him professionally and privately. In true Mandela fashion, the notice was no sooner served than he had arranged for a defense, briefing two high-powered advocates who agreed to act pro bono. Of considerable encouragement during the run-up to the hearing were the offers of support from well-known Afrikaner lawyers and staunch National Party members who, nonetheless, viewed this action as an affront to the legal profession. Mandela, pleased that even in a racist milieu, professionalism could sometimes supersede the color of a person's skin, was further heartened by the outcome. His defense argued that in a state where the rule of law applied, citizens had a right to their political beliefs. The judge agreed. He found in Mandela's favor and ordered the Law Society to pay costs.

Whatever jubilation this occasioned, he went home to an increasingly disapproving wife. As thoroughly as Mandela was embroiling himself in the politics of liberation, so Evelyn was committing her life to the Jehovah's Witnesses. She took to distributing their magazine *The Watchtower,* thrusting copies at her husband and trying to convince him to accept her faith. But he couldn't. For one thing the doctrine preached passivity, the last message Mandela wanted to hear. For another, he found her belief obsessive and wondered if this was to cover some hurt in her life.

He was being more than somewhat disingenuous. He might have devoted his life to the ANC, but these devotions included some of the female office-bearers. When Evelyn heard rumors that he was having affairs she challenged him. Mandela flew into a fury. He had long tried to convince her of the necessity of the struggle but they had no common ground in this regard. Now she was questioning his integrity. He moved his bed into the sitting room. He became cold and distant. In despair, Evelyn appealed to Walter and Albertina Sisulu to intervene. Sisulu did so, and was roundly told by Mandela to mind his own business. He then accused Evelyn of broadcasting their problems. Mortified, for a time he stopped eating at home, occasionally slept out, and took his laundry to his cousin. The atmosphere in the house upset his mother and she returned to Qunu. In trepidation his sister stood by watching two people she loved and respected tearing one another apart.

Throughout the year the rift deepened, with Mandela becoming convinced that their marriage was untenable. Evelyn issued an ultimatum: if he wanted to save their marriage he had to give up the ANC. The animosity deepened. Over their ever-shifting battlefield, they fought, too, for the affection of their children. Thembi, the eldest boy, was most frequently targeted. Evelyn wished to convert him to her faith and read him religious tracts, took him to church, and enlisted his help whenever she distributed copies of *The Watchtower.* Mandela countered with political talk and enrolled Thembi in the Pioneers, a junior section of the ANC. To the young Makgatho he attempted to explain the injustices of the white regime. In a more fatherly role he would take Thembi to the boxing ring at the community center where he worked out whenever he had a free night. Together, father and son would do some road work, skipping, and shadow boxing before putting on gloves for the serious business of sparring. The skinny little boy became an enthusiastic paperweight and an even more enthusiastic ringside critic of his father's abilities. For Mandela these were happy hours when he escaped the dictates of his private and public lives.

In June 1955, the banned Mandela had covertly watched the adoption of the Freedom Charter. Throughout the heated debates surrounding its drafting, Mandela and many of the Freedom Charter's drafters had had to look on impotently, silenced by their banning orders. Now, however, his restrictive notice expired and he decided to visit the Transkei. After fourteen years in the city he still felt "a country boy at heart," as he wrote in his autobiography,[17] and absence had induced in him a need for the "open veld and rolling valleys" of his childhood.[18] He was thirty-eight, he hadn't had a holiday in nine years, he needed a break from a demanding legal practice, he had family affairs in Transkei to sort out, and there was ANC business needing attention. He probably also wanted to escape a tense and unhappy household. A few hours before he left, two-year-old Makaziwe woke up and wanted to go with her father. Mandela had been neglecting his family and he knew it, and now here he was about to leave on a holiday. He carried her back to bed where she quickly fell asleep while he watched over her, guilt darkening his anticipation for the trip. Yet once he was on the road, driving through the country of the Zulu kings, his mood eased. Once more he was travelling through history.

Mandela first visited Durban, spending a day with the ANC leader, Luthuli. From there he drove down the coast then inland to Umtata for meetings with members of the *bunga* and K. D. Matanzima. He and Matanzima were now politically poles apart, and even a long night of heated discussions could not resolve their differences. His next stop was with his mother in Qunu. Again his conscience tormented him. Was he justified in sidelining his family to fight for others? Was politics merely an excuse for abandoning his duties? The questions plagued him, as they did periodically, but they did not dissuade him from his course. For two weeks he relaxed, shuttling between Qunu and Mqhekezweni, reminiscing with his friends, spending time with his mother and his second mother, the regent's widow. He ate the same meals he had eaten as a boy, walked in the *veld,* gazed at the night sky flung with stars. Keeping in touch with his roots, he felt, was important.

In the early hours of the morning – his favorite time on the road – Mandela left Qunu for Cape Town. The rest of his trip was dictated more by ANC business than holiday, but it was hardly a condition he found onerous. He also took time off in Cape Town to buy presents for his children.

His days in Cape Town coincided with nationwide police raids on the offices and houses of known political leaders, and Mandela feared that if new banning orders were issued there would be one for him. This time, although his offices were searched, he remained unfettered, but the threat of a banning order was a daily reality. And eventually, in March 1956, the day came: Mandela was again restricted to Johannesburg, this time for five years. With some despondency he realized that for sixty months his world would be reduced to the same streets, the same mine dumps, the same patch of sky. As he had recently bought a plot of land in Umtata, the recognition that he was trapped in one place was annoying. On the other hand, he had no intention of obeying his banning orders to the letter: he was not going to collaborate with the repressive demands of the state.

Mandela's clandestine activities in the coming months were as much political as domestic. He spent nights away from home and rumors of liaisons with women were fed back to Evelyn who began to think about moving out.

Following page: Part of the preamble and text of the Freedom Charter etched into the wall of the waiting cell at the Palace of Justice, Pretoria.

THE FREEDOM CH[ARTER]

PRE[A]MBLE: SOUTH AFRICA BELONGS T[O]
[I]N [I]T, BLACK AND WHITE AN[D]
CAN JUSTLY CLAIM AUTHORI[TY]
BASED ON THE WILL OF

1. THE PEOPLE SHALL GOV[ERN]
2. ALL NATIONAL GROUPS
3. THE PEOPLE SHALL SHAR[E]
4. THE LAND SHALL BE SHA[RED]
5. ALL SHALL BE EQUAL
6. ALL SHALL ENJOY EQ[UAL]
7. THERE SHALL BE WORK
8. THE DOORS OF LEARNI[NG]
   SHALL BE OPENED
9. THERE SHALL BE HO[USE]
10. THERE SHALL [BE P...]

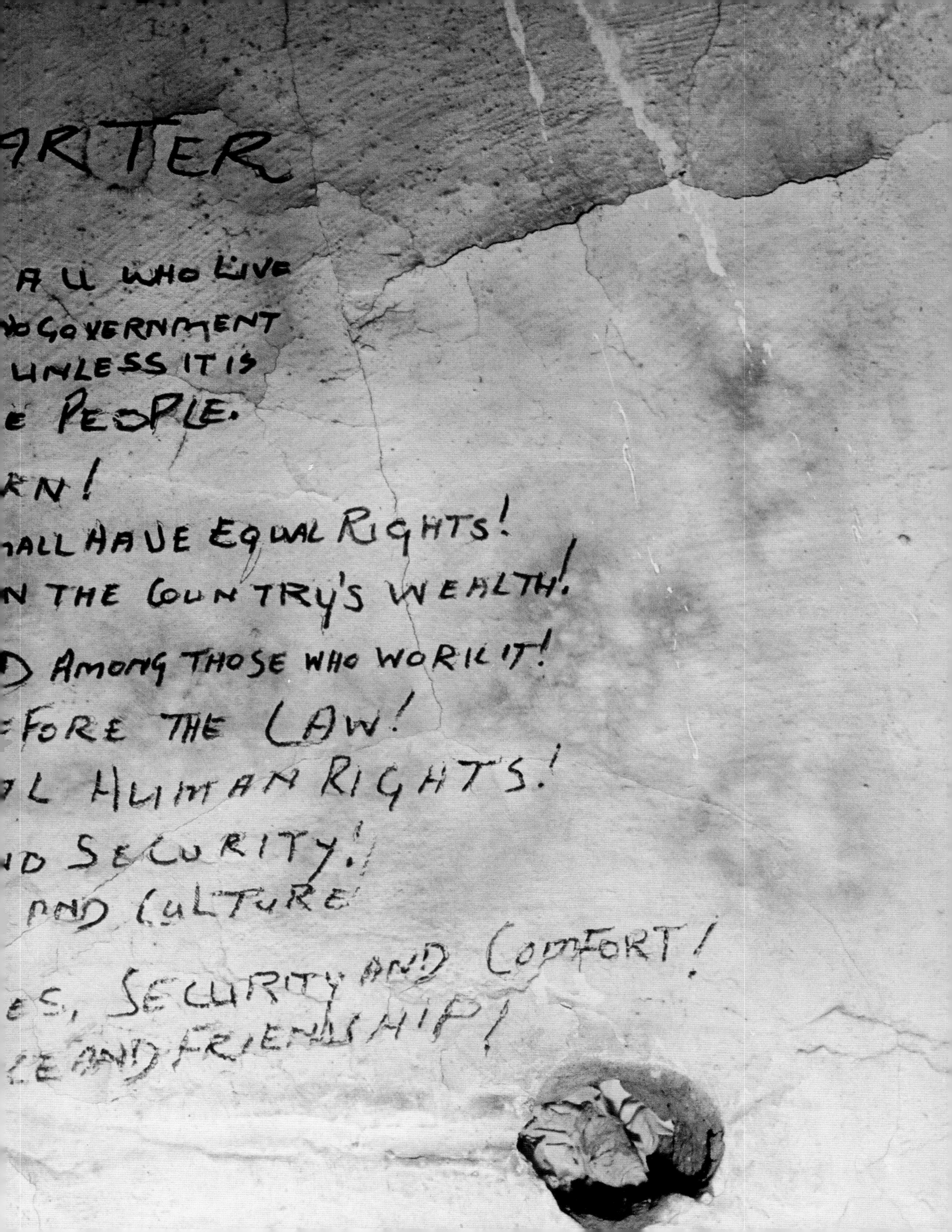

ARTER

A LL WHO LIVE

NO GOVERNMENT

UNLESS IT IS

E PEOPLE.

EN!

HALL HAVE EQUAL RIGHTS!

N THE COUNTRY'S WEALTH!

D AMONG THOSE WHO WORK IT!

EFORE THE LAW!

L HUMAN RIGHTS!

ND SECURITY!

AND CULTURE

ES, SECURITY AND COMFORT!

E AND FRIENDSHIP!

But before she could do so, Mandela was arrested on a charge of high treason. At dawn on December 5, 1956, he was awaken by the security police hammering on his front door. He opened it, expecting trouble. Three white men barged in, terrifying the children. Mandela did his best to calm them while the house was turned upside down: drawers, cabinets, and cupboards ransacked for evidence of his political activities. The violation continued for an hour; then he was summarily arrested and escorted to a waiting car. His tearful children stood watching from the doorway while the car accelerated down the street. The confusion in their faces tore at Mandela's heart.

On his arrest in 1956, Mandela was taken to the Fort, an infamous prison on the rise overlooking central Johannesburg. Here, those arrested on a similar charge would be incarcerated until the state was convinced it had all the political leaders responsible for the Freedom Charter and the Congress of the People. Shortly before Christmas, the group, now numbering 156, were bundled into police vans and taken to the Drill Hall in the city center. Crowds of sympathizers had gathered outside the military building. Among them was the *Drum* journalist Can Themba, who described Mandela entering the makeshift courtroom with hunched shoulders, seeming to "glower with suppressed anger."[19] The charge was high treason and in particular conspiring to violently overthrow the state. The indictments went back four years; clearly the trial would be lengthy. After four days the accused were granted bail – £25 for blacks, £250 for whites – and the trial was set for January 1957.

For all his relief about being free on bail, Mandela's buoyancy was crushed when he got home. Evelyn had left, taking the children. He wandered around a bare house that echoed disquietingly. That she had taken even the curtains devastated him. This final incongruous detail seemed to symbolize what he had lost. Worse was ahead.

In the coming months, as the trial dragged on and on, he would watch his children struggling to cope with the separation. Thembi, at ten years old, crumbled badly. He became withdrawn, his school work suffered. Often he would dress in his father's clothes, even though they were far too big. Mandela felt helpless in his efforts to comfort him. Whenever he could he took the boy boxing, but between the trial and his legal practice, he had little spare time. Makgatho tried to get his parents to reconcile, and when this failed insisted on sleeping with his father during his overnight visits. Little Makaziwe, unable to comprehend the situation, didn't know whether to run to her father or flee from him on one occasion when Mandela visited her crèche. She saw him and stood transfixed. "She had some conflict in her small heart which she did not know how to resolve," Mandela recorded in his autobiography. "It was very painful."[20]

Despite the bitterness and rancor that prevailed at the end of their marriage, Mandela never had anything but respect for his wife, whom he regarded warmly as a strong person and a good mother. Yet he was soon seen about town with his long-standing and supportive secretary, Ruth Mompati, or the lively Lilian Ngoyi, then president of the ANC Women's League, and a fellow treason defendant. But it was another woman altogether who was to catch first his eye then his heart: Nomzamo Winifred Madikizela, known affectionately as Winnie. He initially noticed her at a bus stop, then, coincidently some weeks later, was introduced to her by Adelaide Tsukudu, who would soon marry Oliver Tambo. For Mandela it was love at first sight. The next day, on the pretext of asking her to donate to the Treason Trial Defense Fund, he invited her to an Indian restaurant for lunch. Afterwards they drove to the outskirts of the city and walked in the *veld*. Mandela's thoughts were already turning to marriage.

Winnie Madikizela was from a powerful family and clan that came from the Pondoland district of Transkei, well to the east of Mandela's home terrain. She was bright, had done exceptionally at school but had a reputation for being domineering and rebellious. Some years previously she had come to Johannesburg to study for a career in social work. In 1955, she became the first black social worker at Soweto's Baragwanath Hospital. She was young and beautiful with a taste for fine clothes and shoes. Although her political experience was limited she was a fast learner, fascinated to meet Mandela's friends and colleagues, and quick to champion the cause. In all this she provided the encouragement and support that Mandela had long sought.

The Treason Trial, it soon became clear to the accused, was an insult to their intelligence. The state's witnesses were invariably incompetent and few of them gave coherent testimony. The weeks in court turned into months and still there seemed no end to the proceedings. Mandela attended the hearing, spent whatever hours remained on his legal work, and tried to see as much of his new love as possible. For her part, Winnie was in court whenever she had free time.

Mandela's attitude in court, although serious, even stern, was also aloof. To court reporters and international observers he was a tall and striking figure but they did not number him among the obvious leaders such as Luthuli, Sisulu, and Tambo. Some even considered him a slick young man with his briefcase and immaculate suits. It was only when he delivered his testimony in the final months of the trial that he left no one in any doubt about his commitment and ideals.

Above: A sunny day on a Johannesburg suburban street and a pass raid in action. A black domestic worker grimaces in pain, her arm twisted by the white policeman who is marching her to a group of other women waiting to be transported to jail for not having their pass books.

Following page: Supporters threaten to burst through the gates outside the Drill Hall in Johannesburg during the preparatory hearing for the Treason Trial. On the second day the defendants were surrounded by a wire cage and one had scribbled a note: DANGEROUS, PLEASE DO NOT FEED.

HILDA BERNSTEIN:

I first met Mandela when he came to our house in Johannesburg in about 1956. We've never forgotten it because he was an extremely imposing figure and always had an air of dignified authority which I think arose out of his training as a minor chief. In addition to being tall – of course, you lose height as you get older – he was very broad. He was a boxer at that time, very muscular. One of my children came running into the kitchen and said, "There's a giant in the front room!" Nelson's never forgotten this because, according to him, one of the other children looked him up and down and said, "He's not so big."

We were supporters of the anti-apartheid struggle, tied up, through the Communist Party, with people like Moses Kotane, Edwin Mofutsenyana, Ruth First, Joe Slovo, and Duma Nokwe. My husband Rusty worked as an architect. We met through politics and shared the same set of attitudes and social views. You have to put yourself back into a white South Africa during the apartheid years. We were swimming against the tide which involved us having friendships across the class and color line with a lot of interesting and stimulating people.

Left: Mandela speaks to Peter Nthite, a Youth League leader, during a lunch break at the Treason Trial.

Right: Mandela and Moses Kotane outside the Pretoria Court in October 1958, triumphant at the news that the prosecution had withdrawn charges. However, the Treason Trial resumed in February on the basis of a more precise indictment.

I was banned by the government when the Communist Party was banned, which meant I was banned from meeting other people. My husband was also banned, but there was a special clause in my husband's and my house arrest orders saying we were allowed to meet each other. It sounds ridiculous but this is the way it was.

My husband was one of the accused in the Treason Trial. During the state of emergency after the Sharpeville shootings, they picked up a whole lot of people, including myself and my husband, and detained us in jail for about three or four months. They had never had educated middle-class white prisoners before and didn't really know how to handle us. They tried to interrogate us but we refused to answer questions and we got away with a lot of things we wouldn't have been able to later on. We were "subversives", we were "undermining the authority of the state." I don't know what they were after and I don't know what they found out either.

Captain Swanepoel didn't do the interrogation though I know he was always around. You know, he had a fixation on Winnie Mandela. He couldn't keep his eyes off her, and very often, when the Treason Trial was on and the cars were going between Johannesburg and Pretoria every day, he would find an excuse to stop her car. She was very beautiful.

Nelson and Winnie on their wedding day in June 1958. Mandela was immersed in the Treason Trial and had to be granted a temporary stay of his banning order so that the wedding could be held in Winnie's native Pondoland.

'The day Nelson comes out of prison, we must go and complete the second part of our ceremony. I still have the wedding cake, the part of that cake we were supposed to have taken to his place. I brought it here to Brandfort. It crumbled a bit when they dumped our things. It is now in my house in Orlando, waiting for him.' Winnie Mandela, *Part of my Soul*

In September 1957, the state finally closed its case and the court adjourned for the defense to review the evidence. Technically, the nine months had been a preparatory hearing to present and test the evidence in anticipation of a proper trial. Unexpectedly, three months later charges were dropped against sixty-one of the accused, including Luthuli and Tambo. From a financial point of view this was good news for the firm of Mandela & Tambo. During the trial, what had been a bustling practice faced near collapse. Mandela was in such dire straits that he couldn't make the final £50 owing on the plot of land he had bought in Umtata and had to forgo the property. Tambo now tried to resuscitate the business.

Early in 1958 the court gave notice that the case would go to trial in the Supreme Court on an unspecified date. Some months later this was set down for August. In the meantime Mandela was left battling to salvage his practice while restricted by a banning order. He also had unfinished business concerning Evelyn and Winnie.

His first priority was to divorce Evelyn. She had heard about his relationship with Winnie but he was devoted to the children, and this, she felt, would preserve their marriage, at least in name. Consequently, the divorce papers took her aback but she didn't contest them. Custody of the children would go to her and this was her only concern. Mandela, however, was in for a surprise. Because he had never paid *lobola* for Evelyn, he had no rights over the children in customary law and belatedly had to arrange to make the payment to Evelyn's brother. As he was struggling financially this couldn't have been an easy payment, especially as he was about to pay a second *lobola*.

Mandela never formally proposed to Winnie. Once he had filed for divorce, he told her where she could get a wedding dress made and suggested she inform her family of their intentions. Winnie, swept up in the danger and excitement of their romance, obeyed without a murmur. Her father was set against the union; her sisters wept at the prospect. The man was going to end up in jail. She would be nothing more than his housekeeper. But Winnie had made up her mind.

A date was set – June 14, 1958 – and Mandela was granted a six-day stay of his banning order so that the ceremony could be held in Pondoland. At the reception, Winnie's father couldn't resist warning his daughter that Mandela was already married to the struggle. If your man is a wizard, he advised, you must be a witch – a suggestion that Mandela interpreted as follow your husband's path. Events were to prove that this was Winnie's understanding too.

The couple returned to Johannesburg and moved into a house in Orlando West. There was no money or time for a honeymoon. Within a few months the newlyweds had to settle down to a routine dictated by the trial. Their day began at 4 A.M. Mandela would take his exercise jog through the streets while Winnie prepared breakfast. At daybreak he would catch a bus to the trial, a long and tedious journey to the court in Pretoria. His afternoons were spent at the office; his evenings were filled with political work. Winnie didn't complain. She well understood her situation; besides, she was pregnant, the future was filled with hope. Despite the charge of treason hanging over him, Mandela believed this too. Winnie had given him a second chance.

The Treason Trial lurched on in fits and starts. In October the prosecution withdrew some of the charges and a month later presented a revised indictment. This released sixty-one of the accused to be tried later, while levelling a more specific charge of revolutionary or violent incitement against the remaining thirty, including Mandela. The trial was then rescheduled to start in February 1959. This released him temporarily from the daily haul to and from Pretoria but there was much else on his mind.

In October Winnie had joined a march to protest the pass laws. She had become a member of the ANC Women's League, and was making her presence felt. As a political leader, Mandela approved of her action, but as a husband he had tried to dissuade her. For one thing she was four months pregnant and jail would not be an easy option. Another consideration was financial. Winnie's income was essential. He pointed out that if she were arrested she would likely lose her job and would have great difficulty finding another.

However, Winnie's mind was made up. On the day of the march Mandela saw her off before taking the bus to Pretoria. In the afternoon he learned that his wife had been arrested along with hundreds of other women. She was to spend two weeks in prison until the firm of Mandela & Tambo was finally able to arrange bail for the more than two thousand women arrested. The couple were reunited but one of the eventualities Mandela had dreaded occurred when the hospital fired Winnie. Friends and her father helped them out financially.

The prosecution hoped it would get a conviction in the Treason Trial primarily on the basis that the Freedom Charter was a treasonous document. However vague or sometimes contradictory some of the articles of the charter may have been, the idea that South Africa belongs to all who live in it was anathema to the apartheid regime. If the prosecution could secure jail terms for the 156 they originally arrested, they believed they would smash the ANC – the primary organization behind the charter – and therefore end further protest and challenge.

It's a very important trial because in many ways it was the last major trial that was conducted with some semblance of what may loosely be called the Queensberry Rules. The onus was still on the state, although it did introduce a couple of presumptions against the accused. In the main, however, the principles of the Criminal Procedure Evidence Act were still in force.

The ANC was viewed, at the insistence of the apartheid regime, as a terrorist organization, as a communist organization. The legal team not only smashed the state's case, but in the course of evidence managed to highlight the history of the ANC and its intentions in relation to the future, and so expose the contradictions in the prosecution's case. For instance, they alleged there had been an organization of conspiracy and yet Chief Luthuli, the president of the ANC, the leading organization in the so-called conspiracy, was one of the sixty-one accused whose charges were dropped in 1957. And here was a devout Christian taking the stand and saying that the ANC is a wide church and there's room for all those who are interested in establishing democracy. People like Maulvi Cachalia, who was called as a defense witness, and Helen Joseph and many others all spoke with the same voice.

Nelson Mandela himself gave evidence very well. He made a tremendous impression on, I think, at least one of the judges, Judge Bekker, who was an honest man. Reading Mandela's evidence, you can actually see Bekker viewing him not just as a witness but being particularly interested as a white South African: "Let me ask this man some questions as to whether we can come to terms with him." Nelson was very adept at answering the questions. For instance, the judge asked him, "You want one man one vote?" He said, "Yes." Then Bekker asked, "Would you settle for anything less?" Nelson would evade the question, saying, "Well, you know, I can't speak for the organization. But make us an offer, you know, and we'll consider it!" There seemed to be a rapport.

Although the judges had some unkind things to say about some of the views and some of the evidence offered, the core finding of the Treason Trial was that the Freedom Charter was an acceptable socialist document with some elements of Marxist principle but it was not a blueprint for the establishment of a communist state and they were acquitted on that ground. Nelson Mandela points out that this was a key building block for the platform on which the ANC, in exile under Oliver Tambo, could build an image of itself as a liberation movement, and that this was very important as time went on and the pariah

Mandela and fellow treason defendants during a lunch break in a neighboring garden.

FATIMA MEER:

Prior to the Treason Trial, the "First World" believed the liberation movement was made up of a bunch of "wild communists". All sorts of people came to speak to the treason defendants and went away forming their own very commendable opinion of them, and suddenly the South African government's attempts to portray them as communists was undermined and the moral implication of what was going on in South Africa was exposed. In other words, the Nationalist myth was exploded.

The Treason Trial in fact laid the way for the final break of the West from the Nationalists. Up to that point the Nats had been seen as the bastion of Western and European civilization and Christianity. But evening after evening the accused, even after a heavy day in court, would make themselves available to church people, statesmen, and members of NGOs from all over the world.

Every one of those treason defendants was seen as a hero. The Treason Trial – apart from what the Defense and Aid Fund sent – depended very heavily on local monies. Here too, there was support from the Liberal Party – people like Paton and the Kupers – Christians and Jews. When the whole charge was dropped and the case withdrawn, it confirmed in the minds and hearts of both the non-European and many Europeans that the government was simply persecuting people who did not deserve it. By now the treason

King Kong, the internationally popular musical, was originally conceived in about 1958. It came about because my husband Todd was asked to write a song for a fund-raising concert for the families of "Mr Drum," Henry Nxumalo, the *Drum* journalist who had been murdered, and the musician Victor Mkhize, who had been killed in a car smash. These two events happened quite close together in 1957.

Todd wrote "Sad Times, Bad Times" and in it he was asking, "What did these two men do to deserve what they got?" It was performed with Todd at the piano, and the Manhattan Brothers with Miriam Makeba singing the lyrics. It was very, very powerful and when the idea of *King Kong* was raised, Todd's name came up.

Nelson and Winnie were present on the opening night in the Great Hall at the University of the Witwatersrand. It was a Friday night, February 2, 1959. The following Monday, the Treason Trial was due to resume. In those days the government concession that was made to black audiences was that they would sit in separate rows from whites. They were allowed to come but not to sit in a mixed audience. I remember the Menells decided to sit in the row in front of us. The Oppenheimers were right in front of the show. Three or four or five rows behind us were Nelson and Winnie.

We didn't expect it would be such an exciting production or be so well received. During the interval we all went out into the foyer and there was Nelson. When he heard "Sad Times, Bad Times," he had a completely different perception about what it was saying. Nelson interpreted it as being to do with the Treason Trial. We were all standing together: Nelson, Winnie, Todd, and I. I think Todd left it at that. He suddenly thought, well it also fits the situation of the Treason Trial.

That night as we were going out, the cars were jammed outside the Great Hall and everybody was hooting! They were so excited. Nobody expected the show to go on for

Internal dissent within the ANC had grown since the advent of the Freedom Charter: the Africanists were again agitating for independence, citing a communist influence in the ANC's affairs. Ironically, Mandela, who had once been an ardent nationalist, was now regarded as an enemy. At a meeting in November that almost ended in a physical confrontation, the Africanists walked out. Mandela was irritated. He might sympathize with the sentiments but he regarded the rhetoric as immature. Five months later they would form the Pan Africanist Congress (PAC). In a further irony this organization would have a dramatic hand in determining the course of Mandela's life.

The new year brought fresh demands on Mandela the father. Evelyn approached K. D. Matanzima to persuade Mandela to let the boys be schooled in Transkei. Mandela approved of the discipline at the mission boarding schools, and he believed the rural environment would be good for the boys. Before the new term began, he fitted them out with smart uniforms and then drove them down to the Transkei, a ten-hour journey. He was breaking his ban and had to get back to Johannesburg immediately to register at his local police station as the banning order required.

Then early in February he returned home late one night from a political meeting to find Winnie in pain. He rushed her to Baragwanath Hospital only to learn that it would be some hours before she went into labor. The expectant father was due in court and was not able to return to the hospital until late in the afternoon, by which time Winnie had given birth to a daughter. Mandela proclaimed her a true Mandela. She was named Zenani – "what have you brought to the world?" – a name he thought carried with it a social responsibility.

The trial staggered on through the long, hot summer, but Mandela's home life was greatly changed and happy. His mother had come up to help the young family, and his sister, a nurse, was living with them. The house resounded with conversations and laughter. Whenever he had extra money, Mandela would come home laden with large bags of groceries and bottles of alcohol for his drinks cabinet. At the time prohibition prevented Africans from buying "European liquor" unless they had a permit. Mandela, always a generous host, had acquired a permit so that his guests never went dry. Paradoxically he very seldom drank himself.

Early in the winter, the Treason Trial took another unexpected turn when the court quashed the indictment against the sixty-one. In court, the arguments had been more a matter of legal maneuvering than dramatic evidence and vibrant cross-examination. But despite the defense's successes, the minister of justice was adamant that the trial would proceed irrespective of cost. While the ANC took heart at the prosecutor's apparent tentativeness about the evidence, they were less sanguine about the overall political climate. The leadership decided that in the event of a security crackdown Oliver Tambo should immediately go into exile and rebase the organization in a neighboring and supportive country. Leadership from afar was not an option that had ever interested Mandela, who firmly believed his battleground would be on the soil of the country he loved.

In August, two years and eight months after the initial arrests, the trial restarted with its focus now on the remaining thirty accused. Over the next two months, thousands of documents were put on record and more than two hundred witnesses, mostly from the police force's security branch, took the stand. There was nothing new.

But while their days were absorbed by the trial, in the evenings Mandela and his fellow ANC leaders were busy debating the future. At a conference in December the organization decided to stage a massive anti-pass campaign starting in March and extending through to Freedom Day on June 26, 1960. Mandela's banning order prevented him from attending the conference, but he welcomed the new resolve.

The decade that had seen Mandela move from the political sidelines to the center, came to an end. His fortunes had risen and fallen; his personal life had been characterized as much by joy as by heartache. He was on trial for treason; he was under a banning order, yet elsewhere in Africa, seventeen countries were due to become independent in the coming year.

The man who, in a sense, set the tone for the decade was the British prime minister, Harold Macmillan. He ended a tour of Africa by addressing the South African parliament in February 1960. In the

These racist signs are evidence of the increasingly stringent apartheid laws and of the complete disrespect some of the population had for black people.

"There were sudden shrill cries of 'Izwe Lethu' – women's voices it sounded – from near the police, and I could see a small section of the crowd swirl around the Saracens and hands went up in the Africanist salute. Then the shooting started. We heard the chatter of a machine gun, then another, then another. There were hundreds of women, some of them laughing. They must have thought the police were firing blanks. One woman was hit about ten yards from our car. Her companion, a young man, went back when she fell. He thought she had stumbled. Then he turned her over and saw that her chest had been shot away. He looked at the blood on his hand and said: 'My God, she's gone!' Hundreds of kids were running, too. . . .

". . . One little boy had on an old blanket coat, which he held up behind his head, thinking, perhaps, that it might save him from the bullets. Some of the children, hardly as tall as the grass, were leaping like rabbits. Some were shot, too. Still the shooting went on. One of the policemen was standing on top of a Saracen, and it looked as though he was firing his gun into the crowd. He was swinging it around in a wide arc from his hip as though he were panning a movie camera. Two other officers were with him, and it looked as if they were firing pistols. Most of the bodies were strewn on the road running through the field in which we were. One man, who had been lying still, dazedly got to his feet, staggered a few yards, then fell in a heap. A woman sat with her head cupped in her hands."

Eyewitness account of the Sharpeville massacre by Humphrey Tyler, assistant editor, *Drum* magazine

Right: The mass funeral for the Sharpeville victims – fired on by police while protesting pass laws – in 1960.

den of a government that was racist and fascist (white pretensions to democracy notwithstanding), the nervous Macmillan spoke of a fundamental difference between Britain and the South African government when it came to the aspirations of the African people and the need for a partnership between the various groups. "The wind of change is blowing across the continent," he warned, a phrase which captured the Zeitgeist.

Mandela, from his bench in the dock at the Old Synagogue, with the trial murmuring on about him, thought Macmillan courageous, although he remained wary of British imperialism. The winds of change were indeed blowing, and 1960 would fling both Mandela and his country into times of greater tyranny.

During the tea adjournment on the morning of March 21, the accused learned of the news of a massacre. At Sharpeville, a township in the industrial belt some eighty kilometers south of Johannesburg, sixty-nine people had been shot and 180 wounded when police opened fire on a crowd protesting the pass laws.

Left: A smiling Mandela about to burn his pass outside his Orlando home during the nationwide stay-at-home in March 1960. The stay-at-home led to the government declaring a state of emergency and arresting hundreds of activists, Mandela included.

The protest had been organized by the PAC in an attempt to upstage the forthcoming ANC anti-pass campaign. Riding high on the "wind of change," the PAC trumpeted the destruction of the white regime by 1963. Such rhetoric caught the popular imagination. It also unsettled security forces.

The shootings brought national turmoil and international condemnation. The Johannesburg stock exchange plummeted; the UN Security Council blamed the killings on the Nationalists' racist policies. The government countered that it was a communist conspiracy. Mandela held an all-night meeting with three ANC leaders to consider a response. They had been wrong-footed politically.

The ANC decided to have Luthuli publicly burn his pass on March 26 followed by a nationwide stay-at-home on March 28. On that day, outside his Orlando home, a smiling Mandela burned his pass, the ashes flaking into an aluminum pot. The stay-at-home was observed around the country. In retaliation, the government declared a state of emergency and detained hundreds of activists. But not before Mandela was able to warn some of his comrades. A day or two earlier, Tambo was driven across the Bechuanaland border (now Botswana) into exile; others went underground. A few, including Mandela, decided to face the impending arrival of the security branch.

In the early hours of the morning of March 30, Mandela was woken by six security policemen pounding on his front door. He, Winnie, his mother and sister stood watching as the men searched the house, taking every scrap of paper they found, including transcripts of his mother's accounts of family histories and folk tales. Then, untroubled by the lack of an arrest warrant, they whipped him off to a police station near Sophiatown. Here, together with forty other activists, he spent the rest of the night standing in a dank courtyard before they were herded into a small cell at daybreak. The conditions were appalling: they had not eaten, they were not given blankets, the toilet was a drain hole in the floor and there was no toilet paper. They were not allowed to contact their lawyers.

By the middle of the following afternoon they still had not eaten. The group was hustled back into the courtyard. Mandela stood defiantly with his hands in his pockets. As if he were addressing a child, the commanding officer ordered Mandela to take his hands out of his pockets. Mandela responded that he might comply if they were fed. Some time later they were given a pot of thin porridge. They had to eat it with unwashed hands.

At the same time as the arrests, the government had declared a state of emergency. This brought with it curfews and restrictions on political meetings and demonstrations. More than two thousand activists were held under the emergency regulations in police cells across the country.

SYDNEY KENTRIDGE:

I was an advocate in South Africa in the 1950s, quite new at the bar. Nelson Mandela and Oliver Tambo ran a firm of attorneys in Johannesburg. There were very few black attorneys and no black advocates, so in the nature of things it was struggling, but it always had a good reputation. It was a small firm and its clients were small people, all blacks. But occasionally they would brief an advocate to act for one of their clients. Even more occasionally it was me.

At the end of 1956, over 150 leaders of the ANC and other organizations were arrested and put on trial for high treason. There were seven or eight advocates in the defense team and I was one of the juniors. We were all appearing for all of them jointly. For various reasons, tactical and otherwise, each of us was representing one particular individual and who it happened to be was a matter of chance. I was allocated Nelson Mandela. I was the one who examined him as his counsel and that meant I had to spend a good deal of time talking to him. He was obviously very steadfast and completely committed to his cause, but if you asked him a question about a political issue he would give a really thoughtful reply not a slogan or cliché. He wouldn't have described himself as an intellectual but to me he was a thinker as well as a doer.

He was a very warm person toward everyone who was friendly to him. My political views weren't his but he never picked quarrels. When he gave evidence he had to talk very critically about the government and the police but he was never insulting. He would state his view about why apartheid and everything connected with it was wrong but he was never insulting to individuals. I read a lot of his speeches in preparation for the trial. They were very eloquent, but I would never have called him a firebrand. He was not a fiery speaker, his tone was always quiet. He wasn't a demagogue. He didn't call on people to go and burn down the city hall. That wasn't his style at all.

Right: George Bizos and Sydney Kentridge during the Terrorism Trial of 1970 where Winnie Mandela was one of the defendants. Both men had previously defended Mandela, Kentridge notably during the Treason Trial and Bizos during the Rivonia Trial.

Although this was a treason trial, everyone was on bail so they used to come over from Johannesburg every morning to Pretoria in a government bus – it was an odd arrangement. There was a lot of time out of court when people were talking and sitting around and Mandela was obviously looked up to already not only by the other accused but by the scores of blacks who used to come to listen to the trial. He was already prominent in the ANC, but he'd made his name as a youth leader and wasn't one of the most senior people. My impression is that it was at that trial that his true leadership qualities were first evidenced. Leaders like Chief Luthuli, Z. K. Matthews, and Walter Sisulu were very impressive, great men, but Nelson appealed to the younger ANC members. He was the coming generation. I could somehow tell from the many talks I had with him that this man was a leader – of course I couldn't have guessed he would become the leader he in fact became.

I mainly spoke to him about ANC policy because the state's theory in the Treason Trial was that all these organizations were fundamentally communist, working to overturn the state by violence. In fact at that time their policy had been demonstrations, industrial action, and passive resistance. I didn't have any doubt that Nelson himself had been very much impressed by communist analyses. I was very curious about his attitude and asked him why there was never ever any criticism of the Soviet Union in ANC speeches and publications – it was just after Hungary. He had a very simple answer, "In the whole world, they're our only friends. You don't attack your friends."

The Treason Trial was not by jury but by three High Court judges and none had political views remotely sympathetic to the ANC. Yet it had a remarkable outcome: they acquitted everyone. It was fair. Although these organizations had been heavily influenced by communist theory they were not out to set up a communist state and certainly at that stage they had no plans to carry out their policies by violent means.

The accused had been arrested toward the end of 1956, and indicted toward the end of 1957. The trial began in August 1958 and the acquittal was in March 1961. So the moment the verdict was announced was marvellous. It was pandemonium. The spectators and crowds waiting outside for the verdict cheered and some of the accused were carried shoulder high by their supporters.

The ANC had been a banned organization since April 1960: simply belonging to it became a criminal offense that got people ten years in prison. I didn't see Mandela after he went underground, but people who had been clients of mine in the Treason Trial would say, "Have you seen Nelson? I saw him the other day." I said, "It's all very well to have a cloak-and-dagger operation, but you need less dagger and more cloak!" There was very little cloak, so it was not surprising to hear after a time that he had been arrested. From the end of the Treason Trial I didn't see him again until he was released from prison in 1990.

When the new South African Constitutional Court was inaugurated in 1995, I was an acting justice of the court. The chief justice was there to swear everyone in but Nelson came onto the bench formally to inaugurate the court. I still remember his exact words. "The last time I entered a court it was to find out whether I was going to be sentenced to death." That was literally true. It had been the end of the Rivonia Trial, and he was in court to see if they were going to be sentenced to death. There was a sort of hush when he said that. Everyone was obviously thinking, "Supposing that judge had sentenced Nelson to death?" If he had, the odds are he would have been hanged. I was thinking, "Aren't we lucky? Aren't we lucky?"

After thirty-six hours of enduring appalling prison conditions, Mandela and his fellow treason defendants found themselves being taken off to attend the Treason Trial in Pretoria. His life entered a surreal period. He and the other defendants were being held at Pretoria Local Prison and had to be in court during the day. With Tambo in exile, Mandela informed the prison commander that he needed time to close his practice. It was agreed that on Friday afternoons he would be taken to Johannesburg, could spend the weekend sorting out the paperwork and would be locked up overnight in Marshall Square police station. His arrangement with the sergeant detailed to ensure he didn't escape was equally strange. On the way to Johannesburg the man would stop at roadside shops to buy chocolates, fruit, and dried beef biltong for them both, leaving Mandela to wait unfettered in the car. Or during the weekends he would let his prisoner go downstairs to buy lunch. Nor was he concerned when an anxious Winnie came to visit her husband, and even gave them privacy. This type of "gentleman's agreement" with his guards, Mandela would abide by again many years into the future.

A week later, on April 8, the ANC and the PAC were banned according to the dictates of the Suppression of Communism Act. Mandela's situation became even more peculiar. He was serving a banning order, on trial for treason, incarcerated according to emergency regulations and now, at a stroke, he and his comrades were outlaws, facing ten-year prison sentences simply for being members of the ANC or furthering its aims.

The trial, too, was affected when the defense counsel, on the instructions of the accused, withdrew in protest at the restrictions imposed on their access to their clients by the state of emergency. The accused were left to defend themselves, assisted in so far as it was possible by the two lawyers among them, Mandela and Duma Nokwe. Their strategy over the next five months would be to protract proceedings even further.

Overriding everything were the tedium and frustrations of prison life. Whenever the authorities let her, Winnie would arrange a visit. Yet for Mandela, these occasions were bittersweet. She was pregnant again and he was worried about her and their drastic financial situation. Also, he was missing Zenani's formative years. If the guards were feeling magnanimous they would allow him to cuddle Zenani, but he was always sharply aware of having to let go. Especially when, as the guards ushered mother and daughter from the room, she would beckon him to follow, puzzled that he didn't.

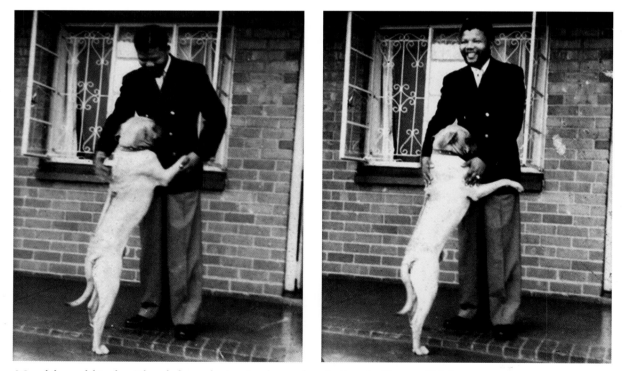

Mandela and his dog Khrushchev relaxing in the garden during the Treason Trial.

When I think of Madiba, it's his huge frame that always gets me. He was such a huge man, with big hands, and then you think of the humility of this big man. I have images of him walking into my husband Yusuf's office at the South African Indian Congress offices and plonking himself down, towering above everybody else, except Yusuf. I met him there for the first time. The offices were in a basement then in West Street, and he used to struggle to come down those stairs!

I think of him on the day I had my twenty-first birthday in 1951. And Yusuf – we weren't yet married – decided we must have a birthday party, so he went off to get some pigeons and got twenty-one – awful little things. And Nelson came to the party and everyone started cooking these pigeons. I don't think Nelson did much cooking, but he stood around trying to help and fiddled around with the rice. It turned out to be a meal they thoroughly enjoyed but I couldn't eat it because the pigeons all turned blue. One of Nelson's first letters from the island referred to the pigeon meal.

We became great friends, Nelson and I, and we saw a lot of each other socially. We used to have lunches together after meetings and into the trials. There was an eating house called Moretsele's, down in Pritchard Street. Moretsele was a lovely huge, plump man who was Transvaal president at one time of the ANC. Often we had no money to pay, but Moretsele would let us off. Nelson had a great sense of humor always, and we just used to talk and laugh and chat. Just friends, meeting for lunch.

In 1956 when they were arrested in what became the Treason Trial, we all went down to the Drill Hall for the first few sessions. There were 156 defendants – you couldn't even get into the court; they had made no arrangements for them to sit.

While the trial was on, Nelson used to come straight from Pretoria to his offices in Chancellor House, and work for a couple of hours before and sometimes phone me to bring him sandwiches and tea. There was always a policeman downstairs, security branch, and one upstairs, but they got accustomed to me bringing sandwiches. I was in Pretoria on the day they were all cleared. It was a very special day. We left Johannesburg early in the morning and I went with Joe Slovo and Ruth First. It was very crowded. And suddenly it was all over: they were all cleared. There was a great deal of hugging and rejoicing. We celebrated first in Pretoria in the streets and in the cars and everywhere else. The treason defendants were so exhausted and relieved that a lot of them just went home.

In 1961 when the trial finished, he went underground. I didn't see much of him except one day when he popped around when I was living on 15th Street, Vrededorp. He was dressed as a night watchman. The disguise wouldn't have fooled people who knew him, but it probably kept the police at bay for a while.

When he was finally caught and tried, we were all in court. I saw him standing there in the dock, dressed in skins and feathers around his head, and he looked like a warrior who was going to bring freedom to his country. When we came out on the day he was sentenced, a huge crowd had gathered. I suddenly felt so relieved: five years, I thought, that's not much. He'll be out in two or three years.

Hemarie Valabe Aminabehn,

Exactly where do I start in writing to you behn? Aug '52 in Aggie's flat when you cooked pigeons for Yusuf and me the night before we appeared in court with Flag and others and when I discovered for the first time that you and Yusuf were united by firmer and more intimate ties than politics offer? Nei, that would take us far back into history. The night in the late fifties when we saw the "10 Commandments"? Perhaps it may be better to remind you of the tasty curry dishes you brought to Chancellor House when I worked there under police escort during the 1960 state of emergency. I well remember how one evening you came with refreshments to the Square which a cop in turn carried into my cell. "Your wife?" he asked almost in a whisper. "No, my sister," I replied. . . . Come March '61 the day the Treason Trial ended, you were amongst those who travelled all the way to Pretoria, who warmly congratulated and cheered us on our discharge, glad to share the victory with those with whom you had fought so hard and long for a new order and a new world. Zami and I met you at a party the same night, but you were soon gone. A few days thereafter I bade farewell to Zami and kids and now I'm a citizen across the waves. It was not an easy decision to make. I knew the hardship, misery, and humiliation to which my absences would expose them. I have spent anxious moments thinking of them and have never once doubted Zami's courage and determination. But there are times when I even fear receiving letters from her, because on every occasion she comes down, I see with my own eyes the heavy toll on her health caused by the turbulent events of the last eight years. Moments in my life are occupied by tormenting thoughts of this kind. But most of the time I live in hope and high spirits as I think of the progress we are making in the sphere of ideas and in important other directions, and the golden friends whose sacrifices at one time or other make these advances possible. They give us the strength and courage to continue striving for what is permanent in the values for which mankind has fought right down the centuries. It is against this background that we think of you Amina. Few of us are likely to forget the forties and the fifties when you were right in the forefront of the youth and women's movements. Indifferent health slowed down your tempo and took away some of the fire that was once in you. But yours is a past you cannot shake away from your life, it is part and parcel of our history. I think of you with pride and fond memories. . . .

Extract from a letter from Mandela to Amina Cachalia written from his cell on Robben Island, dated April 8, 1969.

Hlumelo Vehalie Aninabehu,

I have wanted to write to you ever since I returned in July '62 but until the end of '67 I did not do so simply because you would not have replied. Throughout last year I tried hard & earnestly to reserve a letter for you but pressing problems of one kind or other obliged me to put the matter off. But this is all history; here is your letter.

Exactly where do I start in writing to you, Helu? Aug '52 in Aggie's flat when you cooked pigeons for yourself & me the night before we appeared in court with Flag & others & when I discovered for the first time that you & Yusuf were united by firmer & more intimate ties than politics offer? Nei, that would take us far back into history. The night in the late fifties when we saw the "10 Commandments?" Perhaps it may be better to remind you of the tasty curry dishes you brought to Chancellor House when I worked there under police escort during the 1960 State of Emergency. I well remember how one evening you came with refreshments to the Square which a cop in turn carried into my cell. "Your wife?" he asked almost in a whisper. "No, my sister," I replied. He was even more astonished & suddenly I realised that there was a s.a. even behind bars. Came March '61 the day the Treason Trial ended. You were amongst those who travelled all the way to be there & who warmly congratulated & cheered us on our discharge glad to share victory with those with whom you had fought so hard & long for a new order & a new world. Zami & I met you at a party the same night, but you were soon gone. A few days thereafter I bade farewell to Zami & kids & now I'm a citizen across the waves. It was not an easy decision to make. I knew the hardship, misery & humiliation to which my absence would expose them. I have spent anxious moments thinking of them & have never once doubted Zami's courage & determination. But there are times when I even fear receiving letters from her, because on every occasion she comes down I see with my own eyes the heavy toll on her health caused by the Turbulent events of the last 8 yrs. Moments in my life are occupied by tormenting thoughts of this kind. But most of the time I live in hope & high spirits as I think of the progress we are making in the sphere of ideas & in important other directions & the golden friends whose sacrifices at one time or other make these advances possible. They give us the strength & courage to continue striving for what is permanent in the values for which mankind has fought right down the centuries. It is against this background that we think of you Amina. Few of us are likely to forget the forties & the fifties when you were right in the forefront of the youth & women's movement. Indifferent health slowed down your tempo & took away some of the fire that was once in you. But this is a past you cannot shake away from your life; it is part & parcel of our history. I think of you with pride & fond memories.

My late mother visited me in Sept. '67. She told me then how kind were Yusuf & Agz to her & gave me details of their hospitality. I was quite surprised when she mentioned & pronounced both names perfectly, & realised how things had changed & how her own ideas had developed. I recalled an occasion in Apr. '52 when I returned from a meeting in Krugersdorp which Yusuf & I had attended. She told me that a tall white man

In August, shortly after Mandela had started delivering his testimony, the state of emergency was lifted which meant that he could return to the succor of his family, the comfort of his own bed, and the joy of the small things – being able to take a walk, buy a newspaper – that prison denied. As best he could he took on legal work, operating out of the offices of colleagues, and then Ahmed Kathrada's flat, until he had taken over all the rooms bar the kitchen. Winnie was forbearing, hoping only that he would be at the hospital when the new baby was born.

During the Christmas adjournment of the trial, Mandela learned that Makgatho was ill. Breaking his ban, he drove overnight to the Transkei only to find that the boy required surgery. Mandela drove Makgatho to Johannesburg the following night. The boy was left in the care of his mother while an exhausted Mandela went to make arrangements for the operation. Having taken care of one emergency, he phoned Winnie only to be told that she had gone into labor and been rushed to a nursing home. A previous pregnancy had ended in a miscarriage and now she was weeks ahead of the expected date of birth. By the time he got to the hospital, Winnie had given birth. His daughter was fine but his wife had been placed in an oxygen tent. Over the next few days Winnie rapidly recovered. The baby was named Zindziswa – "you are well established" – after the daughter of the praise singer who had so greatly impressed Mandela during his school days at Healdtown.

In the new year the trial resumed. Counsel for the accused had been reinstated, and the arguments droned on. Then, unexpectedly, toward the end of March 1961, the judges interrupted the defense to request a week's adjournment. It was presumed they had reached a verdict. In the interim Mandela met with his ANC comrades. They had already decided to operate both underground and from outside the country and now needed to implement the M-Plan. As Mandela's banning order expired two days after the adjournment, it was decided that he should clandestinely operate full time for the organization, resurfacing periodically to show that the fight continued.

It was a somber man who let himself into his house that night. Winnie was up and waiting. "I was about to embark on a life that neither of us wanted," he wrote in his autobiography.[21] As she packed a small suitcase for him, he told her what had been decided. Friends and relatives would look after her and their family, he reassured her. She did not ask how long he would be away, and he did not hazard a guess. The next morning he kissed his two daughters goodbye then went to Evelyn's house to say goodbye to Makgatho and Makaziwe. (Thembi was at boarding school in Transkei.) Father and children walked on the *veld*. They did not ask him what was happening but they were subdued, sensing something serious in the wind.

Mandela headed for Pietermaritzburg where he addressed fourteen hundred delegates representing one hundred and fifty religious, social, cultural and political organisations, and called for a national convention in which all South Africans – black and white, Indian and "colored" – would together create a constitution for the country. The audience was excited by his unexpected though secretly prepared appearance, their fists punching the air with the salute: '*Amandla*' (power) and the answering cry: '*Ngawethu*' (to the people). The journalists present felt that here was a man to watch. Yet before any of them or the security police could corner him, he had slipped away as mysteriously as he had appeared. It would be three decades before Mandela would step on to a public platform in South Africa again.

Above: New Age *headlines from 1961*

Left: Winnie and Nelson with their second daughter Zindzi, born during the uncertain years of the Treason Trial

The day after the Pietermaritzburg conference, Mandela drove back to Johannesburg to attend the Monday court hearing for the Treason Trial. If the verdict was guilty, he would be imprisoned. If he were discharged, his life underground would begin.

To the relief and surprise of the accused, a full bench of three judges handed down a verdict of not guilty. To the state's embarrassment they found that the prosecution had failed to prove that the ANC had a policy of violent revolution or was communist. Mandela regarded the verdict as the deliberation of fair-minded men who had done the right thing, rather than a vindication of the judicial system. His skepticism was justified as the state's forces of oppression would become ever harsher in the coming decades. As the jubilant crowd gushed from the court, they broke into the hymn "Nkosi Sikelel' iAfrika" – God bless Africa – its haunting melody ending a trial that had lasted more than four years.

Mandela himself was a free man for the first time since 1956. His banning order had expired a few days earlier and he could have gone home to his family. But his short life as an outlaw was about to begin. That night he slept in a safe house in Johannesburg and in the next few months would shift about the country visiting ANC branches, talking to white newspapers and preparing the ground for the three-day stay-at-home planned for May 31, the day white South Africa would be celebrating the country's reconstitution as a republic. He was becoming the voice of the people, more famous as a creature of the night than he had ever been in the spotlight.

Right: Mandela surrounded by supporters singing "Nkosi Sikelel' iAfrika" at the end of the Treason Trial. Slightly behind to his right is a very young Aziz Pahad and behind Aziz is Winnie Mandela.

Above: Mandela celebrates his bittersweet freedom with Winnie outside court. That night he went to a safe house; his life as an underground leader had begun.

It was not an easy time. Mandela desperately missed his family and he was constantly on the move from empty flat to safe house. He was a man of the shadows, holed up during the day, dashing out in the darkness to meetings and appointments. Although the long days of solitude gave him time to think, for a gregarious person the hours could sometimes be too lonely. Always at the back of his mind were his wife and two daughters, one still a baby.

He adopted various disguises: supplementing his beard with long hair and wearing rimless glasses. Sometimes he was a "garden boy," unobtrusive in threadbare blue overalls; at other times a chauffeur with a peaked cap and a long dust coat. But he had to be careful. There was a warrant out for his arrest and police roadblocks were a frequent occurrence.

Despite a large-scale security operation that saw troops pouring into the townships across the country, the May 31 stay-at-home was more successful than the ANC leadership believed at the time. In hiding, or restricted by banning orders, they had to monitor the situation through the media. Without exception the state-owned radio and the white-owned newspapers played down the impact. Reluctantly, Mandela and his committee called off the strike after the first day. The government hailed this as a victory. Mandela, tense and despondent, gave an interview to a British television crew expressing his anger and frustration. It was his first television appearance: the background was a brick wall. The symbolism could not have been more blatant: Mandela and the black people of South Africa had their backs to the wall.

The "Black Pimpernel."

He told the interviewer, "If the government reaction is to crush by naked force our nonviolent struggle, we will have to reconsider our tactics. In my mind we are closing a chapter on this question of nonviolent policy."[22] For this outburst Mandela was criticized by the ANC executive but he felt that sometimes it was necessary to push the reluctant toward the inevitable.

A month later, Mandela formally proposed at an ANC meeting that they abandon the policy of nonviolence and establish a military wing. Moses Kotane opposed it and the proposal was defeated. The next time Mandela raised the matter the committee authorized him to take it to the national executive. The meeting was held at night and in secret. Though Chief Luthuli, who as president presided over the meeting, initially resisted Mandela's arguments, he ultimately agreed that a military campaign was inevitable. He then proposed that any military movement should be a separate and independent organ, under the overall control of the ANC, but fundamentally autonomous. Having agreed, the matter was then taken the next night to a joint meeting of the executives of the ANC, the Indian Congress, the Colored People's Congress, the South African Congress of Trade Unions and the Congress of Democrats. After an all-night debate, the congresses authorized Mandela to go ahead and form a military organization, separate from the ANC. That body became Umkhonto we Sizwe (MK) – Spear of the Nation – with Mandela as commander-in-chief.

The lawyer relished his new profession. When MK did a practice run at setting off an explosive device, he decided it was worth the security risk to witness the fireworks. One night they drove to a brickworks on the outskirts of Johannesburg where dynamite explosions to loosen the clay were not uncommon. MK's test bomb was a paraffin tin filled with nitroglycerine set off by a timing device fashioned from the inside of a ballpoint pen. The explosion was deemed a mighty success, but even before the debris settled the men had disappeared into the darkness.

At the time Mandela was staying in Berea, a residential area of flats on the hill overlooking central Johannesburg. He felt safe here, mostly because it was a white suburb and one of the last places the police would think of looking for him. His host was a white journalist, Wolfie Kodesh. On the first night Mandela spent at his flat, Kodesh woke in the early hours to find the MK commander preparing to take a jog through the streets. It was 4.30 A.M. Kodesh couldn't believe his guest was serious. A black man running in a white suburb would have attracted attention. He refused to relinquish the door key so Mandela spent an hour running on the spot. Kodesh returned to bed bemused. Eventually he came to join Mandela in this early morning ritual.

Mandela spent his days engrossed in books: Karl von Clausewitz's treatise *On War,* works by and on Che Guevara, Mao Tse-tung, and Fidel Castro, Deneys Reitz's account of guerrilla tactics during the Boer War, *Commando,* and Menachem Begin's *The Revolt,* which impressed him because the guerrillas fought in terrain similar to South Africa where there were no forests or mountain fastnesses.

But for all this mental stimulation and his feelings of security, he was lonely and missed his family. He had released a heartfelt open letter to the newspapers which mentioned his enforced separation "from my dear wife and children, from my mother and sisters, to live as an outlaw in my own land."[23] But it also acknowledged that the struggle was his life and he would never cease from fighting for freedom.

By now the newspapers had dubbed Mandela the "Black Pimpernel" – a reference to the fictional Scarlet Pimpernel in Baroness Orczy's novels of the French Revolution. It had a certain romantic cachet but hardly reflected the danger and anxiety surrounding his life. In fact it was the very ordinary things that could give him away.

Mandela had a penchant for sour milk – *amasi.* Each day he would ferment a bottle of milk on the windowsill. On one occasion he overheard two men remarking in Zulu that this was surely an indication that a black person was living there. When the Zulu cleaner approached Kodesh with a newspaper article about the Black Pimpernel, Mandela acknowledged that it was time to move on.

The Black Pimpernel next donned his gardener's disguise and moved to the quiet leafy suburb of Norwood. Then in October he moved to a farm in Rivonia, a semi-rural area of market gardens, horse stables, and ranch-style houses in large grounds linked by dirt roads and devoid of street lighting. The property had been bought secretly by the Communist Party and was occupied by one of their members and his family to disguise its function as a safe house. Mandela moved into the outbuildings, adopting the name David Motsamayi.

The bucolically named Lilliesleaf farm suited Mandela. The countryside reminded him of his happy childhood. Winnie came out occasionally, bringing the children and fresh vegetables, and he could allow himself the brief illusion that his family was intact. Makgatho was often with her and father and son would enjoy long walks across the *veld.* There was even a pool where they could swim in the hot afternoons. What especially pleased Makgatho was the pellet gun his father bought him. But the security police had

Winnie under surveillance and these visits were always fraught with danger.

During the evenings, Mandela continued his undercover activities, meeting with ANC activists at houses across the city. He was also travelling throughout the country as the chauffeur David Motsamayi, clothed in peaked cap and white driving coat. High up the agenda on these excursions were plans for MK's first declaration of the armed struggle. This was scheduled to take place on December 16, a national holiday commemorating a battle won by Afrikaner *voortrekkers* against the Zulus in 1838.

The targets were buildings symbolizing apartheid rule, such as pass offices, or electricity pylons and telephone lines, installations that would disrupt military communications, alarm the government and the white population, and cause foreign capital to flee. The last thing Mandela wanted was a blood-feud. Animosity between Afrikaners and English-speaking whites was still palpable sixty years after the Anglo-Boer war. How much deeper and longer would be the fallout from a race war? Successive acts of sabotage he believed could help bring the Nationalists to their senses.

The explosions on December 16 occurred in Johannesburg and the coastal cities of Durban and Port Elizabeth. MK suffered its first casualty when one of the operatives was killed in an explosion and another had his arms blown off. Nevertheless, the activists were elated, although Mandela felt some embarrassment as Luthuli had been awarded a Nobel Peace Prize just six days earlier. Fortunately, the links between MK and the ANC were not publicly known.

Early in the new year, the ANC received an invitation to attend a pan-African conference in the Ethiopian capital, Addis Ababa. The leadership felt it was time to elicit support from the independent states and chose Mandela to go.

The trip greatly appealed to him. He was forty-two years old, had never been out of the country, and his mission was important. He spent the night before his departure with Winnie. She was worried about his leaving the country but Mandela was adamant that he would be returning. Touchingly, she had bought him a new suitcase.

The next morning Mandela was to be driven to Bechuanaland, a British protectorate. He was delayed waiting for Walter Sisulu at a secret rendezvous in Soweto. Much later Mandela would learn that Sisulu had been arrested. Kathrada arranged for Ameen Cajee to drive Mandela to Bechuanaland. Mandela remained on edge, worried about roadblocks and the border police, let alone his lack of a passport. They made it safely across the border to the town of Lobatse without alerting the South African security police, but the British authorities were better informed, even down to the £600 in funds Mandela carried.

During the next six months, Mandela would visit twelve African states before spending two weeks in London with Oliver Tambo. The experience dazzled him. In Bechuanaland he watched a lioness saunter out of the bush and felt that this was the Africa of myth and legend. In Tanzania the burden of skin color disappeared in a land now ruled by Africans. While on a flight from Khartoum to Addis Ababa he noticed the pilot was black and experienced a moment's panic. With some annoyance he realized how apartheid had conditioned him to think of Africans as unable to perform certain skilled jobs.

In every country Mandela visited he spoke to the heads of state and explained the ANC's position and the need for funds, arms, and military training. To his consternation he found that in many countries the PAC had a far higher profile than the ANC, whom PAC propagandists had dismissed as a Xhosa tribal army

While in hiding, Mandela went on a tour of African states before heading to London. He ended the trip with eight weeks of military training in Addis Ababa (left) in preparation for his role as commander-in-chief of Umkhonto we Sizwe, the ANC's new military wing. Mandela poses with Colonel Tadesse Biru (top left) in Ethiopia.

infiltrated by white communists. While being careful to give the PAC its due, Mandela argued the ANC's centrality and won pledges of support and financial aid. But it was the advice he received from an Algerian military commander who explained that guerrilla warfare was not about overthrowing the enemy but about bringing them to the negotiating table that made a lasting impression.

In Britain, the self-confessed Anglophile marvelled at the buildings that were the home of parliamentary democracy while abhorring the imperialism that had attempted to destroy his people. On a sightseeing stroll with Tambo, he stopped at a statue of Jan Smuts near Westminster Abbey and jokingly wondered if it would one day be replaced with a statue of them. His stay in Britain was packed with meetings and long chats with old friends now in exile, many of whom thought he had moved closer to the PAC after his experiences in independent Africa. He reassured them that his rhetoric was a matter of image. If the ANC was to receive support from the independent states then it had to present a black face to black Africa, he argued.

Before returning home, Mandela spent eight weeks undergoing military training in Addis Ababa. He went on fatigue marches, learned how to shoot an automatic rifle and a pistol, fired mortars, was taught to make small bombs and attended classes on military science. The program was scheduled to last six months but toward the end of July he was summoned home. As a parting gift, the instructor presented him with an automatic pistol and two hundred rounds of ammunition. Stopping off in Dar es Salaam, an armed Mandela met with a group of twenty-one MK recruits heading to Ethiopia for training. Echoing the words of the Algerian commander, he told them a guerrilla war was not about pulling a trigger but about creating a just society. When he left he was saluted by his own soldiers.

Mandela, still in khaki fatigues, flew to Bechuanaland where he was met by Cecil Williams, a white theater director and member of MK. That night, with Mandela posing as the chauffeur, they drove back to Johannesburg, reaching Lilliesleaf at dawn. There was time to snatch a few hours' sleep before an uneasy Winnie arrived with their daughters. Part of her anxiety might have been the Sabotage Bill being ushered through parliament in response to MK's first explosive attacks. It carried the death penalty for those found guilty. She knew well enough that the state was becoming tougher. While her husband was out of the country she had been subjected to continual harassment by the security police. On one occasion in June, after newspaper headlines declared the return of the Black Pimpernel, police had ransacked her house late at night. People gathered in support and during the fracas some youths set fire to the police motorbikes. For a moment it had seemed as if the police might shoot into the crowd but when the throng dispersed they demanded that Winnie find the culprits. "Don't ask me to do your dirty work," she retorted.[24]

It was Mary Benson, the anti-apartheid activist, who introduced me to Nelson Mandela. Her father was a hospital registrar in South Africa, and after the war she became deeply engaged in the struggle to end apartheid. I was international secretary of the Labour Party at the time and Mary had asked me if I would introduce Mandela to Hugh Gaitskell. I met him and Mary just outside the Tube station at Westminster and took them both to see Hugh Gaitskell in the House of Commons. The issue of sanctions did not arise then. Mandela seemed much more interested in learning about the British system and politics

In London, the self-confessed Anglophile marvelled at the buildings that were the home of parliamentary democracy while abhorring the imperialism that had attempted to destroy his people. His stay in Britain was packed with meetings and long discussions with old friends now in exile including Mary Benson (above) and Oliver Tambo (pictured above with Mandela in Addis Ababa).

ESME MATSHIKIZA:

We saw Nelson when he came on his secret trip to London. We were living in exile in Primrose Hill and one night, past midnight, the doorbell rang. Todd put on his dressing gown and went to open the door, and there were Nelson and Oliver Tambo standing there. It was a surprise, but Nelson had just said to Oliver that he wanted to see Todd. Oliver seemed to be nervous because there was no doubt that this was a highly secret mission. But Nelson, with his slightly stubborn side, was insistent. And so he spent about an hour with us. I had a feeling even then that this man had a vision of where it was that South Africa had to go to. He was way above and way beyond any of us at the time. I said to him "Surely you can't go back now? They'll arrest you." And he said, "I see myself as a leader of the people and the leader of a people must be with the people."

MAC MAHARAJ:

While I was a student in London, working as part of the underground SACP unit, we began to receive requests for books on guerrilla warfare, and it became my task to scour bookshops and libraries for these books and smuggle them in to South Africa. I was aware of the debate at home over whether or not nonviolence was a sustainable tactic and I remember very clearly receiving a request thanking us for the books we were sending, but also asking specifically for books written by the other side in any freedom struggle. We were told to find books by British generals on successful counterinsurgency in the Malaysian world, the Burmese world, anywhere where guerrilla warfare had failed.

When I came home and eventually ended up on Robben Island and began to join in the discussions in the quarry, I suddenly found that the one person who had read all the books we had sent from London was Madiba. And it was indeed Madiba's request. He explained that he very consciously wanted books on failed guerrilla struggles to understand how counterinsurgency had succeeded and what tactics would foil counterinsurgency from succeeding.

BILLY NAIR:

After Madiba's trip abroad in 1962, he came back through Botswana in disguise and came to Durban to meet MK. We met at a safe place that no one, except members of the regional command, knew. And the very first thing he said – he was actually dressed in the typical, partially Arabic gown – was: *"Salaam Alakhum,"* the Muslim greeting. This, incidentally, was a detail given by Bruno Mtolo when he gave evidence in the Rivonia Trial.

Madiba gave us an account of his experiences in Africa, pointing out that it was not sufficient for us only to engage in sabotage; we would need to train people militarily. It was not a campaign to take lives, nor was it against whites. It was to overthrow the regime, if necessary, by force. Where our cadres were trained abroad, they had to be politicized. A first-class military man who is politically unconscious could hit at anybody indiscriminately.

We had lunch with Madiba and exchanged views on the future of MK, and then we handed him over to another MK component to meet Chief Luthuli, Dr. Naicker, and others. But this is where the fault lines appear, so far as security is concerned, because he also met some journalists and it is suspected that one of them was a CIA agent. Madiba's arrest came as a shock to us – if it had been handled entirely by MK I don't think he would have been in trouble.

AHMED KATHRADA:

I was on the MK committee whose task it was to deal with all logistical matters pertaining to Madiba's underground activities. We discussed the proposed trip to Durban and had advised against using Cecil Williams's car again so soon after it had brought Madiba from Bechuanaland. But he was extremely impatient; he wished to report to Chief Luthuli, and the Indian Congress leadership in Natal. His impatience was due to a rumor spread by the PAC that he had become an Africanist during his Africa tour and had in fact joined the PAC. Our committee was overruled by the ANC leadership, and he went in Cecil's car, acting as Cecil's driver. He was arrested on his way back from Durban.

ve known Nelson Mandela as a professional, as a political figure, as a prisoner, as a president, as a pensioner. In a way it's the story of our country, it's the story of my life and it's the story of the South Africa of Madiba.

When I was a student at the University of Cape Town in the 1950s, I used to come to Johannesburg and visit the offices of Mandela & Tambo. They would be jam-packed: rural people, township people, all seeking support for their complaints. I would always be so beautifully received – the only white person on the premises – and someone, usually Ruth Mompati, would greet me, offer me a cup of tea, with such grace. Although they were so busy, sometimes Oliver Tambo or Nelson Mandela would ask, "How is the struggle in Cape Town?" And I had forty-five seconds to describe it. There was an element of grace and courtesy and acceptance from these extremely busy professionals. I was just a student, but I felt welcomed.

Afterwards I met Madiba – it would have been about 1961, 1962 – deep in the underground. It was very, very dangerous. In circumstances where we were all tense and grey with anxiety, and looking all the time over our shoulders, at the windows, at the doors – in strode this calm, serene, majestic person with that huge Mandela smile. It was not something that only came with the presidency – it's just part of his nature – and with it went that total conviction, and again the embrace, the warmth and the strength.

I met him again in Lusaka in 1990 when the two sections of the ANC – from "home" and the exiles – met up. I was waiting inside the airport not wanting to be pushy. Someone said, "Comrade Albie, go forward, go forward." So I went forward to the rope and I saw the crowds waving at this absolutely joyous moment after so many decades, and the sound gets louder and louder and then there is Madiba, with that same huge smile, that same welcome. And to be honest, I threw myself upon him. It was a very important moment for me. The only time I felt the loss of my arm, which happened late in 1988, was at the moment when we reconnected, the two elements of the struggle. And I wanted some physical affection, some acknowledgement, and he stepped back and he said to me, "And how's Stephanie?" Now, after he went to jail, I met Stephanie, we fell in love, we married, we had two children, we were in exile, and I'm sorry to say we divorced, yet somehow he kept track of all that. It was so poignant, a beautiful and a sad moment.

After that we had a lot of dealings while I was part of the negotiating team for the new constitution. There was one very dramatic night where the whole issue was whether amendments to the Bill of Rights could be by the two-thirds or by seventy percent. We had been given a firm mandate of sixty-six and two-thirds – not a third of a percent more. The anxiety was that the National government was getting all sorts of concessions and now we were told, late I think on a Friday afternoon, that if we went up to seventy percent you've got a deal, we've got a constitution. All the things that we'd been spending our whole lives fighting for were now in the balance. Cyril Ramaphosa said, "We've got to go and see Madiba. He's the only person who can think his way through, and possibly give authority to even put that on the agenda." So we drove to Houghton. It's dark. I'd been in exile fo[r] twenty-four years; it wasn't the place ordinary members of the ANC would hang out in unless they were doing underground work some decades earlier. Cyril had been to Madiba's house once or twice but in the daytime. So I remember we were driving around – it's getting later and later – and eventually when we find it no lights are on at all.

It was long before cellphones so Cyril gets out of the car and he shouts, "Tata! Tata!" Nothing happens. He then gets hold of some little pieces of gravel and he throws them up to Madiba's window – nothing. He throws some more. Eventually after about five minutes a light goes on. At last!

Then the door opens. I've never seen Mandela so majestic – in a dressing gown! In a dressing gown, woken up at about 12:30. And again, that enormous smile. "I thought my last moments had come. It's quite a relief to see it's only friends waking me up at this hour." And he just took it in his stride and we went and sat downstairs, Mac Maharaj, Cyril Ramaphosa, myself, discussing with him what to do the next day.

We did respond to the seventy percent and the other side reneged and from ther[e] onwards it was just downhill to the breakdown of the negotiations. And I actually recommended, at that stage, that we stop, on the principle of "see you in court." My proposal wasn't accepted but Mandela listened to all the speakers, he kept a careful record, total democracy. As a politician, he was an excellent listener, interested in ideas and good at judging when the moment was right and when to hold back.

I believe the moment during the negotiations when apartheid fell was when Mandela pointed his finger at President de Klerk and said, "That man cannot be trusted." He was seething but totally controlled, and that was the end of white domination in this country. There were other formal moments, legal moments, constitutional moments, tragic moments after the death of Chris Hani – going on television, holding the country together. But in psychological terms, it was Mandela pointing at de Klerk.

For me Mandela was in his greatest presidential mode, and by that I mean warm and humane and funny, when he announced the winner of the competition for the design o[f] the Constitutional Court which went up on the site of the old Fort prison. We had a gathering inside the prison and he started off saying, "I feel most uncomfortable. In fact, [I] want to leave as soon as these formal proceedings are over. I've spent enough time in my life in prison. I'm fearful people will forget to unlock and let us out afterwards. To make matters worse," and he points to me, "I see among the judges people who have been in prison." It was a very joyous moment.

Nelson Mandela's past and his presence is there in the old Fort. He's been there as a lawyer, he was there in the Treason Trial as a prisoner, he's been there as the president and then finally he came in as a pensioner for the opening of an exhibition of his documents that were seized from Robben Island. Older, a little bit slower, but again tha[t]

After Winnie left Lilliesleaf, Mandela briefed a meeting of the ANC leadership about his trip. The next evening, he and Williams went to visit Luthuli in Natal, rather rashly driving in the same car that had been used to fetch Mandela from Bechuanaland. As befitted a commander Mandela carried his loaded pistol, although posing as a chauffeur.

After briefing Luthuli, Mandela went on to meet with MK saboteurs and then on to a party at the house of a *Drum* photojournalist, apparently unconcerned by security considerations.

The next morning, Sunday, August 5, 1962, he and Williams started the six-hundred-kilometer run to Johannesburg. Mandela chatted about the majestic views and how easy it would be to sabotage the railway line which ran parallel to the road. Shortly after passing through the hamlet of Howick they were overtaken by a car of white men which slowed to a halt and forced them to stop. When Mandela glanced in the rear-view mirror he saw they were sandwiched between two more cars packed with white men. Surreptitiously he slipped the pistol and a notebook with names and addresses into a gap between the two front seats. His life on the run had come to an end. Remarkably, the car was never searched or the charges against him would have been greater and many others would have been arrested.

Some days later Mandela was charged in a Johannesburg magistrate's court with inciting workers to strike and leaving the country without a passport. Instead of a suit, he wore a traditional leopard-skin kaross, proclaiming the heritage and history of his people. With typical vigor, he chose to defend himself, enlisting Joe Slovo as his legal adviser. The trial was set to be heard in October.

Mandela left the courthouse in a police van through cheering and applauding crowds, as the call and response cry of *"Amandla, Ngawethu"* resounded along the streets. The Black Pimpernel may no longer be at large, but he was the hero of the people.

As he was being led away he glanced at the public gallery and smiled encouragement at Winnie who was watching him in consternation.

Rand Daily Mail proclaims the arrest of the Black Pimpernel. Right: Mandela in prison in Pretoria.

A few days later Winnie visited him at the Fort. She was attractively dressed and considerably more cheerful. The supervising guard allowed them some privacy by turning away and they clung together fiercely. Hurriedly they discussed the children and financial matters. Mandela believed the children should be made to understand that he could be jailed for a long time. As for money, he again reassured his wife that friends and family would help. Theirs wasn't the first family to face hardships in the name of a cause. When Winnie left, the guard allowed Mandela to walk with her almost to the main gate. As she went on alone, he stood watching until she turned a corner. In his hands he held a present she had brought him: expensive pajamas and a silk dressing gown.

In the weeks leading up to the trial, Mandela established an exercise routine and enrolled at London University for a correspondence course law degree. He knew that the ANC had established a Free Mandela Committee to publicize his case and ensure there were mass demonstrations at the court and he fully intended to exploit his predicament.

On the first day of the hearing he entered the Old Synagogue, again wearing his kaross. His emphasis on the historic nature of the struggle was echoed by Winnie, defiant and proud in a long Xhosa skirt and beaded headdress. The effect electrified a gallery packed with supporters: they raised clenched fists, shouting *"Amandla."*

MANY YEARS AGO, WHEN I WAS A BOY BROUGHT UP IN MY VILLAGE IN THE TRANSKEI, I LISTENED TO THE ELDERS OF THE TRIBE TELLING STORIES ABOUT THE GOOD OLD DAYS, BEFORE THE ARRIVAL OF THE WHITE MAN. THEN OUR PEOPLE LIVED PEACEFULLY, UNDER THE DEMOCRATIC RULE OF THEIR KINGS AND THEIR AMAPAKATI, AND MOVED FREELY AND CONFIDENTLY UP AND DOWN THE COUNTRY WITHOUT LET OR HINDRANCE. THEN THE COUNTRY WAS OURS, IN OUR OWN NAME AND RIGHT . . .

Nelson Mandela, opening statement to court, October 22, 1962

WHY IS IT THAT IN THIS COURTROOM I AM FACING A WHITE MAGISTRATE, CONFRONTED BY A WHITE PROSECUTOR, ESCORTED BY WHITE ORDERLIES? CAN ANYBODY HONESTLY AND SERIOUSLY SUGGEST THAT IN THIS TYPE OF ATMOSPHERE THE SCALES OF JUSTICE ARE EVENLY BALANCED? WHY IS IT THAT NO AFRICAN IN THE HISTORY OF THIS COUNTRY HAS EVER HAD THE HONOR OF BEING TRIED BY HIS OWN KIND, BY HIS OWN FLESH AND BLOOD . . .? I AM A BLACK MAN IN A WHITE MAN'S COURT. THIS SHOULD NOT BE.

Nelson Mandela, statement in his defense, October 22, 1962

The trial lasted two weeks. Mandela knew he was guilty, and his intention was to justify his cause by questioning the legitimacy of the proceedings. He called no witnesses of his own. Instead, on the final day, he delivered an hour-long political speech. As he had done at the Treason Trial, his argument took a long historical perspective and concluded with the unjust laws that had driven him to desperate measures. After a ten-minute recess the magistrate sentenced him to five years in jail. It was a harsh sentence that brought wails of disbelief from the crowd. Pugnaciously Mandela raised a clenched fist. Three times the court echoed with the call and response before subsiding into the lilting "Nkosi Sikelel' iAfrika." Downstairs Mandela said a brief goodbye to Winnie. This time she was the one giving encouragement.

For the next six months Mandela was jailed in Pretoria. Then, on a cold winter's night, he was handcuffed and bundled into a windowless van with three other political prisoners. Fifteen hours later the men were hauled out on Cape Town docks and, still handcuffed, were shoved into the hold of an old boat.

Left: Lilliesleaf farm in the suburb of Rivonia was both a safe house during Mandela's underground years and the de facto head- quarters of MK. In 1963 while Mandela was on Robben Island, an informant's tip-off led to almost the entire high command of MK being arrested there. These are the original police photographs from the raid. Incriminating paperwork was found at the farm and Mandela was brought back to Pretoria from Robben Island to face a more serious charge of sabotage, carrying with it the death penalty.

Through a porthole above their heads, guards took turns urinating on them. The knock of the diesel engines rose thunderously and the packet pitched into the bay. Their destination was no secret: Robben Island. On his first visit to Cape Town in 1955, Mandela had stood on Signal Hill and gazed at the notorious prison twelve kilometers away. Many famous Xhosa chiefs had been incarcerated there: some, like Makana and Maqoma, had died on the windswept island or in attempting to escape. It was a place of dread and brutality.

Mandela was destined to spend only a few weeks on Robben Island before being carted back to solitary confinement in Pretoria. Baffled at first, he learned that a security police raid on Lilliesleaf in July had captured almost the entire high command of MK.

In October, he and his comrades were charged with sabotage. Through their legal counsel, Bram Fischer, they learned that the state would push for the death penalty. "From that moment on we lived in the shadow of the gallows," Mandela recorded.[25]

The hearing, like the Treason Trial, bumbled slowly into motion at the Palace of Justice in Pretoria. Armed soldiers and policemen surrounded the building while hordes of people gathered in the streets. As he climbed out of the fortified van in a protected yard behind the Supreme Court, Mandela could hear the crowd singing and chanting. The case was not only a major political event in South Africa: the world was watching.

Despite ample preparation time, the prosecution distinguished itself with such amateurish arguments that on one occasion the judge dismissed the indictment. Technically, Mandela was free. The court erupted in commotion but the security police promptly rearrested the accused. A month later they were back in court. When Mandela was asked to plead he said, "My Lord, it is not I, but the government that should be in the dock. I plead not guilty."[26]

The Rivonia Trial, as it became known, continued into the first two months of the new year. Winnie had been placed under a two-year banning order in 1961 and was restricted to Johannesburg. Her attempts to get police permission to be in court were refused. To make matters worse, Mandela heard that their home had been raided by the security forces and a young relative of Winnie's detained. He interpreted the harassment as a dirty tricks campaign by the state to persecute him further. Eventually the minister of justice granted Winnie the necessary permission on condition she did not wear traditional dress. Mandela ruefully noted that this same government was exhorting Africans to embrace their culture in the homelands.

DENNIS GOLDBERG:

When we were charged in the Rivonia Trial they brought Nelson from Robben Island and he was dressed as a black prisoner: he was in leg irons and handcuffs, wearing sandals, no socks, short trousers, a jacket that looked like a house boy's jacket. Now, you know, to put a man into the dock like that is to create an immediate prejudice. He was usually so elegant, such a snappy dresser, and they set out to humiliate him in his clothes, but he held himself so ramrod straight, so dignified. He had lost an enormous amount of weight in prison. I had a small slab of chocolate with me and I nudged him. He looked around below the level of the barrier of the dock, and he nodded his head and I broke off a couple of blocks of chocolate and put them in his hand. He sort of wiped his hand across his face and the chocolate ended up in his mouth with a sharp corner sticking out of this very sunken cheek, and he sucked on this chocolate until it disappeared and then he nudged me again. . . .

George Bizos used to bring us food. Nelson really enjoyed the sausages and the gherkins and the sweetmeats and his cheeks filled out in a very few days. You realized how near the edge our prison diets were: just a few snacks every day would put on weight.

During the preparation of the trial, Nelson wasn't sitting around leaving the lawyers to do it; he was part of the defense team. At one point he took me aside, and standing over me – and he's much taller than I am – he wagged his finger at me and said, "Dennis, when you talk Marxism you must talk about South Africa. Don't come with all these theories of feudalism and the development of classes in Europe, because our people don't understand these things, it is not part of our discipline. I just want you to know that this is important." By that point I think we all feared that the death penalty was a very real threat and I am quite sure he felt that he had to say to somebody who he

Winnie attends the Rivonia Trial with Nelson's mother, Nosekeni Fanny. Winnie had to fight a banning order to be allowed to attend.

thought might not be sentenced to death, what he felt about our fundamental goals.

I first met Nelson Mandela at a meeting after he came back from his visit abroad. He was with Walter Sisulu and saying that armed struggle was inevitable, that we had to achieve victory, and I remember saying to him, "What's victory?" He said, "I can't tell you the answer. The point is, we will carry on our struggle to the limits of our energies and the strength of our people and decide as we reach each stage how far we will go. And it was a sense of realism, not an idealism gone mad that believed we could overthrow the government in 1963 and then be free. They were saying: we are undertaking an armed struggle, but we are not wedded to an armed struggle. It's a long struggle and we will take it step by step until we succeed. The first manifesto of Umkhonto we Sizwe, of which Mandela was commander-in-chief, said clearly that when the apartheid regime was ready to negotiate we would negotiate. It took thirty years.

Before the elections, Mandela did a "meet the press" on Robben Island and he was telling stories in the officers' mess hall. The photographs of B. J. Vorster were still there and Adriaan Vlok, that vicious minister of police, (so-called) justice, and prisons. And Nelson was telling prison stories – quite harsh stories, but you have to end them with a little humorous twist, because you have to give your audience a bit of a lift. It's like cooking sweet and sour, you know. And then we were asked to go for a walk to the lime quarry where the comrades on the island had worked. When we were out of earshot of everybody I said to Nelson, "I think sometimes you must show some anger for the comrades who never get to talk to the press and who don't understand that we laugh at the plight we were in." And Nelson was quite shocked, so everybody waited for Walter, because everybody always waited for Walter, who said, "Dennis, don't be bitter." And I said, "I'm not bitter, I'm angry. There's a difference."

ARTHUR CHASKALSON:

In the weeks leading up to the sentence, Mandela never wavered. He knew what he was going to do. I think they all did. Once the decision had been taken that they were not going to deny the allegations, he started working on his statement from the dock.

A lot of preparatory work had been done. The first work would have been built up in consultations in the court and in prison and there would be questions and drafts on which he would make comments and corrections. The final version was all carefully prepared and typed out, but I think it would have been written out in his own hand first. I brought my wife's South African history books into prison so he could verify certain facts, and make sure he got the sequence right.

Even on the day he was due to make the statement he changed some words. At the end he makes a series of points not unlike Shylock's: "We are human beings." He was rejecting a whole lot of petty apartheid things. This section originally had the word "African" in it. I remember him saying to me just before his speech: "I want to change that 'Africans' to 'we'. Do you think that would be wrong?" So right up till he was actually delivering the speech he was changing it.

The decision to run a political defense, in essence to plead a justification, was undoubtedly correct. It had a huge impact internally and internationally. In fact, it put the government on the defensive; they were called upon to justify apartheid and they got lost attempting to do so. Yutar and his team were totally outclassed – the accused ran rings

I was born at Umtata, Transkei, on the 18th July 1918.

I was only 12 yrs of age when my father died. After my father's death, my cousin, David Dalindyebo, then Acting Paramount Chief of Thembuland, became my guardian. He brought me up and educated me.

I am related to both Sabata Dalindyebo, the present Paramount Chief of Thembuland, and to Kaizer Matanzima the "Chief Minister" of the Transkei. Both of them are, according to Tembu Custom, my nephews.

I took the degree of Bachelor of Arts of the University of South Africa which I obtained in 1942.

Later I studied law and early in 1952, I was admitted as an attorney. The same year, I set up practice in Johannesburg in partnership with Mr Oliver Tambo, a co-conspirator in this case. This partnership was dissolved in 1960 as a result of my being detained during the State of Emergency and as result of Mr Tambo's departure from the Republic. After the State of Emergency I continued practising until March 1961, when I went underground as a result of certain events which I will deal with later in my evidence.

I am married and have five children.

In 1944, I joined the African National Congress. The same year I, and several others, founded the African National Congress Youth League, which became a subsidiary body of the ANC.

In 1946 I was elected to the Executive Committee of the Transvaal branch of the ANC. In 1950 I became a member of the National Executive. In 1952 I was elected President of the Transvaal branch and later, during the same year, the National Executive appointed me deputy National-President of the ANC.

I held these positions until September 1953 when I was served with a notice issued by the Minister of Justice in terms of the Suppression of Communism Act of 1950. The notice ordered me to resign from the ANC and for numerous other organisations specified in the notice.

I have already indicated that in 1944, I became one of the foundation members of the ANC. I served on its National Executive continuously from 1944 until 1952. In 1946, I became the National Secretary and in 1952 its National President.

I have also indicated that during September 1953 I was ordered in terms of the Suppression

of Communism Act, to resign from the ANC and other organisations. Prior to this date, I had been convicted and sentenced to nine months imprisonment, suspended for three years, by the Witwatersrand local division of the Supreme Court for my part in organising the Defiance Campaign which was held to be a breach of the Suppression of Communism Act. In terms of the Suppression of Communism Act the banning provisions of the Act could be applied not only to named Communists but to people who had been convicted under the Act. It was under this clause that I was banned.

After September 1953 I did not attend any meetings except for a brief period of about 4 months when as a result of a judgment of the Appellate Division, the order restraining me from attending gatherings became invalid.

After my ban I still kept in close touch with the ANC and followed its activities. The practice of the ANC, was to keep banned members who were banned informed by sending them important documents such as conference reports and statements issued from time to time.

I am a socialist and am greatly attracted by the idea of a classless society. But I am not a Communist and have never been a member of the Communist

** It is an idea
it is an ideal
live and see
be ~~to~~ ~~I am~~
an ideal for
to die.

for which I have lived;
or which I still hope to
realised. But if I ~~should~~ NEEDS
~~spared to die for~~ it it is
which I am prepared

u only met Mandela once before the trial. I was working as a partner in Kantor's in Johannesburg. James Kantor was a playboy lawyer with a big criminal law practice, but one of the solicitors there was his brother-in-law, Harold Wolpe, who was a Communist Party member and would handle political cases. Mandela was underground at that stage.

I didn't take much notice when on July 11, 1963, seven men were arrested in Rivonia, a suburb of Johannesburg. I had by then decided to emigrate with my family and I was no longer at Kantor's. Suddenly, two days after the Rivonia arrests, Harold disappeared and a couple of days later was arrested trying to get over the border. Extraordinarily, Harold, along with Arthur Goldreich, managed to escape from jail. The security branch was so angry they arrested James Kantor and locked him up in solitary confinement, and I was asked if I would wind up his practice so I left the bar and delayed my departure for Australia.

Although rumors circulated, there was no hard news about what was happening to any of the men arrested at Rivonia. Mandela was on Robben Island, and the other accused were all locked up in solitary confinement. But then Hilda Bernstein came to ask if I would handle the trial. She was asking that I should embark on a case of unknown duration in the defense of people I didn't know, whose actions I knew nothing about and on a charge which had not yet been formulated. Given the mood of the white population I was extremely pessimistic, but I was sickened by her account of her reception from other legal practices in Johannesburg and I agreed to take the case. In the following days Albertina Sisulu and Annie Goldberg, Dennis's mother, came and after a time, Winnie Mandela. She was one of the most spectacularly beautiful young women I've ever seen.

Eventually I was defending all the accused except James Kantor. We put together an outstanding team of barristers: Bram Fischer, George Bizos, Arthur Chaskalson, and Vernon Berrange. The prosecution was handled by a monster called Dr. Percy Yutar, an appalling little man who refused to give us any details about who was even being charged. I was stumbling around in the dark. It was unheard of in legal circles. But Yutar was very taken by publicity so he would tell the newspapers before he told the defense team. One day I was phoned up and told the trial was to begin the next day and that the various accused would be let out of solitary confinement so they could be interviewed by lawyers. "Who are the accused?" I asked. "We won't tell you. You'll find out when you arrive."

Eventually we discovered they had been brought to Pretoria jail. We went there and they brought the accused into the interview room. Then the door opened and Nelson Mandela walked in. That was the first time we knew he was going to be charged because he'd been in prison for over a year. It was a most extraordinary experience. He came in and they all fell on him and hugged him. They were so pleased to see him. When I first met him he had been in his mid-forties but seemed considerably younger because of his youthful and vigorous manner. Now he'd lost a lot of weight and was much paler, his face hollow-cheeked. However, his manner was the same: friendly, easygoing, confident.

All the other accused were dressed in their normal clothes but Mandela was dressed in black prisoner's garb, but despite this he immediately took command and everybody deferred to him. You could see the charisma and immense authority this man exuded. I felt very respectful. You just recognized this was somebody extraordinary. There was no were crowds of spectators on both the white and non-white benches. In Pretoria's Supreme Court, prisoners in custody enter up a steep staircase which emerges in the center. A few minutes before the judge entered, a signal was given for the prisoners to be brought in. The first prisoner was Nelson Mandela. As he climbed the staircase and his head and shoulders appeared above the level of the dock, there was a ripple of excitement among the public. He turned to face them and gave the thumbs up sign of the ANC with his right fist clenched. His deep voice boomed out with the ANC battle cry: "*Amandla!*" The African audience replied immediately in chorus: "*Ngawethu!*"

When we eventually got to the beginning of the trial after all sorts of delays, Mandela was called. The clerk says, "Accused Number One, how do you plead?" and Mandela says "I plead not guilty. It is the government that should be on trial not me." Accused Number Two had the same story. They all did the same. The whole essence of the defense was that the defendants denied nothing but attempted to put the government on trial.

Right from the start, Mandela said, "You are my lawyers. You will do what I want you to do. You are not allowed to cross-examine any witness who is telling the truth. It is of fundamental importance that I, and my fellow accused, accept responsibility for everything because what we did was the only thing we were allowed to do and that was to fight for the freedom of our people. What we must do is turn this trial into a trial of the government." Later George Bizos said they spoke more as gladiators than defendants.

When it came to the defense, Mandela decided that as he was, in effect, pleading guilty, the best way to get his message to the world would be to make an unsworn statement to the court that would allow him to say everything he wanted to say uninterrupted. When Percy Yutar realized this he was very taken aback – almost hysterical – but the judge allowed us to proceed.

It was amazing to sit through Mandela's speech. There was tremendous silence in the courtroom when he stood up and he spoke for a long time, around five hours. He went into the dock ready to die. "What I did was right. I had no alternative. Freedom will come to South Africa one day and even if you hang me it will only give inspiration to others," he said "I plead not guilty." When finally he got to the end, he took off his reading glasses, looked straight at the judge and said, "It is an ideal which I hope to live for and achieve. But if needs be, it is an ideal for which I am prepared to die." There was this intense pause. As he sat down, the court was very quiet and then a sort of sigh went up from all the black people listening.

The only time I despaired was when they had eventually been found guilty. There was a real concern they would be sentenced to death. We asked Mandela if we could bring in some witnesses to give evidence in mitigation – historians, for instance, who could explain that if you deny people the opportunity to vote and refuse to talk to them, revolution is the natural consequence. But Mandela said no. He prepared a note for what he would say if the death sentence was passed, "I meant everything I said. The blood of many patriots in this country has been shed for demanding treatment in conformity with civilized standards. If I must die . . . I will meet my fate like a man."

IN PRETORIA'S SUPREME COURT PRISONERS IN CUSTODY ENTER UP A STEEP STAIRCASE WHICH EMERGES IN THE CENTER. A FEW MINUTES BEFORE THE JUDGE ENTERED A SIGNAL WAS GIVEN FOR THE PRISONERS TO BE BROUGHT IN. THE FIRST PRISONER WAS NELSON MANDELA. AS HE CLIMBED THE STAIRCASE AND HIS HEAD AND SHOULDERS APPEARED ABOVE THE LEVEL OF THE DOCK, THERE WAS A RIPPLE OF EXCITEMENT AMONG THE PUBLIC.

Joel Joffe

Right: An evocative photograph of the stairs that led the Rivonia defendants to the dock.

Following page: The front cover of the charge sheet listing the names of the accused. The back cover (on p. 129) lists the verdicts.

AHMED KATHRADA:

When Madiba was first arrested in August 1962, Joe Slovo managed to smuggle me in for consultations on the grounds that I was going to be a defense witness. So we saw him a few times together and he asked us then, "Chaps, is Rivonia clean?" Joe reported that he was told by Arthur Goldreich that everything had been removed, which was not true. Had they found nothing at Rivonia I don't know what evidence they would have had against Madiba. It was there at Rivonia they found his diary, they found his notes.

Right from the word go, Madiba was regarded as the leader during the Rivonia Trial. And right from the day of our arrest, the police had drummed it into our heads that we were going to hang. But during the ninety-day period, we had nothing to do with Madiba; he didn't even know for a time that we had been arrested.

After the ninety-day period was up, we were brought together in Pretoria to consult with our lawyers and prepare the case. Bram Fischer told us, "Chaps, prepare for the worst," and they seemed to have enough evidence to hang us. Madiba started telling us at every consultation that we had to fight this as a political case. Where they hadn't got evidence against us we would not volunteer any. Where they had got evidence we would admit it. We all accepted that we should fight it as a political and not a legal case.

Right through, we had to steel ourselves because in every interrogation they'd drum it into us about the death sentence. They were not very bright chaps, the security branch, and they used the usual tactics – the soft one, and then the threat that if you don't cooperate they bring in Captain Swanepoel. Sergeant Van Zyl said to me, "Just give us two bits of information. . . ." They wanted to know where I had been staying underground and the location of the farm to which my colleagues had moved from Rivonia. They could have tortured me to death, but I couldn't tell them this because I didn't know. Van Zyl said, "Just give us this and we won't charge you. We'll see you go out of the country. We'll give you a good sum of money." But all the time very sympathetic: "Your people are such nice people. Why must you protect the Jews and kaffirs?"

Then comes Swanepoel. Tough chap. Terrible fellow; a real sadist. He comes with some paper and pretends to be reading to me, "This is what your friends are saying about you." And some of it may be true, I don't know and this is where you have to be very, very strong. So you go back to your cell and you're facing this death sentence and you're not allowed to talk to your colleagues, and you don't know who is saying what. I began to notice that Govan Mbeki's hair was turning white and I became very frightened because people in certain stressful circumstances can lose their hair or go white. . . . I thought Govan must have broken down until we met one day and he says, no, it's just that his black hair dye has worn off!

With the exception of Mlangeni and Motsoaledi and possibly Dennis, the police never ever assaulted the rest of us, not even Swanepoel. They came close, but they never touched us. But the worry is there. I don't know what I would have done had they tortured me, because you can't blame anybody who breaks down under torture.

It was our collective decision that Madiba should make the statement in the dock. We had seen Madiba's speech, we had discussed it, we agreed with it. We were aware that this speech could hang us, especially the last part of it. When we were discussing it, Madiba said, "Apart from anything else, we owe it to the people in the struggle. If we show any weakness in our defense or if we decide to appeal, it means we are showing weakness."

He reads this statement. After we were found guilty there was this period of mitigation. Harold Hanson was a very senior advocate and his speciality was to plead in mitigation. When he saw Madiba's statement he said, "I can't do this because you fellows are asking for the death sentence." Bram Fischer managed to convince him of the need for it.

Until the last day when the judge says, "Stand up for your sentence," the expectation was death. Prepare for the worst, right from the word "go."

Arthur Chaskalson told me much later something I didn't know – he wasn't trying to keep it a secret – apparently the day before we were sentenced, one of the senior lawyers went to ask de Wet, "Are you going to hang them?" and he said, "No." They didn't tell us because he could always change his mind. On the 11th we were found guilty. And then there was mitigation. On the 12th we were sentenced. So right up to that time the expectation was death.

In your mind you have now reconciled yourself to the worst. Fear is there, naturally, but you can do nothing about it now. They've found you guilty so you have to steel yourself to accept the worst. When he pronounced life there was this collective sigh of relief.

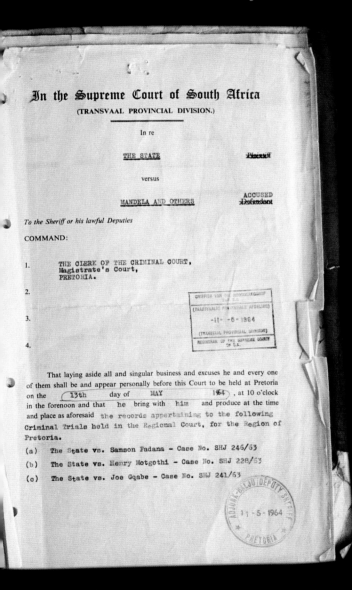

GEORGE BIZOS:

The formation of Umkhonto we Sizwe in December 1961, and the adoption of violence, albeit selected violence, was used as an excuse for the introduction of detention without trial. It was information given by people in detention that probably led to the discovery of Lilliesleaf farm.

The Rivonia Trial marks the end of the Queensberry Rules period. The witnesses would come directly from the cell with the investigating officer who had interrogated and probably tortured them. Those witnesses would have to repeat that information, extracted under duress, if they wanted to avoid a jail sentence.

Percy Yutar was a good prosecutor, an adept cross-examiner for whom irony and sarcasm were part and parcel of his armory, but he was overzealous and made some fundamental mistakes. He drew up a political indictment: the State versus the "National High Command," a ridiculous situation – what are you going to do, send an amorphous body to prison?

Arthur Chaskalson prepared and Bram Fischer delivered an outstanding argument, based on authority, that the indictment was excipiable – it was prejudicial to the accused – primarily because it named hundreds of co-conspirators. We asked for particulars. Back from the prosecution came a reply that angered the judge: "These particulars are well-known to the accused." De Wet said that was presumptuous: it presumed that the accused were guilty.

The world at large did not understand that the quashing of that indictment was not a final judgement. The Rivonia defendants were immediately rearrested, unleashing a flood of protest from organizations, trade unions, and NGOs throughout the world demanding their release.

The nationalist newspapers had been calling for the death sentence, as had the South African Broadcasting Corporation. If the trial had been speedy, it is likely we would have received a death sentence. The respite we got as a result of the quashing of the indictment enabled us to prepare properly.

Yutar expected perjuries and apologies. Instead, the defendants said, "Yes, I did it. But we have been knocking on your door for over thirty years to negotiate with us. You haven't. You should be in the dock." This was the defense we put in cross-examining witnesses and that was the statement made deliberately by Nelson Mandela from the dock, not in the witness box where he could be cross-examined. I later categorized this as the "Mandela defense." We wanted a clear statement of what the ANC was about and why it had done what it did. It had a tremendous effect overseas, and here, and for years thereafter copies of the version printed in the *Rand Daily Mail* were found under the brown-paper cover of schoolbooks in Soweto and elsewhere. It was a clarion call for the liberation of the people in South Africa.

It wasn't only Mandela. Walter Sisulu, a man of limited education, but an ardent believer in freedom for the people of South Africa, put up a tremendous performance, with dignity and even a sense of humor. I had had the advantage of having worked with Sisulu for a couple of months on his statement and I was confident he would do well. Yutar could not resist the temptation of showing how clever he was and completely underestimated Sisulu.

He was persuaded by the notion that Africans need Indian and white agitators to write their speeches. We were confident that Sisulu had the resources to manage very well on his own and his ninety-day detention didn't appear to affect him at all. It is said that if you have a strong belief in the righteousness of your cause you actually develop a sort of resistance.

Yutar said, "Sisulu, now let us come to the so-called grievances of the African people that you purport to represent." Sisulu lost his temper in a controlled way and said, "Dr. Yutar, I believe you have a son similar to mine. Mine was arrested this morning when he came here with his mother and he's in a cell somewhere in Pretoria. How would you feel if that happened to your son?" Then he added, "Dr. Yutar, I just wish that you had been a black man for one day in this country and then you wouldn't say the things that you said. Now let us deal with what you call 'so-called grievances.'"

And then Govan Mbeki, of course an intellectual, also scored. He said, "We didn't do this in order to win a civil war. We did it to put pressure on the government to come to the negotiating table." Somewhere Yutar had picked up a quotation by Mbeki describing the nationalist party policy as granite-like. "Ah," says Yutar, "but you call it granite. You could not possibly have believed that they would soften!" And Mbeki said, "You know, Dr. Yutar, fissures do occur in granite, and because they are so brittle they disintegrate more easily."

The possibility of a death sentence was always there, but I think over the course of the trial, the tide had turned, in the international community in particular, in favor of the accused and against the death sentence and it would have been a very serious step to take. Verwoerd said that if the judge sentenced them to death they would have carried it out. De Wet was an Afrikaner to the core, but he was not an apartheid ideologue; he hated all intellectuals. He was a shy man in many ways, patronizing, unsure of himself, but not a bloodthirsty man and I think that, given a free hand, he would probably not have imposed the death sentence.

In his first draft of his famous speech from the dock, Mandela's last paragraph ended with the words: "It is an ideal for which I am prepared to die . . ." I read this and I said, "Nelson, you know, you'll be accused of seeking martyrdom. Surely you've done all these things not for the purposes of dying, but for accomplishing them and living happily. Do me a favor. Just add the words, 'And if needs be' before 'for which I am prepared to die.'" And he did. I don't know if it made any difference.

Part of my job was maintaining contacts with diplomats and I saw the British consul-general the night before sentencing. He was in his cups and he kept me there till 11:30, but he told me I mustn't worry, there would be no death sentence and there would be one acquittal – Rusty Bernstein. As it turned out, he was one hundred percent correct – but we couldn't tell the accused. How could we rely on it? Anthony Sampson later got the inside story and it was obvious that the British must have warned of the possibilities of a death penalty and were told not to worry. Just before the sentence, the advocate Harold Hanson went to de Wet and said, "Are you going to impose the death sentence?" and the judge told him, no. Hanson told Bram and no one else. As far as the accused were concerned, they didn't know.

This is perhaps the most significant and poignant document in African history. These notes, in the scrawl of a lawyer, were written either the night before, or, more likely, during the session on the very day Mandela and his fellow Rivonia defendants were facing the possibility of the death sentence. They present, too, a curious historical puzzle. Mandela's biographer, Anthony Sampson, was unable to decipher line eight. It has also defeated other close associates. When Sampson showed it to Mandela it baffled even him. A solution is offered here. The key lies in the second word and so the line reads, "That army is beginning to grow." (Skeptics should note the similarity of the "ar" in the word "standards" immediately above with the beginning of the mystery word.) An alternative – "That army is busy and growing" – does not materially affect the sense. In August 2005, this interpretation was presented to Mandela for his comments. A transcript of our conversation appears on page 336. In it Mandela himself offers the word "army" and so for the first time this amazing document can be read as a whole. Since they are Mandela's private thoughts – notes to himself – they are more direct and authentic than any more formal statement. They present a developing logic in his position and argument. And they are the backbone of the stance that was to sustain him in the years of adversity and triumph.

1. Statement from the dock.

Thursday 11th June, 1964:   Before de Wet JS.

For State: Dr. Yutar, Mr. Krogh, Mr. Klasmann.
For Defence: Mr. Fisher QC, Mr. Berrange QC, Mr. Bizos & Mr. Chaskalson.

Verdict :- Accd. 1 :- Guilty all 4 counts.
" 2 :- Guilty all 4 counts.
" 3 :- Guilty all 4 counts.
" 4 :- Guilty all 4 counts.
" 5 :- Guilty Count 2 - Not guilty counts 1, 3 & 4.
" 6 :- Not guilty all counts and discharged
" 7 :- Guilty all 4 counts.
" 9 :- Guilty all 4 counts.
" 10 :- Guilty all 4 counts.

Friday: 12th June, 1964: Before de Wet JS :-

For State: Dr. Yutar, Mr. Krogh, Mr. Vorster & Mr. Klasman.
For Defence: Mr. Hanson QC, Mr. Fisher QC, Mr. Berrange QC,
             Mr. Bizos & Mr. Chaskalson.

Sentence :- All accused sentenced to imprisonment
for life   and in those cases where
the accused were convicted of more than one
count, all counts are taken together
for the purpose of sentence.

       All accomplices who gave evidence
and were given indemnities are declared
immune from prosecution.

12/6/64.

Boshoff JWB.   Claassen & G. M.
           O' Hagan E.S.C. 7 Judgments
           while N.R.D.
       Abovenamed Judgments were
today referred to Dr. Yutar.
                    (sgd.) 12/6/64

The prosecution closed its case at the end of February 1964 and the defense was given a month to prepare. Their counsel thought Mandela and Sisulu had an even chance of being hanged. Nevertheless, as "accused number one," Mandela and his fellow accused decided that instead of giving testimony he would read a statement. Legally this would not help his case, but he was more concerned with highlighting the grievances of the people he represented. Once again, Mandela turned to history and tradition to explain his political beliefs and motivations. He touched on Marxism, on the great democracies, and he emphasized how legislation had stripped Africans of dignity, destroyed their family life, and shredded their society.

While the defense concluded its case, all-night vigils for the accused were held at St. Paul's Cathedral in London and half-hearted attempts were made by various British officials to dissuade the Nationalist government from taking a hard line. In a gesture of support that appealed to Mandela, he was elected president of the student's union at the University of London. Of more political weight was a UN Security Council resolution (not ratified by Britain or the U.S.) urging the South African government to end the trial and grant amnesty to the defendants. With an equanimity that showed Mandela's tough single-mindedness, he wrote examination papers for his law degree courses a few days before the verdict. He passed.

On Thursday, June 11, the court found Mandela and the main accused guilty on all counts. That night the men agreed that even if they were sentenced to death they would not appeal. They had fought on a moral stance; an appeal would negate their position. The next day the court was packed, and crowds stood outside the Palace of Justice waving banners. Inside, the last moments were playing out. Mandela smiled at Winnie and his mother, who had travelled up from the Transkei. Two pleas – one by the writer Alan Paton – were entered in mitigation. When they had finished, the judge nodded at the accused. He was breathing heavily and refusing to meet Mandela's eye. After a short preamble he sentenced them to life imprisonment. The court erupted in joy. As he was being hustled out of the dock, Mandela searched for Winnie and his mother in the public gallery but to no avail.

In the dark hours of the following morning, Mandela and six of the Rivonia defendants – Walter Sisulu, Raymond Mhlaba, Govan Mbeki, Ahmed Kathrada, Elias Motsoaledi, and Andrew Mlangeni – were flown in a drafty Dakota directly to Robben Island. They arrived shortly after dawn: the sky was low and grey, a bitter wind howled off the sea.

PART TWO

Out of the Darkness, 1964–1990

he group of prisoners was driven to an isolated cement building, the old jail. At the door they were ordered to strip while the guards stood around, automatic weapons cradled in their arms. Naked and shivering in the cold, they were thrown the island's uniform: plain khaki shirts, short trousers, a thin jersey, a canvas jacket, and shoes without socks. Kathrada, being Indian and therefore regarded by the authorities as higher up the racial hierarchy, received long pants and socks.

The old jail proved temporary; a few days later the men were handcuffed and taken to a wing that had been built within the prison especially for politicos – the bleak Section B. Their cells lined both sides of a long corridor. Each had a small barred window and two doors – a metal grill inside, a wooden door outside. At night both doors were locked. Their bedding was a sisal mat and three blankets. The cells were so cold and damp from the recent building work that the men slept fully dressed. When Mandela lay stretched out his head touched one wall, his feet almost the other. At the door on a piece of white cardboard was his number: 466/64 – the four hundred and sixty-sixth prisoner jailed on the island in 1964. His cell window looked onto a courtyard.

"I was forty-six years old, a political prisoner with a life sentence, and that small cramped space was to be my home for I knew not how long," he wrote in his autobiography.[1]

Physically Mandela was in fairly good health, although thinner and weighing less than he had done prior to his incarceration. He was, however, suffering from high blood pressure and needed a low-salt diet. For a man in his mid-forties, the cold, the damp, a mat on a concrete floor, a poor diet, and manual labor were daunting prospects. From the outset, Mandela took up issues with the prison authorities with the agreement of and on behalf of all the prisoners. Now he demanded to see the head of the prison. Among his list of complaints was a protest about the short trousers.

Previous page: The watchtower and barbed-wire confines of Robben Island.

Right: Mandela and his fellow Rivonia defendants were placed in cells so cold and damp from recent building work that the men slept fully dressed. When Mandela lay stretched out his head touched one wall, his feet almost the other.

For Mandela the snappy dresser, short trousers were an insult: a deliberate attempt to strip them of their dignity. At the start of his five-year sentence in 1962 he had demanded long trousers and been accorded his wish. But the concession came with solitary confinement. The isolation ate at his mind until he caught himself about to talk to a cockroach. After a few weeks he surrendered the long trousers in return for the company of the general cells. Now he was again petitioning the monolith. Initially his complaints were ignored, but Mandela persisted. Two weeks later he came in from the work yard to find a pair of old khaki trousers on the floor of his cell. They gave him more pleasure than a pin-striped suit until he discovered that he alone had been favored. He returned the trousers, wanting to know why they couldn't all be given long pants. The guards sneered that he should make up his mind about what he wanted. It would be three years before they all were issued long trousers.

There were other deprivations. According to the prison classification system, political prisoners fell into category D, the most restrictive. Usually they would rise through the categories every two years but could as easily be knocked back on the whim of a prison commander. Despite his two years in prison, Mandela entered Robben Island for the second time as a category D prisoner, allowed to send and receive a letter every six months and entitled to one visit during that period. His letter could be only five hundred words long and was subjected to a vindictive censorship – as was the incoming mail. His first letter from Winnie was so heavily censored that very little was left but the greeting. In the terrible isolation from his family, Mandela came to cherish the biannual letters. "A letter was like the summer rain that could make even the desert bloom," he recorded.[2] Knowing this, the authorities occasionally withheld letters out of spite.

In August, two months after his arrival on the island, Winnie was allowed a thirty-minute visit. The visiting room was a cubicle in a shed near the harbor, some distance from the cells. A three-foot-wide passage divided by wire separated husband from wife. They had to shout to be heard. Guards loomed behind them, monitoring their conversation, which had to be conducted in English or Afrikaans.

Mandela stared anxiously at his elegantly dressed wife. She was thinner, she seemed tense and stressed. He didn't know that she was under her second banning order and because of this had been dismissed from her job at the Child Welfare Office. He longed to touch her, to be able to speak privately to her. But no: "We had to conduct our relationship at a distance under the eyes of the people we despised."[3] Half an hour flashed past so quickly Mandela couldn't believe the guard's gloating, "Time up! Time up!" In the months ahead he would relive that visit repeatedly, knowing it would be six months before he saw her again. In reality, he would not see her for another two years.

OURS IS NOT TO ASK FOR EQUALITY ON A LOWER SCALE; OURS IS TO FIGHT TO WIN ON AN EQUAL BUT HIGHER LEVEL.

Nelson Mandela, on Robben Island

AHMED KATHRADA:

On the night of sentence, the seven of us were woken up. I was chained to Govan Mbeki and put on the plane, past midnight, very cold and we landed at Robben Island early on a cold, windy and rainy Saturday morning. It was June 13, 1964. Now the first thing we had to do on Robben Island was change into prison clothes. In prison they had these gradations of apartheid – whites getting the best, then colored and Indians and Africans – so when it came to clothing, my colleagues, who were all older than me, had to wear short trousers with no socks, while I was given long trousers.

Then it came to food, and again there was discrimination. One's gut reaction was to reject it, but Madiba said, "No, you are wrong. Ours is not to ask for equality on a lower scale; ours is to fight to win on an equal but higher level." One of the colored prisoners was also very angry about this and he wrote a letter to the authorities complaining, and just as Madiba predicted, they replied, "If you are so concerned about this, we'll get you reclass-ified as a Bantu and you'll get their food and you'll get equality in that way."

A young Ahmed Kathrada before his incarceration on Robben Island.

So, from the start our struggle was for equality, and after three years they conceded and equalized the clothing. As in most, if not all improvements in prison, this came about as a result of a combination of pressures: pressure from the prisoners, from the struggle in the country, and from those in exile; and, as important, pressure from civil society organizations and individuals throughout the world.

Madiba was called fairly early on by the authorities, who said, "We are prepared to exempt you from work." But his attitude was, "You know, I'm just a prisoner," and he would accept no special treatment for himself although they offered it. He would volunteer to do everything everybody else did, including getting down on the floor and polishing. He was tough. When we were not allowed newspapers, the bulk of the news came from the communal cells because they had access to the common prisoners and newspapers. They even had radio there. So when we got hold of any news we sent it back to them. Here again, Madiba volunteered to transcribe the news – and that's when the comment came back, "We cannot understand the writing." So we had to exempt him from doing this.

When it came to hunger strikes the ANC had decided among ourselves that the older people and the people who were sick shouldn't take part, but Mandela took part in all the hunger strikes, Walter as well. In other words he refused to accept any treatment that would be special. At work it was the same thing. He was the toughest among us. He could work without fading. And yet they charged him for not working. They could have charged any of us, but they charged him.

BILLY NAIR:

Sixty-one of us arrived together on Robben Island in March 1964. We were badly beaten up by the guards and I managed to smuggle out a letter to my attorney. As soon as the lawyers began to act, Dennis Brutus and I were removed to the isolation block. Madiba and the other Rivonia defendants arrived in June 1964, but we spent about nine months in isolation before joining them and the other political groups.

In the first years we had porridge without milk and very little sugar and thin as water. You breakfasted at about six-thirty or seven and by about nine you were emptied, looking forward to lunch. Indians and colored prisoners would have mealie rice which used to be boiled at two or three in the morning, so by the time we had it at twelve we were eating rocks. And then, for good measure, a little bit of boiled pumpkin, turnip, carrots, just thrown on top, not necessarily all at once. You'd get pumpkin running for a year, two years, every lunch hour.

The Africans had the same breakfast, but for lunch they'd have boiled mealies, yellow mealies. I liked something rough, so I used to exchange my food with an old man from the Transkei who was doing a life sentence for attempting to assassinate Matanzima. He had hardly any teeth so I used to exchange the samp or mealie rice for his mealies. For supper, Africans had more porridge and Indians and coloreds a quarter loaf of bread with a little bit of lard, and black coffee which was largely chicory. Four days a week you'd get beans, on the other days four little squares of meat.

Of course we had visits from the big boys in Johannesburg and Pretoria. If they changed our diet it would mean changing diet for the entire prison system, they said. They could not discriminate against the rest of the prison populace. The International Red Cross visited us at least once a year and they said it was ridiculous: if the system applied to us, it must be worse for the rest. Of course, there was a great deal of smuggling going on in the kitchens – we were not too sure whether it was caused by the deliberate attempts of the authorities to keep diet to a minimum or whether the smuggling itself resulted in a reduced diet. But it was only as a result of the battles we fought on Robben Island that the prison diet changed throughout the country.

The sporting facilities we enjoyed in later years were hard to come by. We mixed the cement for the tennis court and laid it with assistance from the builders. Initially, they'd only allow us tennis and table tennis, but on weekends we were allowed to play six- or seven-a-side soccer. Govan Mbeki was referee, Mandela and Sisulu were linesmen. Finally, about two years before my release, we were able to get a quarter-size billiard table from the International Red Cross so some of us learned billiards for the first time.

Our food improved when we were graded A-class prisoners and we could buy a limited amount of our own food – not much, somebody would buy jam, somebody would buy canned fish, once or twice a month – we would have a little party over the weekend and share this with the guards.

Madiba was eventually prescribed a special diet because of high blood pressure and he used to have a quart of milk for the day, and other stuff, too; and all this he used to readily share. When Tokyo Sexwale, now a multi-millionaire businessman, and Terror Lekota, our present minister of defense, came to Robben Island with the Black Consciousness movement in the 1970s, they landed in our section on weekends. After a little while they were allowed to come over to our side on Saturdays and Sundays. These two rascals were not used to prison food and they used to go into Madiba's cell looking for biscuits. Madiba would go in there in the afternoon after work and all the stuff would have disappeared – seriously!

The older guards were replaced in about 1966 with a younger set. Madiba was very good with them. A new chap would be posted to Robben Island, he's anxious to meet him, he's heard about Mandela, terrible, dangerous. The first time he comes, he's taken to Madiba's cell, sits down and Madiba accommodates him, opens up a packet of biscuits and makes tea for him. The guard confesses, "But we were told you are a terrorist!" Madiba says, "No, no." And the guard – not only one, dozens of them – began to get a different picture.

Although I had been at meetings with Madiba before his arrest, we didn't become close until we met on the island. He gave me his life story, personally, and I gave him mine – even details of the girlfriends – but he didn't reveal everything. He's quite a shark, a big shark. He was quite a playboy in his day, even during the Treason Trial.

Then, of course, we had political discussions of a wide variety. We would conduct classes in the quarry. I did the trade union movement; Madiba, Walter, Govan Mbeki, and others did the history of the ANC. We also had detailed discussions on the origin of man. We had a resource second to none: the State Library, which supplied material – even Marxist literature – to Ahmed Kathrada and 'Sbu Ndebele who were the librarians then. In that way, through those essays and discussions, we educated the entire ANC component in the prison. Many of us became UNISA students and some of us got one, two or more degrees.

Madiba is a democrat of the first order. When overseas visitors came to discuss prison conditions for instance, they usually wanted to meet Madiba, and perhaps Walter or Govan Mbeki. But Madiba used to insist, to the chagrin of some of us, that they have a conference about general conditions and would involve people from other organizations.

Madiba is also, first and last, a gentleman of the first order. He wants to ensure that he listens to you, to whatever problem you've got. He sits down and listens and then he'll respond – and there, too, he's casual, slow and laborious at times. When Madiba got angry he would sometimes simply walk out in a huff, just knowing that he was going to blow, although on occasion, yes, he lost his temper.

Even before making a personal decision, Madiba would like to sound out somebody. In prison the first person he'd go to was Walter Sisulu. He'd go to Walter, and if he wasn't satisfied, he'd go up to the next guy, Raymond Mhlaba. Then he'd go to a few others, even me, and Mac. There were a number of rumors about Winnie while he was still on the island. He probably discussed this with Walter but he kept it [to himself]. . . . He gave me the impression that he'd remain faithful to her irrespective of what happened, and he was conscious of the fact that his imprisonment and their long separation probably was the cause of the problems. But, he was disappointed. And it goes to show the Madiba character: he was not oblivious to what was happening, he was steadfast. He meets the rough tide as it were, head on.

As Mandela had come to realize from his previous prison experience, it was the guards who held sway over their day-to-day lives. If they were to improve their lot even slightly, they had to win the confidence of these men. For the most part the guards were Afrikaners from poor homes, ill educated, with their own vulnerabilities. To be posted to Robben Island was to be imprisoned by one's career.

Reasonableness and a controlled temper were Mandela's response to the daily humiliations inflicted by the guards. He was also careful to position himself as a prisoner of conscience in the hands of an illegitimate regime. He would not be subservient, and he would certainly never call the guards *baas* [boss], as many of them insisted.

There were, however, a few occasions when the normally controlled Mandela unleashed his temper. One of these occurred in 1968 when he officially complained that a guard was withholding study materials. The captain hearing his complaint responded with an insult and Mandela let rip. His fury was formidable and deliberate and the captain clearly felt reprimanded. Another incident took place some years later. The imperious head of the prison, Lieutenant Prins, declined Mandela's request for a visit from Winnie on the basis that he did not really want to see her, and that she turned their meetings into opportunities for publicity. Mandela rose from his chair, moving around Prins's desk. The lieutenant backed away but Mandela checked himself, releasing instead a tirade that condemned Prins as a contemptible man without honor. Even when he reentered Section B, Mandela was visibly unsettled and panting from the encounter. Prins duly charged him with threatening behavior, to which a once again unflappable Mandela replied with a countercharge of misconduct. The matter was eventually dropped.

Right: All day long the Robben Island prisoners sat in rows in the courtyard smashing stones into gravel.

The vagaries of prison life and prison staff notwithstanding, the daily routine was punishing enough. At 5.30 A.M. the prisoners were woken with the clanging of a bell and a guard went through the corridor shouting in Afrikaans, "Wake up! Get up!" For the next hour the men were expected to clean their cells, wash, and shave. Each cell had a sanitary bucket and a one-liter bottle of water. Before they were allowed to breakfast in the courtyard, the buckets had to be emptied into the communal toilets and scoured clean. The job was messy and the stench powerful. Prior to breakfast Mandela jogged around the courtyard, initially the only opportunity he had for exercise. A breakfast of maize porridge arrived in a metal drum. Mandela, the man who loved good food, found it barely edible. To wash it down he received a mug of "coffee" – ground maize roasted black then brewed with hot water.

All day the men sat in rows in the courtyard smashing stones into gravel with five-pound hammers. During the wet winter months the yard was cold; during summer the heat baked within the walls. The work was relentless: there were no breaks and if anyone slackened they were yelled at by the vigilant guards. Day after day the men sat breaking stones, forbidden to talk.

Lunch was boiled kernels of maize washed down with a concoction called *phuzamandla*. In its traditional form this was powdered maize with a pinch of yeast stirred into water or milk until creamy and tasty. The brew served to the prisoners was little thicker than water and as flavorsome. An hour later work resumed through the afternoon until 4 P.M.

The men had half an hour to shower in cold brackish water in a communal bathroom. In an icy midwinter, this alone was torment, although it gave them another hasty opportunity to talk. Not until eight years later would they be given warm water to bathe in. Supper was eaten in their cells: yet more maize porridge, sometimes with a soggy piece of vegetable or, every other day, a gristly piece of meat. The night duty guard was locked in at change of shift around 5 P.M. Sleep time was 8 P.M., but those who had permission to study – which included Mandela who was continuing with his law degree – were allowed to work later; for matric students until 10 P.M. and for university students until 11 P.M. There was never a "lights out"; in each cell a bare forty-watt bulb burned through the night. On weekends the prisoners remained locked in their cells except for a daily one-hour exercise break in the courtyard.

EDDIE DANIELS:

When I came out of jail in 1979, I was escorted home by security police and put under house arrest. There was a young lad standing on the *stoep* and I shook hands with him and walked inside. When I got inside my sister-in-law asked me if I had seen Danny and I said, "No, where's Danny?" She said Danny was on the *stoep* waiting for me. Danny is my son. I had not recognized him. When I went away he was a year old. I went outside and he was crying and I cried too, and I hugged him. I had been in jail for fifteen years and I had a hard stone in my chest. Slowly and surely it disappeared.

When I heard I was going to Robben Island I didn't think I would survive. We in the Liberal Party had collected affidavits from prisoners who had gone there after Sharpeville, and they were brutally handled. In prison they shackled me and handcuffed me. When I got to the harbor they took off my shackles and put me in this dirty, stinking dark hold in this little boat and I had no one to share my fears with.

For the first three days I was kept in my cell away from everybody. Then after that I was allowed to go and work in the yard. We got a hammer and the common-law prisoners would bring us big slabs of slate and we had to break the slate up into gravel. Then we'd pile the gravel and bring the bucket. We were given a quota – fill so many buckets a day – but we refused and we got punished for that. We did work, we worked hard.

Right: In 1964, the prison authorities allowed the Daily Telegraph, *a conservative London newspaper, to visit Robben Island. This was the only time Mandela consented to being photographed while in prison, on condition that Sisulu joined him.*

The first day, we knocked off about four o'clock. I walked into the bathroom and there was this big man standing in front of me. He shook my hand. Mr. Mandela was the first person to extend the hand of friendship to me on the island. I belonged to the Liberal Party and refused to join any organization that had a racial tag, but the ANC was very good to me. Now I'm a member of the ANC, but in prison I did not join anyone.

The psychological pressures on us were immense. We'd be locked up twenty-three hours a day on weekends, half-an-hour exercise in the morning and half-an-hour in the afternoon and if it was raining we'd be locked up all day. The corridors are quite narrow. Some of the exercise was just walking up and down. Sometimes you might bump up against someone and you'd think to yourself what does that mean? You would go back to your cell and brood.

In this terrible bleak, harsh environment Mr. Mandela and Mr. Sisulu were beacons. They carried themselves with dignity. They and Mr. Kathrada were very good to me. I don't say I wouldn't have been able to survive without them but they made it easier. In later years when we had easy access to one another, if I felt demoralized I could go and hug Mr. Mandela or Mr. Sisulu. They were always open to listen to your tales of woe. Both were compassionate but Mr. Sisulu had a quality of warmth and often people would find it easier to go to him and hug him.

Mr. Mandela was very good to me. In the mid 1960s Kathrada and I both had operations. Afterwards I was very sick, lying on the floor. Mr. Mandela comes back from work from the quarry and wanted to know, "Why wasn't Danny at work?" So he came into my cell and comforted me and encouraged me to get better. Then he was locked up in his cell and I in mine. Next morning he comes into my cell with his bucket under his arm. There's no waterborne sewerage. He puts his bucket down on the ground, sits down next to me and again encourages me. He gets up, puts his bucket under one arm, puts mine under the other, goes to the common toilet, empties my bucket, cleans it and brings it back. Now this man is the leader of the most powerful organization in prison. He's an international figure. He could have instructed any of his members to look after me, but he came.

All kinds of people were trying to get me released – lawyers, Mrs. Suzman, the head of the Methodist church – and I knew I could be released at any time, so I kept a diary, noting what assaults had taken place, the names of the guards and so on. But one day, there was a big raid. They had discovered a radio battery in the main section and they were beating people up. We could hear the screams. It was terrible.

Mr. Mandela and I were walking in the yard, when they brought one chap back – I think it was Peter Magano. He was standing there, shaking with pain and Mr. Mandela walked around him and he came back to me and he said he deliberately walked around him because if he was called as a witness he could testify as to what he saw.

Then they discovered my diary. The lieutenant who is in charge of the beatings said, "Tell Daniels I'll be seeing him later." Hell, I was frightened. The word flashed around that I had kept this diary that's been discovered and people began to say, "What did you say about me?" So I'm waiting now to be called to the front. As we are locked up, the guard says to me, "The lieutenant says he'll see you in the morning."

All night I shivered with fear. Next morning I go into the yard, to finish my plate of pap. Then I come back to my cell. And who's sitting in my cell? On my little bench? Madiba. What a thrill! My morale went up, just to see Mr. Mandela there. He came to comfort me. He didn't criticize me or ask what I'd said about him. He just said, "Danny, I know you'll handle this." I was never sent for.

In such harsh and heartless conditions it takes a particularly sanguine man to face the future. Mandela did so without hesitation. He might be serving a life sentence but he refused to believe it meant he would die behind bars. This optimism persisted even in the darkest times and could be felt by the other men in Section B.

There were about thirty of them: most were from the ANC; others were from the PAC and the Unity Movement. The ANC group established a committee known as the High Organ consisting of the four men who were in the national executive of the ANC, with Mandela as the head. Its purpose was to maintain the political cohesion and discipline of members of the ANC and its allied organizations, including MK, to provide political education for prisoners and to take up issues with the authorities and decide on complaints, strikes, and "go-slows." After a few years Mandela and his colleagues were able to persuade members of the other political organizations jointly to set up a prisoners' committee to improve prison conditions in the name of all prisoners. In time, even non-ANC prisoners, such as Neville Alexander who had many political disagreements with Mandela, eventually regarded him as a master of political debate: not a philosopher but a pragmatist, a strategist with an eye for the long game. Indeed, Mandela played politics the way he played chess or checkers: slowly, considering every option before he moved and often delaying his move simply in order to wear down his opponent.

The first six months on the island dragged past. Apart from Winnie, there had been a succession of visitors during August who Mandela believed were part of a government attempt to quiet any rumors that the Rivonia defendants were being badly treated. First came an English travel writer who published an article in *The Times* about Mandela's "light and airy" cell;[4] then a journalist from the *Daily Telegraph* who reported that Mandela was being treated satisfactorily despite being told the contrary; followed by a couple of lawyers, one from Britain, the other from the United States. The two were never heard of again. Nor did the outside world hear anything of Mandela for another twelve months. Winnie was refused permission to visit him and the two censored letters he received from her were his only news of the family.

In early 1965 the stone-breaking in the yard was replaced by a more grueling regime in a lime quarry. Initially told this work would last six months, it turned into thirteen years. Their task was to break through layers of rock to reach the lime which was then dug out with pick and shovel. The pit was scoured by relentless south-east winds in summer and blasted by icy north-west gales in winter. There was no protection from the heat or cold. Worse, the blinding glare of the sun striking off the white stone seared their eyes as they swung their picks into the dazzling seams of lime. Repeated requests for sunglasses were ignored or derisively dismissed and it was three years before they were allowed to buy their own dark glasses. By then it was too late for Mandela and some of the others; their eyesight was irreparably damaged. Despite the merciless conditions, Mandela preferred work in the quarry to that in the claustrophobic courtyard. He enjoyed the walk to and from the pit, he relished the open air, he even appreciated the physical exertion. Better still, they were soon able to dictate their own work pace. Nevertheless, each evening they returned exhausted to their cells, caked with a powdery dust that the cold shower never completely rinsed away.

A few hardened criminals serving long sentences for crimes such as murder, rape, and armed robbery were joined with the political prisoners. Mandela saw them both for what they were – agents provocateurs – and as potential converts to the struggle. Some gangsters were aggressive toward the political prisoners, taking their food and breaking up their conversations. In the quarry they sang songs intended to belittle and provoke. Rather than rise to the challenge physically, Mandela's group responded by singing louder. This unofficial singing competition ended when the gangsters fell silent and the guards ordered the activists to stop. But the point had been made and Mandela and his colleagues were eventually able to convert one of the men to the ANC's cause. When another of the thugs, quaintly named Bogart after the actor, was badly assaulted by a guard, he came to Mandela for help. Mandela demanded to see the commanding officer on the man's behalf only to find out that Bogart had withdrawn the charge. Mandela felt humiliated and outmaneuvered by a system that could so easily smother injustice with a bribe.

Toward the end of the year subtle changes put the prisoners on alert. There was a lump of fat covering their breakfast porridge, fresh meat with their supper, they received new shirts, and in the quarry the guards behaved less aggressively. A few days later the International Red Cross arrived. Mandela was allowed to see the representative privately. He told him they needed proper clothing: long pants, socks, and underwear. He complained about the food, visits, letters, study conditions, the hard labor in the quarry, and the demeaning attitude of the guards. The representative went away; the old ways resumed.

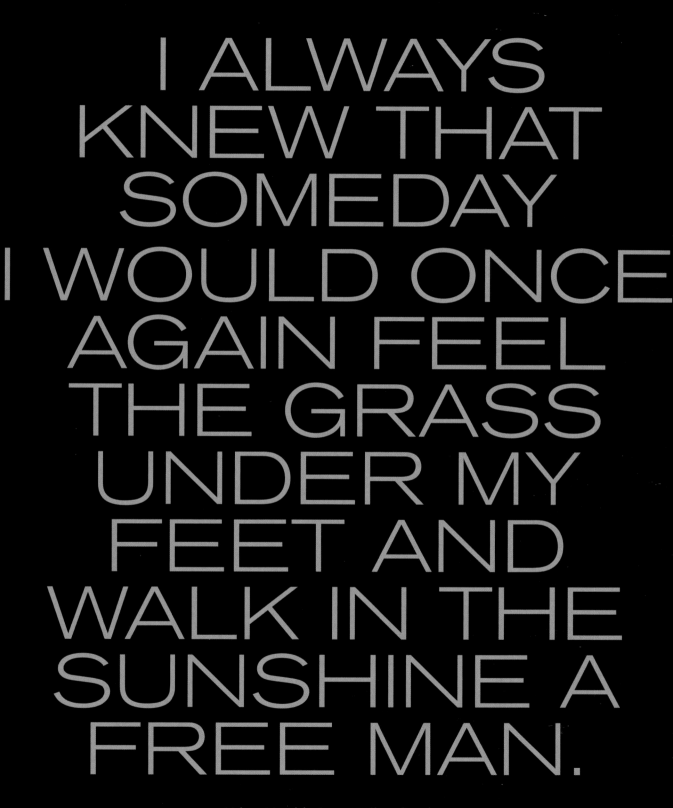

I ALWAYS
KNEW THAT
SOMEDAY
I WOULD ONCE
AGAIN FEEL
THE GRASS
UNDER MY
FEET AND
WALK IN THE
SUNSHINE A
FREE MAN.

Nelson Mandela, Long Walk to Freedom

MAC MAHARAJ:

Madiba was part of the leadership that said we had to build a common front, not only with all classes within the African community, but also with colored and Indian people and with people in the white community, however few, so that we truly represent our country. That search for unity was another characteristic of the man – something we saw in prison in a number of ways. For instance, in the single-cell section, although those of us from the congress movement led by the ANC were the overwhelming majority, there were people from other political groups there including the YCC led by Neville Alexander, members from the PAC, Eddie Daniels from the Liberal Party and Toivo ja Toivo of SWAPO. We consistently held discussions with fellow political prisoners, urging the need to stand together and fight not just to improve our conditions, but as part of the overall fight against apartheid. In a sense it was an extension of the struggle – on a different terrain, but it was the same struggle. In the end, although the prison authorities said it was illegal to do so, we founded a prisoners' committee around 1967 to which all the organizations sub-scribed. And when it came then to appointing a chairman, at the behest of Mandela we proposed and accepted Fikile Bam from the YCC, an organization that had only existed for a few months, that disappeared from history on the arrest of its leaders and that was bitterly anti-ANC. When some of the ANC prisoners heard this, they protested, but we said: No, this is not a question of status, this is a question of making sure that the smaller organizations do not feel that we as a majority are just steamrolling them. We changed the chairmanship of that prisoners' committee every year, but we kept on giving it to members of other organizations. You may translate that message as reconciliation, but I translate it as unifying – just as I translate the reconciliation of the era of 1994 as nation-building.

Right from day one, Madiba stood up for the rights of all prisoners, even for the criminal prisoners, and there were a few of them put in our section to act as provocateurs and to intimidate us. There was one occasion in the early years when we were still working breaking stones. We were sitting in three rows, not allowed to talk to each other. The criminal prisoners used to bring in the rocks on wheelbarrows and drop them at our feet and we had to break them. And they used to go around terrorizing us. But one day a very vicious prisoner, Bogart, a terrifying looking chap who had several murder cases behind him, got beaten by a guard in our presence. Madiba went up to protest. The guard tried to ignore him, but Madiba insisted on being taken to the officer in charge. We had been told repeatedly that as a prisoner you speak for yourself, you don't speak for others, so the whispers went around: hey, Madiba, you can't trust that prisoner, he has treated us viciously. Don't stick your neck out. Eventually Madiba came back from the office and told us what had happened. When Madiba raised the question of the assault, the officer turned to Bogart and says, "Were you assaulted?" And he says, "No, *baas*, I wasn't." And the officer says, "You see, Mandela, not only are you taking up somebody else's problems, which is against the prison regulations, but I can charge you for false claims and under that I can administer lashes to you. Now, I'm letting you off, but I don't want you to come to me with these problems." It turned out later that the prison authorities had simply given this prisoner a packet of pipe tobacco and that was it. When Madiba came and told us this in the bathroom some of us were laughing and told him, we told you so! But Madiba insisted that his stance was correct. We will fight for anybody who suffers injustice, he said, and that includes that criminal prisoner, who was brought here to terrorize us.

every year on July 18, Madiba would give me a birthday present. Sometimes it would be a book, sometimes a packet of biscuits or chocolates. We were only allowed to buy these things over Christmas and he would keep his until July 18. By that time, of course, I would have squandered all mine, so I never had anything to reciprocate with!

Madiba was a very striking, commanding personality, but he was also a nice person, very polite, very courteous and his demeanor always of royalty. Although we were made to wear short pants and sandals, somehow his demeanor was never reduced by that. His whole person was chief-like: he walked with a certain gait, in a very dignified way. He always took his time. If the guards were rushing us a bit, he just wouldn't respond, he would walk very deliberately, slowly, taking his time. Occasionally he would lose his cool if the guards, particularly officers, were abusing us, and then he would stand his ground. He was also a very good storyteller with a good sense of humor. Of course, he'd been through quite a lot of things: he'd travelled abroad, he'd had military training, and he'd been to Ghana and Ethiopia. He loved telling us stories about those particular experiences.

If you listened carefully he never stuck to one version of any incident and over a ten-year period I was able to tell when he was adding a little bit more. I never tired of hearing the stories because I was always looking out for the version he was going to tell.

We spent a lot of time together because we were both lawyers and he was studying law so we used each other for testing out what we'd learned the night before and arguing about cases. I was not allowed to study law – there were certain courses we were not allowed to study: politics, law. So I took a whole range of subjects including jurisprudence – none of the guards were any the wiser as to what it meant. Madiba had permission to study for a further law degree because they had given him permission during his first sentence and once they'd allowed him to start they couldn't take it away.

He was studying English law. He would read a chapter overnight on a specific topic and the next day come and deliver a lecture on it at the quarry and then I would do the same. We actually quite liked going to work because it was where we could exchange ideas. We were not allowed to communicate once we were inside, but there's very little they can do to you once you have been sentenced to jail. They would punish us with a *"drie-maal tye,"* when you didn't get food for a day or two. But it wouldn't stop us from talking to each other or from singing, all sorts of things we were not supposed to do but which we just defied.

Conditions were very bad in the beginning. For starters, most of us landed up there during the winter of 1964, one of the worst winters for thirty years. Africans wore shorts and sandals; Indians and coloreds had long pants and socks and they had some jerseys, but we didn't get socks or jerseys or hats or berets. And we just had two blankets and a mat to sleep on, so it was pretty tough.

Circumstances on the island reached crisis point in July 1966 when the political prisoners in the main section of the prison initiated a hunger strike, protesting against the poor conditions. Section B learned of this through a note wrapped in plastic and smuggled to them in their food drum. In an act of solidarity, all the political prisoners in Section B joined in. Several years later Mandela began to doubt the efficacy of hunger strikes in the South African prison system. He began to favor more militant action: "go-slows," work stoppages, refusals to clean up, which had the potential to impact directly on the authorities. To weaken the strikers' resolve, the prison kitchen improved the quality of the food daily. On day four the evening meal was topped with hunks of meat and fresh vegetables. "The food was positively mouth-watering," wrote Mandela. "The temptation was great."[5] As they were being driven hard at the quarry, their tenacity was sorely tested.

Suddenly, after two years of petitioning the state, and in the midst of the strike, Winnie was granted permission to see her husband. In the preceding months Mandela had been subjected to a malicious form of harassment: occasionally he would return from the quarry to find newspaper clippings about Winnie on his bed. He knew that she was under constant persecution by the police, that they had tried to prevent her family from living with her, and that a security branch officer had broken into their Orlando home while she was dressing. These matters tormented him and emphasized his impotency to act in the way he felt a husband should.

Right: During their first years in the high-security confines of Robben Island, the outside world heard almost nothing of Mandela and his fellow prisoners, and for their part, contact with the outside consisted of a handful of heavily censored letters.

When he sat gazing at his wife through the smudged square of glass, he thought she looked thin and drawn. They talked about the girls and their education, about his mother's declining health, about their poor financial situation. At the back of his mind was the worry that Winnie was too gullible, too willing to trust people. "Time up," the guard shouted when their thirty minutes were over. "I always preferred Winnie to leave first so that she would not have to see me led away, and I watched as she whispered a good-bye, hiding her pain from the guards," he would write in his autobiography not many years later.[6] A hungry and heartsick Mandela returned to his cell. There was soon to be some relief, at least for his stomach if not his heart, when the hunger strike was called off. But if their meals improved slightly, the state's campaign to undermine Mandela continued. Later in the same month he received a hand-delivered letter from the Department of Justice informing him that he had been listed as a member or supporter of the Communist Party. It was yet another attempt to denigrate him. Mandela emphatically denied the allegation and threatened to take up the matter in court. Four months later that allegation was dropped from the list.

At the same time as one battle ended, another began when he learned that the Transvaal Law Society intended to remove him from their rolls because of his conviction in the Rivonia Trial. That once before they had failed in a similar action didn't appear to deter them. Mandela immediately told the prison authorities that he wished to contest the action and defend himself. While he prepared his brief he demanded a proper table and chair to work on, time off from the quarry, and access to a legal library. He applied to the Supreme Court for documents and records and a list of the prospective witnesses and their testimony. A slew of correspondence followed, but Mandela remained adamant about his requests. Meanwhile, the prison authorities refused to accede to his demands. Several months and many letters later, Mandela's game of chess came to an end   the Law Society dropped the matter.

HELEN SUZMAN:

I first met Nelson Mandela on Robben Island in 1967. I was then the only Progressive Party MP left in Parliament and I had read in the newspapers quite alarming reports about the harsh treatment the political prisoners were getting on Robben Island, so I thought I should use my clout as an MP to get permission from Piet Pelser, the minister of justice and prisons, to visit.

I was taken straight to the single-cell section which was where the political prisoners were kept. And as I walked in I saw Eddie Daniels whom I knew. "Don't waste your time talking to us," he said. "Go and talk to Mandela. He's our leader. He's at the end of the cells." I hadn't gone specifically to see Mandela, I went to find out about the conditions, but I was pleased to be guided to him. He stuck his hand through the bars of the cell and said, "Pleased to meet you." And I said, "Pleased to meet you." I was struck immediately by the man's very imposing stature. He's very tall and stands well, and has a very easy way of communicating. He told me that their conditions were bad, particularly because there was a guard in charge of them, Van Rensburg, who had a swastika tattooed on the back of his hand. "This man's very tough on us when we're in the quarry breaking stones," he said. He also said they only had bedrolls to sleep on and it was very cold in winter because Robben Island is very exposed. Their clothing – they had these shorts and things – meant they were very uncomfortable with the weather conditions and they didn't have enough letters, enough visits, they didn't get newspapers, all those things.

Left: Progressive Party MP Helen Suzman was the sole voice of parliamentary opposition to the ruling Nationalist Party and its rigid regime. She campaigned tirelessly for the improvement of prisoners' living conditions, although she refused to support the demands of Mandela and the other political prisoners to be released unless they renounced violence.

So when I got back to the mainland I wrote to Pelser and said I'd like to speak to him because I had learned some very interesting things. I told him about the guard and I said, "I am going to raise this in your vote which is in two weeks' time, I believe." He said, "Don't do that. It's dynamite. I can't send that guard away immediately. It's very bad for discipline. But I will see that he is gone." And he did get rid of him. Terrible chap.

It was a number of years before I was allowed to go back because Jimmy Kruger took Pelser's place and he was a really nasty piece of work. Every time I went to see him about anything it was, "*Ja*, you and your *kommunis* friends. What do you want now?" Eventually I got permission but it took about seven years, although I used to have a yearly visit to the political prisoners at Pretoria where Bram Fischer and the others were being kept, no trouble. But not to the colored or Indian or black prisons.

Anyway, eventually I got permission and the first thing Nelson said to me was, "Why has it been such a long time?" I explained and we had a long chat again. Conditions had improved – not only through me I might add – although I raised them every year under the Prisons Vote. It gave me the opportunity of addressing things and asking questions – whether beds had been provided, whether more visits had been provided, whether they were now allowed newspapers, whether they were allowed to study. The Red Cross used to visit and they did a lot to get conditions improved.

I visited Mandela during his last years of imprisonment at Pollsmoor and Victor Verster where he was under very different conditions. By then we were talking politics. I was convinced that this was the one man who could lead us to a peaceful resolution of the problem, and that's the sort of speech I kept making in Parliament, year after year.

I believed this man was our last chance. To keep these people in jail for life was ridiculous. By then, they were already beginning to start to talk and eventually Mandela was moved from Pollsmoor to Victor Verster where he lived in a cottage and was looked after by a guard. I had lunch with him on one occasion and we exchanged books. By then we had got to know each other quite well and we could talk about politics quite openly. When he came out of prison in February 1990, he phoned me and he said, "When are you coming to see me?" and I said, "Well, I'm coming home over the weekend." He said, "Well, come and see me when you're home."

It was obvious from the start that he was a clear leader. The prisoners themselves acknowledged him as a leader and you could not help but be impressed with this man when you met him. He seemed so rational and sensible in the way he reacted to everything. He understood the situation about politics and power.

As the years went on there appeared to be a change in the authorities' approach. Under pressure, Mandela and his comrades were issued long pants; in the quarry they spent as much time talking as working. A guard gave them illegal access to a newspaper (although Mandela was caught reading it and put in isolation on a spare diet of rice and water for three days). Then, in early 1967, he received his first visit from the only opposition member in Parliament, Helen Suzman of the Progressive Party. The authorities removed Mandela from his cell nearer to the entrance and put him in one right at the end of the passage, in the hope that when Suzman entered, the prisoners would all stop and talk to her and take up all her time before reaching Mandela. The prisoners, however, beat this maneuver by each insisting that Mandela would speak on their behalf. In the presence of the prison commander she listened to his grievances. Shortly afterwards conditions for the political prisoners improved marginally, and a particularly abusive guard was transferred.

These triumphs aside, the remaining two years of the decade brought considerable grief and anguish to Mandela. In the spring of 1968 he saw his mother for the first time since the Rivonia Trial. She was frail and shrunken. Her obvious ill health worried him and he dreaded that this might be the last time he would see her. That she had made the long and difficult trip from Transkei with his son Makgatho, his daughter Makaziwe, and his sister Mabel touched him deeply. In the short time he was allowed to speak to his family, he pushed the thought of her frailty to the back of his mind and gazed with fatherly pride and some amazement at his adult children. Paternal urges welled up in him and he couldn't resist advising them to continue their studies. The forty-five minutes especially allotted for this visit sped past and Mandela was soon watching them depart, his sister supporting their weakened mother. After the visit he returned to his cell unusually subdued and withdrawn.

Right: In 1969, Mandela's eldest son, 23-year-old Thembi, was killed in a car accident. Already distraught over Winnie's incarceration and still grieving the death of his mother, this tragedy left Mandela heartbroken.

The daily grind continued: the long hot hours in the quarry; the tortuous thoughts in the small hours. Then, some weeks later, he returned from the quarry to a telegram from Makgatho: his mother had died of a heart attack. Grief brought with it the ever-present recriminations: had he made the right choice in putting the people's welfare before his family? While he had worked as an attorney he had been able to support his mother, but that had ended with his imprisonment. Her death made him question his own life. "My family had not asked for or even wanted to be involved in the struggle, but my involvement penalized them," he agonized in his autobiography.[7] His request to attend her funeral was denied.

Unable to fulfill his responsibilities as the eldest son and bury his mother, Mandela had to suffer his sorrow in silence and frustration. His fortitude was tested again in May 1969 when the security police detained Winnie under the Terrorism Act. She was thrown into solitary confinement in Pretoria and denied visitors. It was not long before Mandela got to hear about her being dragged away in the middle of the night with Zindzi clutching at her skirt. His nights were now fraught with worry; a mental hell that he couldn't escape. Three months later came more bad news: another telegram from Makgatho; another death. This time his son Thembi, killed in a car accident.

"I do not have words to express the sorrow, or the loss I felt," he would record later. "It left a hole in my heart that can never be filled."[8]

Mandela was mourning his mother; he was distressed about his wife and young daughters who were being cared for by family friends, and now the tragic death of his son. He lay on his bed staring at the ceiling. He did not emerge to eat his lunch. Later that afternoon Sisulu crouched beside his bed and read the telegram. He offered no words of comfort: there were none. He reached over and clasped his friend's hand.

Thembi had never visited his father on the island even though he lived in Cape Town. He had never written. He was married; he had two children who had never seen their grandfather. The failure of their relationship caused Mandela considerable pain. He remembered the boy he had taken boxing, the boy who had worn his jacket, the boy who had never got over his parents' divorce. His request to attend his son's funeral was denied.

EDDIE DANIELS:

Although Mr. Mandela and Mr. Sisulu could comfort us, we couldn't comfort them. When Mr. Mandela's son was killed he was called to the office and informed that he had been killed in a car accident. When he came back into the yard, you could immediately see he was down, the way he walked. Usually, I would shout "Dalibunga!" – that's his circumcision name – and he would shout "Danny!" right across the yard. I loved him, you know, I still do. And perhaps in a small way he reciprocated. But this time he didn't look at anybody. He came down the ramp and walked into his cell. We all knew something was wrong, but we all held our distance. The atmosphere was such that Mr. Sisulu was the appropriate person and he went in and Mr. Mandela told him what had happened and he knelt next to Mr. Mandela and held his hand and comforted him. Then he came out and told us and we would go in, one by one, and sympathize with him.

Mr. Mandela would go into his cell and wrap his blanket around him tight, to keep his pain inside him.

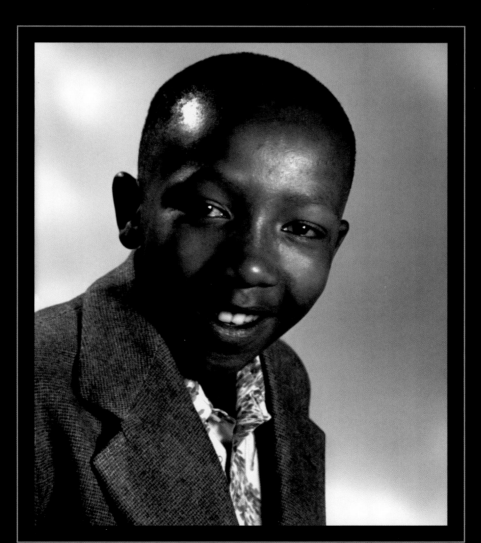

Dear Evelyn,

I write to give you, Kgatho and Maki my deepest sympathy. I know more than anybody else living today just how devastating this cruel blow must have been to you for Thembi was your first born and the second child that you have lost. I am also fully conscious of the passionate love you had for him and the efforts you made to train and prepare him to play his part in a complex modern industrial society. I am also aware of how Kgatho and Maki adored and respected him, the holidays and good time they spent with him in Cape Town. . . . Throughout the last five years up to March this year, Nobandla gave me interesting accounts of his attachment and devotion to the family and the personal interest he took in all his relatives. I last saw him five years ago during the Rivonia Trial and I always looked forward to these accounts for they were the main channel through which I was able to hear something of him.

The blow has been equally grievous to me. In addition to the fact that I had not seen him for at least sixty months, I was neither privileged to give him a wedding ceremony nor to lay him to rest when the fatal hour had struck. . . .

Extracts from a letter from Mandela to his first wife Evelyn on the death of their son Thembi, dated July 16, 1969.

Mandela wrote drafts of all his letters in large notebooks before transcribing them meticulously onto writing paper. Once in the prison post, these letters were subject to heavy censoring and many of them were never sent. The letters featured here are from notebooks that were held by policeman Donald Card. Card was a detective with the security police and a state witness at the Rivonia Trial. From 1969 to 1970, with the help of an informer, Card was tasked with decoding messages in the letters sent and received by Robben Island inmates. According to Card, although he had by then resigned from the police force, Robben Island Prison sent him in 1971 an envelope containing letters and two foolscap notebooks they had confiscated from Mandela. These remained on top of Card's cupboard for thirty-three years until he returned the material to Mandela in September 2004.

The Commanding Officer
Robben Island

My eldest son, Madiba Thembekile, aged twenty-four, passed away in Cape Town on July 13, 1969, as a result of injuries he sustained in a motor-car accident.

I wish to attend, at my own cost, the funeral proceedings and to pay my last respects to his memory. I have no information as to where he will be buried, but I assume that this will take place either in Cape Town, Johannesburg or Umtata. In this connection I should be pleased if you would give me permission to proceed immediately, with or without escort, to the place where he will be laid to rest. If he will already have been buried by the time you receive this application then I would ask that I be allowed to visit his grave for the purpose of "laying the stone," the traditional ceremony reserved for those persons who miss the actual burial.

It is my earnest hope that you will on this occasion find it possible to approach this request more humanely than you treated a similar application I made barely ten months ago, in September 1968, for leave to attend my mother's funeral. Approval of that application would have been a generous act on your part, and one which would have made a deep impression on me. Such a humanitarian gesture would have gone a long way in softening the hard blow and painful misfortune of an imprisoned man losing a mother, and would have afforded me the opportunity to be present at the graveside. I might add that I last saw my late son a little more than five years ago and you will readily appreciate just how anxious I am to attend the funeral.

Finally, I should like to point out that precedents exist when Governments have favorably considered applications of this nature.

Letter from Mandela to the commanding officer of Robben Island requesting permission to attend Thembi's funeral, dated July 22, 1969. The request was subsequently denied.

Dear Evelyn,

This afternoon the Commanding Officer informed me of a telegram received from attorney Mendel Levin of Johannesburg in which he reported the death of Thembi in a motor accident in Cape Town on July 13.

I write to give you, Kgatho & Maki my deepest sympathy. I know more than anybody else living today just how devastating this cruel blow must have been to you for Thembi was your first born & the second child that you have lost. I also am fully conscious of the passionate love that you had for him & the efforts you made to train & prepare him to play his part in a complex modern industrial society. I am also aware of how Kgatho & Maki adored & respected him, the holidays & good time they spent with him in Cape Town. In his letter written in October 1967 Maki told me that Thembi helped you in buying them all they needed. My late ma gave me details of the warm hospitality she received from him when she visited me on the island. Throughout the last five years up to March this year, Nobandla gave me interesting accounts of his attachment & devotion to the family & the personal interest he took in all his relatives. I last saw him five years ago during the Rivonia trial & I always looked forward to those accounts for they were the main channel through which I was able to hear something of him.

The blow has been equally grievous to me. In addition to the fact that I had not seen him for at least sixty months, I was neither privileged to give him a wedding ceremony nor to lay him to rest when the fatal hour had struck. In 1967 I wrote him a long letter drawing his attention to some matters which I thought it was in his interest to attend to without delay. I looked forward to further correspondence to & to meeting him and his family when I returned. All these expectations have now been completely shattered for he has been taken away at the early age of 24 and we will never again see him. We should all be consoled & comforted by the fact that he had

My dear Kgatho,

. . . I think of your mother who must have been severely shocked to lose a son so early in his life and who had already begun to take over some of the heavy duties of a parent that will now press on her from all sides. I think more particularly of you and Maki because I realize fully just how hard a blow Thembi's death must have been to both of you. He sincerely loved you and you, in turn, were very fond of him. He was not just a brother, but the person to whom you naturally turned for advice and assistance. He was the shield that protected you against danger, and that helped you to build up the self-confidence and courage you need to deal with the numerous problems that you meet as you grow. . . .

I think it fit and proper to highlight but one striking virtue of his which created a deep impression on me. His love and devotion to you, Maki, Zeni, and Zindzi and to relatives generally created the image of a man who respected family ties and who was destined to play an important role in the upbringing, education and development of the children. He had already developed himself to a position where he had become the object of his sisters' love, admiration, and respect and a source of pride to the family. From 8115 I was kept constantly informed of his un-flagging interest in all of us and details of his hospitality during his recent visit with his family to Johannesburg were outlined. The late Fanny never missed the chance of saying something compli-mentary about him whenever she visited me here, and I sincerely regret that death has denied him the opportunity to bring this magnificent gift of his in full play in the service of the family. . . .

Extracts from a letter from Mandela to his son
Makgatho on the death of Thembi, dated
July 28, 1969.

My Darling,

. . . I hope you received the Xmas card I sent you and Kgatho and that you enjoyed your Xmas and new year. It was a real pleasure for me to get your undated letter in November 1967. The language and style were good and the writing clear. It pleased me very much to hear that you were enjoying yourself in school and that you liked English the best. I was also happy to know that your ambition is to become a doctor or scientist. Both are strenuous professions and you must work hard and steadily during school terms and have a good rest during school holidays. I see that you are afraid of being kidnapped one day when you have discovered a dangerous drug. Do not worry much, darling, about kidnappers. Their world is getting smaller and smaller and their friends fewer. One day there will be a new world when all of us will live in happiness and peace. That world will be created by you and me, by Kgatho, Zeni, and Zindzi; by our friends and countrymen. When you become a doctor or scientist and you use your knowledge, training, and skill to help your people who are poor and miserable and who have no opportunity to develop, you will be fighting for that new world. . . .

Extract from a letter from Mandela to his
daughter Makaziwe, dated February 16, 1969,
but not sent until after Thembi's death when it
was updated on July 29, 1969.

16. 2. 69

My Darling,

I was indeed very happy to learn that you, Kgatho, Zeni & Zindzi had passed your respective examinations. Please accept my warm congratulations. Your success in all the examinations that you have written about up to now show that all of you have the ability to study and I do hope this will inspire you to work even harder this year. You are now doing the final year of the Junior Certificate and I feel certain that when the time comes to sit for the examinations at the end of the year, you will again pass, provided you work hard and continuously right from the beginning. I expect you to tell me in your reply your subjects this year, and the titles of your English and Xhosa/Zulu setworks. I should like to read them. But for the time being I say: "Well done!"

I believe you, Zami & Kgatho were expected to go down to Umtata to visit Makhulu's grave and to pay your last respects to her. Did you succeed? I was very sorry to receive the news of her death for I had hoped to be able to look after her in her last days on earth and to bury her when she died. But mummy and others tell me that relatives and friends, led by Paramount Chief Sabata, attended in large numbers and gave a burial that aroused deep feelings. I know that Zeni & Zindzi attended and would be equally happy to be told that you were also able to do so.

I hope you received the Xmas card I sent you and Kgatho and that you enjoyed your Xmas and New year. It was a real pleasure for me to get your undated letter in November 1967. The language and style were good and the writing clear. It pleased me very much to hear that you were enjoying yourself in school and that you liked English the best. I was also happy to know that your ambition is to become a doctor or scientist. Both are strenuous professions and you must work hard and steadily during school terms and have a good rest during school holidays. I see that you are afraid of being kidnapped one day when you have discovered a dangerous drug. Do not worry much darling, about kidnappers. Their world is getting smaller and smaller and their friends fewer. One day there will be a new world when all of us will live in happiness and peace. That world will be created by you and me, by Kgatho, Zeni & Zindzi; by our friends and country men. When you become a doctor or scientist and you use your knowledge, training and skill to help your people who are poor and miserable and who have no opportunity to develop, you will be fighting for that new world.

In your letter you told me that Kgatho was doing first year matric and

August 3, 1969.

My Darlings,

On July 17 I received a telegram from Kgatho in which he told me that Buti Thembi, your beloved brother, had died in a car accident. The accident occurred in Touws River, near Cape Town on July 13. I am told that apart from him two Europeans, who came recently to this country from Italy, also died. Your brother will be buried in Johannesburg today. In the telegram Kgatho informed me that he was sending the full details of how Thembi died. But my letters take a very long time to reach me and, at the time of writing, Kgatho's letter had not arrived, and I am thus not in a position to give you more particulars on the matter.

I write on behalf of Mummy and myself to give you our deepest sympathy. All of us were very fond and proud of Thembi and he, in turn, was devoted to us, and it is indeed very sad to think that we will never see him again. I know just how he loved you. Mummy wrote to me on March 1 and advised me that he spent his holidays with his family in Johannesburg, and that during that period he took you out several times and gave you much pleasure and joy. Mummy has also informed me that he had invited you to spend the forthcoming December holidays with him in Cape Town and that you were looking forward to a lot of fun. There you would have seen the sea. Places like Muizenberg and the strand where you could swim. You would also have seen the Castle, a large stone fort which was completed about the year 1679. Here the Governors of the early Cape lived. It was also here that the famous African king, Cetywayo, lived was kept for a time after the Battle of Isandhlwana in January 1879 when the Zulu army defeated the English. In Cape Town you would also see table Mountain which is about 3,599 feet high. From the top of the mountain you would see Robben Island across the waves. Thembi's death means that you will not be able to spend your December holidays down there, and you will also miss the pleasures and beautiful places I have mentioned above, and we are all very sorry that our Thembi is really gone. He meant much to us and we will miss him.

. . . I write on behalf of Mummy and myself to give you our deepest sympathy. All of us were very fond and proud of Thembi and he, in turn, was devoted to us, and it is indeed very sad to think that we will never see him again. I know just how he loved you. Mummy wrote to me on March 1 and advised me that he spent his holidays with his family in Johannesburg, and that during that period he took you out several times and gave you much pleasure and joy. Mummy has also informed me that he had invited you to spend the forthcoming December holidays with him in Cape Town and that you were looking forward to a lot of fun. There you would have seen the sea. . . . From the top of the mountain you would see Robben Island across the waves.

It was not possible for Mummy and myself to attend his funeral. Both of us are in jail and our request for permission to go to the funeral was not granted. You also did not attend, but when you return from school Kgatho will arrange for you to be taken to see the grave and bid your departed brother farewell. Perhaps one day Mummy and I will be able also to visit the grave. But now that he is gone, we must forget about the painful fact of his death. Now he sleeps in peace, my darlings, free from troubles, worries, sickness, or need; he can feel neither pain nor hunger. You must continue with your schoolwork, play games and sing songs.

This time I have written you a sad letter. On June 23 I had written you another letter which was just as sad, because it dealt with the arrest of Mummy. This year has been a bad one indeed for us, but happy days will come when we will be full of joy and laughter. What is even more important is that one day Mummy and I will come back and live happily together with you in one house, sit at table together, help you with the many problems you will experience as you grow. But until then Mummy and I will write to you regularly. Tons and tons of love, my darlings.

Affectionately,
Tata

Extracts from a letter from Mandela to his daughters Zeni and Zindzi after the death of Thembi, dated August 3, 1969. As often happened, the girls never received this letter.

It was not possible for Mummy and myself to attend his funeral. Both of us are in jail and our request for permission to go to the funeral was not granted. You also did not attend, but when you return from school Kgatho will arrange for you to be taken to see the grave and bid your departed brother farewell. Perhaps one day Mummy and I will be able also to visit the grave. But now that he is gone, we must forget about the painful fact of his death. Now he sleeps in peace, my darlings, free from troubles, worries, sickness or need; he can feel neither pain nor hunger. You must continue with your schoolwork, play games and sing songs.

This time I have written you a sad letter. On June 23 I had written you another letter which was just as equally sad, because it dealt with the arrest of Mummy. This year has been a bad one indeed for us, but happy days will come when we will be full of joy and laughter. What is even more important, is that one day Mummy and I will come back and live happily together with you in one house, sit at table together, help you with the many problems you will experience as you grow. But until then Mummy and I will write to you regularly. Tons and tons of love, my darlings.

Affectionately,
Tata.

MISSES. ZENI AND ZINDZI MANDELA,
c/o MRS NIKI IRIS XABA,
HOUSE NO. 8115 ORLANDO WEST, JOHANNESBURG.

MAC MAHARAJ:

On Saturdays and Sundays we were locked up twenty-three hours a day, with only two half hours to get out and collect food and have a bit of exercise walking around the quadrangle. So weekends were a dread and Robben Island can be very, very cold. One Sunday a priest arrived and he preached to us from the corridor with our doors locked. Eventually, after several protests, the authorities agreed to let us out and the guard in charge said as we congregated there, "All those who are Catholics, put up your hands." And Billy Nair, who was a member of the Communist Party, an ardent member of the Natal MK regional command and a real prankster, shouted in response, "Nelson Mandela!" So Madiba was in an awkward situation and had to go to the service. The next time we were given this opportunity it was a priest from a different denomination and the guard said, "All those who

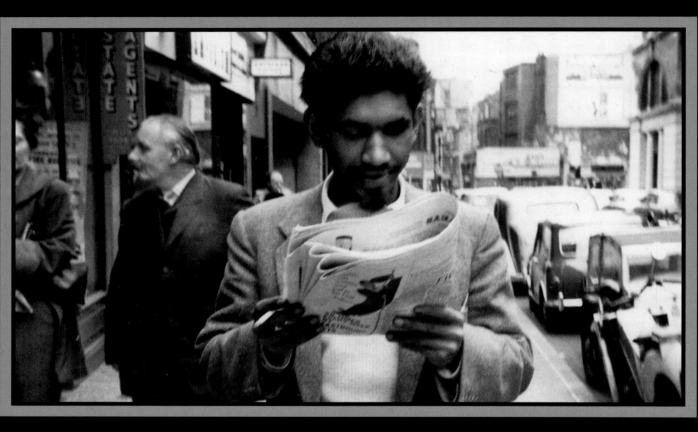

are Methodists, put up your hands." And again Billy shouted, "Nelson Mandela!" So there was Madiba attending every religious service. But as it happened, he turned the tables on us because again he used it to show his open-mindedness, that whatever his private beliefs – and I think he still treats religion as a private issue – we need to respect all religions.

Later we demanded to be allowed to have the service outside in the quadrangle in the sun, but Neville Alexander and Govan Mbeki used to refuse to come out because they said they were "principled atheists." They refused to attend any service. It didn't matter if it was the Anglican priest, Father Hughes, who came with a portable organ and where the singing was such a wonderful relief. He loved listening to African voices singing, and at times he would just stop the organ and listen. But one Sunday, Govan, the first of these two recalcitrant committed atheists, crept out of his cell to join us in the sun and we all said, Oh, Zizi – his clan name – welcome, and he just mumbled under his breath and attended the service. . . .

The services got even more interesting when we began to steal newspapers from the priests because now we could combine singing with those wanting to worship and those wanting to smuggle newspapers. And then Father Hughes announced that he would be taking those who were Anglicans for communion. Of course those of us who were not religious didn't go to that, but when the few who went came back and reported that they had communion bread and a thimbleful of wine, the queue began to increase for communion as well.

DENIS HEALEY:

1970 was my last year as defense secretary and in September I visited South Africa to look at our naval base in Simonstown. David Astor, then editor of the *Observer,* had corresponded with Mandela and sent him books and he had kept me informed about Mandela on Robben Island. So I asked Botha – who was prime minister at the time – and he gave me permission to visit him. I think Botha agreed more with surprise than reluctance.

Left: A young Mac Maharaj in 1958 in Oxford Street in London where he attended the London School of Economics and was active in trade union and anti-apartheid structures.

Mandela was brought out of his cell to talk to me in a visitor's room. He'd shaved off his beard and he was very pale. The jailers insisted on sitting in the room with us but it was clear Nelson was greatly respected by them. When I said I was going to see him, they said, "Well, he is a very remarkable and fine man." And indeed he was. It was very unusual then for white people to respect black people, but he exerted a great moral authority.

I had a long talk with him – a good two hours – and I was enormously impressed. He wanted to know what was going on in Europe and above all what European attitudes were toward South African apartheid. I was able to tell him that – apart from a group of Dutch who had supported the *Broederbond* – the Europeans were overwhelmingly anti-apartheid. Mandela was really concerned about what we could do to put pressure on the South African government. But the trouble with sanctions is they only work against a democratic country because there the country knows why the sanctions are being imposed. In a dictatorship, the government pretends the sanctions are against the people of the country. I told Mandela that we were doing what we could, but we had no influence over the South African government. I had been very lucky to be able to get to see him – I was the only member of a foreign government who was able to see him in jail.

I was very impressed by how much the white South Africans who'd met him respected him. Those who hadn't met him regarded him as a devil. I would say he's a saintly person: he was never vindictive against the people who demonized him. It struck me very much when I met him and, even more remarkably, when he came out of prison. It wasn't part of his character at all. After my visit I got a very bad press from the white South African media. They said I was a "bastard nigger-lover," a "Kaffir *boetie.*" But I remained a very strong anti-apartheid supporter: Mandela has always been one of my heroes – not just as a political thinker, but as a human being. When you think what he went through for all those years in jail, it's amazing how intact he is mentally as well as morally. He's a good man with a capital G.

Mandela now heard that Winnie had been placed on trial, that the case had been withdrawn, that she had been rearrested and landed up in the hospital suffering from malnutrition, bleeding gums, and fainting fits. Again the case went to trial and again it collapsed. The thirteen months of solitary confinement, interrogation, poor food, and little exercise she suffered also extracted a devastating psychological toll on Winnie and she was no sooner released than she was slapped with a five-year banning order and house arrest. But her petition to visit her husband was granted. Suffering from high blood pressure and bronchitis, she made her third trip to Robben Island in November 1970. Husband and wife spent thirty minutes together, monitored by wardens, separated by the pane of glass. For Mandela, who had loathed solitary confinement, the knowledge that his wife had endured it for almost five hundred days was unbearable.

For the first five years of the decade Winnie was under constant harassment. Bricks were thrown through her windows, shots were fired at her front door. A gunman was found prowling the yard; two men broke into the house and tried to strangle her in bed. In 1974 she was sentenced to six months' imprisonment for violating her banning order. Once again, Mandela was distraught at the news.

With both the Mandelas imprisoned, the minister of justice, Jimmy Kruger, chose December 1974 as a propitious time to visit the man on the island. He wanted Mandela to abandon the armed struggle and recognize the Transkei government where Matanzima ruled with a despotic grip. If he did so, he would be released to live there. For his disingenuousness the minister received a lecture on the history of the ANC and the Freedom Charter, and a comparison between the ANC's armed struggle and that of the Afrikaner rebels in 1914. All of this came as news to the ignorant Kruger. He left, returning a month later to hear if the offer had been reconsidered. Again he was told the answer was no. Kruger promptly lambasted Mandela in Parliament as a committed communist. There were two further repercussions: the security police again raided the Mandela home and shortly afterwards, vandals cut the telephone wires and smashed windows and doors.

Despite such worries, Mandela found that the cell gave him the opportunity to meditate on his life, his feelings, and his thoughts. At an age when most men would be set in their ways, he was imprisoned in a place that could ferment bitterness and a desire for revenge, yet he found value in his circumstances.

"In judging our progress as individuals," he would write to Winnie, "we tend to concentrate on external factors such as one's social position, influence and popularity, wealth and standard of education . . . but internal factors may be even more crucial in assessing one's development as a human being: honesty, sincerity, simplicity, humility, purity, generosity, absence of vanity, readiness to serve your fellow men – qualities within the reach of every soul. . . ."[9]

Ten years after his arrival on the island, conditions had improved, although the improvements were always precarious and likely to be withdrawn on a whim. For instance, he and the others in Section B were issued long pants and individual uniforms which they were allowed to wash themselves. They had access to the courtyard throughout the weekend; they could play chess or checkers or cards, and in the quarry their discussions were seldom interrupted. But then a relaxed commanding officer was replaced by a tyrant with a cohort of brutal guards. On a winter night in 1971, while the prisoners were on a hunger strike, drunken guards stormed into Section B, woke the men, and made them strip and line up naked in their individual cells. While the guards abused them, their cells were searched. After an hour in the cold, Govan Mbeki collapsed with chest pains. When Toivo ja Toivo, the leader of SWAPO who had recently been brought to the island fought back, he was savagely assaulted. Incidents such as this were not uncommon during the short, barbarous reign of Colonel Piet Badenhorst.

Mandela was determined to resist the commander's ruthlessness. He laid a complaint that was ignored. He had a message smuggled out asking for his colleagues to agitate for Badenhorst's dismissal. He organized a deputation to confront the commander. This time they were given an audience. Mandela threatened "go-slows," work stoppages, and hunger strikes unless privileges were restored and the beatings ceased. Badenhorst was surprisingly amenable. Some weeks later three judges and the commissioner of prisons visited the island. In the presence of the commander Mandela relayed their complaints to the judges. Three months later Badenhorst and his gang were transferred. "Ultimately," wrote a reflective Mandela, "Badenhorst was not evil; his inhumanity had been foisted upon him by an inhuman system."[10]

IN JUDGING OUR PROGRESS
AS INDIVIDUALS, WE TEND TO
CONCENTRATE ON EXTERNAL
FACTORS SUCH AS ONE'S
SOCIAL POSITION, INFLUENCE,
AND POPULARITY, WEALTH AND
STANDARD OF EDUCATION . . .
BUT INTERNAL FACTORS MAY
BE EVEN MORE CRUCIAL IN
ASSESSING ONE'S DEVELOP-
MENT AS A HUMAN BEING:
HONESTY, SINCERITY, SIMPLICITY,
HUMILITY, PURITY, GENEROSITY,
ABSENCE OF VANITY, READI-
NESS TO SERVE YOUR FELLOW
MEN – QUALITIES WITHIN THE
REACH OF EVERY SOUL.

Nelson Mandela, in a letter to Winnie

Dade Wethu,

I believe that on Dec 1 you and 21 others will appear in the Pretoria Supreme Court on a charge under the Sabotage Act, alternatively, for contravening the provisions of the Suppression of Communism Act. I am informed that you have all instructed Mr. Joel Carlson to act in the matter. . . .

Since our wedding day in June 1958, you have, under some pretext or other, been dragged 3 times before the Criminal Courts and once before a Civil one. The issues involved, at least in part of this litigation, are better forgotten than recalled. They caused us much grief and concern. This will be the 5th occasion, and I suspect that here there is much that lies beneath the surface, and the proceedings are likely to be the bitterest experience of your entire life to date. There will be those whose chief interest will be to seek to destroy the image we have built over the last decade. Attempts may be made to do now what they have repeatedly failed to achieve in former cases. I write to warn you in time of what lies ahead to enable you to prepare yourself both physically and spiritually to take the full force of the merciless blows that I feel certain will be directed systematically at you from the beginning to the end of the trial. In fact, the trial, and the circumstances surrounding it, may so far influence your thoughts and actions that it might well constitute an important landmark in your entire career, compelling you to re-examine very carefully values you once fondly cherished and to give up pleasures that once delighted your heart. . . .

. . . I do wish you to know that you are the pride of my heart, and with you on my side, I always feel I am part of an invincible force that is ready to win new worlds. I am confident that, however dark and difficult times might seem to be now, one day you will be free and able to see the beautiful birds and lovely fields of our country, bathe in its marvellous sunshine and breathe its sweet air. You will again see the picturesque scenery of the land of Faku where your childhood was spent, and the kingdom of Ngubengcuka where the ruins of your own kraal are to be found.

I miss you badly! Tons and tons of love and a million kisses.

Devotedly,
Dalibunga

Extracts from a letter from Mandela to Winnie, encouraging her to stand firm for her upcoming trial, dated November 16, 1969.

My Darlings,

It is more than 8 years since I last saw you, and just over 12 months since Mummy was suddenly taken away from you.

Last year I wrote you 2 letters – one on the 23rd June and the other on the 3rd August. I now know that you never received them. As both of you are still under 18, and as you are not allowed to visit me until you reach that age, writing letters is the only means I have of keeping in touch with you. . . . The mere fact of writing down my thoughts and expressing my feelings gives me a measure of pleasure and satisfaction. . . .

. . . I last saw our brave and beloved Mummy in December 1968. She was arrested on the 12th May last year about two weeks before she was due to visit me. Her visits brought me joy and inspiration and I always looked forward to them. I must confess that [I] miss her very badly. I also miss you, darlings, and hope you will be able to write me long and nice letters in which you tell me everything about yourselves. . . .

I have in my cell the lovely photo that you took during the 1968 Christmas, with the Orlando West High School in the background. I also have the family photo which Mummy sent in March 1968. They make it somewhat easy for me to endure the loneliness of a prison cell and provide me with something to cheer and inspire me every day. . . . Perhaps one day, many years from now, Mummy will return, and maybe it will then be possible for her to arrange for me to have the little things that are precious to my heart. . . .

The dream of every family is to be able to live together happily in a quiet and peaceful home where parents will have the opportunity of bringing up the children in the best possible way, of guiding and helping them in choosing careers and of giving them the love and care which will develop in them a feeling of security and self-confidence. Today our family has been scattered; Mummy and Daddy are in jail and you live like orphans. We should like you to know that these ups and downs have deepened our love for you. We are confident that one day our dreams will come true: we will be able to live together and enjoy all the sweet things that we are missing at present.

Tons and tons of love, my darlings
Daddy

Extracts from a letter from Mandela to Zeni and Zindzi during Winnie's imprisonment, dated June 1, 1970.

16.11.69

Dade Wethu,

I believe that on Dec 1 you & 21 others will appear in the Pretoria Supreme Court on a charge under the Sabotage Act, alternatively, for contravening the provisions of the Suppression of Communism Act. I am informed that you have all instructed Mr Joel Carlson to act in the matter.

From the particulars of the charge it would seem that you would require me to give evidence on your behalf & I look forward to an early consultation with you and Counsel. I would certainly consider it irregular & unjust & contrary to the elementary principles of natural justice to force you to start a long and protracted trial on a serious charge without arrangements having first been made for us to meet. We have not seen each other since Dec. last year & a meeting between us would go a long way towards easing the strains & stresses of the last 5 months & putting you in a better physical condition & frame of mind. Only after such a meeting could you have some-thing approximating a fair trial, & I sincerely hope it will be possible to arrange it. I am also keen to discuss the question of how you should conduct your defence & to anticipate the tactics the State will most certainly use.

Since our wedding day in June 1958, you have, under some pretext or other, been dragged 5 times before the Criminal courts & once before a Civil one. The issues involved, at least in part of this litigation, are better forgotten than recalled. They caused us much grief & concern. This will be the 5th occasion, & I suspect that here there is much that lies beneath the surface, & the proceedings are likely to be the bitterest experience of your entire life to-date. There will be those whose chief interest will be to seek to destroy the image we have built over the last decade. Attempts may be made to do now what they have repeatedly failed to achieve in former cases. I write to warn you in time of what lies ahead to enable you to prepare yourself both physically & spiritually to take the full force of the merciless blows that I feel certain will be directed systematically at you from the beginning to the end of the trial. In fact the trial & the circumstances surrounding it, may so far influence your thoughts & actions that it might well constitute an important landmark in your entire career, compelling you to re-exa-mine very carefully values you once finally cherished & to give up pleasures than once delighted your heart.

Already the months you spent in detention have been a severe test for you & when you come to the end of the case, you will have got a deeper understa-

Dade Wethu

. . . During the 8 lonely years I have spent behind bars I sometimes wished we were born the same hour, grown up together and spent every minute of our lives in each other's company. I sincerely believe that had this been the case I would have been a wise man. Every one of your letters is a precious possession and often succeeds in arousing forces I have never suspected to be concealed in my being. In your hands the pen is really mightier than a saber. Words flow out freely and naturally and common expressions acquire a meaning that is at once challenging and stimulating. The first paragraph of your moving note, and more especially the opening line, shook me violently. I literally felt every one of the millions of atoms that make up my body pulling forcefully in all directions. The beautiful sentiments you have repeatedly urged on me since my arrest and conviction, and particularly during the last 15 months, are clearly the result more of actual experience than of scholasticism. They come from a woman who has not seen her husband for almost 2 years, who has been excluded from her tender children for more than 12 months and who has been hard hit by loneliness, pining and illness under conditions least conducive for recovery, and who on top of all that must face the most strenuous test of her life. I understand perfectly well, darling, when you say you miss me and that one of the few blows you found hard to take was not hearing from me. The feeling is mutual, but it is plain that you have gone through a far more ravaging experience than I have ever had. . . .

Extract from a letter from Mandela to Winnie, dated June 20, 1970.

Dade Wethu

. . . What a world of difference to your failing health and to your spirit, darling, to my own anxiety and the strain that I cannot shake off, if only we could meet; if I could be by your side and squeeze you, or if I could but catch a glimpse of your outline through the thick wire netting that would inevitably separate us. . . .

. . . In spite of all that has happened I have throughout the ebb and flow of the tides of fortune in the last 15 months, lived in hope and expectation.

Sometimes I even have the belief that this feeling is part and parcel of myself. It seems to be woven into my very being. I feel my heart pumping hope steadily to every part of my body, warming my blood and pepping up my spirits. . . .

By the way the other day I dreamt of you convulsing your entire body with a graceful Hawaiian dance at the B.M.S.C. I stood at one end of the famous hall with arms outstretched ready to embrace you as you whirled toward me with the enchanting smile that I miss so desperately. I cannot explain why the scene should have been located at the B.M.S.C. To my recollection we have been there for a dance only once – on the night of Lindi's wedding reception. The other occasion was the concert we organized in 1957 when I was courting you, or you me. I am never certain whether I am free to remind you that you took the initiative in this regard. Anyway the dream was for me a glorious moment. If I must dream in my sleep, please Hawaii for me. . . .

Keep well my darling: do not allow yourself to be run down by illness or longing for the children. Fight with all your strength. Tons and tons of love and a million kisses. Devotedly, Dalibunga

Extracts from a letter from Mandela to Winnie while she was in prison, dated August 1, 1970.

My Darling,

. . . You cross-examined me very closely on my health on Dec 12. . . . Don't be disturbed, darling, I hope to outlive Methuselah and be with you long after you have reached the menopause, when not even Zeni and Zindzi will fuss over you, when all the gloss you now have will be gone and your body, your lovely face included, will be all wrinkles, skin as tough as that of a rhinoceros. I shall nurse and look after you in every way. Now and again we will visit the farm, walk around with fingers of my left hand dovetailing with those of your right, watching you dart off to pluck some beautiful wild flowers, just as you did on Sunday March 10. You were dazzling in that black [and] white-spotted nylon dress. Every day will always be March 10 for me. What does age and little blood pressure matter to us? Nothing! . . . But you are a witch! Always casting spells on your man. . . .

Extracts from a letter from Mandela to Winnie, dated December 28, 1970.

Dादेwaहन   20ᵗʰ June 1970.

Indeed, "The chains of the body are often wings to the spirit." It has been so all along, & so it always will be. Shakespeare in _As You Like It_ puts the same idea somewhat differently:

"Sweet are the uses of adversity,
Which like a toad, ugly and venomous,
Wears yet a precious jewel in the head."

Still others have proclaimed that "only great aims can arouse great energies."

Yet my understanding of the real idea behind these simple words throughout the 26 years of my career has been superficial, imperfect & perhaps a bit scholastic. There is a stage in the life of every social reformer when he will thunder on platforms primarily to relieve himself of the scraps of undigested information that has accumulated in his head; an attempt to impress the crowds rather than to start a calm & simple penetrating exposition of principles & ideas whose universal truth is made evident by personal experience & deeper study. In this regard I am no exception & I have been victim of the weakness of my our generation not once but a hundred times. I must be frank & tell you that when I look back at some of my early writings & speeches I am appalled by their pedantry, artificiality & lack of originality. The urge to impress & advertise is clearly noticeable. What a striking contrast your letters make, Inhlope. I hesitate to heap praises on you but you will pardon my vanity & conceit, Ngutyana. To pay you a compliment may amount to self-praise, for on my part you & I are one. Perhaps under the present conditions this type of vanity may serve as a powerful lever to our spirits.

During the 8 lonely years I have spent behind bars I sometimes wished we were born the same hour, grown up together & spent every minute of our lives in each other's company. I sincerely believe that had this been the case I would have been a wiser man. Every one of your letters is a precious possession & often succeeds in arousing forces I have never suspected to be concealed in my being. In your hands the pen is really mightier than a sabre. Words flow out poetically & naturally & common expressions acquire a meaning that is at once challenging & stimulating. The first paragraph of your moving note, & more especially the opening line, shook me violently. I literally felt every one of the millions of atoms that make up my body pulling forcefully in all directions. The beautiful sentiments you have repeatedly urged on me since my arrest & conviction, & particularly during the last 13 months, are clearly the result more of actual experience than of scholasticism. They come from a woman

GEORGE BIZOS:

Mandela has never been guided by ideology. He was bored with Marxism and with political theory even though he was surrounded by members of the Communist Party whose tactical skills he respected and whose nonracism he embraced. People like Dr. Dadoo, Bram Fischer, Michael Harmel, Rusty Bernstein, J. B. Marks, and others contributed to his move away from the Africanist exclusivity he espoused as a young man.

We've known one another ever since we were at university and we have never discussed political theory. We've discussed poverty, we've discussed the amelioration of poverty, we've discussed minimum wages, the franchise, what sort of constitution we're going to have, what sort of bill of rights we're going to have, but never have we had an ideological discussion. He was never an ideologue – and perhaps that is the reason why he is the man he became. Even while he was awaiting trial, he was not prepared to be confrontational with people who regarded him as their enemy. The brigadier who was in charge of security shouted at him when he asked for a steady table, "Mandela, it is about time you realized you are a prisoner, and not in your office here ordering people about." Mandela said, "Brigadier, have you finished?" The man said, "Yes." Mandela said, "Thank you," and turned around. He came back after lunch and said, "Guess what? I got a better table than you chaps have got here!"

When I went to Robben Island in August 1964, it was winter. Mandela arrived, wearing a pair of shorts, no socks, rough shoes, on the back of a *bakkie,* with eight guards, two in front, two at the back, two on each side. He jumped off the *bakkie* and had to walk some distance to the concrete *stoep* in front of the consulting room. I snaked through the front two guards and embraced him. The guards were absolutely shocked – they were young – that a white man should embrace a black man in prison! And what did he say? "George, you know this place has already made me forget my manners. I haven't introduced you to my guard of honor." And he proceeded to introduce each one of them by name. So he may lack belief in any of the fashionable ideologies of liberation, but he has a very, very strong belief in democratic principles and an abhorrence of any form of discrimination.

RICHARD STENGEL:

Mandela has a wonderful memory but he's not very introspective. You have to interpret what he says through narrative or stories. I was constantly probing for some psychological detail or insight. I remember once when talking about Robben Island I said, "How is the man who emerged after twenty-seven years different from the man who went in in the 1960s?" I kept pressing him in different ways and one day he finally got frustrated and said, "I came out mature." It was a sort of Robben Island/ANC word, and of course the clichés are true: the experience did harden them and make them mature and "mature" was the nearest he came to answering that question. The man at the Rivonia Trial was this passionate young man who I think was probably not in control of his emotions. The man who came out was in very rigorous control of his passions and his emotions. People say Mandela's not bitter; he's terribly bitter, but he's learned to control it. It's not an absence of bitterness or anger. Nobody gets rid of those things, but some people learn how to harness and control them.

He told me that the daily humiliations he had to suffer when he first got to Robben Island taught him control. How could you get through the days, the weeks, the months, the years without it? And what is so singular about Mandela, so unique and extraordinary, is that he never lost his dignity and power through that process. Eddie Daniels who was with him on Robben Island told me whenever he felt down he would look out of the window onto the courtyard and if he could just see Mandela standing there, or walking, it would fill him with optimism again and pride. That's what a leader in a very fundamental way has to do. The guys that are on the line with you have to look at you and think, "Oh, he's not scared. He's doing this. I can't be scared either." He fulfilled that role for his comrades.

Robben Island taught him patience too. Any normal human being dealing with bureaucracy gets frustrated but Mandela dealt with bureaucracy for twenty-seven years. Perhaps it was not so much that he learned patience, but he learned to feign it because that's how he got things accomplished. He learned not to appear angry. He was virtually powerless, this very powerful man, but he learned how to make friends with his captors. He and his fellow prisoners developed a kind of resilience, a flexible way of dealing with authority without compromising their values.

The mini-politics of Robben Island taught Mandela a lot about politics and he developed great shrewdness and emotional intelligence in dealing with his rivals. For instance, Govan Mbeki was a real rival in prison and there was no love lost between them. Govan had his own following of straight-from-the-shoulder Marxists. Mandela was a pragmatist and when, during the final stages of negotiations with the government in the late 1980s, he proposed Govan as the first to be released, it was a brilliant tactical move and Govan was sort of neutralized when he came out. I've spent time in American politics as a speech writer and although – largely because he had been away for so long – Mandela was naïve about many things, whenever we talked about politics or political strategy he was so shrewd. Politics is his hyper-talent.

INVICTUS

Out of the night that covers me,
Black as the pit from pole to pole,
I thank whatever gods may be
For my unconquerable soul.

In the fell clutch of circumstance
I have not winced nor cried aloud.
Under the bludgeonings of chance
My head is bloody, but unbow'd.

Beyond this place of wrath and tears
Looms but the Horror of the shade,
And yet the menace of the years
Finds and shall find me unafraid.

It matters not how strait the gate,
How charged with punishments the scroll,
I am the master of my fate:
I am the captain of my soul.

W. E. Henley

The poem Invictus *by the Victorian English poet William Ernest Henley with its emphasis on dignity and personal responsibility was a great source of inspiration for Mandela on Robben Island.*

of my generation, it was the Rivonia Trial that brought Mandela to our attention. I had been almost totally conditioned by the very conservative political background of my family and the little villages in which I grew up. And when I went to Potchefstroom University there were fewer than a thousand students so it was pretty easy to control the overall ethos. Although I slipped into a very easy and predefined role of the campus rebel, it was always rebellion within a very clearly demarcated and safe framework. With the exception of Professor Z. K. Matthews, who came to address us once, I had never ever encountered a black person who was not a laborer or a domestic servant. It never occurred to me that a black person could be a lawyer or a doctor or even a teacher. This meant Matthews made an even greater impression.

There were many things that made me feel a bit uneasy, but I had no framework of reference within which I could evaluate them. I became politically conscientized as a student in Paris between 1959 and 1961 and when I came back I was in a very uneasy position. I had totally broken from everything I held sacrosanct but I felt I had not had time to establish a new foundation for my beliefs. It was the Rivonia Trial that shaped my political thinking more than anything else. I remember the sense of outrage that such people could be brought to court because they made such a tremendous impression of dignity, of a sense of direction, of knowing what they wanted and how to get it, and not having any sentimental remorse about it because they were confident that what they were doing was the right thing.

From then on Mandela became a kind of iconic figure for me although I knew very little of him apart from the little bit that could be reported in the newspapers and the text of his statement from the dock, which made a tremendous lifelong impression. It remained like that for all the years he was in jail except that as international agitation grew and as pressure on the government grew I wrote an article here and one abroad pointing out how important it was for a man like that to be present in the increasingly fluid situation in which we found ourselves.

The 1976 uprisings and the Biko murder were absolutely pivotal events in my conscientization. Toward the end of the seventies I started being contacted by the ANC whenever I was abroad – in Australia, in Dublin and London, and in the Scandinavian countries. I think I started knowing more about my country outside it than I ever did here. From then on, I became involved in campaigns for Mandela's release, and in trying to explain the cause of the ANC to people who had totally demonized it. In my writing, from Kennis van die Aand onwards, I saw it as necessary to try to change the conditioning of Afrikaner minds – not as necessary in the sense of campaigning, or of propagandizing the political situation, but because of my own experiences. As a result of contacts I was having with ANC members abroad, some of whom became very good friends, I started meeting more and more people locally – in many cases not in a specifically political context, but as friends. And that caused the influence to penetrate that much more deeply.

Because he figured so prominently in all those things, my curiosity about Mandela grew and grew. Occasionally from people who had spent some time on the island with him and otherwise just from the perceptions of people in the townships who worshiped him

In a very particular context it became obvious that he was an exceptional kind of person. And in the late eighties, and specifically on the Dakar expedition in 1987, [a meeting in Dakar, Senegal, where fifty Afrikaner intellectuals met ANC leaders] I found out what a staggering hero Mandela had become and I became more and more eager to do something, to find out more.

The best way I can illustrate my impression of Mandela is through for me the most important morning I spent with him. Shortly before the second elections in 1999 he invited me to tea at Genadendal. It was unforgettable because of the grandfatherly way he spoke about things and the kindly, understanding way in which he spoke about the soft spot he had for Afrikaners. He insisted on speaking Afrikaans for much of the conversation and the few books over the years he has signed for me he always signed in that lovely handwriting in Afrikaans. He has the quality that I think many really great people have of making you feel, even if you have only one minute to spend with him, that for that one minute you are the most important person in his life.

The specific moment there, which is still a key moment in my whole life, was when – I can't remember what led up to it – he put out his hand and put it on my wrist, and said, "I want you to know one thing. When I was in prison you changed the way I saw the world."

I'm quite sure he said that to many writers and, I realized afterwards, that I don't think he was addressing me as an individual but as a writer. He was thinking of what writing and literature did to the shaping of his thinking in prison. I remember feeling very specifically then, "Please God," and I said that as an atheist, "just let me die now. Nothing that happens after this can top that."

I still feel moved almost to tears every time I tell this because of the extent of the man's humanity and compassion. I really felt I was in the presence of a saint. Thank God he has too many human faults ever to be mistaken for a saint. I think that is his saving grace.

FIKILE BAM:

Nelson was very serious about learning to understand the Afrikaner – his mind and how he thought. Because in his mind, and he actually preached this, the Afrikaner was an African . . . and whatever solution there was going to be on the political issues, was going to involve Afrikaans people. They, after all, were part and parcel of the land, apart from the point that they were the rulers of the land, but . . . they had grown up and they had a history in the country, which he wanted to understand.

And hence he put a lot of work and effort in learning to speak Afrikaans and to use it. . . . He had absolutely no qualms about greeting people in Afrikaans, and about trying his Afrikaans out on the guards. People who came in around about 1976 did have a problem and inhibition about Afrikaans, but not Nelson. He wanted to really get to know Afrikaners, as part of the people who belonged to the country.

Fikile Bam, "The Long Walk of Nelson Mandela"

I must draw your attention to the abuse of authority, political persecution, and other irregularities that are being committed by the Commanding Officer of this prison and members of his staff. . . .

During the last 14 years of my incarceration I have tried to the best of my ability to cooperate with all officials, from the Commissioner of Prisons to the Section Guard, as long as that cooperation did not compromise my principles. I have never regarded any man as my superior, either in my life outside or inside prison, and have freely offered this cooperation in the belief that to do so would promote harmonious relations between prisoners and guards and contribute to the general welfare of us all. My respect for human beings is based, not on the color of a man's skin nor authority he may wield, but purely on merit. . . .

Improper Interference with Social Relationships
(a) My youngest daughter, Zindziswa, sent me photographs on 3 different occasions one of which I actually saw in my file in 1974 when W/O Du Plessis and I were looking for the copy of a letter I had written to a former minister of justice. When I asked for the photo, he told me we should deal with one thing at a time and, for that day, I left the matter there. When I subsequently asked for it, the photo had disappeared. . . .

I might add that I had no trouble with letters from my daughters until Zindziswa complained to the United Nations about the systematic persecution of my wife. Of the 6 I got in 1973 only 3 were mutilated. Of the 11 which came in 1974, 7 were heavily censored and in 1975, 6 out of 16. But the picture for 1976 is totally different. Of the 9 I have received since the beginning of the year only 1 reached me unsullied. . . .

It is futile to think that any form of persecution will ever change our views. Your Government and Department have a notorious reputation for their hatred, contempt, and persecution of the Black man, especially the African, a hatred and contempt which forms the basic principle of a multiplicity of the country's statutes and cases. . . .

Extracts from a twenty-five page letter from Mandela to the commissioner of prisons, complaining about the abuse of authority, dated July 12, 1976.

The Commissioner of Prisons
Pretoria

1. Attached please find a copy of a letter of complaint dated the 12th July, 1976 by the abovementioned prisoner addressed to the Commissioner of Prisons – annexure A.

2-1. BACKGROUND
Nelson Mandela considers himself as the leader of the prisoners on Robben Island and to retain and improve this image amongst his fellow prisoners he, from time to time, acts as the mouthpiece of the prisoners, by raising the so-called general complaints directly to the Commissioner of Prisons or the Honorable Minister – the highest authority possible.

2-2. Official records are kept of the complaints and requests by prisoners and the way of disposal and I am quite satisfied that the head of the prison sees them daily and that we comply with the provisions as laid down in Regulation 103.

2-3. They also have the opportunity to raise their complaints with the inspectorate when such visits take place.

2-4. The International Committee of the Red Cross visited Robben Island recently and they – including Mandela – had a golden opportunity to lodge their complaints through an international organization with the commanding officer; with senior officers representing Headquarters; with the Commissioner during an interview between the Commissioner of Prisons and the delegates of the ICRC and finally with the Honorable Minister. . . .

2-7. Before I comment on the various issues raised by him, I must draw your attention to the introduction of his letter where he systematically and in a psychological manner brought the reader under the impression of his own importance, self-esteem and the very high level at which he as a prisoner communicates and very clearly creates the impression that the guards, the head of prison and even the Commanding Officer are of no importance and not capable of solving his problems. . . .

Extracts from a letter from the officer commanding, Robben Island, to the commissioner of prisons, Pretoria, regarding Mandela's letter of complaint, dated July 27, 1976.

---

(15) G 138

DEPARTEMENT VAN GEVANGENISSE
PRISONS DEPARTMENT

C.P.-S. /M-5/

CONFIDENTIAL

The Officer Commanding
Prison Command
Private Bag ROBBEN ISLAND
7400

FOR ATTENTION : SECURITY

The Commissioner of Prisons
Private Bag X136
PRETORIA
0001

U. verwysing
Your reference .... 19..

My verwysing   Serial No.   27/7/1976
My reference   913

Telefoon
Telephone   11   Uitbr. 2
                          Ext.

SERIAL NO. 913 : NELSON MANDELA : LETTER OF COMPLAINT
TO THE COMMISSIONER OF PRISONS

1.   Attached please find a copy of a letter of complaint
      dated the 12th July, 1976 by the abovementioned
      prisoner addressed to the Commissioner of Prisons -
      annexure A.

2-1. BACKGROUND
      Nelson Mandela considers himself as the leader of the
      prisoners on Robben Island and to retain and improve
      this image amongst his fellow prisoners he, from time
      to time, acts as the mouthpiece of the prisoners, by
      raising the so-called general complaints directly to
      the Commissioner of Prisons or the Honourable Minister -
      the highest authority possible.

2-2. Official records are kept of the complaints and requests
      by prisoners and the way of disposal and I am quite
      satisfied that the head of the prison sees them daily
      and that we comply with the provisions as laid down
      in Regulation 103.

2/......

-2-

2-3. They also have the opportunity to raise their
      complaints with the inspectorate when such
      visits take place.

2-4. The International Committee of the Red Cross
      visited Robben Island recently and they -
      including Mandela - had a golden opportunity
      to lodge their complaints through an international
      organization with the commanding officer; with
      senior officers representing Headquarters; with
      the Commissioner during an interview between the
      Commissioner of Prisons and the delegates of the
      ICRC and finally with the Honourable Minister.

2-5. Brigadier du Plessis visited Robben Island
      on various occasions during which Mandela
      lodged his complaints and requests which received
      the necessary attention.

2-6. Regulation 103(3)(a) makes the provision that
      if a prisoner has valid grounds for requesting
      an interview with the Commissioner, Deputy or
      Assistant Commissioner he may submit a written
      request for such interview together with the
      grounds in support thereof to the commanding officer.
      Nelson Mandela, nor any other prisoner in the single (isolation)
      cells, made such an application.

2-7. Before I comment on the various issues raised by
      him, I must draw your attention to the introduction
      of his letter where he systematically and in a
      psychological manner brought the reader under the
      impression of his own importance, self-esteem and
      the very high level at which he as a prisoner
      communicates and very clearly creates the im-
      pression that the warders, the head of the prison
      and even the Commanding Officer are of no
      importance and not capable of solving his problems.

3/....

Increasing numbers of MK soldiers were now being incarcerated on the island. These men were more militant than Mandela's generation, more belligerent toward their captors. Once again Mandela found himself mediating between the authorities and his comrades. It was an uncomfortable position but one he was adroit at handling, further consolidating his status among both his comrades and the prison staff. With the soldiers came war stories and encouraging news of the ANC in exile. At the Rivonia Trial Mandela had warned the regime that the intensity of the opposition would increase, but he took no pleasure in the knowledge that his prophecies were coming true. He also had a sense that the world outside the island was changing. The bush war in Rhodesia was escalating and a 1974 coup d'état in Portugal had brought a new government to power, ending centuries of colonial rule in Mozambique and Angola. Slowly South Africa was being enveloped by independent Africa.

By this time the prisoners had created an intellectually vibrant environment. The quarry had become less a site of labor than of education, in a sense the campus of the Robben Island "university," as it became known. With many of the prisoners studying for degrees they organized discussion groups, tutorials and lectures. The prisoners became both students and teachers. Sometimes the lectures were academic in support of their studies, sometimes unofficial talks on political topics such as a history of the Indian struggle (taught by Kathrada) and a history of the ANC (by Sisulu). Mandela himself gave a course in political economy.

Although education was always a priority for Mandela and he encouraged both his comrades and the guards to study, the men of Section B also developed a penchant for amateur dramatics. An early performance was Sophocles' *Antigone,* with Mandela in the role of Creon. Creon stood for everything Mandela was not: an uncompromising leader hidebound by the dictates of authority. Yet the play spoke of their condition: men of conscience, epitomized by Antigone, striving for justice against a harsh regime. Unbeknown to the actors, news of their performance filtered back to the mainland and inspired the dramatist Athol Fugard's play *The Island.* Suddenly Robben Island gained a new and grim reality on the stages of Cape Town, London, and Broadway.

Mandela took great interest in the vegetable garden the prisoners were allowed to keep in the 1970s. For years he had petitioned to start one and eventually they were allowed to cultivate a narrow patch on the edge of the courtyard. Soon they were producing tomatoes, chilies, radishes, onions, and sweet melons, which they shared not only among their comrades but among the guards. "The sense of being the custodian of this small patch of earth offered a small taste of freedom," Mandela recorded in the manuscript that he had secretly begun to write.[11]

The idea for the autobiography came from Walter Sisulu and Ahmed Kathrada. As Mac Maharaj, who had been sentenced to twelve years for sabotage in what became known as the "little Rivonia Trial" in 1964, was due for release in 1976, it was felt he could smuggle out a copy and have it published on Mandela's sixtieth birthday in 1978. For four months Mandela spent his nights writing in secret. Each day, the previous night's pages were copied in a minute script by Maharaj onto sheets of thin paper which he and Laloo Chiba then hid in Maharaj's study books. The five hundred pages were wrapped in plastic cocoa containers and buried in three separate places in the courtyard.

Shortly after he finished his autobiography, Mandela heard from Winnie that she had been released from prison and her banning order had expired. He made arrangements for her to bring Zindzi when next she visited. At fifteen, Zindzi was a year under the minimum age for visitors, but Winnie doctored her birth certificate to get her through. Mandela put on a freshly pressed shirt and carefully combed his hair to see his wife for the first time in a year and his daughter for the first time since she was three years old. He thought she had the fire and beauty of her mother. Initially there was an awkwardness, but he asked her about her friends, her school and told her anecdotes from the short time they had shared as a family. He noticed she was holding back her tears. As was he.

"I have been fairly successful in putting on a mask behind which I have pined for my family, alone, never rushing for the post when it comes until somebody calls out my name," he would write to Winnie. "I also never linger after visits although sometimes the urge to do so becomes quite horrible. I am struggling to suppress my emotions as I write this letter."[12]

Despite completing his memoirs in 1976 and Winnie's freedom, 1977 also brought disaster. Toward the end of the year the authorities found one of the manuscript packets and Mandela, Sisulu, and Kathrada had their study privileges withdrawn for four years. In a further twist, although Maharaj smuggled out his copy, it would be eighteen years before the updated manuscript would appear as *Long Walk to Freedom.*

. . . I was informed that you cancelled my study privilege permanently with effect from 1st January 1978, on the allegation that I abused the said privilege by using study material to write my memoirs.

I must point out that I was appalled to note that, in taking such a drastic decision, you violated the fundamental principles of natural justice, and you did not even consider it necessary to inform me beforehand of the case against me. . . .

In this regard I regret to tell you that you did not at all act in good faith. Not only did you conceal the fact that you were investigating an allegation against me, but you also denied me the opportunity of contradicting any relevant facts which I might have considered prejudicial to my interests.

It is unlikely that I would have contested my handwriting which appeared in any material in your possession. But there have been occasions in the past when some of us were accused of having abused their study and privilege on the strength of material which was not in their handwriting, and their studies were saved simply because they were able to establish that the accusation was false. To the best of my knowledge and belief, neither you nor any of your staff members are handwriting experts, and any opinion you may have on the identity of a particular handwriting would be quite valueless. . . .

For example, if you had given me the opportunity to state my case before you withdrew the privilege, I might have convinced you that last year I had no permission to study and, therefore, could not have abused any study privilege. This is quite apart from the fact that, in any case, in the enlightened world of the Seventies, I see nothing wrong whatsoever in incarcerated freedom fighters writing out their life-stories and preserving them for posterity. Such privileges have been granted freely by all sorts of regimes since Roman times. . . .

Extracts from a letter from Mandela to the commissioner of prisons regarding his study privileges being cancelled after discovery of the *Long Walk to Freedom* manuscript, dated December 6, 1977.

whatever I used to read in prison – even the *Reader's Digest* – if I came across a little thing by say Balzac or someone, I made a note of it. And in that way I filled about seven notebooks with a collection of random things, including a poem by a young Afrikaner Antjie Krog, on the Immorality Act, which I must have copied down in 1967.

I used to keep the notebooks in my cell. And they confiscated them because of some offense. In the end, so much material had been confiscated, especially from the communal cells, that they had no space so they set aside one cell and put everything in there.

On weekends we had nondisciplinary guards who worked in the hospitals and on the ferries and they didn't know what was happening. So one weekend Laloo Chiba and I went to them and said, "Look, just open this cell. We want to clean it." They were very happy – here were prisoners who wanted to work! They opened up and we literally stole back everything, all the copies of my letters, nine hundred of them, and these notebooks.

The idea for Mandela's autobiography came about when Walter and I were just walking, as we generally did, talking about things, and I suggested that Madiba's sixtieth birthday was coming and we should get him to write. We knew the risks involved, not only to us but to the whole community, but we had to take that chance. The leadership of the ANC – the High Organ – of Madiba, Walter, Govan Mbeki, and Raymond Mhlaba discussed it, but the only other ANC people who knew about it were Mac Maharaj, Laloo Chiba, and myself.

The process was that Madiba would write whatever he could. For a while he pretended to be ill, and stayed in the cell, so that he could sleep during the day and work at night. Madiba had registered to study Afrikaans and he was allowed *Die Huisgenoot.* Guards were not allowed to bring anything into the sections – no newspapers, no magazines, no books – so these chaps who looked after us at night were bored; they had nothing to do but walk up and down the passage. The nasty ones would try to trap us with this rule: if you're studying Standard eight you sleep at eight and if you're studying Standard ten you sleep at ten and at university you sleep at eleven. But Madiba struck up good relations with some of these night chaps and gave them *Die Huisgenoot,* so they allowed him to write late.

Every night Madiba wrote about ten to fifteen pages in his handwriting. It was given to Mac the next morning when we were opened up so that he could transcribe it in very small handwriting the next evening. At the same time Mac would be making notes of queries. He would then conceal the transcribed part temporarily while passing on the original version to me so that I and Walter could go through it and make our comments.

Madiba's writing was very neat, very symmetrical, but not legible, so I had to read it to Walter, which was quite a task! Walter's handwriting was worse – so much so that when he registered at UNISA, one of his assignments came back, saying, "Please, please, Mr Sisulu. We cannot understand." So I had this triple task of reading the manuscript to Walter, making my own comments, and writing some of Walter's before returning it to Madiba. He would then do the final version, whether he accepted our comments or not. Generally he did.

Mac and Chiba were experts at tiny handwriting and concealment. We used to order things as part of my stationery when I was studying – anything, not really having in mind what I was going to use it for: glue, parchment, mapping pens, india ink. So we had this huge collection of things. What these chaps did was reduce these two books – Madiba's book and the collection of eight essays that we wrote and that Mac subsequently edited as *Reflections in Prison* – to less than fifty or so pages on thin paper.

Then Chiba constructed what roughly could be called an album, just made up of maps. He did such a beautiful job it looked like it was factory-made, but in the covers he concealed these fifty pages. Mac was being released in 1976 and was given the task of taking it out. He didn't even try to hide it. He just walked out with it – it just looked like maps.

We buried the unedited version in cocoa containers in the garden. The idea was that as soon as the final transcript reached England, Mac would send me a pre-arranged message on a birthday card or something indicating that it was safe and we would then destroy what was buried. We thought it was safe in the garden – who was going to interfere in the garden? Some of the guards used to steal our tomatoes, but they wouldn't dig.

Then suddenly one day they started building this wall. Early in the morning when they opened us up as usual to take out our slop buckets, two or three of us saw what was going on. We did manage to rescue some of it, but because of the three handwritings they found there – Mandela's, Mac's, and mine as well as comments by Sisulu – the three of us were punished with deprivation of studies. They could do nothing to Mac as he was already abroad. On that occasion the three of us lost our studies for four years.

We recently got access to some of our prison files. In them it appears that the prison authorities feared charging us because we would then have been able to make the autobiography a public document. They therefore amended the prison regulations in December 1977 to enable them arbitrarily and without charging us to deprive us of our study privileges.

MAC MAHARAJ:

For the version of Madiba's memoirs I was to smuggle out we used very thin paper and wrote on both sides. Tiny handwriting, yes, because we had to conserve space, but we were already masters of tiny handwriting for clandestine communications between our section of the prison and the communal section. Laloo Chiba became the expert, so much so that his eyesight suffered because we had no magnifying glass. I didn't want to know what happened to the original version in case I got caught, but it turned out that it was buried in the little prison garden.

I did smuggle my version out and sent it off to London when I was house-arrested in Durban. When I left South Africa six months later I went to London and retrieved it from Rusty Bernstein and it was transcribed, although for one reason or another it was never published. About a year after Madiba's release I retrieved the material and gave him a set and that's how it was used as the basis for *Long Walk to Freedom*.

... Gambians, Mali, Guinea, S/Leone & Liberia.
... (Sic Saliewa - either Liberia or Mali?) - who
... ... expressed impression & uncaware ... role of "Voice"
(was 1° a "mouthpiece" thing) Also H Kwame not aware too.
1st day - Friday - phoned Barden - says ga to be away. Appltd & monday.
OK not arrived - & agreed & & could only act together.
But 1st went to Bureau - met editor of Voice (another hotel
fib - took to another)
    Saw Barden monday - told him I would wait for OK before
discussions start - just pd respects. A few days late OK arrived
together c Robbie.
    Debate betw us 3:- OK says Aradeba - draw full memo, compliment &
knows ∴ Barden will block on way to Kwame. meanwhile obliged him
to pass it to Kwame. I - No - & knew Barden - will gave 1 to
Nupama. But Robbie OK felt Memo & & died the memo. ... Beginning
of may. There was ga to be a Conf of f/fighters towards end of may.
Bureau - attitude wait until then to see Kwame. But I didn't
wait until then. Barden couldn't be moved. See Bureau
was a new scam - quite friendly ... Adamafio who struck me as more
favourable - us - but he was sec & only - Barden who blocked
the way. & then saw michael Dei-Anang (new Pleugh)
& Saliewa, Kwame) He also - wait & 28th may (a Conf):
The impression wh I got from ambassador was not confirmed by
their experiences. They were well disposed, happy to see me but
as far as seeing Kwame they were adamant. Then saw
Ako Adjei , new F/Affairs — let cat out of bag - astonished as usual →
[NB OK was present] (1) repeats best policy & H lup - we return by 1st week
... a lecture. (2) UN waste of time (3) Critical org ∴ cant assist
Any replies. Contra to ambassador - my impression H was
not just Bureau - but also a segment of ministers. But still convinced
H Kwame not aware.
    Memo given in - but had to leave & Nigeria.
        & Ghana - wanted by students Ghana University but
Njorsana (Zam's cousin - but separate in cafe) consulted - says
no - University centre of opposition - Kwame - dont compromise
yourself. Same said by ambassador who was in Congo (at height of
death of Patrice) was coming back into favour (check OK) I also
personally experienced this when I met lectures informally.
    Spent a lot of time c "Liberty Flag, Dr ... Loner - very good, really
entertained me.
        After we went to London — OK discussed discussed came with
Kwesi Armah → said will letter to Kwame, gun 1 to me, & dont know
about G, He get 1 to Kwame - This done - solved problem
Gave OK - private phone no to phone Kwame wherever he was
in Ghana.

KATHRADA (2)

on 8th line from bottom. under the secretaryship of Alfred Nzo, & .. co-ordinating committee was established & consisting of representatives from the various areas. ANC men played a prominent part in organising the solidarity boycotts.

p 6   Insert at arrow.
The original fares were restored.

p 9 ⑥ delete portions enclosed in brackets.
add at arrow after "consumers." In spite of this, ~~due~~ thanks mainly to the widespread influence of the Congresses & the high level of political consciousness among the masses, the boycott caught on. Within a short time the blacklisted products began to disappear from ~~th~~ Indian and African shopwindows and shelves. Company travellers ~~who~~ turned back from shops, without orders. Congress offices received reports, of spontaneous boycotts ~~often from~~ remote and unlikely areas.

p. 11 ⑦ substitute for paragraph marked :-

June 26 is our national day. In 1957 we commemorated as a "Day of Abstinence" by calling upon the people: — not to do any shopping; — not to eat ~~for~~ during the day; — not to use electric lights in their homes but to use candles instead; - ~~and to light take part in bon~~ to display ~~th~~ ANC flags, and to take part in bonfire ceremonies at night. A balloon carrying a huge ANC flag was released over JHB. This novel form of demonstration was highly successful. Reporters from a daily newspaper in Johannesburg visited bazaars and shops ~~a~~ in the centre of city at the peak hours and found them empty. The only customers they found were whites. Indian shopkeepers in Johannesburg also reported "no business" for the day.

pp 11-14 delete ~~the~~ all the pages from "True in 1949 (p 11) ... to "high expectations" (p 14.)
This whole portion on the 1949 riots will have to be fitted in in the earlier ~~portion~~ chapters. The portion has ~~to~~ been re written. See later on. (P 6 of this)

p 14 ⑧ insert at arrow.
sentenced her and about 15 men to death for the alleged murder of the chief. The sentences were later commuted to life imprisonment.

...ove and following page: In 1974 the government introduced the compulsory use of Afrikaans as the medium of instruction...
...pils from Standard 5 onward. The rise of Black Consciousness in Soweto spurred by the victory of Frelimo in Mozambique...
...ne and on June 16, 1976, thousands of youths marched through Soweto in protest. The police opened fire and a number...
...dren were killed. Soweto became a battleground of stone-throwing youths against police with automatic rifles, tear gas, armo...
...icles, and helicopters and sparked a series of insurrections that lasted two years and spread throughout South Africa. Rob...
...nd was swamped by a new breed of young activists as hundreds of youths were jailed. Others escaped to join the MK train...
...ps abroad.

...ht: In August 1976, the first news of the Soweto uprising reached Robben Island. Mandela smuggled out a message which...
...ntually published by the ANC in 1980. It gives a contemporary indication of the significance he attached to the uprising in...

WE WHO ARE CONFINED WITHIN THE GREY WALLS OF THE PRETORIA REGIME'S PRISONS REACH OUT TO OUR PEOPLE. WITH YOU WE COUNT THOSE WHO HAVE PERISHED BY MEANS OF THE GUN AND THE HANGMAN'S ROPE. WE SALUTE ALL OF YOU – THE LIVING, THE INJURED, AND THE DEAD. FOR YOU HAVE DARED TO RISE UP AGAINST THE TYRANT'S MIGHT.. . .

WE FACE THE FUTURE WITH CONFIDENCE. FOR THE GUNS THAT SERVE APARTHEID CAN-NOT RENDER IT UNCONQUERABLE. THOSE WHO LIVE BY THE GUN SHALL PERISH BY THE GUN.

UNITE! MOBILIZE! FIGHT ON!

BETWEEN THE ANVIL OF UNITED MASS ACTION AND THE HAMMER OF THE ARMED STRUGGLE WE SHALL CRUSH APARTHEID AND WHITE MINORITY RACIST RULE.

AMANDLA NGAWETHU! MATLA KE A RONA!

Nelson Mandela, in response to the Soweto uprising

In April 1977 the government invited twenty-five South African journalists to visit Robben Island hoping to dispel rumors about the harsh treatment of political prisoners. The men resented being treated as "zoo animals" with the cameras following their every move as they worked.

"They showed us around the place hoping to convince us that everything was fine and that prisoners were being treated well – but didn't show us any prisoners. We told the authorities the fact that they weren't showing us prisoners could mean that Mandela was dead – and that we thought they might be covering it up. Eventually they got so worked up and worried about us speculating about this that they pointed him out to us, and there he was. Hardly any of us knew what he looked like because by that time he'd already been inside for twelve years and nobody was allowed to see photos of him. He looked cross – definitely angry. Then he turned around and looked the other way."

– Eric van Ees, United Press International foreign correspondent.

Above (left to right): Mandela; Toivo ja Toivo, Namibian independence leader; Justice Mpanza, ANC stalwart. Right (left to right): APDUSA member Frank Anthony, MK member Sandy Sejake, Sisulu. Opposite: Mandela.

The Head of Prison
ROBBEN ISLAND

We strongly protest against the purpose for and manner in which the visit to this prison of the local and overseas press and television men on the 25th April was organized and conducted by the Department of Prisons. We resent the deliberate violation of our right of privacy by taking our photographs without our permission, and regard this as concrete evidence of the contempt with which the Department continues to treat us.

On the 26th April fellow-prisoner Nelson Mandela was informed by Major Zandberg that the Minister of Prisons had finally agreed to the repeated requests by the press over the years to visit Robben Island. We also learned that the minister had authorized the visit provided no communication whatsoever would take place between pressmen and prisoners.

The Minister planned the visit in the hope that it would white-wash the Prisons Department; pacify public criticisms of the Department here and abroad, and counteract any adverse publicity that might arise in the future. To ensure the success of the plan we were not given prior notice of the visit, on that particular day the span from our Section was given the special work of "gardening" instead of pulling out bamboo from the sea as we normally do when we go to work. Some 30 liters of milk was placed at the entrance to our Section, quite obviously to give the impression that it was all meant for us, whereas in truth we receive only 6.5 liters a day.

Most of us know that a section of the press here and abroad is sympathetic to our cause, and that they would have preferred to handle the operation in a dignified manner. Nevertheless, the Minister's disregard for our feelings had led to the situation where total strangers are now in possession of photographs and films of ourselves. The impropriety of the Minister's action is sharpened by the Department's persistent refusal to allow us to take and send our photographs to our own families.

We stress the fact that the way in which the Minister planned this visit in no way differs from previous ones. In August 1964 reporters from "The Daily Telegraph" found those of us who were here at the time "mending clothes" instead of our normal work at the time of knapping stones with 5lb. hammers. As soon as the reporters left we were ordered to crush stones as usual. At the end of August 1965 Mrs. Ida Parker from "The Sunday Tribune" found us wearing raincoats on our way back from the lime quarry – raincoats which were hurriedly issued to us at work on the very day of her visit, and which were immediately taken away when she left. The rain coats were not issued to us again until a year or so later. . . .

At all times we are willing to have press and television interviews, provided that the aim is to present to the public a balanced picture of our living conditions. This means that we would be allowed to express our grievances and demands freely, and to make comments whether such comments are favorable or otherwise to the Department.

We are fully aware that the Department desires to protect [sic] a favorable image to the world of its policies. We can think of no better way of doing so than by abolishing all forms of racial discrimination in the administration by keeping abreast of enlightened penal reforms, by granting us the status of political prisoners, and by introducing a nonracial administration throughout the country's prisons. With few or no skeletons to hide the Department will then no longer stand in any need for resorting to stratagems. . . .

We stress that we are not chattels of the Prisons Department. That we happen to be prisoners in no way detracts from the fact that we are, nevertheless, South African and Namibian citizens, entitled to protection against any abuses by the Department.

Finally, we place on record that we cannot tolerate indefinitely any treatment we consider degrading and provocative and, should the Minister continue to do so, we reserve to ourselves the right to take such action as we deem appropriate.

The Single Cells Section
ROBBEN ISLAND

19 May 1977

The Head of Prison
ROBBEN ISLAND

We strongly protest against the purpose for and manner in which
the visit to this prison of the local and overseas press and
television men on the 25th April was organised and conducted
by the Department of Prisons. We resent the deliberate viola=
tion of our right of privacy by taking our photographs without
our permission, and regard this as concrete evidence of the con=
tempt with which the Department continues to treat us.

On the 26th April fellow-prisoner Nelson Mandela was informed
by Major Zandberg that the Minister of Prisons had finally agreed
to the repeated requests by the press over the years to visit
Robben Island. We also learnt that the minister had authorised
the visit provided no communication whatsoever would take place
be=tween pressmen and prisoners.

The Minister planned the visit in the hope that it would white=
wash the Prisons Department, pacify public criticism of the De=
partment here and abroad, and counteract any adverse publicity
that might arise in the future. To ensure the success of the
plan we were not given prior notice of the visit, on that parti=
cular day the span from our Section was given the special work
of "gardening" instead of pulling out bamboo from the sea as we
normally do when we go to work. Some 30 litres of milk was
placed at the entrance to our Section, quite obviously to give
the impression that it was all meant for us, whereas in truth
we receive only 6½ litres a day.

[margin note: Not true. I didn't even see any milk JM.]

Most of us know that a section of the press here and abroad is
sympathetic to our cause, and that they would have preferred to
handle the operation in a dignified manner. Nevertheless, the
Minister's disregard for our feelings has led to the situation
where total strangers are now in possession of photographs and
films of ourselves. The impropriety of the Minister's action is
sharpened by the Department's persistent refusal to allow us to

---

-2-

take and send our photographs to our own families.

We stress the fact that the way in which the Minister planned this
visit in no way differs from previous ones. IN August 1964 re=
porters from "The Daily Telegraph" found those of us who were here
at the time "mending clothes" instead of our normal work at the
time of knapping stones with 5 lb. hammers. As soon as the re=
porters left we were ordered to crush stones as usual. At the end
of August 1965 Mrs. I. da Parker from "The Sunday Tribune" found us
wearing raincoats on our way back from the lime quarry - raincoats
which were hurriedly issued to us at work on the very day of her
visit, and which were immediately taken away when she left. The
rain coats were not issued to us again until a year or so later.

We emphatically state that under no circumstances are we willing
to cooperate with the Department in any manoeuvre on its part to
distort the true state of affairs obtaining on this island. With
few exceptions our span has been kept inside for several months
now, but our normal work is still that of pulling sea-weed, and
the Department has given no assurance that we will never be sent
out to the quarry again.

We also cite the example of the cupboards we have in our cells.
Any television-viewer is likely to be impressed with this furniture
and would naturally give all the credit to the Department. It is
unlikely that such television-viewers and newspaper readers would
be aware that the cupboards have been painstakingly built with
crude tools in a crude "workshop" from cardboard cartons and
from driftwood picked up on the beaches by prisoners, that the costs
for beautifying them have been borne by the prisoners themselves,
and that they have been built by a talented fellow prisoner, Jafta
Masemola, working approximately 8 hours a day on weekdays at the
rate of R1,50 (One Rand fifty Cents) a month.

[margin note: Rubbish!]
[margin note: The same for other prisoners.]

Atlall times wer are willing to have press and television inter=
views, provided that the aim is to present to the public a balanced
picture of our living conditions. This means that we would be
allowed to express our grievances and demands freely, and to make
comments whether such comments are favourable or otherwise to the
Department.

We are fully aware that the Department desires to protect a favourable

---

-3-

image to the world of its policies. We can think of no better
way of doing so than by abolishing all forms of racial discrimi=
nation in the administration by keeping abreast of enlightened
penal reforms, by granting us the status of political prisoners,
and by introducing a non-racial administration through-out the
country's prisons. With few or no skeletons to hide the Depart=
ment will then no longer stand in any need for resorting to
stratagems.

The actual execution of the plan was entrusted to Gen. Roux and in
his presence, the reporters and cameramen stormed down upon us like
excited visitors to an agricultural show. From all that we have
seen of Gen. Roux, we are convinced that he has no respect
whatsoever for our feelings and dignity. The way he handled
the visit is no different from his conduct when he visited this
prison on the 15th November 1976. On that occasion he conducted
his interviews with us individually in a cloak-and-dagger fashion
in the hope of finding us at a complete loss when confronted with
the unexpected. That there were no ugly incidents as a result
of the provocative action on the 25th April was due solely to our
sense of responsibility.

[margin note: Very interesting.]

We are fully aware that we cannot prevent the publication of such
articles on prison conditions here as the Minister might authorize.
But we are equally aware that, whatever the law might be, the
taking of our photographs by the press for publication purposes or
otherwise without our consent, constitutes an invasion of our privacy.
That privacy has been blatantly violated by the very people who,
within the framework of the law, are considered to be its guar=
dians. And, having violated that privacy, the Department had the
temerity to ask us for permission to make us objects of public
scrutiny.

We stress that we are not chattels of the Prisons Department. That
we happen to be prisoners in no way detracts from the fact that we
are, nevertheless, South African and Namibian citizens, <u>entitled
to protection against any abuses by the Department</u>

[margin note: I suppose all other S.A. citizens are also entitled to protection against them.]

Finally, we place on record that we cannot tolerate indefinitely any
treatment we consider degrading and provocative and, should the
Minister continue to do so, we reserve to ourselves the right
to take such action as we deem appropriate.

-4-

F. Anthony
J.E. April
L. Chiba
T.T. Cholo
E.J. Daniels
T.L. Daweti
M.K. Dingake
M.S. Essop
J. Fuzile
K. Hassim
T.H. Ja-Toivo
A.M. Kathrada
N.R. Mandela
J. Masemola
G. Mbeki
R. Mhlaba
K. Mkalipi
W.Z. Mkwayi
A. Mlangeni
E. Motsoaledi
J. Mpanza
P. Mthembu
B. Nair
J.N. Pokela
S. Sijake
W.U. Sisulu
M.M. Siyothula
J.B. Vusani
R.C. Wilcox

The young activists who arrived on Robben Island in the aftermath of the riots were even more aggressive than the MK soldiers of the early 1970s. Mandela realized it would not be an easy task to convert them to a more pragmatic position given their impatience with the apartheid regime and the torture they had suffered at its hands. News of the rise of Black Consciousness had reached the island before the Soweto uprising and while Mandela could understand its attraction, he believed it was sectarian and limited. His attitude was to listen to the opinions of the young lions, and, when questioned, emphasize unity against a common enemy. Gradually many were won over although there were some instances of physical fights between different factions inside the Black Consciousness group.

In early 1977, when work had slowed down almost to a standstill, the authorities officially abandoned all pretence at manual labor. Mandela now filled his days with reading, writing letters, attending to the legal requirements of his fellow prisoners, gardening, and playing tennis on the makeshift court painted in the courtyard. He also increased the Monday to Thursday exercise regime in his cell that included running in place, push-ups, sit-ups, and knee-bends.

But despite the improved conditions Robben Island remained a prison. Mandela worried about Makgatho; he'd heard that Makaziwe's marriage was on the rocks and wrote to her concerned for her welfare but suggesting that divorce offered a second chance. He wanted her to abandon her nursing ambitions and register for a degree in medicine instead.

Of Zindzi, he wrote to Winnie stressing that she must not neglect her studies. He sent a letter to Zeni concerned that she was too young to marry Prince Thumbumuzi of Swaziland and should graduate first. But he soon warmed to the marriage. Once the couple's daughter was born, the young family made a journey to the island. Their status gave them diplomatic privileges and the meeting was held in the consultation room; Mandela was able to hug and kiss his daughter and grandchild. "It was a dizzying experience," he wrote. "To hold a newborn baby, so vulnerable and soft in my rough hands, hands that for too long had held only picks and shovels, was a profound joy."[13]

With his study privileges still withdrawn, Mandela turned to other books, particularly Tolstoy's *War and Peace*. Each day he listened to a news summary broadcast over the prison's intercom system and looked forward to the once-a-week diversion of a movie – mostly Westerns and action features. Later they were able to choose documentaries although Mandela would never turn down a film starring Sophia Loren. Their meals had also improved.

In his neat cell with its shelves of legal books and his tidy desk on which were two photographs – one of Winnie, the other of a graceful African woman snipped from a *National Geographic* – Mandela would receive those who sought his legal or personal advice. To his fellow prisoners he was a man with gravitas. They called him by his preferred clan name, Madiba, while to the prison staff he had become Mandela or even Mr. Mandela. The familiar Nelson had long since fallen out of use.

Dear Madiba,

In the early seventies, when you were still a young man and when we were still not allowed in our cells photos of our loved ones, we came across this picture in the National Geographic. *It is a photo of an Andamanese woman running effortlessly on the beach – a glorious celebration of life.*

You fell in love with the photo. I used a broken blade to carve a frame from a tomato box plank. We gave you the framed picture as a birthday present. You kept it on your bookshelf. The regime got the press to photograph your cell in 1978. And there in the media was splashed your bookcase (made out of cardboard) and this framed photo (which the press said was Winnie!). . . .

And so, having traced the National Geographic *of the late sixties/early seventies, I thought we would frame it much like the one we gave you in prison, and give it to you on this your 86th birthday to share with aunt Graça and the family as a remembrance of a little thing that brought beauty and hope into a desolate cell 30–35 years ago. Happy birthday and may you in the bosom of your family have a truly wonderful and joyous day.*

Mac and Zarina, Milou and Sekai Jo

Letter from Mac Maharaj to Mandela on his eighty-sixth birthday, July 18, 2004.

With the coming of the 1980s Mandela took stock of his circumstances and seemed to sense the future. He had recently been awarded the Jawaharlal Nehru Human Rights Award in India; he was able to resume his legal studies; and a Free Mandela campaign initiated by Oliver Tambo in London had been taken up by *The Sunday World,* a Johannesburg newspaper edited by Percy Qoboza.

On the mainland there was a new prime minister, P. W. Botha, a belligerent man with an admonishing finger who soon came to believe that his country was facing what he called a "total onslaught." His assessment was not all paranoia: the war along the northern border of Namibia was intensifying, ANC bombs had damaged three oil-from-coal refineries and the townships were becoming sites of militancy.

Although Botha was against releasing Mandela, on March 31, 1982, Mandela and three others were told to pack their possessions. The suddenness, the secrecy, the transfer, unsettled him. He was given no time to say goodbye to his comrades as the guards hurried him out to the waiting ferry. Between the mainland and the island he looked back in the fading light. "A man can get used to anything, and I had grown used to Robben Island . . . and while it was never a home . . . it had become a place where I felt comfortable."[14]

Mandela was moved with Walter Sisulu, Raymond Mhlaba, and Andrew Mlangeni (they would be joined a few months later by Ahmed Kathrada) to Pollsmoor Prison in Tokai, a suburb thirty kilometers south of Cape Town. Nearby were the historic vineyards of Constantia, and pine forests covering the slopes of the peninsula's impressive mountains. However, none of this was visible from inside the high concrete walls.

The men were taken to a large room on the top floor. They had proper beds, sheets, blankets, and towels. A separate bathroom section was equipped with hand basins, showers, and a toilet. What Mandela drily called the penthouse opened onto a rooftop terrace. But even this was enclosed by high walls and from only one corner could they glimpse mountain ridges. Although the food was better and they had a radio that could receive the BBC World Service, Mandela missed the "university," the fellowship and the discussions. He again cultivated a garden where he could escape from the daunting concrete edifices and maintained his early morning exercise routine.

The move to Pollsmoor brought with it greater access to Mandela for the outside world and his family. Journalists visited him, as did a conservative British politician, Lord Bethell, and an American academic. More importantly, the availability of newspapers and magazines meant he was connected to events beyond the prison walls. He followed Botha's introduction of a tricameral parliament (in which whites, coloreds, and Indians had their own houses), wryly noting that it was a ruse and not a reform. He was disappointed at the nonaggression pact Botha inveigled Mozambique into signing and then mourned the killing in Maputo a few months later of his old friend Ruth First by letter bomb. As other ANC operatives had been assassinated in Maputo, in retaliation MK exploded a car bomb outside the Pretoria offices of the South African Air Force leaving nineteen people dead and more than two hundred injured. Although horrified at the death toll, Mandela saw the escalation of violence as inevitable given the government's attacks, raids, and assassinations both inside the country and in London, Paris, and neighboring capitals.

But the news and the stream of visitors paled against his need for Winnie. "Your love and devotion has created a debt which I will never attempt to pay back," he told her. "So enormous is it that even if I had to pay regular installments for another century I would not settle it."[15] In May 1984 he enjoyed his first contact visit with her. A guard escorted his beaming wife into the room and they were able to hold and kiss one another for the first time in twenty-one years. "I held her to me for what seemed like an eternity. We were still and silent except for the sound of our hearts," he would record in his autobiography a decade later.[16]

AS WE ENTERED THE
NEW DECADE MY HOPES FOR
SOUTH AFRICA ROSE ONCE AGAIN.
SOME MORNINGS I WALKED OUT
INTO THE COURTYARD AND EVERY
LIVING THING THERE, THE
SEAGULLS, THE WAGTAILS, THE
SMALL TREES, AND EVEN THE
STRAY BLADES OF GRASS SEEMED
TO SMILE AND SHINE IN THE SUN. IT
WAS AT SUCH TIMES WHEN I
PERCEIVED THE BEAUTY OF EVEN
THIS SMALL, CLOSED-IN CORNER
OF THE WORLD, THAT I KNEW
THAT SOME DAY MY
PEOPLE AND I WOULD BE FREE.

Nelson Mandela, Long Walk to Freedom

Surinder Singh

Release Nelson Mandela
and all political prisoners of South Africa and Namibia!

Anti-Apartheid Movement 13 Mandela St London NW1 0DW 01-387 7966

BOB HUGHES:

My family immigrated to South Africa when I was fifteen, just after the Second World War, and we went from wartime austerity to what was virtually a paradise. We were a good working class family and, like everyone else, had a black servant who lived in a little hut at the bottom of the garden. When she was sacked for stealing, she took the blankets she'd been supplied with her and I was told to go and get them back. It was the first time I came up against the reality of life for black people in the townships and it started me asking questions.

We eventually returned to England and I joined the Anti-Apartheid Movement in about 1972, becoming chair in 1975. It's very difficult to describe those years: there was anger at the system of apartheid, anger at the way successive British governments either gave direct support to the South African government or at best were lukewarm in their opposition. There was passion, argument, and despair that we were never going to get anywhere. But there was also excitement. The South African security tried to burn us out on one occasion. A lot of the ANC exiles used to have their flats and houses burgled regularly. Because they'd come from a society where they had expected to move at any time they always kept money in the drawer and it was never taken. It was a calling card: "We know who you are; we know where you are; we're watching you."

Right: Bob Hughes (far right) and others march through London in an anti-apartheid march.

The Free Nelson Mandela campaign came out of the general strategy discussions we used to have with the ANC. At the time we were using every possible line of attack: the sports boycott, the economic boycott, the academic boycott, the arms embargo.

Because of the treason trials I knew about Mandela, but in those pre-television days when all we had were flickering news images in the cinema, none of us had any real sense of those people. There was no communication with Mandela: we never heard his voice, we never saw him. It was obvious from his closing speech at the Rivonia Trial that you were dealing with someone of tremendous character and vision, but his strength also came from the people around him. We projected him as Mandela, prisoner of conscience, man of principle, leader of the ANC. And we projected him in the image of Martin Luther King Jr. as a man of huge charisma, but no one knew that for sure then.

When the news came of his release there was some internal trepidation in the Anti-Apartheid Movement because when you build someone up as a prisoner of conscience and a great leader of men you can't help wondering whether he would be the person we built him up to be. In fact, he was more.

I met Mandela first at the Namibian independence anniversary celebrations. I saw him and Joe Slovo and just introduced myself. We had about half an hour's discussion about the negotiations which had started before the dignitaries arrived and he said, "Don't for one minute think they are going to go smoothly. There are going to be side-trackings, we're going to go backwards, it'll look as if it's going to collapse. But we are going to get there because we are determined." You could feel the inner strength, the strategy, the vision. You could just feel he was someone who knew what he wanted and knew where he was going, and yet he's the most modest of men.

I once had the temerity to tell him off. The ANC was very worried. He was up at four doing radio interviews first thing in the morning and he didn't finish until last thing at night. We were having lunch at Oliver Tambo's house and I said to him, "You're working too hard." And he said, "There's a lot to be done. You know as well as I do the struggle is only starting now, it's only the beginning not the end." And I said, "Do a couple of hours and take a half hour just to read or put your feet up." "I agree entirely," he said; "I should. But I've got twenty-seven years to make up." What can you say to that?

There was an unbreakable bond that kept the leaders of the ANC together: Tambo, in many ways, was the unsung hero, Mbeki, Sisulu, Ma Sisulu, Joe Slovo. They were soul-mates. I marvel still. Many people have made their way through struggles and on achieving

power the trappings of power have taken over and they have become isolated from the causes they have held so dear. You can never say that about Mandela and the ANC. I'm not saying they didn't make mistakes but they never ever lost their sense of purpose. This wasn't a theory. It was a genuine movement of liberation not just of a country but of a whole people.

The magnanimity of the ANC was epitomized by Mandela who came out and showed no sign of bitterness. I would not have shown the sereneness of character that Mandela epitomized. It was not a policy decision; it was what he believed. And it held together because the ANC was made up of remarkable people, bound together by their belief in a nonracial, nonsexist, democratic South Africa. And there was no shoving people aside. It was a collective leadership with the recognition that Mandela was something special. It was a privilege to have known them.

My anti-apartheid attitudes and activities were bundled together with the campaign against racial discrimination, the movement for colonial freedom and those kinds of activities in the late fifties and early sixties which any young socialist worth his salt was involved in. Rivonia landed like a hand grenade in that, because it articulated the nature of apartheid as organized injustice. When Mandela spoke from the dock, it was the kind of courageous nobility that leapt straight from history books. At the time I believed history was the product of tides in institutions and that personalities bobbed along on that current. Rivonia made me think, "No, it's people, individuals with two arms, two legs and a brain. They make the difference."

In the 1960s the anti-apartheid movement was in its infancy. The focus then was to

sustain political campaigning and of course sport became an absolutely core issue. We picketed the 1969 Springbok tour and got a tremendous turnout. An astounding 12,000 on the streets in Cardiff – that would be quite an event in London, but in Cardiff it brought the city to a halt. We even picketed the South African bowls team. This busload of old ladies and old men got the driver to stop outside the bowling club in Sophia Gardens in Cardiff so they could wind the windows down and spit on us! They were screaming insults at us in Afrikaans. Of course we thought it was a huge joke.

It was to me that Margaret Thatcher made her famous comment that Mandela was little better than a terrorist. She said to me, "I think sometimes the Right Honorable gentleman all the time. There was never any question in my mind that Mandela would do a deal. At the time I was talking to Thabo Mbeki and others who were saying there's a nudge here, there's a stumble there. Although the scenery did not seem to be shifting, the performance was. All kinds of subtleties were developing.

I'm ready to give credit to de Klerk because Nelson has. After Mandela was released the then South African embassy called to ask if we would be prepared to see Mr. de Klerk. I called some chums to ask what the attitude – particularly Mandela's – would be and the message came back, "Yes, by all means see him." So I arranged for de Klerk to come to the shadow cabinet. The natural thing if someone sticks out a hand is to stick out yours and automatically curve your lips, so before he arrived I said, "There are going to be a few snappers here and if I catch anyone smiling . . . I'm requiring self-constraint." There's not a single bloody photo of one member of the shadow cabinet with a smile. Not one . . . de Klerk came and everyone was very courteous, but it was frigidly formal.

I met Mandela for the first time in Stockholm when he came to collect the Nobel Prize. It was his first visit outside South Africa after he came out of Pollsmoor. Ingvar Carlsson, the Swedish prime minister, invited us and when Glenys and I arrived he asked us to come to the head of the reception line. Can you imagine! Mandela came up the stairs toward us, dazzling television lights behind us. He squinted, put his hands over his eyes, and said, "Neil Kinnock!" Maybe they told him who to expect, but there's no reason in the world for him to have recognized me. Amazing.

I was astounded by the state he was in. As a constituency MP I've dealt with people who had been in prison for twelve years or so and come out in their forties and they haven't looked as good as Mandela did. I said this to him later: "The prisoners I work with are never like you and they've only served half the time you did." And I remember him saying, "Maybe that's the difference. They served. Served, eh?" He's got a voice like cracked glass.

Oliver Tambo and Mandela were like two great old chums even after that separation. They reminded me of a couple of old fellows who last saw each other when they were demobbed in 1946. They'd been the best of mates through those years, and they were still laughing at the same things. Oliver had had one bout of illness but he was pretty fit still, busy and intense and always ready for a laugh. He kept alive that network with fantastic discipline. Denis Healey and I used to comment long before the end of apartheid, that we'd met a lot of exiles but the sense of duty, of commitment from these South Africans, was exceptional.

There were a couple of semipublic occasions when Mandela talked about the steadfastness of comrades in the anti-apartheid movement. He said, "You never forgot us." He has said that sometimes, when the prospect of victory seemed very distant, the knowledge that people you'll never know and will never meet are making the case, keeps determination going. That's probably one of the most gratifying things I've ever heard in my life. It's like throwing stones in the dark and then someone comes out of the dark, and says we knew you were throwing stones and each stone refreshed our determination.

CHRISTO BRAND:

I arrived on Robben Island in the beginning of 1979. Four of us were sent to B section where the leaders were. We were told we were going to meet the biggest criminals in the history of South Africa. When we walked into the single-cell section I saw old people sleeping on the floor – I saw Sisulu, I saw Mandela, but they were not names I knew. I had never heard of Mandela until I arrived on Robben Island.

Mandela was very friendly, he greeted us politely in Afrikaans. He was a man in his sixties and yet he treated even us young guards, who were of lower rank, respectfully. He always let us feel we were his superiors, but he also motivated us. "The future of the country is in studies," he would say. "You must study." He was always with a book, studying something.

You know, when I started working on Robben Island my uncle visited me, and he asked if I'd seen Mandela. And my father asked, "Who is Mandela?" And then he said he remembered something about the trial, but if the man has been so long in prison they should release him, because he is worth nothing outside now. And my uncle said, "No, they should have hanged him. They were lucky they survived the death sentence." So that is how our family was: my uncle thought he was a traitor and my father thought he should be released.

Mr. Mandela was always very concerned about our families, even inside the prison. The first year I arrived on Robben Island we were not allowed to talk to the prisoners, but we did get an opportunity to talk a little bit when I was taking him to the visiting booth. I would talk about his family, and always he asked me, "How is your family? And what is your father doing?" He never discussed politics, but he was interested in our family relationships. He is a family man.

At Pollsmoor in 1985 when negotiations were taking place, Mandela was isolated alone in the cell away from his colleagues. And I was told that I had to give him a message about visiting minister Kobie Coetsee. My wife was out, so I went to the prison with my eldest son, Riaan. When I walked into Mandela's cell, he jumped up and he greeted my son. He wanted to hold him, but my son was afraid of these people behind these bars and held onto me tightly. Mandela rushed over to his cabinet and opened it to get some sweets for him – and after that I used to take my son to his cell whenever I went to deliver a message.

Mandela sent that boy a letter on his sixteenth birthday, telling him that he must study very hard because he was one of the leaders of the country and its future depended on him. He let him feel that it was very important to study. And every time we meet each other the first thing he asks me is, "How are your children? How's Riaan? How's the wife?"

You know, I see Mandela as a father. After 1986 when my own father passed away, I became very close to him. When I had a motorcycle accident, I received a letter from a lawyer saying he wanted to sue me, and Mr. Mandela put his studies aside to write a letter back. I took the letter home for my wife to type, but I destroyed the draft Mandela wrote because we were monitored by the security branch and if they found the letter I would have been in trouble.

Today I can say that Mandela is still the same person and treats me with the same respect as the first day I met him in prison. I would like to thank him for his friendship and his helpfulness and his kindness, for always giving me a chance and for listening to me. And I want to thank him for having such hope for me and such respect for me. And I feel very sorry that I didn't always have the same respect for him. I would also like to thank him for everything he has done for the country. I didn't believe when I saw him in prison that things would change like that.

AHMED KATHRADA:

There were very few guards who were working with us at Pollsmoor, just a small group who understood political prisoners, and that's when this close relationship started with Christo Brand. At Robben Island one-to-one contact with guards was very difficult except for the guards who worked in our section whom we bribed. We didn't bribe Christo; he is just a good human being who understood no politics. His wife used to bake a Christmas cake for me, illegally, in prison. She still bakes for me and now it's twice a year: at Christmas and my birthday. They're just good people.

Before we had visits, Christo would warn me that today you can't talk because you are being bugged. During other visits we were free to talk about anything because he had told us we were not bugged. And over the negotiations, we could guess what Madiba was doing but we had no real idea, so Christo Brand came to me one afternoon and he'd tell us, "Last night we took Mandela to Kobie Coetsee's house." So in this way he would keep us informed.

Madiba paid almost as much attention to his physical appearance as to his plants, and his insistence on a certain brand of hair oil sparked what became known as "The Pantene Crisis." No substitute would do, and Christo Brand was instructed by the prison chiefs to scour the pharmacies of Cape Town on Mandela's behalf. . . . Brand finally managed to locate the last remaining stock of Pantene — possibly in the whole of South Africa! — and bought the few he managed to find. No one wanted to go through that particular "mass action" again. A few years later, some of us conspired to give Madiba a surprise birthday gift. I managed to acquire two bottles of Pantene from a friend in the U.S. Walter and I, together with Brand, went off to Pretoria, and in the presence of a media contingent, surprised him with the two bottles, which were presented to him by Brand from behind a huge cardboard cut-out in the shape of a Pantene bottle. He thoroughly enjoyed the surprise.

Ahmed Kathrada, Memoirs

Right: Mandela and Christo Brand on Mandela's birthday.

FREE
NELSON MANDELA
Musik und Solidarität gegen Apartheid!

Ngubengcuka,

. . . I perhaps need to remind you that when you first wanted to visit us in 1977 my colleagues and I decided that, because of your position in the implementation of the Bantustan scheme, we could not accede to your request. . . .

Again in February this year when you wanted to come and discuss the question of our release, we reiterated our stand and your plan was not acceded to. In particular, we pointed out that the idea of our release being linked to a Bantustan was totally and utterly unacceptable to us.

While we appreciate your concern over the incarceration of political prisoners, we must point out that your persistence in linking our release with the Bantustans, despite our strong and clearly expressed opposition to the scheme, is highly disturbing, if not provocative, and we urge you not to continue pursuing a course which will inevitably result in an unpleasant confrontation between you and ourselves.

We will, under no circumstances, accept being released to the Transkei or any other Bantustan. You know fully well that we have spent the better part of our lives in prison exactly because we are opposed to the very idea of separate development which makes us foreigners in our own country and which enables the Government to perpetuate our passion up to this very day.

I accordingly request you to desist from this explosive plan and we sincerely hope that this is the last time we will ever be pestered with it.

Ozithobileyo,
Dalibunga

Extracts from a letter from Mandela to K. D. Matanzima reiterating the prisoners' refusal to be released to the Transkei, dated December 27, 1984.

The year 1985 began with a call by Oliver Tambo to make South Africa ungovernable, and apartheid unworkable. Simultaneously, Botha, on a governmental tour through Europe, was urged repeatedly by heads of state to release the man who had become the world's most famous political prisoner. Botha returned home to tell Parliament he would let Mandela go if he would reject violence as a political strategy. Defying the admittedly feeble attempts by the prison authorities to prevent him issuing a reply, Mandela released a statement which was read by his daughter Zindzi to a packed Jabulani stadium in Soweto. It was the first time his words had been heard in public for more than two decades.

The words rang out in Zindzi's dramatic voice and struck a chord with people determined to achieve their freedom. Two months later, amidst the simmering unrest in the townships and the dreaded "necklace" method of killing perceived traitors by igniting a gasoline-filled tire around the victim's neck, Winnie vented her wrath. The previous year she had broken her banishment and returned defiantly to Soweto. She was being hailed as the mother of the nation. "We have no guns," she told a crowd at Munsieville, near Johannesburg, "we have only stones, boxes of matches, and petrol. Together, hand in hand, with our boxes of matches and our necklaces we shall liberate this country."[17]

Privately the ANC was appalled by her advocacy of necklacing but didn't admonish her. Mandela too was shocked.

The violence in the country continued to escalate alarmingly. Although most of the fighting was in the townships, a few bombs were detonated in white areas at fast-food restaurants and shopping malls. On July 20, the government declared a state of emergency which gave the security police draconian powers. Torture, disappearances, and assassinations became ever more widespread. Meanwhile, along Namibia's northern border, a war was being fought ineffectually by white soldiers, who, although brainwashed into accepting the total onslaught, had no heart for the conflict.

The state of emergency brought with it economic repercussions. Chase Manhattan Bank refused to renew short-term loans; other banks withdrew credit; the exchange rate plummeted; calls for sanctions became more strident, and some international companies withdrew their products. The financial crisis deepened, the economy staggered. Within the country, business people and Afrikaner intellectuals realized only Mandela's release would stop what looked like a slide into anarchy and civil war.

Toward the end of this year of horror, Mandela underwent prostate surgery. It was a routine procedure, but Botha's cabinet took fright: what if Mandela died? Civil war would follow was the considered response of the commanding officer at Pollsmoor Prison.

Once the decision to operate was taken, Winnie immediately caught a flight to Cape Town, finding herself on the same plane as the minister of justice, Kobie Coetsee. Little did she know, but Coetsee had already been asked by Botha to sort out the Mandela question. After takeoff, Winnie strode into the first-class section and spent most of the two-hour flight with the minister. To Mandela's surprise, shortly after Winnie arrived at the hospital so did Coetsee.

Mandela was in for more surprises. He returned to Pollsmoor to find he was now imprisoned in a ground floor group of cells. Again, what was meant as an improvement came with drawbacks: to see his comrades three stories above, he had to apply for permission from Pretoria which could take up to two weeks. Access to his family, lawyers, and international figures was easier, but the rooms were musty and damp, there was little natural light, and he couldn't get to his beloved garden. Nevertheless, he decided to accept the situation which gave him a degree of political autonomy – although he well knew that this was a lonely position fraught with pitfalls. He wrote to Coetsee proposing talks about talks.

The day before Christmas, Mandela was taken on a drive around Cape Town city. "I felt like a curious tourist in a strange and remarkable land," he noted.[18] On the way back to Pollsmoor, the colonel driving him stopped at a small shop in a quiet area to buy two Coca-Colas. Mandela was left in the unlocked car wondering why he shouldn't escape. He wondered, too, if he hadn't been set up. It was with some relief that he saw the colonel returning. It was the first of many such trips, some of which were whole-day excursions to distant beaches and towns.

NTHATO MOTLANA:

My relationship with Mandela goes back to the late 1940s when I was a wild-eyed youth leader. He was fond of coaching me and the relationship went on for many years although when the guys were swept up in the Treason Trial I was a houseman at Livingstone, so I missed all that. When Mandela was finally convicted in 1964 and sent to Robben Island, he formed a little trust to look after his family, consisting of a teacher, Mzadume, Desmond Tutu, and me. I joke with Madiba that I looked after him and his family from 1964, and he never paid me – and Madiba says he can't anyway.

When I was finally allowed to visit him on Robben Island, I got there at the end of the month, which meant that I got two hours – an hour for the previous month and one for the month coming. I was there talking to Madiba about my role as the family doctor and how Winnie and the girls were faring, but you can't do that for two hours – you run out of stories! So I started talking about some of the things that interested us both, like boxing and about Muhammad Ali who was at his peak then, and the guard would say, "You're not talking about family, you're talking about boxing!" And it was the most uncomfortable thing to stand there for two hours and not talk about anything and to have this guard standing behind Mandela, looking at me, and recording everything we talked about. But even under those circumstances, the guy who commanded the space that was occupied by all of us was Mandela. He would indicate to this guard how he should stand, how he should behave. He was confident, tall, his demeanor, his carriage was stately. Gravitas . . . Mandela's got something.

When Madiba's prostate problem arose, I had arranged for Dr. Geslter, a classmate, a first-class urologist, and someone one could trust, to see him. The ANC in France sent one of France's top urologists, the ANC in Britain sent a top British urologist, and the ANC in the United States sent an American one – and there was also a urologist provided by the prison, Dr. Laubscher. So there was a whole gang of us and the question was who was going to do the operation. We all wanted our own candidates and so finally we said to Madiba, "Who would you prefer to operate on you? Because we can't make up our minds." And Madiba points to Dr. Laubscher, an Afrikaner! I learned later that Dr. Laubscher lectured at Cape Town University and he did a wonderful job – but to choose him in preference to all these world experts!

In February 1985 Zindzi Mandela read a speech – a response
to Botha's offer of conditional release – on behalf of her father
to a packed Jabulani stadium in Soweto.

am not less life-loving than you are. But I cannot sell my
the people to be free. I am in prison as the representative
National Congress, which was banned.

"What freedom am I being offered while the organization
being offered when I may be arrested on a pass offense? Wha
with my dear wife who remains in banishment in Brandfo
for permission to live in an urban area? What freedom an
seek work? What freedom am I being offered when my very

"Only free men can negotiate. Prisoners cannot enter into
I cannot and will not give any undertaking at a time whe
freedom and mine cannot be separated. I will return

YOUR FREEDOM AND MINE CANNOT BE SEPARATED. I WILL RETURN.

Nelson Mandela, from Pollsmoor Prison

13 February 1985

The Commissioner of Prisons
PRETORIA

THE SUBJOINED LETTER IS FOR THE ATTENTION OF THE STATE PRESIDENT,
MR P W BOTHA :

"The State President,
CAPE TOWN

Sir,

Copies of the Hansard parliamentary record of

25 January to 1 February 1985 were delivered to us on

8 February.

We note that during the debate in the House of Assembly you

indicated that you were prepared to release prisoners in our

particular category provided that we unconditionally renounce

violence as a means of furthering our political objectives.

We have given earnest consideration to your offer but we

regret to inform you that it is not acceptable in its present

form. We hesitate to associate you with a move which, on a

proper analysis, appears to be no more than a shrewed and

calculated attempt to mislead the world into the belief

that you have magnanimously offered us release from prison

which we ourselves have rejected. Coming in the face of such

unprecedented and widespread demand for our release, your

remarks can only be seen as the height of cynical politicking.

We refuse to be party to anything which is really intended to

create division, confusion and uncertainty within the

The State President,
CAPE TOWN

Sir,

Copies of the Hansard parliamentary record of 25 January to 1 February 1985 were delivered to us on 8 February.

We note that during the debate in the House of Assembly you indicated that you were prepared to release prisoners in our particular category provided that we unconditionally renounce violence as a means of furthering our political objectives. We have given earnest consideration to your offer but we regret to inform you that it is not acceptable in its present form. We hesitate to associate you with a move which, on a proper analysis, appears to be no more than a shrewd and calculated attempt to mislead the world into the belief that you have magnanimously offered us release from prison which we ourselves have rejected. Coming in the face of such unprecedented and widespread demand for our release, your remarks can only be seen as the height of cynical politicking. . . .

Just as some of us refused the humiliating condition that we should be released to the Transkei, we also reject your offer on the same ground. No self-respecting human being will demean and humiliate himself by making a commitment of the nature you demand. . . .

The intensification of apartheid, the banning of political organizations and the closing of all channels of peaceful protest conflicted sharply with these principles and forced the ANC to turn to violence. Consequently until apartheid is completely uprooted, our people will continue to kill one another and South Africa will be subjected to all the pressures of an escalating civil war. . . .

The peaceful and nonviolent nature of our struggle never made any impression on your government. Innocent and defenseless people were pitilessly massacred in the course of peaceful demonstrations. You will remember the shootings in Johannesburg on 1 May 1950 and in Sharpeville in 1960. On both occasions, as in every other instance of police brutality, the victims had invariably been unarmed and defenseless men, women and even children. At that time the ANC had not even mooted the idea of resorting to armed struggle. You were the Country's defense Minister when no less than 600 people mostly children were shot down in Soweto in 1976. You were the Country's Premier when the police beat up people, again in the course of orderly demonstrations against the 1984 colored and Indian elections, and 7000 heavily armed troopers invaded the Vaal Triangle to put down an essentially peaceful protest by the residents. . . .

At no time have the oppressed people, especially the youth, displayed such unity in action, such resistance to racial oppression and such prolonged demonstrations in the face of brutal military and police action . . . Those who "cooperate" with you, who have served you so loyally throughout these troubled years have not at all helped you to stem the rapidly rising tide. The coming confrontation will only be averted if the following steps are taken without delay.

1. Your government must renounce violence first;
2. It must dismantle apartheid;
3. It must unban the ANC;
4. It must free all who have been imprisoned, banished or exiled for their opposition to apartheid;
5. It must guarantee free political activity. . . .

Despite your commitment to the maintenance of White supremacy, however, your attempt to create new apartheid structures and your hostility to a non racial system of government in this Country and despite our determination to resist this policy to the bitter end, the simple fact is that you are South Africa's Head of Government, you enjoy the support of the majority of the White population and you can help change the course of South African history. A beginning can be made if you accept and agree to implement the five-point program on pages 4 – 5 of this document. If you accept the program our people would readily cooperate with you to sort out whatever problems arise as far as the implementation thereof is concerned. . . .

Extracts from a letter from Mandela, Ahmed Kathrada, Walter Sisulu, Andrew Mlangeni, and Raymond Mhlaba (in Pollsmoor Prison) to President P. W. Botha rejecting a conditional release, dated February 13, 1985.

In the mid 1980s, the violence in the country escalated alarmingly. Although most of the fighting was in the townships, a few bombs were detonated in white areas at take-away restaurants and shopping malls. A state of emergency was declared which gave the security police draconian powers: torture, disappearances, and assassinations became ever more widespread. This page, above: The funeral of a UDF (United Democratic Front) leader, tortured to death by police. Right and below: Residents fleeing the violence in the squatter camps.

Opposite, clockwise from top left: Mourners are teargassed at a 1986 funeral; Cosas (Congress of South African Students) supporters burying a comrade at Duduza in 1985; a woman escapes a squatter camp in the Cape with a piece of corrugated iron, all that is left of her house after battles between vigilantes; white farmers at a mass funeral for a family killed by ANC landmines; police charge UDF supporters holding a rally for the release of political prisoners outside Pollsmoor Prison in 1985; vigilantes at a squatter camp.

My dreams these days are policed
by a million eyes
that baton-charge my sleep
and frog-march me into a
shaken morning.

Chris van Wyk, Injustice

The next two years passed with ever-increasing contact between Mandela and the government's man, Coetsee. In 1986 he also met twice with a group of eminent people selected from the Commonwealth countries to mediate a solution to the impasse in South Africa. Yet during the group's May visit, South African forces struck at ANC offices in the neighboring capitals of Zambia, Zimbabwe, and Botswana. The eminent people went home in despair. The following month the state of emergency was renewed. In the face of this blatant aggression, Mandela told Coetsee he wanted to meet with Botha. It was a decision he kept to himself, knowing it would not find favor either upstairs or in Lusaka where Tambo and the ANC headquarters were based. For months there was no response.

In the new year the meetings with Coetsee resumed, now including the head of the National Intelligence Services, Dr. Niel Barnard. Mandela met his colleagues to reassure them that he was pressing for talks between the government and the ANC. They accepted his rationale with minor quibbles: Sisulu wanted the government to take the initiative; Kathrada thought that by Mandela initiating talks it would appear the ANC was capitulating. A message from Tambo smuggled to Mandela expressed concern about the secret talks and wanted to know what Mandela was discussing with the government. Mandela sent a firm rejoinder setting the record straight: he was talking to the government to persuade it to meet the national executive of the ANC.

Page from Mandela's diary noting his trip to the hospital and his visits by Kobie Coetsee and Helen Suzman.

Later that year the process of releasing the prisoners began when Govan Mbeki (still on Robben Island) was set free. But the rejoicing that accompanied his freedom was overtaken by disturbing events emanating from the Mandela home in Soweto. The "Mandela United Football Club" Winnie had formed for protection had turned into a murderous vigilante gang. From Pollsmoor Mandela instructed his wife to disband the group, but his wishes were ignored.

During 1988, meetings between Mandela and the government continued. But so did the violence in the townships, while KwaZulu became a war zone, and along the Namibian border the fighting intensified until the South African forces capitulated fearing the political repercussions of a high body count among the conscripted white soldiers.

In July Mandela turned seventy. A pop concert in London's Wembley Stadium to celebrate his birthday was broadcast around the world, giving him almost mythic status. He was also nurturing the knowledge that Botha would see him in August. But, again, other events overshadowed him. A turf war between Winnie's football club and a rival gang led to the Orlando house being torched, destroying family papers, letters, and a slice of wedding cake that Winnie was saving for his release. Yet public sentiment in Soweto was roused against Winnie, and a group of respected UDF (United Democratic Front) and COSATU (Congress of South African Trade Unions) leaders and church leaders formed the Mandela Crisis Committee to control her excesses. A few days later, ill and coughing badly, Mandela was diagnosed with the early stages of tuberculosis. This time he was hospitalized for four months; the meeting with Botha dropped off the agenda.

Once the hospital treatment was completed, Mandela recuperated in a clinic not far from Pollsmoor. Now he had a view of the mountains he couldn't see from the prison, and an exercise bike on which he spent hours "spinning." The staff adored him; flowers and boxes of chocolates arrived daily from well-wishers. His contacts with Coetsee resumed.

RELEASE MANDELA

& all political prisoners

In 1977, they offered to release Mandela to the Transkei because they wanted credibility for the Transkei bantustan. He turned it down. Then in 1982 I was called to a visit, and there was my brother with some of the top brass of the prison service with a message that they were prepared to release me alone. I was so surprised I couldn't ask for details, but in my mind I had already decided I was not going to accept it. I still don't know how this came about and by the time I came out my brother was dead. All the family knows is that the initiative came from a minister. They said, "All we want from him is that he won't take part in politics."

Then came February 1985 at Pollsmoor. Madiba was called one morning to the office with this message from P. W. Botha. He was prepared to release Madiba provided he gave up violence. But being Madiba, he comes back from the meeting cool as anything, and starts reading the paper. "Oh, by the way . . ." he tells us eventually. We met and discussed it that night and Madiba says we cannot accept this. Then he drafted this letter and we all signed it, rejecting Botha's offer.

We were not leaders, we were not policymakers. Oliver Tambo and the national executive made the decisions. We did not even give instructions from inside. We discussed things but no policy matters went out as policy. Even now people say, "You fellows made policy," but it's just not true. The one major "deviation" – and it wasn't a deviation from policy – was when Madiba took the initiative in the negotiations. That was the one time he did something major without consulting us and it transpires he did it deliberately, because he expected opposition from us.

After three years or so in Pollsmoor, the five of us together, they removed him from us. Our immediate reaction was to protest, but he said, though not in these words, "Cool it chaps. Something may come out of this." In retrospect we can now guess that he must have decided it was time to talk. Again it was not contrary to policy. The policy of the ANC, even MK, was to force the enemy to the negotiation table by all means. We knew we could not win against the South African Army, the most powerful army in Africa. Eventually we would have won, not through the armed struggle alone, but it would have taken years and years and a lot of bloodshed.

So, what I'm saying is, he did not part from policy because the aim had always been to get them to communicate and Madiba must have had that in mind. When he took the first steps he made an application to see us. They would not allow him to see us all together. They may have had political and technical reasons, because when you're five sitting together and you're taping it, it's not always easy to say who's saying what.

He saw Andrew Mlangeni and Raymond Mhlaba and there it was straightforward: "Why did you wait so long? You should have started talks long ago." Then it came to Walter. His attitude was that in principle there was nothing against it but the initiative should have come from the other side. Madiba's reply was, "Look, once you've agreed in principle, the other's a detail." Then the last one was me. I was totally opposed to the talks. I can't specifically explain why, but I think I must have thought that the momentum of the struggle was increasing and that maybe we would be negotiating from weakness and we can't show weakness now. Of course, in retrospect I was wrong.

it was amicable. They never said, "Stop. I don't agree with you. These are my views."

After that we were allowed to meet him and when he was transferred to Victor Verste we saw him quite a few times, but by that time all of us had accepted that he was doing the right thing. Outside, however, the rumors went around that Madiba was selling out and a decision was taken in some quarters: don't visit him – because by then Madiba was allowed to see whomever he wanted to. So you even had a situation where Ma Sisulu would not visit him, because she had been told he was selling out. Eventually Ma Sisulu came to see Walter in prison and she put to him the rumors about selling out and he assured her that there was nothing of the sort. The message also went abroad and back came an inquiry from Tambo asking what he was doing. Madiba put it very succinctly: "I am trying to get the government to talk to you." When Madiba started the negotiations he made it clear to the other side, "We are prisoners. We don't negotiate. You have to negotiate with the ANC. You have to un-ban them, allow them to come back, release the political prisoners, then only can negotiations take place on an equal level."

Above: Members of Minister Coetsee's team who held a series of meetings with Mandela while he was in prison. General Willemse (the Commissioner of Prisons), Mandela, Dr. Niel Barnard (head of the National Intelligence Service), Minister Kob Coetsee, and Fanie van der Merwe (Director General of Justice).

Previous page: In July 1988 Mandela turned seventy. A pop concert in London's Wembley Stadium to celebrate his birthday wa

As long as P. W. Botha was president, I was not optimistic about political change, but onc[e] de Klerk took over he was determined to find political solutions to the problems. The nigh[t] before he made his great statement in Parliament he rang me up at midnight and said yo[u] can tell your prime minister she will not be disappointed. So the British were in a muc[h] closer relationship with the de Klerk government than any other country at the time. Man[y] people believed that would count against us, but I saw Mandela a few days after he wa[s] released and he walked up to me, shook me by the hand, and said, "Please give my bes[t] wishes to Mrs. Thatcher!" He knew what we had been trying to do.

You could perfectly well argue that we could have imposed more sanctions, but w[e] would not have been able to influence de Klerk to the extent that we did. The assumptio[n]

TELL MRS THATCHER

Mrs Thatcher and Mr F W de Klerk appear by kind permission of Luck and Flaw.

STOP SUPPORTING APARTHEID!

SUNDAY 25 MARCH

SOUTH AFRICA **FREEDOM** NOW — Assemble Hyde Park 12-1pm / March to Trafalgar Square / Rally 2.30-4pm

ANTI-APARTHEID MOVEMENT 13 MANDELA ST · LONDON NW1 0DW · 01 387 7966

was that the British government woul[d] have nothing to do with the ANC, but I wa[s] seeing these people every day inside th[e] country as were my colleagues i[n] Zambia. While we were supposed to b[e] having no contact with the ANC I wa[s] having drinks with Oliver Tambo i[n] Hampstead! We didn't advertise that fo[r] very obvious reasons – and I didn['t] advertise that vis-à-vis my ow[n] government either actually. Thatcher wa[s] quite clear about what she wanted t[o] happen. She did not want any mor[e] economic damage inflicted on Sout[h] Africa; she wanted Mandela released an[d] us to try to help with some kind o[f] peaceful change. Beyond that I never go[t] any instructions. Whether Charles Powe[ll,] her private secretary, bothered to tell he[r] that I was talking to the black leaders [I] don't know – but nobody ever tried to sto[p] me.

After Mandela came out of jail, I use[d] to see him regularly because negotiation[s] with the government were very fraugh[t.] There was a lot of violence in the townships and undoubtedly a lot of it was fomented b[y] rogue elements of the security forces but quite a lot of it wasn't. From time to time h[e] would break off the negotiations – he is a truly wonderful man but he is also quit[e] emotional and he has quite a temper – and he would throw up his hands in horror and say[,] "It is impossible! These people are lying and cheating and I can't go on having anything t[o] do with it." But in the end he would go back to the negotiations because people like Slovo[,] who were more cold-blooded about it, understood: "We have to negotiate these people ou[t]

About six weeks after Mandela's release, I said to him, instead of meeting at you house, why don't we just get out and have lunch in the best restaurant in Johannesburg? About five minutes before we arrived we told them who the guest was and there was a sharp intake of breath. So I walk in with him and at least half the old mining magnates are here – most of whom would have voted to keep him in jail. And he proceeded to go from table to table, shaking them by the hand as if they were his natural constituency. And then of course at the end of the meal he did what he always does, which is to dive into the kitchen to shake the hands of everyone who had helped to feed us. Classic Mandela – disarming, co-opting, and genuinely inclusive.

Mandela was due to go to England for a Wembley concert and he wanted to meet Mrs Thatcher. Again this was classic Mandela: his whole approach is to co-opt people. You are in jail, you start working on your guards and, at de Klerk's inauguration, the minister of justice came up to me and said, "You have to help me persuade him to release Mandela!" Having worked his way up from the guard in the prison, through the prison commandant he had converted the minister of justice too! This ability to win over people is a fantastic skill – and I found him doing exactly the same to me. First of all he kept urging me to join the ANC – and I had to explain that as the Thatcher ambassador that wasn't going to be possible! And then, he kept referring to me as his "adviser." I had to keep reminding myself that I was actually Thatcher's ambassador rather than his assistant!

"How do I tackle Mrs. T?" Mandela asked me, so we did a dress rehearsal. "You must stop all this nonsense about banks and the markets immediately. It is completely hopeless!" I said, pretending to be Mrs. Thatcher. He thought it was hilarious. I went to see her before she met him and said, "Please remember he's been waiting twenty-seven years to tell you his side of the story." So she glared at me and said, "You mean I mustn't interrupt!" And I said, "No, please don't." Just before he came through the door, she gripped me by the elbow and said, "Is he like Robert Mugabe?" and I said, "I can assure you that there are no two human beings on earth less like each other than Mandela and Mugabe." Then he came in and after a wary hour or so they got on well, because his charm never fails to work, particularly on women. She did go through her, "Stop all this nonsense about the banks and mines immediately!" and gave him what you might describe as a course in economics over lunch which actually he quite enjoyed. In the end, the meeting went on for about three hours and the press outside No. 10 began to chant "Free Nelson Mandela!"

Mandela wanted to have a party at the Albert Hall because he loves music, especially African music. So this was done in front of members of the royal family and the lineup included Phil Collins and Ladysmith Black Mambaso. The place was really jumping and during the interval we had a drink in the bar and I said, "When Ladysmith comes on, you've got to stand up and do your jig because that's what people have come for!" And he said, "But I am sitting next to Her Majesty!" Anyway, halfway through the second half he stands up and starts to do his jig – horrified glances across the royal box! But the Duke of Edinburgh feels that he probably has to do something too and so he stands up and then, after about fifteen minutes, to our amazement the monarch stands up and does a little jig

IQBAL MEER:

My uncle Ismail Meer's flat in Johannesburg, Kholvad House, became quite famous as a meeting place for the ANC and other political activists. There were always people coming and going. As a boy I was aware of Mandela's presence but he didn't particularly engage with the children then: it was always very serious.

In the late 1980s I received a message in Britain that the South African authorities would make arrangements for me to visit Mandela in Victor Verster Prison. He wanted to see me about handling his autobiography – probably because I'd handled my aunt Fatima's biography of him, *Higher Than Hope,* which eventually came out when he was released. I hadn't seen Mandela for nineteen to twenty years so you can imagine I was pretty nervous. When I walked in he was impeccably dressed in a smart three-piece suit even though it was a fiercely hot day. I said, "Can I take my jacket off?" and he took it from me, folded it neatly and put it on the back of the chair. Then he took off his own jacket and his waistcoat and folded them too so that he and I should be exactly the same. Then his guard came in with tea and a Swiss roll. I didn't take a piece, but he said, "Iqbal, you'd better eat it, because I've paid for it."

I have always held Mandela in awe. He has such a commanding presence. He is always cool, calm, and collected. When he was released the world recognized him as an icon so inevitably I looked at him differently. But he was always very commanding.

CYRIL RAMAPHOSA:

I first met Madiba when he was in Victor Verster Prison. The first stage of the negotiation process had really started with him being allowed to consult with his colleagues from various formations of the liberation movement and I was in the delegation that went to see him from COSATU. We were ushered into his house and we sat in the lounge and waited with bated breath for the moment when we would set eyes on him. When he came in we saw this tall slender man with a towering presence and you just could not mistake him for anyone else in the world. You knew immediately, without any shadow of doubt, just by looking at him that you were in the presence of an incredibly important leader. He stood out, head and shoulder, not only in terms of his height but also in terms of his personal aura, his presence. And as he stretched his hand to greet, and to mention our names it seemed like he knew us. In my case it seemed like he had known me for years and years and he asked about me, my family, my children, it was unbelievable.

When we knew that Walter Sisulu, Ahmed Kathrada, and the others were going to be released we formed a national reception committee and I was asked to be the chairman. Once Walter Sisulu was released we realized we had an even bigger task at hand to organize Mandela's release, this man the world had been waiting for for years and years. More than anything else we were also worried about his safety. We didn't want him to be released into the hands of the South African police or the South African defense Force or the South African security police; he had to be our responsibility. We had to create a very clear distance between him and his former jailers and handlers. So therefore in a strange way we had to create our own state apparatus and security precautions – but we didn't know anything about security. We were not even militarily trained like our ANC colleagues in exile. It looked like a joke, but we had to create a semblance and an aura of security around Madiba. And then we also had to prepare him for the political intervention that he would have to make. We had to work with him to craft his speech and his speeches thereafter. And then there was the personal aspect as well. Where would he live? Which bed would he sleep on, which house should he go to? Again there was a security aspect to this – which car could he drive in? Who could stand guard outside his house? Who would drive him around? For a while I was his chauffeur, which was fun, and in many ways we became very close.

Madiba saw me first and foremost as his colleague. I also became his secretary, the secretary general that is, but he was – and is – a father to me in many, many ways. I was also able to confide in him on personal matters, and he was also able to confide in me when he went through his own personal crises. So it was a wonderfully mutually beneficial relationship, more special than I can describe. I had a very close relationship with Walter and with Oliver Tambo as well, so I have been blessed to have rubbed shoulders with all these giants of our movement and in a way to have walked with history.

STANLEY MOGOBA:

I arrived on Robben Island in 1964, just before Nelson Mandela. I was a junior prisoner, not part of the leadership core of the Rivonia defendants who from the very start were held separately. I was only doing three years on Robben Island, but while I was there in isolation, I had a spiritual experience which actually brought me toward the ministry of the church. Eventually I became a leader in the Methodist church and that brought me into a special relationship with Mandela and Winnie because they were both raised as Methodists.

Jack Scholtz, the president of our church, and I were given a mandate by the church assembly to visit Mr. Mandela in Pollsmoor. The government was very suspicious, but finally agreed. We were very cautious about the way we should handle this visit because we feared we might discuss things with Mr. Mandela that might incriminate him, but as soon as he came into the room he took over the leadership of this meeting and suggested the points of discussion. The government had asked General Willemse to remain in the room with us to watch what was happening. At the end of the discussion we suggested to Mr. Mandela that we have Holy Communion and he agreed, but just as were about to get to the table he looked at General Willemse and said, "But you ought to be with us too." So it was an historic occasion, I think, to kneel at the table and have Holy Communion with Mr. Scholtz and myself and then Mr. Mandela and the general at Pollsmoor Prison.

Later on Mr. Mandela invited me to visit him at Victor Verster Prison. That visit confirmed to me that he would soon be out – it was like prison, but it was not a prison. The essence of this visit was that he was worried about the rift between the ANC and the Inkatha Freedom Party and about the isolation of Winnie. He was convinced she was being left alone to make decisions without any help. He was also concerned about the whole situation of the country and it was this that gave me the clear impression that he was actually on the way out of Victor Verster.

Early in December 1988, Mandela was discharged from the clinic and driven to Victor Verster Prison near the winelands town of Paarl. Once on the property he was taken down a winding dirt road through a belt of dense scrub and trees to a white house shaded by pine trees. Inside were modern furnishings and a hi-tech kitchen. A warrant officer, Jack Swart, was on hand as his personal chef. The garden was big, with a swimming pool.

The following afternoon Kobie Coetsee called, bringing a case of wine as a housewarming present – a gesture that was well-meaning, although both men appreciated the irony. He assured Mandela this was to be his last prison: a place where he could have discussions in privacy and comfort.

January brought with it grim news. In Soweto, Winnie's gang had continued their reign of terror. She had watched while a boy named Stompie Seipei, accused of being an informer, was beaten and assaulted. Some days later his battered and stabbed body was discovered in a riverbed. The Mandela Crisis Committee found itself confronting the wife of the most revered man in the country. Criticism of her also came from the Mass Democratic Movement inside South Africa and from the ANC in exile. A deeply troubled and distressed Mandela, desperately wanting to believe in his wife's innocence, cautioned her to say nothing, to ensure the football club tracksuits were never used again and to be vigilant against a "third force" trying to sow dissension.

In the same month P. W. Botha suffered a stroke, and it was not until July that the two finally met. Mandela was nervous. A tailor had made him a suit for the occasion; he had a new tie, shirt, and shoes. But after almost three decades he'd forgotten how to knot a tie and the commanding officer of the prison had to help him. Then, at the official presidential residence Tuynhuys, the National Intelligence head, Barnard, noticed that Mandela's shoelaces were undone. He knelt and quickly tied them. He had hardly finished when the door opened and Mandela was ushered in to greet the president.

As things turned out, their thirty-minute chat was an amiable meander through history although Mandela scored a point by mentioning the 1914 Afrikaner Rebellion and how like his own struggle it had been. Before anyone could shout "Time's up!" Mandela asked for the release of all political prisoners. Botha, renowned for his temper, just shook his head and said he was afraid he couldn't do that.

Reassured by the respect he had been accorded, Mandela went back to his garden house to celebrate his birthday – attended by most of his family including his daughter Makaziwe who felt he had opened up to her for the first time as a father. "It was a deep, deep pleasure to have my whole family around me, and the only pain was the knowledge that I had missed such occasions for so many years," Mandela noted.[19]

In the last quarter of the year political events moved swiftly. An election brought F. W. de Klerk to power, and in October he released the Robben Island contingent, including Sisulu and Kathrada. Two months later he met with Mandela. The meeting, in the same room in Tuynhuys, was, however, of a different order. De Klerk listened and Mandela felt that here was a man the ANC could do business with.

His instincts were right. At the opening of Parliament on February 2, 1990, de Klerk announced the unbanning of the ANC, the PAC, and the Communist Party. Seven days later – a Friday – he again met with Mandela to tell him that he would be released that weekend in Johannesburg. To de Klerk's surprise, Mandela informed him that he would need a week to prepare and he wished his first free steps to be taken out of Victor Verster Prison. They compromised; the date could not be postponed but he could leave from the prison. De Klerk poured whiskies in celebration. Mandela raised his glass in a toast but only pretended to sip the drink.

On the hot summer afternoon of Sunday, February 11, 1990, at 4 P.M., a suited Nelson Mandela, at first unsmiling, his hand clasping that of his wife, walked toward the prison gate. His life, he felt, "was beginning anew." His "ten thousand days of imprisonment were at last over."[20]

DENNIS GOLDBERG:

After sentencing in the Rivonia Trial, we were taken back to the prison in an armored convoy with the sirens shrieking, and when we arrived Colonel Aucamp, the head of prison security, said to me, "You're lucky. You should have been hanged, all of you. You will never get out of here on your own feet. We will carry you out in a box." He was smiling like a cat that had licked the cream. At the time I was amazed at the viciousness of his response, but they really were bitter that we got away with our lives. But whether or not he had heard Colonel Aucamp that day, when Nelson Mandela was released, he stopped the car inside the prison grounds and he walked out. And it seemed to me a moment of such triumph, that this man, dressed in a suit, elegant as ever, should walk out on his own feet to meet the crowds.

PART THREE

Free at Last, 1990–present

Emerging from the prison gates to where a huge crowd of well-wishers and journalists waited, television cameras rolling, photographers crouched behind their lenses, Nelson Mandela's demeanor relaxed: a broad smile broke across his face and he raised his right hand in the ANC salute. Beside him Winnie held her arm high in victory, but this was a different woman to the one who had seen him go to jail. Yet despite the controversy surrounding her, Mandela had refused to leave prison without her at his side; he still desperately believed in her.

They lingered briefly among the crowd to the roar of *Amandlas,* which gave Mandela a "surge of strength and joy," before heading for Cape Town's Grand Parade where people had been gathering since the morning to welcome him back.[1] The site of the Grand Parade was well chosen: a place of history that Mandela would now stamp with a new seal. It was on this ground that the colonial armies had paraded, it was here that Queen Victoria's birthday had been celebrated every year for fifty years. It was here that in 1882, the manacled Zulu king, Cetshwayo, had been brought up from his dungeon in the nearby castle to watch the queen's soldiers. Perhaps his ghost returned now to smile in triumph.

Standing on the balcony of the city hall, overlooking the parade, Mandela faced the jubilant crowd. Some had climbed trees and statues to get a view of their hallowed leader. There had been shops looted earlier, and a youth shot dead. Armed police ringed the square and the vibration of helicopters reverberated off the city buildings. In the background the granite face of Table Mountain pulsed with heat. Wearing his wife's glasses (he'd forgotten his own at Victor Verster), Mandela read a speech which dedicated his life to the people, thanked those who had supported him through the bleak three decades, adding, "Our struggle has reached a decisive moment. We call on our people to seize this moment so that the process toward democracy is rapid and uninterrupted. We have waited too long for our freedom. We can no longer wait. Now is the time to intensify the struggle on all fronts."[2] To most whites and some Western leaders, his adherence to the party line and his upholding of armed resistance were disappointing; to the firebrands, his defiance showed he was still a freedom fighter. These were certainly sentiments he would not regret, but he would be bedeviled by his allowance that de Klerk was a "man of integrity."[3]

Right: A black youth holds up the front page of a newspaper proclaiming Nelson Mandela's release after nearly three decades in prison.

Mandela spent his first night of freedom at the residence of Archbishop Desmond Tutu in the exclusive white suburb of Bishopscourt. The townships of the Cape Flats would have been his choice, but security considerations dictated otherwise. The next day he and Winnie flew to Johannesburg but were diverted from their Orlando matchbox house – which had been rebuilt – as it was surrounded by thousands of people. Again Mandela slept in a house in a white suburb. The next day he spoke at a packed and roused stadium of a hundred thousand people in Soweto, and finally that night, returned to Orlando. 'It was only then that I knew in my heart that I had left prison. For me, No. 8115 was the center point of my world, the place marked with an X in my mental geography.'[4]

But it was not to be an easy night. At 10 P.M. Winnie left the house, only returning in the early hours of the morning. From the moment he left jail, Winnie wouldn't enter his bedroom while he was awake. Nor were his relations with his children any easier.

Zindzi complained, "From the day my father was free, we had to share him with the rest of the world."[5] To her mother she said, "You know we were better off with Daddy in prison. We had access to him, we could talk to him as a father. Now that all has gone."[6] His son Makgatho was battling with his legal studies in Durban and rarely saw his father; his daughter Maki was in Canada. She would return to South Africa later in the year but still only saw her father sporadically. On one occasion when he tried to hug her she flinched away, a replay of her indecision before him as a child. "You are a father to all our people," she told him, "but you have never had the time to be a father to me."[7]

FRIENDS,
COMRADES, AND
FELLOW SOUTH
AFRICANS. I GREET
YOU ALL IN THE
NAME OF PEACE,
DEMOCRACY, AND
FREEDOM FOR ALL.
I STAND HERE
BEFORE YOU NOT
AS A PROPHET BUT
AS A HUMBLE
SERVANT OF YOU,
THE PEOPLE. YOUR
TIRELESS AND
HEROIC SACRIFICES
HAVE MADE IT
POSSIBLE FOR ME
TO BE HERE TODAY.
I THEREFORE PLACE
THE REMAINING
YEARS OF MY LIFE
IN YOUR HANDS. . . .

Mandela addresses the people from the balcony of Cape Town City Hall on his release from prison, February 11, 1990, flanking him are Walter Sisulu and Cyril Ramaphosa

DESMOND TUTU:

Mandela is a deeply loyal member of the ANC and he derives considerable strength from that organization whether physically or in spirit. On the island of course he had his comrades around him: Walter Sisulu, Govan Mbeki, Ahmed Kathrada, and all of those others. He also derived considerable strength from Winnie who was beautiful, incredibly brave, and an extraordinary stalwart of the struggle until latterly when things may have gone a little wonky. He loved her very, very, deeply. And then he was aware just how much the international community was rallying to him. People might think that twenty-seven years was an utter waste, but I beg to differ. That time was actually crucial in the evolution of a moral giant.

I think there are many influences in Mandela's life. He was a Methodist and received much of his education from mission schools and institutions and although he isn't someone who carries his faith on his sleeve, even unconsciously that would have had some effect. And then the fact that he is an African, someone who has taken in the tenets of *ubuntu* with his mother's milk.

We tend to forget that when Mandela went to prison he was relatively young. He was the commander of Umkhonto we Sizwe so he wasn't someone who would flinch from using force and violence. He was appalled at the miscarriage of justice that had happened in the Rivonia Trial, just as he was in the many other instances where black people were the accused, and when he went to jail he was angry. But he grew in his understanding of the fears and apprehension of a minority who thought they were going to be swamped and by the time he got out he was ready to go more than just a second mile.

Mandela and Winnie in Archbishop Desmond Tutu's Bishopscourt garden the day after Mandela's release.

When Inkatha were threatening to boycott the election, the presiding bishop of the Methodist Church Stanley Mogoba and I convened a meeting between Madiba and Chief Buthelezi, who wanted a number of things including their appearing together at a political rally. Many of the ANC would have rejected this out of hand but Madiba was ready even to go into an Inkatha stronghold which would have required very considerable physical courage. At one point he said to Buthelezi that if they won the election he would offer him a high position in government, which was quite amazing. All he wanted was Inkatha's agreement that they would participate in the elections and I saw then that he was ready to put his whole reputation on the line even when others were engaging in brinkmanship. It wasn't spineless, because you know just how angry he could become, as he did after the Boipatong massacre, for instance, when they had alerted Mr. de Klerk that something was going to happen and the government did nothing. He is not a soft touch but he is an interesting mix of almost regal arrogance with an incredible modesty and humility.

In negotiation Mandela always tried to ensure that he didn't make the other person feel that he was rubbing his nose in the dust. After their public debate on television he got up to shake hands with de Klerk so graciously. It was a very small gesture and yet it was so pregnant with significance since so many were getting angrier and angrier with the last apartheid government. Mandela was quite clear that you didn't win in order to humiliate the other; victory did not mean riding roughshod over the vanquished. When the Truth and Reconciliation Commission subpoenaed P. W. Botha, for instance, I think he felt in part that it was a humiliation to have to come at our bidding. Madiba sent word to him to say that if you are feeling that they are somehow seeking to embarrass and humiliate you I, the president, would be ready to attend a session and sit side by side with you.

We are an incredible country. We deserve to celebrate the victory over apartheid and the fact that we have the kind of stability that we have in our country despite crime, and despite poverty and HIV/AIDS. We are still in many ways a beacon of hope for the world.

I think the youth of today are thrilled that Mandela was their president, although I suspect that we may sometimes romanticize places like Robben Island and I worry that we forget too easily. Amnesia is not good: first because the younger generation is not aware of the price that was paid and so it might be easy for them to devalue the freedom they have today; and second because forgetting may make it easy for the atrocities of the past to be repeated.

Mandela outside his Orlando house during the first press conference following his release.

GEORGE SOROS:

It didn't really surprise me how Mandela behaved when he came out of prison. He is a man of very high moral standards, believing, in the old-fashioned mold of Gandhi, that goodwill can carry everything before it, and the world is as good as you make it through your behavior. There is a parallel with the experiences friends of mine had in Hungarian prisons after 1956. Those who managed to go through prison without compromising themselves came out very strong. When people take personal punishment for standing up for principles and prevail, it strengthens them tremendously and they stand as an example for the rest. Most Hungarians after 1956 compromised with the regime, but there was great respect for people who hadn't compromised. That is the quality Mandela has: he came out of prison and he was clean. He had a moral authority that made him the equal or the superior of the Afrikaners and they recognized that. There's a similarity with Lech Walesa in Poland. They embody a certain kind of moral integrity that few others have.

Top: Mandela, flanked by security guards, delivers his address to the people at the FNB Stadium in Soweto.

Above: From left to right, singing "Nkosi Sikelel' iAfrika," are the Reverend Frank Chikane, Kathrada, Winnie, Mandela, and Walter Sisulu.

Following page: Mandela surrounded by children in Soweto shortly after his release.

COMRADES,
FRIENDS, AND THE
PEOPLE OF SOWETO
AT LARGE,
I GREET YOU IN THE
NAME OF THE
HEROIC STRUGGLE
OF OUR PEOPLE TO
ESTABLISH JUSTICE
AND FREEDOM
FOR ALL IN
OUR COUNTRY. . . .

Mandela's address to the people at a
"welcome home" rally at the FNB Stadium in Soweto,
February 13, 1990

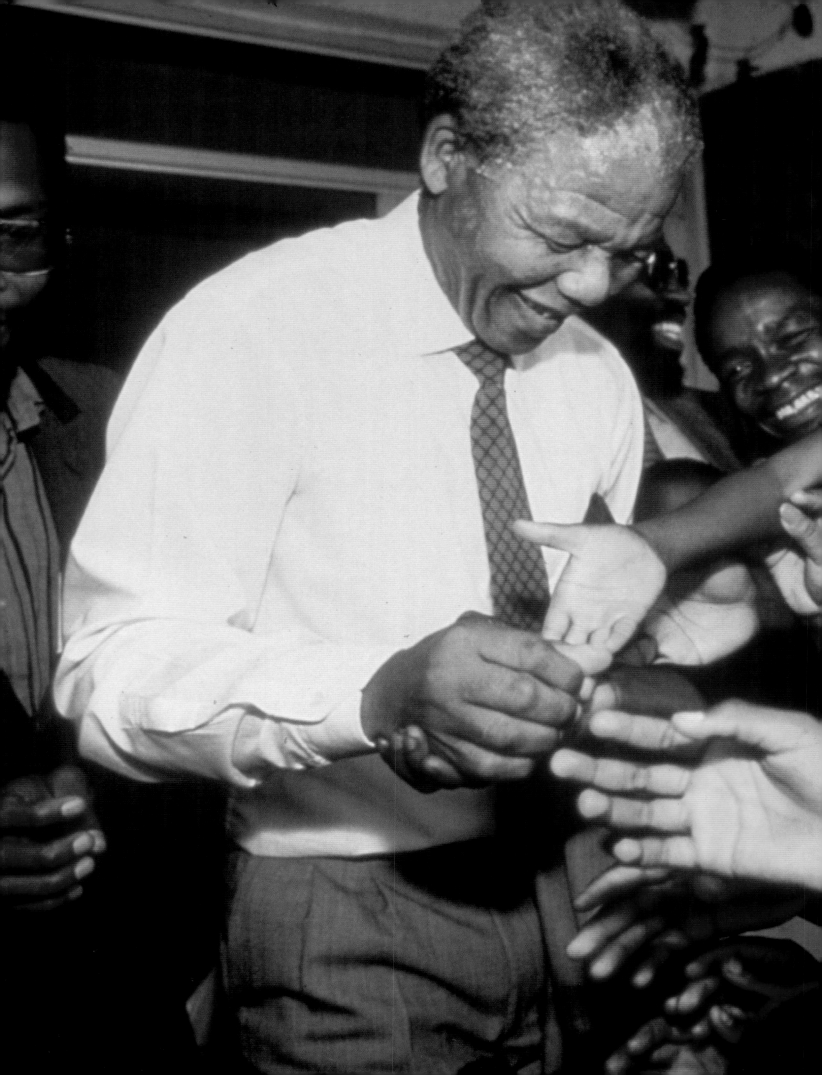

was in Soweto when Mandela arrived two or three days after his release from prison. He was staying in this little matchbox house in Orlando West, and Walter Sisulu's son Zwelakhe was there, acting as the spokesperson. Zwelakhe saw me and he went in and chatted to the old man who out of the blue said he wanted to see me. So I was hauled over the fence and ushered into this poky, tiny room and there he was! It was just amazing to be there alone with him so soon after his release.

That first impression in fact was a lasting one. It struck me that one of the great things about this man was that on the one hand he was an international icon, a man who could stride the world, and yet he had a common touch toward the smallest individual of his flock. He paid the minutest attention to me, and he said to me simply, not in a condescending way, that the stuff I had written over the years had been meaningful to them in prison. He wasn't trying to flatter me or make me feel good or anything – although of course I felt very proud. While I was there, somebody stuck a head around the door and said that some people from Qunu, his home town in the Transkei, were there. He hadn't seen them for a long time and he turned to me and said, "Excuse me. There are some people I have to meet." And these three elderly men came into the room and he broke into Xhosa. I speak Xhosa so I was able to follow the conversation and he was asking in the most minute detail about the relationships between people in the village – who had married, and how was so-and-so, and didn't they have a granddaughter now – and so on, while the world stood still and waited for his next great move to transform South Africa, Africa, human relations globally.

I recall a story that the lawyer George Bizos told me once. He said that on one occasion during the Rivonia Trial he had said to Mandela that he wouldn't be able to be in court on the following Monday because it was his daughter's birthday. Mandela asked her name and her age and he just nodded and George told me that ever after, all the years that he was in prison, his daughter got a birthday card from Nelson Mandela.

Later on, I asked for an interview with Mandela for a book I wanted to write about the transition phase and I was called one morning to say that they had had a security scare and could they send Mandela around to my house to do it because he hadn't been to my place before and they liked him to stay somewhere different every time this happened. We talked and talked for many hours that day and broke off for lunch and he suddenly said 'Oh, this is in Rivonia! Where is Lilliesleaf? I'd like to see it." It was only a kilometer away so we got in my car – to the great consternation of his bodyguards – and we drove off to Lilliesleaf. The family that owned it wasn't there, but Mandela was immediately recognized by the maid who gave us a tour. He remembered having a pellet gun there and shooting a dove which fell to the ground, and Arthur Goldreich's young son who was only about five said, "Oh, David" – this was Mandela's code name at the time – "what will its mother do?' And he was so stricken he said he'd never killed anything after that. He'd even rescued bugs in his cell and once reprimanded a guard for killing a cockroach.

Anyway, we wandered around the house, and he suddenly said, "You know, I buried some weapons here, twenty paces from the kitchen," and he walked out and measured off twenty paces, but after he got to about eight or nine he came up against a wall because now it's a suburb and no longer a farm. Apparently this weapon was a ceremonial pistol that had been given to him in Ethiopia, and he'd wrapped it up and buried it deeply so that a plow wouldn't reach it. He had then gone off to Durban and his arrest followed.

After this we went back to the car and the bodyguards were very agitated because word had got around and people were crowding around the car, and he was greeting everyone and chatting with them and asking them about their lives. He was about to get into the car when a "traditionally" built African woman emerged from a house right at the top of the road, and began to half run, half waddle up the long slope, ululating. And he got out of the car again and he stood in the middle of the road applauding and he waited until she got all the way up to the top, panting, and he just threw his arms around her. It's this simply amazing human personal touch that makes him a truly great man.

In the interview he gave me that day, he gave minute details of the forty-seven meetings he had had with the government while he was still in prison. He revealed how worried he had been that his colleagues would think he was up to some deal cutting, but he realized this was a great opportunity and he decided to go ahead. The others were indeed concerned, and certainly in Lusaka the leadership was deeply apprehensive. But the conversations went on and laid the basis for the subsequent decision to unban the organizations, which the government side came to realize were not the bloodthirsty terrorist, communist organizations of their imaginings and indeed of their propaganda. And Mandela personally laid the basis for that.

I think the key to South Africa's achievement lies in the fact that Nelson Mandela went to prison as a militant and while he was there decided strategically that the ANC would never be able to overthrow the regime in South Africa by military means alone. He says today that he probably realized this even before founding Umkhonto we Sizwe, but thought it would be an additional means of applying pressure. He became convinced that in the end it would have to be resolved at the negotiating table and, to that end, while he was in prison he set about trying to get himself into the mind of the Afrikaner people. What was it that was making them so apparently racist, so resistant to change? He learned the language, he asked for more Afrikaans literature, and he questioned the guards to try to understand what was motivating the Afrikaner people, and he came to realize that it was primarily their fears. In the end I think he latched on to one of the great truths of human relationships, which is that the identity of a people is an important thing. And he came to realize that the real conflict in South Africa was the conflict over whose country this was. And he realized that unless he could allay the Afrikaner fears the negotiating process would go nowhere. So while insisting that there had to be one person, one vote, he was intent on assuring the Afrikaner people that their language, their faith, their church structure, everything would be safeguarded, and that one could have a constitution that would do that.

And when you reflect on this, what South Africa has achieved has been extraordinary. Too often we are simplistically compared with the racial conflict in the south of the United States, but ours was a much more profound conflict than simply a matter of park benches or segregated schools and buses, lunch counters, and so on. This was a conflict over whose country South Africa was and therefore the true comparison is rather with the conflict between the Israelis and the Palestinians, or between the Greeks and the Turks of Cyprus. And if you look at it in that context you begin to realize just what South Africa has achieved – and Mandela was the catalyst that made it happen.

No matter how the rebuffs from his children stung him, Mandela had learned well to compartmentalize his life. His friends found him warm and gentle, more at peace with himself than the man who had gone into prison. "He knew exactly who he was," said Ismail Meer. "He had gone through this period of fire and purified himself. . . ."[8] And who he was now, above all else, was the man who would lead the country to a negotiated settlement and democracy. The first steps along this path meant rallying the forces and halting the violence that had gripped the province of KwaZulu-Natal.

Here Chief Mangosuthu Buthelezi controlled the Inkatha Freedom Party which was fighting an internecine war against the ANC with – as was subsequently established – the backing of elements within the state apparatus. Buthelezi was one of the first people on Mandela's telephone list after his release as he wished to thank him for his support through the prison years and arrange a meeting to resolve the differences. But initial attempts came to nothing. The killing continued. In early February, just three weeks after his release, Mandela flew to Durban. He visited grieving families and saw the burnt corpses of ANC supporters, victims of the strife. These images uppermost in his mind, he addressed a hundred thousand-strong, mainly Zulu crowd, exhorting them to 'Take your guns, your knives, and your *pangas,* and throw them into the sea! Close down the death factories. End this war now!'[9] No one listened. The next month 230 people would be killed.

Toward the end of February, Mandela traveled to Lusaka to consult with his ANC colleagues. The next month he visited Zimbabwe and Namibia. Behind the scenes, ANC attempts to meet with the Zulu king floundered but there was agreement with the government that talks about talks would start in April.

On March 26 in Sebokeng township, near Johannesburg, an ANC demonstration ended with twelve dead and hundreds wounded when police opened fire. Mandela suspended the talks, warning de Klerk through the media that he couldn't talk about negotiations while the state continued to murder people. With this bad taste in his mouth he embarked on a tour to Tanzania, Egypt, and Sweden to visit Oliver Tambo, and in April attended a pop concert in London in his honor. Back in South Africa he met privately with de Klerk. He came away realizing that de Klerk was playing for time, hoping that he might prove a man of straw in the face of escalating violence while the government sought to woo Inkatha and colored voters in the Cape into an anti-ANC alliance. Talks were rescheduled for early May.

Right: Mandela with his grandson Bhambatha in Qunu during his first visit to the Transkei in almost three decades.

Before then Mandela headed for Qunu, to his mother's grave, marked by a few stones and broken bricks as were most graves in the cemetery. He felt regret, remorse "and a longing for what might have been had I chosen to live my life differently."[10] Nor was Qunu the idyll of his imagination: the village was degraded, the surroundings littered. He went on to Robben Island, this time to persuade twenty-five MK prisoners to accept the government's offer of amnesty. Being back, as a visitor, was disconcerting but he had no time for nostalgia. Early winter was in the air when the first round of talks ended positively with a joint working group established to probe a way through the obstacles. Mandela, about to leave on a six-week tour of Europe and North America, met privately with de Klerk who wanted him to end the ANC's call for international sanctions. Mandela said no, not until apartheid was dismantled and a transitional government had taken over.

Despite his domestic unhappiness with Winnie, she accompanied him on the trip. They had moved into her seven-bedroom house in Soweto where Mandela felt uncomfortable with the extravagance, and stories abounded of her heavy drinking. Yet for six weeks she was the perfect consort, solicitous and vibrant. Everywhere Mandela was fêted. Before he flew from London to New York he made a courtesy phone call to the British prime minister, Margaret Thatcher (who he was scheduled to meet on his return). She sternly warned him that his program was too rigorous. "If you keep this up," she insisted, "you will not come out of America alive."[11] Amused but unheeding, Mandela flew to New York and a fifteen-mile-long tickertape motorcade through the streets, the largest the city had ever known. He went from meetings to banquets to addressing a joint session of both houses of Congress in Washington to discussions with President George H. W. Bush. Back in London, he held a three-hour meeting with Thatcher, the first fifty minutes of which she let him speak uninterrupted. But she refused to apply the sanctions he requested.

Nelson Mandela's "thank-you tour" of the U.S. in 1990 drew huge crowds and attention.
Above: The cover of Time *magazine, July 2, 1990, marking the visit.*

Opposite: Mandela receives applause after addressing the UN in New York in June 1990, urging it to maintain sanctions against South Africa until apartheid was abolished.

PRINCE BANDAR:

I was aware of South Africa's apartheid problems and of the ANC's fight against them since I was in elementary school. Saudi Arabia was a member of the nonaligned group, so our support for the ANC and for Mandela in jail and our opposition to the apartheid government was part of our life, part of the consciousness of the nation.

When I became ambassador to Washington at the end of Reagan era, the Americans had just begun to put pressure on South Africa to change. One day I got a call from the national security adviser to President Reagan, Judge Clark, inviting me to meet with the black leader of South Africa. He was going to call on President Reagan and it would be nice if I could meet him there and show support. The first thing that came to mind was Mandela – and I wondered how did he get out without it being announced? Then I thought maybe it's a designate, or Oliver Tambo. . . .

My answer was, of course, I will come over. The White House sent the details to my office, but the names didn't ring a bell and my political section told me this man is not from the ANC, this is Chief Buthelezi. And I said, wait a minute – this is the guy who's going to be the leader of South Africa? I turned down the request to meet with him in the White House and Judge Clark said, "This is not a very smart move, Prince Bandar. This man is going to be the next president of South Africa when apartheid collapses and you'll regret not getting to know him early." I said, "Well, I'm very sorry, but my country's committed to the ANC and to Mandela or whoever he designates and therefore I cannot attend. We will see." A few years later, when President Mandela came to Washington during the Clinton era, I was present at the White House reception ceremony as dean of the Diplomatic Corps. That afternoon I happened to run into Judge Clark and I couldn't resist saying to him, "Judge, well you can see, thank God I didn't meet your man then, the president who never was!"

Right: Mandela meets the Kennedy family in Boston. From left to right, Senator Ted Kennedy, Jacqueline Kennedy Onassis, Winnie, Mandela, and Congressman Joe Kennedy. Ted Kennedy and his family had visited Winnie during her exile in Brandfort.

Below: Winnie and Mandela meet Rosa Parks, American civil rights pioneer, in Detroit.

I first met Mandela on his "thank-you tour" just after he left jail. The White House asked me to suggest to him that he shouldn't go to Cuba from America. And I said to them, "Why do you ask me? He's your guest." Apparently they did send feelers out, but he would not give. When I asked Mandela what it was all about, he said, "I don't know. I am not going there to support a regime or a president. Cuba has supported me and the ANC all along and just as I'm going to Brazil, or to Germany, or to Saudi Arabia, or America, Canada, Britain, I just want to say thank you. If this is going to cause embarrassment or unpleasantness and the president doesn't want to see me, that's fine."

President G. H. W. Bush told me later that when he met Mandela he realized why he was a great man. He was impressed by the fact that he would not sell his principles just to please a superpower. Both men tell this same story. After Mandela left jail, President Bush phoned him and one of his grandchildren answered the phone. Bush said, "Can I speak to Mr. Mandela?" and he said, "Who are you?" and he said, "I am George Bush," and he said, "Well, stay on the line and let me see if my grandfather is available." So he goes to tell his grandfather, "Grandfather, there is someone on the phone. He says he is George Bush. He wants to talk to you." And his grandfather started laughing knowing that this young man didn't know he was talking to the most powerful man in the world.

BILL CLINTON:

The Republicans were quite surprised when I got elected and they basically decided to assault my legitimacy from the day I became president. It was tough. I lived through an eight-year onslaught and when they started trying to run me out, Mandela was especially helpful. I remember asking him one day to go over one more time the moment when he realized that he was letting go of his anger and hatred. "Well, I hated them for fourteen years," he said, "and I'm not sure, when I was young and strong, if I wasn't kept alive on my hatred. But one day when I was breaking rocks I realized they had taken so much from me. They had abused me physically; they had abused me emotionally; they had taken me away from my wife and children; I wouldn't see my children grow up; eventually it would cost me my marriage. They'd taken everything from me except my mind and my heart. And I realized I would have to give those things to them – and I decided not to give them away." Then he looked at me and smiled and said, "And neither should you." And I said, "OK! I got it!" He knew how mad I was for what they did, for the way they treated me and my family and my friends. It was horrible; half the stuff has never come out. He knew how angry I was, and he said, "I'd have to give my heart and my mind away and I decided not to." And he smiled and said, "And neither should you."

Not long before the vote on the impeachment, I saw Thabo Mbeki in Washington and I asked how President Mandela was. He said, "Oh, he's fine, but he did tell me to give you a message. I have no idea what he's talking about but he said you would know. He said I should remind you 'not to give them away.'" Right there before the House voted! It was amazing. And I went, "Right!"

The Republicans were worried because they wanted to impeach me and knew they had no constitutional, legal or historical basis to do so, but they knew that the U.S. press had made such a big deal out of it that they could get it. They were worried, however, about the fallout in the minority community and so they voted to give Mandela the Congressional gold medal. Mandela called me and he starts off, "My President. . . ." Whenever he said "My President," I knew he was telling me something we were going to do and I was going to do it whether I wanted to or not! He said, "The Congress has voted to give me this gold medal.

As the president of South Africa I cannot turn down such an award. I may be old, but I'm not foolish. I understand what is going on here so here's what we are going to do. I'm coming in a day early and we are going to have dinner at the White House and I will tell America what I think about what they are doing." So he comes and says how all these world leaders are dependent on me and how I've helped solve all these problems and how it's not for him to tell America what to do but they ought to leave me alone and let me go back to work. Boy – was he stirring the water! I got a standing ovation at the UN, which is unheard of for an American, but I don't think one network carried his speech on the evening news.

Mandela will never know how much he helped me get through that period. Thinking about what he went through that was so much worse helped me keep my head up and keep going: keep going to work, give the State of the Union address, blow it off. I realized the more I thought about him walking down that road, the more I realized how he had demanded that he be judged, evaluated, and characterized by who he was and what he did and what he said, not by what others had done to him or said about him. I realized that in a small way, not only I but anyone who was willing to develop the kind of emotional and spiritual discipline he had, the kind of pain threshold he had, to hold onto their dignity instead of their anger, could achieve this result. I'll never be able to repay him for what he did for me in those months.

Our connection is a political affinity, but I don't think it is entirely that. He knew the Democrats had supported the embargo on South Africa and that the Democrats had been against apartheid and against his imprisonment. He knew we basically had an interest in the same sort of social mission on domestic things. But from the beginning it was more than political; there was just something about us that clicked. Maybe he was just being nice to me as a younger man. But whatever happened, over time, I was really glad about the moments we were together.

Interestingly enough we did actually have a dispute to do with various economic and security issues that were rooted in the apartheid years before his presidency. He was trying to govern a genuinely multiracial democracy and he included his former tormentors in his government and he needed not to be asked to do anything that might run the risk of eroding the support he needed from some quarters. So we had a real working relationship as two presidents, which included an enormous amount of commonality and a few disagreements. He didn't always agree with everything I did on foreign policy either and our government bureaucracy was a little harder on him than I was. I got that: he was in prison for twenty-seven years and he was determined to stick with any country that helped the ANC when he and the other leaders were in prison. Mandela prides himself on being a loyal friend and just as he was loyal to me so he was to Castro and the Libyans and others that America didn't always get along too well with. The movement and the ANC would have faced bankruptcy, division, destruction in the absence of the critical financial support that came from these quarters that America may have found unsafe. It took forever and a day before the American political system actually stood up against apartheid and you can't blame Mandela for being loyal to those countries that stood up for the ANC and against apartheid before we did. So the official position of the United States government was one of more dismay than I personally felt. I knew Mandela was neve going to back out on those who kept step with him over those twenty-seven years.

He's got so much to teach us about forgiveness. It isn't about being soft-headed and kind-hearted and essentially weak or forgetful, although the Bible says God both forgives and forgets. Mandela found that forgiveness was a strategy for survival. Because he found a forgiving heart under the most adverse circumstances, because he learned to hate the apartheid cause without hating the white South Africans, he had space left inside to learn and grow and become great. To me he represents a great political leader. He had the discipline to stay the course for almost three decades, through enormous punishment, to achieve the political objective he sought. And he did it in a way that, in the end, had the support of people across the racial divide. In the process he freed not only black South Africa but, as Martin Luther King said about America, he freed white South Africans, too. It's a terrible burden oppressing someone else; it's like being in chains yourself.

Most of us act as if we have no control over the way we react. I tried to convince Yasser Arafat not to start the *intifada* in 2000. Mr. Sharon, before he was prime minister, went up on the Temple Mount. He was the first Israeli politician to do so in thirty-three years and the Palestinians felt it was desecration. President Arafat said, "It's humiliating, we have to prevent it," but I said, "No, you don't. You have another option. You could have a little Palestinian girl go with flowers, give them to Mr. Sharon and welcome him and invite him to the Al Aqsa Mosque and say when Temple Mount is yours he can come back every day. You have a choice." Mandela always understood that. That's the difference between a person who is just a politician and a person who is a great human being.

I used Mandela's model of peace-making over and over and over again – in Northern Ireland, in the Middle East, in the aftermath of the conflicts in Bosnia and Kosovo – and regretted that so few people seemed able to follow it. They thought they had paid too high a price, but if you think of what Mandela went through, arguably they hadn't paid the price long enough to be purged of their own anger.

I like the fact that – in the parlance of my part of America – he is determined to die with his boots on. It meant a lot to me that we went to Barcelona together in 2002 to close the world AIDS conference – he knew I'd been in South Africa and he supported the work I'd tried to do. He's never asked for a retirement check. In 2000 he hauled me all the way to the peace center in Arusha in Tanzania. He called me and told me I was coming to help end the conflict in Burundi and I said, "Yes, sir." He said, "We are going to do a good cop bad cop routine and for once I'll be the bad cop and you be the good cop." He said, "They'll either have to do it for me or they'll have to do it for you. You've just got to come." So I showed up. "Here's what we're going to do," he said. "We're going to make peace, and all the parties are going to sign up." Darn it, if that's not what happened. He's never quit. You know I like that.

For me, Mandela is also a personal friend with whom I have shared parts of my personal life. I don't know how conventionally religious he is, but he is a very godly man because he's the living embodiment of the importance of second chances in life: giving them and getting them, and becoming bigger through adversity. But Mandela's not just great: he is a good man. Not because he is perfect – he still has his flashes of anger and regret – but in the big moment, in the big ways, there is nobody like him.

KOFI ANNAN:

I will never forget the last speech Nelson Mandela gave to the United Nations General Assembly before retiring as president of South Africa. It was September 1998, but I recall it as if it were yesterday. We had been chatting in a private room beforehand, and, as ever, he was making everybody around him feel completely relaxed through his unique mix of humor, warmth, informality and dignity. Once inside the general assembly, he had the vast chamber spellbound. "This is probably the last time," he said, "that I will have the honor to stand at this podium to address the general assembly. Born as the First World War came to a close and departing from public life as the world marks half a century of the Universal Declaration of Human Rights, I have reached that part of the long walk when the opportunity is granted, as it should be to all men and women, to retire to some rest and tranquillity in the village of my birth.

President Clinton and President Mandela on Robben Island.

"As I sit in Qunu and grow as ancient as its hills," he went on, "I will continue to entertain the hope that there has emerged a cadre of leaders in my own country and region, on my continent and in the world, which will not allow that any should be denied their freedom as we were; that any should be turned into refugees as we were; that any should be condemned to go hungry as we were; that any should be stripped of their human dignity as we were."

Those were heartrendingly moving words, uttered with the utmost gravity. You could have heard a pin drop in the general assembly hall. But the silence was soon followed – as always after Madiba speaks – by thunderous applause. If the high hopes he expressed for Africa and the world that day come true, it will be in no small measure thanks to Madiba himself. People often ask me what difference one person can make in the face of injustice, conflict, human-rights violations, mass poverty, and disease. I answer by citing the courage, tenacity, dignity, and magnanimity of Nelson Mandela.

Throughout our years of friendship, Mandela has been a source of support and inspiration to me – both personally and as secretary-general. I am honored to participate in this book – a fitting tribute to Madiba's journey. If just one small part of what he has sought to achieve for his fellow human beings is translated into reality, if we live up to just one fraction of the standards he has set, then Africa, and the world, will be a far, far better place.

On his return to South Africa, Mandela put in three short trips to Uganda, Kenya, and Mozambique before scheduling a meeting with de Klerk about the ever-increasing violence. The state of emergency had been lifted the previous month (although it still applied in KwaZulu) but some fifteen hundred people had been killed by July, more than the total number of political deaths the previous year.

Before their meeting took place, two major events occurred. Hundreds of Zulus were bussed into Sebokeng for a demonstration and although the ANC tipped off the minister of law and order, the police did not intervene in the ensuing battle. The next day Mandela went to the morgue to see thirty bodies that had been hacked to death by broad-bladed *pangas*. More than Buthelezi he blamed de Klerk. Three days later the security forces arrested about forty ANC members – including Mac Maharaj – for plotting to overthrow the government in a plan called Operation Vula. It was an outdated moribund plan and nine months later the case was abandoned. What disturbed Mandela was the way these events always preceded negotiations.

In the midst of the horror, Joe Slovo proposed a controversial idea that Mandela found appealing: a suspension of the armed struggle. After several hours of discussion he persuaded the ANC executive to accept the tactic, and their good faith was signed into the Pretoria Minute, an agreement of undertaking with the government, in early August. But the violence continued.

In the following weeks Mandela visited township after township in the wake of atrocities, hearing always the rumor of police collusion with the Inkatha *impis*. On the one hand he was holding talks with the government; on the other he seemed impotent to stop the killing. Yet at the end of a month in which thousands died in Transvaal townships, the government ratified regulations allowing Zulus to carry cultural weapons – *assegais,* fighting sticks, battle axes – in accordance with traditional or religious custom. With a signature, de Klerk had licensed Inkatha's weapons of war.

Mandela became increasingly convinced that there was a hidden hand, a third force, a maverick death squad at work behind the unrelenting bloodshed. An official commission found the allegations groundless, but Mandela believed the report was a whitewash. He considered returning to the armed struggle. By year's end he was accusing de Klerk of playing a dangerous double game, and the security forces of orchestrating the slaughter. His demands for official investigations were ignored.

Berating him from the wings was his wife, frequently to be seen in an MK uniform talking of "shooting our way to freedom."[12] Around her now swirled stories of abductions and murders, and witnesses for her upcoming trial disappeared or left the country. Mandela publicly welcomed the trial as an opportunity to settle the rumors, but when she was charged in October he had difficulty raising funds for her defense. Eventually the Swedes and the Libyan president, Qaddafi, contributed to what would be onerous legal fees. This wasn't his only financial worry: an anonymous donor stopped paying for Winnie's house, which put pressure on his resources.

Undeterred, Winnie sailed into the new year by throwing a party for five hundred guests. A troubled Mandela, never at home in the vulgar excess of her house and unsettled by the enforced bonhomie of the party, ushered in 1991 with a speech cajoling the children to attend school once term started. In those heady days of "liberation before education," school wasn't a priority for many teenagers.

If his words fell on deaf ears, then, equally, his eight-hour discussion with Buthelezi later in the month to promote peace and stop the "killing talk" went unheeded.[13] Despite the establishment of a monitoring committee and a joint accord, four hundred people were killed in the first three months of 1991 as the reprisals and the vendettas exacted their bloody toll.

The following month Mandela devoted crucial time to supporting his wife during her trial. He urged his friends to show their loyalty, yet sat stony-faced through the hearing. Judgement was reserved until June. The weight of the damning evidence lodged heavily on his mind.

Come April, Mandela again met with Buthelezi to warn him of the government's hidden hand. But the Zulu chief brushed aside his concerns, refusing to see de Klerk as a conspirator. However, Mandela distrusted de Klerk. His phone calls met with polite condescension, his demands that the ministers and police heads be purged were disregarded. Exasperated, the ANC suspended talks.

As the townships burned and ran with blood, Mandela's image took a battering while his rival gained stature internationally for dismantling apartheid. To further hamper him, Winnie was found guilty and sentenced to six years' imprisonment. She immediately appealed and left court defiant, clenched fist in the air. However, the verdict troubled Mandela, and he walked out of the building with his face set and severe, nevertheless recording in his autobiography, "As far as I was concerned, verdict or no verdict, her innocence was not in doubt."[14]

Politically, though, a sea-change was soon increasingly noticeable. The violence continued but first the independent Afrikaans newspaper, *Vrye Weekblad,* then the *Weekly Mail* and its sister newspaper in London, the *Guardian,* broke stories about death squads and police financing and supplying weapons to Inkatha. Mandela took no pleasure in the revelations but de Klerk was compromised, and at a conference in September Mandela, de Klerk, and Buthelezi agreed to a national peace accord. Pointedly, Buthelezi refused to shake hands with either Mandela or de Klerk to seal the pact. So what was agreed among the leaders had no effect in the hostels, the townships and the villages, where the killing continued.

With Mandela now president of the ANC, the first round of official negotiations began in December at Johannesburg's World Trade Centre. CODESA 1, as it became known – the Convention for a Democratic South Africa – was scheduled to last three days. On the second day de Klerk asked to be the final speaker and Mandela conceded what had been his privilege. But the president had a hidden agenda and lashed into the ANC. When he was finished, a furious Mandela stalked to the podium to berate the man who had abused a courtesy. The next day they shook hands, but for Mandela a trust had been betrayed.

Nelson Mandela and President de Klerk at the National Peace Convention in 1991.

MY ORDEAL STARTED FIVE MINUTES AFTER I AND MY WIFE WENT TO BED AT ABOUT 10 P. M. WE HEARD GUNSHOTS FOLLOWED BY SCREAMS FROM MY NEIGHBOR. . . . I WENT TO THE DOOR TO SEE WHAT COULD BE GOING ON. I SAW TWO MEN CHOPPING MY NEIGHBOR WITH AXES. TWO WHITE MEN WITH AUTOMATIC RIFLES WERE STANDING BEHIND THEM. THE ATTACKERS SHOUTED IN ZULU: "LET US KILL THESE DOGS." I AND MY WIFE DECIDED TO RUN AND HIDE IN A SWAMP. . . . WE HAD TO GO THROUGH A BARBED WIRE FENCE TO REACH THE SWAMP. I TRIED TO LIFT THE FENCE SO THAT MY WIFE COULD CREEP UNDER IT, BUT BECAUSE OF HER PREGNANCY, SHE COULD NOT. . . . WITH BULLETS RICOCHETING IN THE GROUND PAST ME, I HAD NO CHOICE BUT TO RUN AWAY, HOPING THEY WERE LOOKING FOR ME AND WOULD NOT HURT A PREGNANT WOMAN. . . . IN THE MORNING, I CRAWLED OUT OF THE SWAMP AND WENT TO A FRIEND'S HOUSE WHO LIVED NOT FAR FROM THE SWAMP. HE GAVE ME CLOTHES AND ACCOMPANIED ME BACK HOME BUT MY WIFE WAS NOT THERE. I FOLLOWED THE SAME ROUTE I TOOK WITH HER THE PREVIOUS NIGHT. I FOUND HER STILL LYING UNDER THE FENCE BUT COVERED WITH A BLANKET. I LIFTED THE BLANKET AND SAW IT WAS HER. SHE HAD BEEN SHOT AND HACKED.

Simon Moloi on the Boipatong massacre, recorded in Reporting South Africa *by Rich Mkhondo*

The feud between Inkatha and the ANC, which dated back to the mid-'70s, grew worse during the 1980s. With the release of Mandela, the killing – financed on the IFP side by certain security force elements – moved from Natal into the townships around Johannesburg. The violence drew the country to the brink of anarchy as the leaders lost any control over their supporters. Above: Street fighting in the townships between Inkatha Freedom Party and ANC supporters.

IQBAL MEER:

We couldn't understand when Madiba came out with the idea of reconciliation, firstly because of what he'd been through and secondly because the right wing was so strong, and the Nationalists had become so weak. There were bombs going off all over Johannesburg and we couldn't understand why he adopted this reconciliatory attitude – but we came around. I asked him several times about this and he kept on saying, "Now look, Iqbal, we must never forget what has happened to us, but we must always be ready to forgive." There was just no answer to that. "Always remember what has happened to you so that it doesn't happen again." I asked him where that vision of reconciliation came from and he said, "I've had twenty-seven years to think about it."

And it worked. On one visit to Johannesburg before Mandela was installed as president I entertained him at the house I always stayed in. We arrived back at my house, which was one of these typical South African compounds with six or seven town houses surrounded by high walls and barbed wire and gates: a white enclave, really. We had a lovely meal and typically Mandela went out of his way to thank the cook. After he had gone, there was a knock on the door. It was the chair of the residents' association, who said, "Did you know your house was surrounded by black people?" When I told them who had been visiting he said, "Why didn't you tell us? We would have liked to come and shake his hand."

Mandela has unique qualities: he's always ready to speak his mind, but he has the subtlety to negotiate. He never hides anything, yet he has this capacity to reconcile factions and get them together. For instance, although Chief Buthelezi's Inkatha party had fought with the ANC and felt the ANC treated him very badly, Mandela brought him into government. When the president leaves the country, you have to appoint an acting president – and who does he appoint? Buthelezi! Even if it was only for forty-eight hours, Buthelezi had real power. Who else would have thought of it? It was a masterstroke! I once heard him on the phone talking to Buthelezi and he used his Zulu nickname. It's that kind of tact and diplomacy that means that even Buthelezi holds him in respect.

EBRAHIM EBRAHIM:

I was sentenced to fifteen years on Robben Island in 1964. I was in the general cells, but I was on the disciplinary committee and we would regularly report to Mandela and the rest of the leadership, although we were not allowed to see them or communicate with them. Whenever there were political disagreements we would turn to Comrade Mandela, and he, together with Walter Sisulu, Govan Mbeki, and others, would then give us direction. Mandela was a constant source of inspiration to us.

After my release in 1979 I went into exile, but I was kidnapped, sentenced to twenty years, and sent back to Robben Island, this time to the isolation cells. Mandela had by then been transferred first to Pollsmoor and then to Victor Verster Prison.

When I got to the island I again joined the disciplinary committee and Mandela would call the four of us, as the leadership of the Robben Island prisoners, to his house at Victor Verster. There he would read all the communications that he had had with P. W. Botha and F. W. de Klerk and also would relate his contact with Oliver Tambo and he would then discuss with us what he was doing and why he was doing this. And he asked us to go

Left: Mandela visits a black township beset by the violence that was sweeping the country.

back to Robben Island and report to the general membership there to get their approval. You must realize that Mandela believes strongly in collective leadership – he would never take a decision without consulting.

When I was finally released early in 1991 Mandela came over to Ahmed Kathrada's brother's place and we had lunch. He said he was very happy that I was out of prison and that he expected to see me at the ANC office the very next day! He was a workaholic and he expected people around him to be workaholics as well.

I was at a meeting in Pretoria one night during the first government and he rings me at eleven o'clock at night, and he says he wants a report that day. I said, "Mr. President, I am here in Pretoria at a meeting and I can't give you that report now." And so he said he wanted it on his desk first thing in the morning. And I had to get up at five in the morning and write a report to see that it got to his office at eight o'clock! But he was a very friendly person to work with – he would always inquire about your health, your family, how you were doing, and you could go and see him in his office any time you wanted.

Those of us who had come in early in the struggle had always thought there would be a violent revolution and that we would be taking over Parliament, and we couldn't understand at first why we should negotiate and compromise. But Mandela said that if we wanted to build a common South Africa we had to get all the peoples of this country together. He said it was the historic task of the ANC to unite the peoples of South Africa around cultural, racial, and religious lines.

Internationally, of course, he also believed in peace and security and was very strong against the position of the United States vis-à-vis Libya, Cuba, and Iran. He said that when we were struggling, these were the countries that supported us and he said to the Americans and to Bill Clinton himself, you cannot choose our friends for us, we will choose our friends. Of course the Americans didn't like that, but because of Mandela's powerful influence on the world they had to accept what he was saying.

The negotiating process was a national imperative for Madiba. He wanted it to proceed in a smooth manner and he had taken many risks by moving ahead while he was still incarcerated and he therefore had a deep vested interest in seeing it bear fruit. So anything and anyone who sought to derail it or stand in its way was in a way taking a stand against Madiba personally. Madiba is what he is today because he was formed, shaped, and molded by the ANC, so when de Klerk attacked the ANC during the CODESA negotiations it was like a vicious attack on Madiba himself. As we listened with shock to de Klerk's pronouncements Madiba just started boiling. I was sitting next to him and he said, "Do you hear what he is saying? We can't allow that! We cannot allow de Klerk to get away with this, I have to respond." And in a way maybe I share the blame of winding him up, because I encouraged him and as soon as de Klerk stood down, Madiba immediately walked up to the stage, and you could see and hear his anger. It was right for him to respond in the way that he did because de Klerk's attack on the ANC was unjustified and it was like it was an attack against Madiba himself, and Madiba being the leader that he is, you don't take him lightly. There are moments when Madiba is pliable, moments when Madiba is compromising, when he understands the viewpoint of his adversaries and tries to find solutions that are mutually beneficial, but then there are moments like this when if he is pushed too far he hits back. In more ways than one can ever explain, that was a defining speech, because it immediately revealed the true character of Madiba and of the ANC in these negotiations. If it had not happened, I think our people might have lost confidence in the ability of the ANC to deliver a negotiated settlement.

To have been elected as secretary general of the ANC and to have had this confidence invested in me by the people of our country was a special privilege. But to have participated together with the other ANC leaders in the drafting of the constitution of our country was an historic honor. We had great and special moments of going through processes where we knew that every sentence we were pronouncing, every paragraph we were reading, every document we were looking at was going to cement and consolidate the political settlement that we were crafting. The many hours we spent in negotiations, endless hours arguing differing, were stepping stones, special stepping stones enabling us to move to our real historic goal. Roelf Meyer and I were put in a very special and privileged position where when all the negotiators succeeded in the task that they had they came to report to us. And when they failed to reach settlement they came to us, too, and we then tried to resolve what they couldn't resolve and if we failed we took it to Madiba and de Klerk. Our approach was always that there is no problem without a solution.

Madiba has the ability to listen. He listens to his colleagues, to his adversaries and in listening he is able to take in new ideas and new thoughts. Many leaders don't listen; they think they know it all. Where Madiba doesn't know anything he concedes it. He also admits when he is wrong. There are not many leaders who admit to making a mistake either. And he is forthright. I can tell you with certainty in all the years that I worked with him, I have never for one moment found him to be devious. Honesty, integrity, forthrightness, and truthfulness have been the foremost hallmarks of Madiba's make-up and it is a joy to deal with a person like him. His other important quality is loyalty to his friends. Madiba is loyal to a fault. Even when his friends and comrades falter and go wrong, if they have dealt with him with honesty and they have done some good, he will be loyal to them to the end. I couldn't think of a more loyal person.

Six weeks after CODESA 1, the National Party suffered a setback when it lost a by-election to the Conservative Party. Suddenly its authority to conduct negotiations on behalf of white South Africa was questioned. De Klerk called for a whites-only referendum. In March the electorate came out in his favor: sixty-nine percent wanted the process to continue. Mandela watched from the sidelines, interpreting the vote as support for negotiations rather than de Klerk. As his closest advisers knew, he was facing a crisis of another sort.

The *Sowetan* newspaper had picked up a story that Mandela thought would damage Winnie's appeal hearing. He tried to get the story killed, inviting the night-editor to his house to discuss his concerns. But the timing was unfortunate. That night Winnie held one of her wild parties, in celebration of Zindzi's engagement. The editor found a distressed Mandela sitting dejectedly in his study, while champagne corks popped throughout the house. The story appeared a few days later, along with accounts of Winnie's wild behavior.

Fourteen days later Mandela called a press conference to announce his separation from his wife. With Tambo and Sisulu on either side of him, he told the television cameras, "I part from my wife with no recriminations. I embrace her with all the love and affection I have nursed for her inside and outside prison from the moment I first met her." He rose stiffly, forlorn, despondent, his emotional distress barely concealed. "Ladies and gentlemen," he appealed to the journalists, "I hope you will appreciate the pain I have gone through."[15] No one spoke while he left the room. A few weeks later a miserable Mandela moved into a house in the upmarket suburb of Houghton, formerly a whites-only residential area, bought for him by a well-wisher. If there was a moment's reprieve in the gloom, it came when, for the second time, he met a woman called Graça Machel, and was greatly taken with her.

But all was not well on the political front. CODESA 2 started and deadlocked almost immediately. Mandela met de Klerk but the president was convinced the ANC was derailing the talks. Then, on June 17, an Inkatha war party, aided by white men with blackened faces, slaughtered forty-five people in the Vaal township of Boipatong. Mandela broke off talks. Both leaders accused one another of pushing the country ever closer to the brink of civil war. Three months later in the Ciskei, an ANC march went horribly wrong thanks to cavalier leadership when Ciskei soldiers opened fire killing twenty-eight people, many of them shot in the back while running away. Mandela was as angry with his own militants as he was with de Klerk.

In the aftermath of this catastrophe came a revelation in *The Sunday Times* detailing Winnie's dalliance with a lover and the fraudulent cashing of checks. The newspaper had acquired a letter from Winnie to her lover and published it in the public interest. The letter and the humiliation pushed Mandela deep into himself. Friends worried that he was about to suffer a nervous breakdown. Simply getting out of bed took effort. Slowly he compartmentalized the hurt and regained the iron in his soul. Depression and self-pity were luxuries he could not afford, especially as the Ciskei atrocity had brought the two sides back to the table. Later in the month, Mandela and de Klerk were again snapping and snarling at one another but Mandela's steely resolve won the day. The summit ended with a Record of Understanding that committed the government to a constitutional assembly and a transitional Government of National Unity.

Left: A somber Mandela at a press conference following the funeral of his longtime friend and comrade Oliver Tambo. "When I looked at him in his coffin, it was as if a part of myself had died," Mandela recorded.

Once again the political success was cold comfort. Just days later he sat unsmiling at Zindzi's wedding, an ostentatious reception organized by Winnie in the ballroom of the five-star Carlton Hotel. Toward the end of the party he made a speech lamenting his failures as a father, wondering if his children might have said, "We thought we had a father and one day he'd come back [from prison]. But, to our dismay, our father came back and he leaves us alone almost daily because he has now become the father of the nation."[16] It was a moving confession, indicative of how desperately he wanted to normalize the nation-family.

And indeed, secret talks at remote bush lodges continued between the negotiating parties throughout December, largely thanks to Mandela's ability to convince his comrades to accept various compromises. In February 1993, the parties announced an in-principle agreement to a five-year Government of National Unity. In April talks reconvened, but April was to be a black month.

Early on the morning of April 10, Chris Hani, a former MK commander, the general secretary of the Communist Party and one of the most popular black leaders, was shot dead in his driveway. Fortunately a neighbor noted the getaway car's license-plate number and contacted the police. Fifteen minutes later the assassin, a Polish immigrant, was arrested. Soon afterwards the police took into custody two members of the Conservative Party. But as the news spread, the country exploded in rage. Rioting and looting left seventy dead in the Cape and Natal. The panic among whites was as palpable as the anger among blacks. Mandela flew back to Johannesburg from Qunu to broadcast a message on national television. There was much at stake.

"Tonight," he began, "I am reaching out to every single South African, black and white, from the very depths of my being. A white man, full of prejudice and hate, came to our country and committed a deed so foul that our whole nation now teeters on the brink of disaster. A white woman, of Afrikaner origin, risked her life so that we may know, and bring to justice, this assassin."[17]

That the political leadership prevented the country from going up in flames owed much to Mandela's speech, and if there was a moment when he became the embodiment of the future it was then. Yet two weeks later he regarded himself as the "loneliest man in the world" when his long-standing friend, partner, and comrade, Oliver Tambo, died. "When I looked at him in his coffin, it was as if a part of myself had died," he recorded.[18]

When I first went to South Africa I remember standing on the seafront at Cape Town looking out at Robben Island and it seemed so impossible that Mandela would ever emerge from that place. We've gotten used to the idea of Mandela as one of the most famous faces in the world, but then even to speak his name in public was forbidden let alone to see his image. He was a spirit and a presence on Robben Island. During the state of emergency, however, something changed and his name was on everybody's lips. And then his daughter Zindzi read out his famous speech at that rally in Soweto in February 1985. "Your freedom and mine cannot be separated." It was one of the most inspiring things I ever heard, one of the most magnificent speeches of the twentieth century.

It was very clear at the time that Mandela held the solution. Everybody you spoke to in the emerging political organizations said, "Mandela." Many of them had never met him, many had been born after he'd been put away, but he represented such a powerful idea. There was also an acute awareness of the sacrifice he had made. Remember, many people had grown up seeing their parents forced into a position of compromise, joining the police, working for the apartheid state. Apartheid couldn't have survived without black collaboration. And to the people who had grown up with the shame of that, Mandela represented something pure.

My first glimpse of Mandela after his release was at a rally in a squatter camp in 1990. I had seen him on television surrounded by world leaders and here he was in the dust and misery of the squatter camp outside Johannesburg completely at ease with the people. He has a magnificently regal presence but there was a great humility in it. There is that paradox in his personality: humility in the presence of the poorest of the poor and a wonderfully regal bearing when he is confronted with his political enemies and anybody who might try to talk down to him.

I will never forget the day Chris Hani was assassinated. As I raced to the scene, I remember thinking that everything depends on how Mandela handles this. He went on television that night and told people not to be vengeful and to remember that the prize was a peaceful nonracial democracy. Had Mandela come out and said it's the fault of the whites, the people were so angry there would have been nothing the security forces could have done to stop an uprising. It was an amazing moment, truly statesmanlike.

But you can't be a statesman all the time and there were times when his animus toward de Klerk really showed through, not because of the past but because he knew that sections within the authorities were fomenting the violence and the government was doing nothing to stop it. I remember being at CODESA negotiations when Mandela stood up and went for de Klerk on stage. It was electrifying. My first reaction was this is not the time or place; South Africa doesn't need this. But when I thought about it, I realized there was a justifiable rage and anger about what was happening to his people. The public venting of anger like that was very necessary. It took a lot of the heat out of the situation – and Mandela's anger was never used to inflame.

He was capable, however, of making some very stinging attacks on the white population under de Klerk, but they were never racist. It was always because of an issue.

like violence or economic selfishness, never the color of someone's skin. You have to set what Mandela achieved in the context of South Africa, which was a society more bitterly divided by racial division and hatred than anywhere else. It could have gone atrociously wrong and that it didn't was because of leadership. Mandela took the simplest idea: we will create a society where you won't be judged by the color of your skin, you won't be damned by what happened in the past, and in which it will be recognized that every one of us has a human dignity that no state or force can take away. These are the kinds of grand concepts that get talked about by philosophers or universities or by theologians. To put them into political practice in a place like South Africa takes remarkable courage.

Mandela's not always peace and gentleness. But the one overriding point about him is that he engages with the real world as a human being willing to admit his own flaws. That's what makes him heroic. Being heroic is going into the dirty, nasty business of politics and doing the deals and facing the anger sometimes of your own supporters, facing the anger of your enemy and keeping at it with your eye on the overriding principle. He never forgot the overriding principle.

It's interesting that at the same time in the early nineties as Mandela in South Africa, you had Milosevic, Tudjman, and the other propagators of ethnic hatred in the former Yugoslavia, and the extremist regime in Rwanda. In Rwanda and Bosnia powerful men stoked up ethnic hatred and turned people against each other for the sake of power. Less than a month after President Mandela's inauguration I was in Rwanda and I couldn't believe I had gone from seeing such evidence of good and decency in South Africa into the hell that Rwanda was. The big difference was leadership: Mandela made the right choice, the moral choice, and saved his country. You just realized, driving through those roadblocks manned by men with machetes and bloodshot eyes, thank God South Africa had Mandela. To this day, when I contemplate the horror I've seen, the treachery and the betrayal practiced by politicians and the powerful against the people in this world who have nothing, I think of Mandela and I smile.

I saw Mandela the day he and Winnie announced they were divorcing. It was the one time I saw his self-possession slip in emotional terms. I could detect a great sadness. He was as gracious as ever but very shaken by it, desperately wanting not to believe it. That day we were sitting in his office, I could sense it broke his heart.

It's impossible to imagine what it must have felt like for Mandela to see his marriage disintegrate. It must have been excruciatingly painful. And the fact that he saved the country is no consolation to those in his family who lost out. There isn't a right or wrong about those decisions: it's just what happened.

His son and his mother died while he was in prison and yet he came out with that extraordinary capacity to forgive. We should all ask ourselves how would we have behaved in that terrible situation; and it is in asking that question that we begin to get the real measure of Mandela.

TONIGHT I AM REACHING OUT TO EVERY SINGLE SOUTH AFRICAN, BLACK AND WHITE, FROM THE VERY DEPTHS OF MY BEING. A WHITE MAN, FULL OF PREJUDICE AND HATE, CAME TO OUR COUNTRY AND COMMITTED A DEED SO FOUL THAT OUR WHOLE NATION NOW TEETERS ON THE BRINK OF DISASTER. A WHITE WOMAN, OF AFRIKANER ORIGIN, RISKED HER LIFE SO THAT WE MAY KNOW, AND BRING TO JUSTICE, THIS ASSASSIN.

Televised address to the nation by Nelson Mandela after the assassination of Chris Hani, April 13, 1993

Left: Tribute to Chris Hani, a popular black leader whose assassination caused mass unrest and threatened to send the country into turmoil.

Perhaps because of Tambo's death, Mandela pressed de Klerk and the government ever harder both at home and by rallying international support, particularly from Britain. He wanted an election date. In early June it was agreed: April 27, 1994. But triumph was followed by a slap in the face: the Appeal Court upheld Winnie's conviction for kidnapping but overturned the finding of accessory to the assaults. The sentence was reduced to a suspended two-year term of imprisonment and a fine of R15,000 (then over $5,000). (Five years later the evidence before the Truth Commission would not corroborate this finding.)

Across KwaZulu-Natal and in the townships, Zulu *impis* remained rampant, each death bloodily avenged by ANC supporters. Mandela, in turn, castigated the government's hit squads, Inkatha, and the ANC for the slaughter. There was another boil rising angrily on the body politic: militant right-wing Afrikaners led by a demagogue, Eugene Terre'Blanche of the Afrikaner Weerstands Beweging (AWB). Early in June he and three thousand supporters in khaki uniforms with swastika-like insignia on their sleeves stormed the World Trade Centre, smashing their armored car through the plate-glass entrance, urinating in the conference chamber, and shouting insults. Eventually they retreated outside to cook meat on barbecues and drink beer. Actions like this in retrospect make the AWB seem ludicrous; at the time they posed a very real threat.

The bloodshed – especially the killing of eleven Cape Town churchgoers when five men from the PAC's armed wing fired automatic weapons at a congregation of white and black people – gave the settlement a desperate urgency. In the discussion chambers the negotiators worked long hours, finally arriving at an interim constitution shortly after midnight on November 18, 1993. All that was needed now was the election.

For all the success at the World Trade Centre, and their jointly awarded Nobel Peace Prize that December, Mandela and de Klerk were locked in an increasingly stormy relationship. At the root of it was the fact that although F. W. de Klerk was the state president, many in the international community and within the country saw Mandela as the next, if not already de facto, president.

The historic year of 1994 began with a massacre in Cape Town, this time in a pub mostly frequented by white and colored students and young people. Again PAC gunmen burst in and sprayed the crowd with automatic fire, killing three young women and a nearby restaurant owner. The mayhem up to the election continued unrelieved: a litany of killing and bomb blasts.

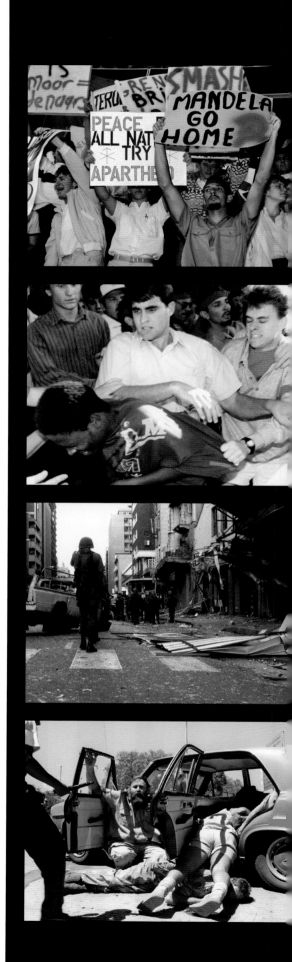

In March the AWB swaggered into the apartheid state of Bophuthatswana randomly shooting at people in the streets. Bophuthatswana police retaliated, shooting dead a number of bearded Afrikaners while the rest retreated in disarray. In the same month an Inkatha *impi* marched on the ANC headquarters at Shell House in downtown Johannesburg. Mandela warned de Klerk of Buthelezi's provocative action and de Klerk alerted the police who took no precautions. When some of the demonstrators fired at the building Mandela cautioned the guards, "You must protect that house even if you are to kill people."[19] At the end of the afternoon fifty-three lay dead.

The elections and the new constitution were anathema to Buthelezi and he had decided to boycott the election. Mandela tried his best to plead with and persuade him to change his mind, all to no avail. In this he was supported by de Klerk. Despite a standby team of international mediators led by Henry Kissinger and Lord Carrington, the Zulu chief remained unyielding. In the end it was a Kenyan professor, Washington Okumu, who convinced him to meet with Mandela and de Klerk, a meeting that led to a change of heart in Buthelezi. Inkatha was brought into the election seven days before it took place.

In the final weeks, despite AWB bomb blasts in and around Johannesburg which killed twenty people, the political spotlight was on Mandela and de Klerk. In a televised debate that went mostly in de Klerk's favor, Mandela finally leaned across and shook his opponent's hand. "We are going to face the problem of this country together," he said, effectively softening what proved a knockout blow.[20] Although this endgame had been rehearsed, it fitted with Mandela's style of conciliation, a lesson he'd learned as a boy from an unruly donkey. The donkey had tried to unseat him by backing into a thorn bush, much to his embarrassment and the amusement of his friends. Humiliation, he realized, was a cruel fate. "Even as a boy," he confided in his autobiography, "I defeated my opponents without dishonoring them."[21]

Left: With the release of Mandela, white supremacist militancy increased, mainly through the AWB and their leader Eugene Terre'Blanche. From top to bottom: Mandela was met with wide opposition from students when he went to speak at the conservative Pretoria University in 1991; white students attack a black student at the same protest; the aftermath of an AWB bomb outside ANC headquarters at Shell House in Johannesburg in 1994; the final outcome of the fiasco of Terre'Blanche's decision to take on the government in Bophuthatswana.

Above: Chief Buthelezi, leader of the IFP, and Mandela shake hands on a deal which finally brought Inkatha into the election just days before it took place. President de Klerk looks on, with Pik Botha to his right.

NADINE GORDIMER:

The night before the Nobel Prize ceremony, George Bizos and I and others came out onto the balcony of the hotel in Oslo to see this torchlight procession of young people carrying their joyous anti-apartheid banners and singing freedom songs. As we stood watching, de Klerk and his then wife Marike came out, and stood there with absolutely closed faces, lips down. After a minute they turned their backs and walked in; they obviously simply couldn't tolerate it. And I thought this was so blatantly ungracious if nothing else. Of course, he's changed a lot since then, but the fact is he was getting the Nobel Peace Prize along with Mandela, so it was not a time to show offense at the fact that people were singing freedom songs on behalf of the liberation movement that overcame him.

GLENYS KINNOCK:

I was there when Nelson Mandela received the Nobel Prize in Norway. I didn't know if I was excited or frightened and I was sure not a word would come out of my mouth. My eyes filled with tears. He must have gotten used to people reacting like that. What struck me was how normal he was and his warmth and that twinkling smile. I just feel so honored I have a moment like that in my life to remember.

There were very strong links between London and keeping the action against apartheid going. I worked with Adelaide Tambo here raising money. I loved Oliver. We always called him President Tambo, but there was never any doubt that Nelson was the leader in waiting. When freedom did come, there was this man in jail who was the icon, the hero.

Winnie was my hero as well then. We knew the tragedy of her life. You can't excuse what she became, but you can understand how difficult it was for her to deal with the agony she suffered. Nevertheless she was crucial in raising the idea that women could do something specifically to help other women.

I always identified quite strongly with the Black Sash movement. Because of the nature of the apartheid system it was white women who stood quietly and peacefully outside government buildings in South Africa identifying with the struggle of black women. A lot of the fundraising we did was for women. We used to raise money for sanitary towels, for books, and things for kids. It was a drop in the ocean but also a way of giving something tangible for political activity. When we were standing outside the South African embassy for hours in the dark with candles, it was the women I was thinking of.

From the very outset, the ANC understood that not only were women part of the liberation they also had to have a political role. The first speaker of the South African

Parliament was an Indian woman, Frene Ginwala. In other freedom movements once th
uniforms came off, women weren't expected to be part of things any more. All thos
women in the leadership of the ANC were very strong. It took amazing courage to provid
that kind of leadership and Adelaide Tambo was very much a leader alongside Olive
Mandela has played an amazing role in giving that message of sexual equality. He had
long time to think about these things and he understood that freedom and equality fo
black people did not depend on men; he knew it had to be everybody.

The first visit I made to South Africa was very soon after he was released. Barbar
Follet, whose first husband had been killed in South Africa, and I had decided we would g
as soon as they were free. When we arrived at the airport, the doors opened and there wa
Adelaide Tambo and about one hundred women all cheering. We hugged and sang an
cried. And she said, "Come on. We're going to visit Nelson. He says your first visit shoul
be to him." And we sat and had coffee and talked about old times, and what he knew abou
what we had been doing – it was amazing!

Mandela really likes women. He loves to sit and chat. It's lovely now that he has Graç
as his rock. She's wonderful and she cares for him in such a loving way. I marvel tha
Mandela who has spent so much time incarcerated and suffering has kept that strengt
alive. He is one of the most remarkable people who has ever lived. We sang, "You sha
overcome." And in the end he did.

*Left: In December 1993, Mandela and de Klerk were awarded the Nobel Peace Prize for their efforts in negotiating a pea
settlement for South Africa. Behind the scenes, the relationship between the two leaders was far from harmonious.*

Above: Archbishop Tutu watches the Nobel Prize ceremony on television from his home in Cape Town.

Above and following page: Mandela on the campaign trail and (right) casting his vote on election day at Ohlange High School near Durban. Mandela chose to vote near the grave of John Dube, one of the founders of the ANC.

WE HAVE STRUGGLED HARD FOR THIS DAY. FOR THE DAY WHEN ALL SOUTH AFRICANS – COLORED, AFRICAN, INDIAN, AND WHITE – COULD TOGETHER CHOOSE A GOVERNMENT THAT WOULD REPRESENT THE INTERESTS OF THE MAJORITY OF OUR PEOPLE.

Nelson Mandela's election campaign speech to the people of Manenberg, Cape Town

THE MOMENT FOR WHICH I HAD WAITED SO LONG CAME AND I FOLDED MY BALLOT PAPER AND CAST MY VOTE. WOW! I SHOUTED, YIPPEE! IT WAS GIDDY STUFF. IT WAS LIKE FALLING IN LOVE. THE SKY LOOKED BLUE AND MORE BEAUTIFUL. I SAW THE PEOPLE IN A NEW LIGHT. THEY WERE BEAUTIFUL, THEY WERE TRANSFIGURED. I TOO WAS TRANSFIGURED. IT WAS DREAMLIKE.

Desmond Tutu, No Future without Forgiveness

Left and following page: Whites and blacks line up for hours to cast their vote on April 27, 1994, in South Africa's first democratic elections.

NEVER, NEVER, AND NEVER AGAIN SHALL IT BE THAT THIS BEAUTIFUL LAND WILL AGAIN EXPERIENCE THE OPPRESSION OF ONE BY ANOTHER. . . . THE SUN SHALL NEVER SET ON SO GLORIOUS A HUMAN ACHIEVEMENT. LET FREEDOM REIGN.

President Mandela's inauguration speech, May 10, 1994

Ten days later, contrary to the prophets of doom, the election occurred peacefully. People who had waited all their lives to vote lined up for hours in the hot sun to cast their ballots. Mandela, ever aware of history and the power of symbolism, traveled to Durban to vote near the grave of John Dube, one of the founders of the ANC. "[It] brought history full circle," he wrote, "for the mission he began eighty-two years before was about to be achieved."[22] Five days later, de Klerk conceded defeat and the ANC threw a victory party at the Carlton Hotel. For the first time Mandela cried in public. He was cheered and adored and he shed tears. "People of South Africa," he called out, "this is a joyous night. I look forward to working with you for our beloved country."[23]

On Monday, May 9, 1994, the new members of parliament took their oaths and Mandela was sworn in as president. MPs and visitors in the public gallery rose to applaud and cheer, wail and cry. A solemn Mandela, with a white rose in his lapel, looked on. The island within kept him serious and dignified. Afterward, he was driven to the Grand Parade to address the crowds gathered there. He had stood on that city hall balcony four years previously: this time he came from parliament, not prison.

The following day he was inaugurated as president in Pretoria, an event that stopped the nation. Heads of state, dignitaries, and celebrities from around the world jetted into the country. For two days prior to the event Mandela had been receiving a stream of well-wishers that included Hillary Clinton, Fidel Castro, Yasser Arafat, Julius Nyerere, Prince Philip, and the priest who had been the refuge of Sophiatown, Father Huddleston. His invitation list included three of his prison guards. Yet this moment of Mandela's glory reflected the unhappiness of his family life. His daughter Zeni was at his side; his estranged wife, initially seated among the less important guests, had finagled herself into a place of more significance. Evelyn, his first wife, was not invited but then neither had she voted. Also missing was his son, Makgatho, who was preparing for a law examination in Durban.

Mandela is sworn in as President of South Africa.

But on that bright day he belonged to the people. Before the huge crowd of the invited and the public who had flocked to celebrate the first black president, Mandela was sworn in by Chief Justice Michael Corbett (who had once intervened to remove the brutal commander Badenhorst from Robben Island). Mandela's thoughts were again on history. He felt that the day had dawned because of the sacrifices thousands of people had made. "I was simply the sum of all those African patriots who had gone before me. . . . I was pained that I was not able to thank them and that they were not able to see what their sacrifices had wrought."[24]

Immaculately suited, wearing large glasses, the lawyer, the activist, the Black Pimpernel, the freedom fighter, the prisoner now the president took the oath. From his notes he read, "Never, never, and never again shall it be that this beautiful land will again experience the oppression of one by another. . . . The sun shall never set on so glorious a human achievement. Let freedom reign."[25]

Mandela sat down to applause and shouts as a praise poet declaimed:

You are a stalwart, you are a catalyst to unite,
You are the father of a new nation in the making.[26]

Overhead jets laid smoke trails in the colors of the new flag – black, green, red, blue, and gold – across the autumn sky. Helicopters, flags slung from their undercarriage, thundered past the grand amphitheater of the Union Buildings that for so long had been the seat of white supremacy. People in the crowd raised their arms and shouted. A woman sobbed, "Those planes killed my son. But now they belong to us. They belong to the people."[27]

FERGAL KEANE:

Seeing Mandela sworn in as president was the most extraordinary moment. I was sitting behind General Viljoen, the leader of the right-wing Freedom Front party, and I'll never forget that among the first guests to come in were Fidel Castro and Yasser Arafat and everybody was standing up including all these right-wing guys and clapping! Jets flew over trailing the new colors and helicopters flew over with flags and then Nelson Mandela came in. It was a beautiful moment, it really was. I saw these white generals and admirals and air force people now serving him, and the striking thing about it was that he looked as if he had been doing it all his life. It was effortless, absolutely effortless. You could tell from the reaction of the white officers that they had no problem serving this man because he radiated calm and authority.

Celebrations for the inauguration of President Mandela. Left: Jets fly over the crowds at the Union Buildings in Pretoria; Mandela and his daughter Zenani. Above: The "three presidents" of South Africa – former president F. W. de Klerk, and future president Thabo Mbeki raise hands with President Mandela; the "rainbow nation" celebrates the birth of South Africa's Government of National Unity. Following page: The "dancing president."

Once the rejoicing was over the business of governing began. Mandela was faced with a Government of National Unity and a cabinet made up of former enemies. Somewhat surprisingly, a camaraderie characterized the early cabinet meetings while the two sides settled down, with the Afrikaners expressing an earnest desire to cooperate. If there was any undercurrent, it was in the abrasive relationship between Mandela and de Klerk, but at least for the time being any grazes were minor. Similarly it was with his minister of home affairs, Mangosuthu Buthelezi.

In the official residences and the corridors of power Mandela got to know his staff, always surprising them with his astonishing memory for their names and family details. He was courteous and friendly, but there were black days when word would go out that Madiba was in a bad mood. More poignantly, the striking face with its broad infectious smile could be sad and dejected in the office behind the closed door.

Zindzi thought her father was lonely. To a close colleague he confided, "I have no friends."[28] And although he had no contact with Winnie, his obsession with her continued and he appointed her deputy minister of arts – an appointment he came to rue. At least he had his grandchildren even if, occasionally, he felt they were guilty of cupboard love. Not that his days were empty. His schedule was as punishing as ever and his presidency was as much about ushering the country into its new democracy as about international statesmanship. During his term Mandela would broker peace efforts in the Democratic Republic of Congo (formerly Zaire), Angola, Indonesia, and Northern Ireland. He traveled often, visiting the U.S. a number of times, on one occasion lending Clinton moral support during the time he faced impeachment. Finally, in his last months in office Mandela persuaded Qaddafi, a friend he had kept despite Western contempt, to surrender the men responsible for the Lockerbie bombing.

Right: Mandela won thousands of Afrikaner hearts when he walked into Ellis Park before the 1995 Rugby World Cup final wearing a Springbok jersey.

At home, Madiba magic was ever present: the icon of the emerging nation. He took to wearing distinctive bright loose-fitting shirts first introduced to him by President Suharto of Indonesia. When a child asked why he liked the style he replied, "You must remember I was in jail for twenty-seven years. I want to *feel* freedom."[29] More significantly, he donned the Springbok rugby jersey in a moment of sheer political brilliance at their victory in the 1995 Rugby World Cup, capturing the hearts of a largely Afrikaner crowd; the same year he visited Betsie Verwoerd, the widow of apartheid's architect, in the dusty Afrikaner-only town of Orania; he went to the Wilderness home of P. W. Botha to chat; he had tea with his prosecutor, Percy Yutar: he was set on nation-building.

Yet behind these efforts were the realities of politics and his divorce from Winnie which brought profound sadness and humiliation. His life roller-coasted through peaks and valleys.

In January 1995 Mandela learned that before the election de Klerk had granted thousands of policemen indemnity from prosecution. His anger almost ended the coalition. Two months later Winnie's house was raided by the fraud squad, amid allegations of shady diamond deals and financial mismanagement. Mandela dismissed her from government for flouting cabinet rules. Yet he could shut away the embarrassment and in the same month appeared relaxed and smiling when he received the Order of Merit from the British queen on a state visit to South Africa. From this high he plunged, in August, to instituting divorce proceedings against Winnie. There were rifts opening in government too. However, a woman had entered Mandela's life, Graça Machel, the widow of the Mozambican president Samora Machel.

The year 1996 heralded the start of a new order: personally and politically. In February, Mandela launched the Truth and Reconciliation Commission, which would lay bare some of the wounds of the past. The next month he revealed his own pain, telling the Rand Supreme Court about his life with Winnie: "The bedroom is where a man and a woman discuss the most intimate things. There were so many things I wanted to discuss with her, but she never responded to my invitations. I was the loneliest man during the period that I stayed with her."[30] His divorce settled, and Graça Machel still a figure in the background, Mandela sought company among the famous and the rich. He would clear space in his diary for pop idols like Whitney Houston and the Spice Girls; he was entertained at the stately houses of the mining Randlords, Harry Oppenheimer and Clive Menell. And he spent time at Qunu in his recently built home, a replica of the house at Victor Verster Prison.

DAVID OWEN:

I have never forgotten the speech Mandela made after he came out from prison. He said, among other things, "I am a disciplined member of the ANC." I remember thinking: this man is not going to be able to be depicted as the white man's prisoner. Nobody will be able to say he has made deals with them. Having spent so much of my time negotiating over these things I knew that he had to carry the ANC and that it was not going to be easy if he had appeared to be a soft touch in going along with the honeyed sycophancy that surrounded this deeply emotional moment. That made me believe this man was made of iron.

Although it was helpful to Mandela that there had been reconciliations in Rhodesia and particularly in Namibia, what happened in South Africa with the Truth and Reconciliation Commission was amazing. I studied it carefully because when Cyrus Vance and I found ourselves in Yugoslavia in 1992 we were asked by the international community to recommend whether or not there should be a war crimes tribunal. We recommended that there should, but we were very conscious of the arguments that were developing from the Truth and Reconciliation Commission approach.

The difference was that in South Africa there had already been a transition of power whereas there was still fighting in Yugoslavia. But the European tradition is more of a reach for the law and absolute justice for war crimes. The African personality has a lot to teach us about reconciliation. The Truth Commission has been a phenomenal success, especially the readiness to take it right out into the small towns and communities. This was not an elitist top-down process like the court in The Hague. I think it was right to have a court procedure in Bosnia, but I still wish it could have been matched with a Truth Commission in which you had to earn your amnesty by coming face to face with the crimes that you had been associated with. The construction of that was very clever and Mandela was the architect of all that.

Right: Mandela and Archbishop Tutu at the publication of the Truth and Reconciliation Commission's report in 1998. Established by Mandela in 1995 and chaired by Tutu, its purpose was to look into the crimes and atrocities committed during the apartheid era. Intended to build a new society without retribution, its basic premise was that any individual was eligible for amnesty if they were prepared fully to disclose and confess their crimes. Public hearings were held between 1996 and 2001, and victims were invited to tell their stories and witness confessions. In this way many families finally discovered how and when their loved ones died. The commission took statements from more than 21,000 victims of apartheid and received applications for amnesty from 7,100 perpetrators, of which only 1,146 were granted.

Where Mandela's greatness was shown was in the way he handled the issue of P. W. Botha's refusal to go to court. Mandela pleaded with him and eventually they forced him to go, but there was a technical mistake in the way they had made the application and he was released. Everyone was demanding that he be brought back, but it was Mandela who said, just let him go. We have made our point. There were many moments where Mandela showed a readiness to compromise, but his handling of P. W. Botha was extraordinary. He could see that the path to reconciliation was by just ignoring him, and letting him stew in his own juice. That is greatness.

IN A GARDEN THERE IS
ALWAYS ONE FLOWER MORE
BEAUTIFUL THAN ANOTHER.
YOUR LETTER IS THAT
FLOWER IN THE GREAT
GARDEN OF
MESSAGES OF COMFORT I
HAVE RECEIVED. . . . ONE DAY
WE SHALL MEET, EITHER
ALONG THE PATH OF
STRUGGLE OR ON THE
MAGNIFICENT ROAD TO
FREEDOM AND THEN,
LOOKING INTO YOUR EYES, I
SHALL BE ABLE TO EXPRESS
MY FULL GRATITUDE.

Letter sent by Graça Machel to the imprisoned Nelson Mandela in response to his letter of condolence on the death of her husband Samora Machel, the former President of Mozambique, in 1986

A relaxed Mandela with Graça Machel in 1997 at Heathrow Airport, London.

In May a new liberal constitution, regarded as one of the most progressive human rights manifestos in the world, was adopted by parliament. But the very next day, a disgruntled de Klerk took his party out of government. It wasn't exactly a blow for Mandela as it meant that the ANC could get on with the business of fashioning the country unhindered. But it was yet another betrayal.

By now, the man who still maintained his early morning exercise regime and made his own bed was letting his deputy president Thabo Mbeki increasingly shoulder responsibility for the daily management of government. He still retained a guiding hand over his cabinet, while Mbeki was able to feel his way into leadership: any mistakes being absorbed by the dazzling Mandela shield. Throughout the rest of the year and the next, he gradually withdrew from national politics, stepping down as president of the ANC at the end of 1997. That Christmas he spent with Graça Machel at Qunu: she had become his consort, her smiling dignified presence at his side both on international tours and at important state functions.

A few months later the couple moved into a new house in Houghton, and on Mandela's eightieth birthday they married. Despite rumors in the weeks preceding the event, the marriage was only announced once the vows were taken. The next day the Mandelas threw a lavish wedding reception that Mandela enjoyed hugely, doing the famous Madiba shuffle around the confetti-strewn dance floor.

True to his word, after the June 1999 general elections, Mandela handed over the presidency to Mbeki, clearly emphasizing that other aging African presidents would be wise to relinquish their bony grip on power. He had reason to be proud of the legacy he was handing on to his successor after the first five years of democracy. Perhaps too much had been promised, but much had been achieved. Improvements in housing, clean water, basic health care, land resettlement, and electrification were all underway, delivered by government departments which themselves had undergone radical reorganization.

As promised, in June 1999 Mandela handed over the presidency to Thabo Mbeki. Here he acknowledges the crowds at Mbeki's inauguration.

Although he claimed he was retiring, his mission remained that of an international peace mediator. At home he devoted time and attention to the well-financed charity, the Children's Fund, which had emerged from a pledge he'd given on Youth Day (June 16) 1994 that he would give R150,000 of his salary to aid children's welfare. As much of Graça's efforts went into child-related ventures, and the couple were a formidable force at raising funds. Late in 2001, Mandela also began campaigning for HIV/AIDS awareness, to fight a disease that affected millions of South Africans and was controversially handled by the government. For his troubles he would incur ANC and government wrath.

He also turned to his memoirs to fill in the years after his inauguration. But even while taking a break to write at a friend's bushveld lodge, his peace was disturbed by sad news: the death of his dearest friend Walter Sisulu. Immediately, Mandela returned to Johannesburg to the grieving household. As he was helped up the steps to the Sisulu house he looked suddenly frail, an old man. But some days later at the funeral he was concerned not only to mourn his friend but to celebrate a life that had been quietly brave and true. Poignantly, he said, "Those of us who are singled out to stay the longest bear the pain of seeing our comrades go."[31]

Eighteen months later, he had to bear the pain of his son Makgatho's death. Their relationship had long been difficult, and they had not spent much time together. Troubled by the anguish of familial duty that had haunted his life, Mandela spent hours at his son's hospital bedside. Then, in a bold gesture to destigmatize AIDS, a sorrowful Mandela, his eyes red with grief, announced that the disease had killed his son.

The moment was typical Mandela: it spoke of his strength of mind, his acceptance of his destiny, and his courage to face the consequences. It evoked a classical stoicism in the sense that the power to achieve one's ambitions, even in a world of human expedience, rests with the individual. Afterward he would continue to raise funds for his children's charity at international events, continue to inspire those who met him, continue to laugh with his grandchildren.

At Mandela's wedding reception, Thabo Mbeki had seen Mandela as King Lear, not the mad old man, but the benighted father who had sacrificed so much. On Robben Island, Mandela and his comrades had turned frequently to Shakespeare for solace and insight. One among them had a copy of the plays and they circulated this, each selecting a quotation. On December 16, 1977, Mandela chose a passage from *Julius Caesar:*

Cowards die many times before their deaths;
The valiant never taste of death but once.
Of all the wonders that I yet have heard,
It seems to me most strange that men should fear;
Seeing that death, a necessary end,
Will come when it will come.

IN A PEASANT SOCIETY A PERSON WALKING WITH A STOUT STICK, A STAFF – NO LONGER THAN AN ORDINARY WALKING STICK AND LESSER THAN A POLE – IS A COMMON SIGHT. ONE ALWAYS HAS IT AROUND.

IT AIDS ONE TO MAINTAIN A STEADY, FIRM GAIT. IT IS A CRUTCH ONE LEANS ON, HELPS YOU NOT TO FALTER IN YOUR WALK. IT IS ALSO A WEAPON TO HELP ONE DEFEND ONESELF AGAINST ANY UNFORESEEN DANGER THAT MAY ARISE IN THE JOURNEY. WITH IT ONE FEELS SECURE AND SAFE.

SUCH WAS XHAMELA TO ME.

Obituary tribute by Nelson Mandela to Walter Sisulu

PERSPECTIVES

AHMED KATHRADA:

I'm often asked if the many years Nelson Mandela, Walter Sisulu, our other comrades, and I spent in jail changed our thinking about the way to bring democracy to South Africa and if so whether we had any regrets about the activities and offenses that led to our lengthy imprisonment. It seems surprising to people that we could emerge from such hardship and humiliation and talk of forgiveness and reconciliation with the enemies who caused our suffering.

But the principle of a negotiated settlement did not originate on Robben Island. I have worked with Nelson Mandela and the other senior ANC leaders since the mid-1940s, and although not formally expressed, the concept of a nonracial and democratic South Africa has been ANC policy since its inception in 1912. It was these fundamental policies that Chief Luthuli, Mandela, Sisulu, Tambo, and the other ANC leaders sought to achieve.

For many years the ANC attempted and failed to achieve these goals through petitions, resolutions, and deputations. In 1949 these methods were replaced by a policy of boycotts, noncollaboration, and peaceful passive resistance, but this met only greater repression culminating in the 1960 Sharpeville shootings. Less than a month later the ANC and PAC were declared illegal. It was under these intolerable conditions that Mandela founded Umkhonto we Sizwe, the armed wing of the ANC. He never envisioned a military victory: MK was launched as part of the overall political struggle, which included the international community. When in the mid-1970s some overenthusiastic MK cadres arrived on Robben Island making wild assertions about imminent victory over the army, Mandela calmly brought them down to earth, pointing out that, in the armory of legitimate weapons of struggle, each had its place and that its use should be governed by time and circumstance. The goal at all times was to pressurize the enemy to the negotiating table.

Even after his release Mandela was careful not to call off the armed struggle prematurely, insisting that it remain in place until change was "irreversible." In the Pretoria Minute signed by the de Klerk government and the ANC on August 6, 1990, he committed the ANC only to a "suspension" but not a "cessation" of the armed struggle, and in fact the disbandment of Umkhonto we Sizwe did not take place until December 1993.

Mandela himself has always been committed to the principle of reconciliation, nation-building, and nonracialism. He played a key part in the drafting of the Freedom Charter, which reflected these principles, and at the Congress of the People of 1955, at which it was adopted, he and the other banned congress leaders invited all organizations and political parties, including the ruling Nationalist Party, to take part. During his evidence in the marathon Treason Trial, Mandela highlighted his commitment to nonracialism and reconciliation. And in his famous address to the court during the Rivonia Trial, in the face of a possible death sentence, he once again proclaimed it.

Thus, when Mandela emerged from prison, he did so with a commitment to negotiation that remained unchanged from the day we first met. In stretching out the hand of forgiveness and reconciliation, he and the rest of the ANC leadership, those who had been in prison and those who returned from exile, were basically continuing a policy that runs like an unbroken thread from the earliest days of the organization. It is in this consistency of purpose, coupled with his refusal both personally and politically to harbor feelings of bitterness toward those responsible for his suffering, that the seeds of his greatness lie.

RICHARD STENGEL:

When I visited Robben Island and walked into Mandela's little cell I just gasped. Mandela is not only physically large, he's large in every sense. And here was this tiny space that even a toddler would feel cramped in and somehow Mandela had stuffed his largeness into it.

One day when we were working on the book, Mandela wasn't feeling very well and he wanted me to come up to his bedroom. It was almost like a hotel room. There were hardly any personal effects in it. Everything was incredibly orderly and he was sleeping on one single side of this enormous king-sized bed, as though it was a tiny, narrow single bed. The rest of it was so perfectly made you could bounce a quarter off it. He would just slip out and fold the sheets over.

There's a lovely image in the Mandela documentary made by Angus Gibson and Joe Menell where they film him in Oslo when he went to receive the Nobel Peace Prize. He is shown making the hotel bed. He would never leave a room without making the bed. It was part of the prison experience that would refine him as an orderly personality. You have to travel light when you've been in prison for twenty-seven years. And he does.

Mandela is resilient in every way. I've never seen any human being as refreshed by a night's sleep as Nelson Mandela. You would see him the night before and think he's had it; he can hardly stand up; he is so tired. He'd have a night's sleep and the next morning he would literally seem twenty years younger. He is totally refreshed by every evening's sleep. Again that speaks of his natural resilience.

Mandela revisits his Robben Island cell in 1994.

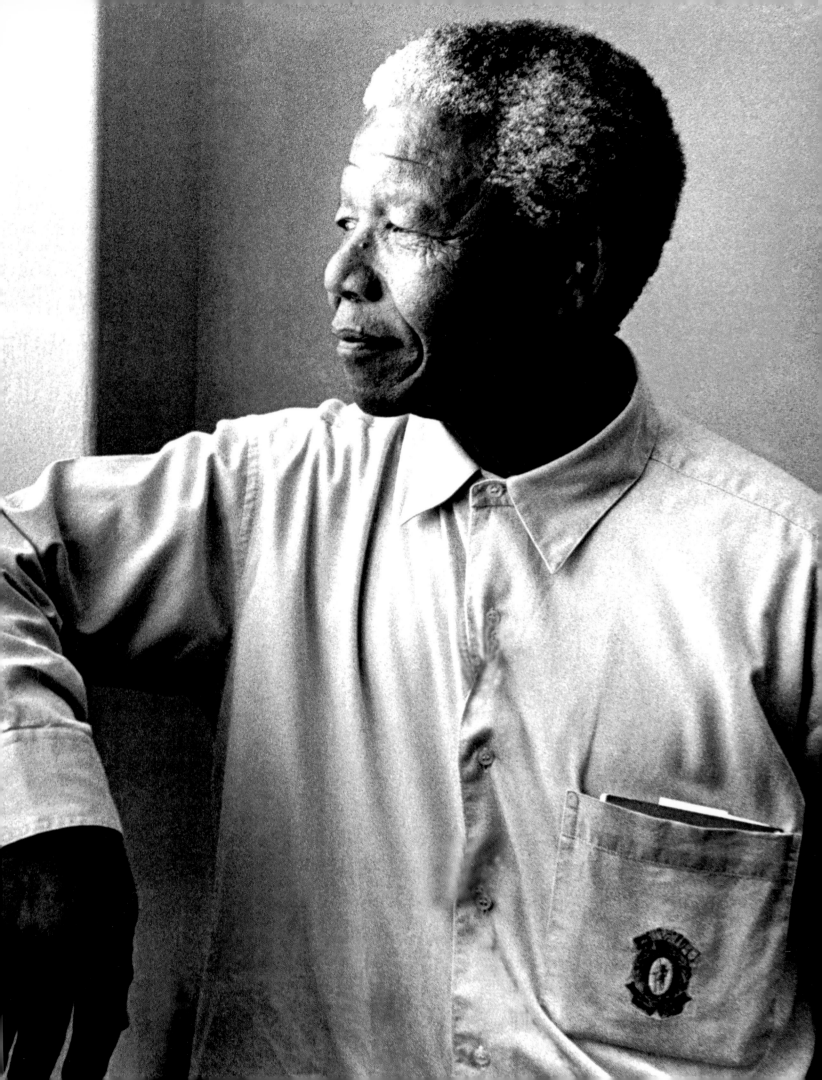

PETER PRESTON:

There were two nights in the *Guardian* office which had exactly the same feeling to them. One was the night the Berlin Wall came down and the other was the night Mandela got out. We ran with a huge picture of Mandela surrounded by people leaping up and down. It was impossible not to feel emotional.

In the early 1990s we merged the *Weekly Mail* in Johannesburg with the *Guardian Weekly,* and held a press launch. I met Mandela for the first time and what stuck with me was his gentleness and courtesy. He exudes a sort of calmness and gentleness, which is totally at odds with what you could possibly expect given the history. At around the same time, the *Mail & Guardian* sponsored a cricket match. About thirty people came to a buffet lunch, including Mandela. I had polio a long time ago and one arm is not tremendously good at holding anything, but as we were lining up for food, Mandela happened to be just behind me. As I was reaching for the salad, he said, "Can I take the plate and help you serve the food?" Afterward I thought I can't think of anybody anywhere else in the world in that position who would have been sufficiently aware to do that.

Mandela is remarkably media savvy. As soon as the government changed, the *Weekly Mail,* which had emerged from the anti-apartheid *Rand Daily Mail,* became the hound of the ANC, so it's not been best beloved by the administration over the last decade. Mandela was very understanding: he has a real laid-back grasp of the media and understands democracy in a way that a whole lot of Western politicians don't.

PALLO JORDAN:

After his release, Mandela came into an ANC collective where there was a strong tradition of first among equals. The only other people who were his peers politically were Oliver Tambo, Joe Slovo, and Walter Sisulu, who was his mentor. Everyone else had come into the movement after Mandela, and they had never been at the level of leadership he was before he went to prison. My argument was not that Mandela is our equal but that if you don't insist on that tradition you then endow the office of president with certain prerogatives that it never had before. It was clear that Mandela would never serve more than two terms as president of the ANC, so his successor would inherit these prerogatives and it would be difficult to reverse the process.

Then there was the age factor – and, I suppose, the baggage of Robben Island. One of the methods they had employed on Robben Island to deal with problems was not to sort them out in open, heated debate, but to do it in caucuses. Prison probably required that sort of management of conflict. But Mandela wanted to transfer that after his release when he was the leader of an organization operating in circumstances of relative normality and it was quite problematic.

At the first national congress held in Durban in 1991, for instance, an interesting argument developed on the floor of the conference to do with the position of women in the ANC. The Women's League had lobbied for a target of one-third of the national executive committee and all supporting committees to be held by women. There were just one or two people holding out in opposition to it, one being Terror Lekota, who had been on the island with Mandela and it was clear that nothing that was being said by anyone else was going to change his and his supporters' minds. Mandela got up and said, "Look, I appeal to Terror, why don't we solve these problems the way we used to solve problems on the island?" Now here was an issue of principle that was being debated publicly on the floor and he was appealing to Terror: don't let's debate this matter in public, let's go and caucus it somewhere.

It made for, I would say, a problematic style of leadership when he was president. In 1994, in preparation for the conference at the end of that year, he gave to me a submitted proposal of a recommended list of candidates. Instead of leaving it to the membership to elect whomever they preferred, he was trying to create a balanced leadership so all the provinces were represented, men and women, young and old. Interestingly it was something that Nehru had done, which was why it was called the "Indian Option." Quite a number of us opposed it on principle. I'd seen the consequences of recommended lists in Eastern Europe, and I used that exact example at the conference in arguments against it. It ended up in sort of stalemate in that particular session of the meeting, and then we had a tea break. And again, consistent with this "let's solve things the way we did on the island," Peter Mokaba and I were sitting together and Mandela comes over and tries to talk us around, and we said, "No, please, on this one you're not going to swing us!" And he retreated. In the end the thing was never presented.

In government, Mandela was less willing to back down in an argument, and that's what led to my first head-on clash with him. Again, it was issues of civil liberties, which to me are sort of life-and-death issues. He then called me to his residence in Cape Town for breakfast. At the end of the breakfast he says to me, "You know, I'll give you this friendly warning: in the national executive committee of the ANC you are there because the membership elected you, but in the cabinet you are there because I put you there. I just want to remind you of that." I said, "But why?" He said, "No, no, no, I've noticed you opposed me. In NEC, fine, but here just remember I should [rule]." I was a little bit mind-blown by the whole experience. In the ANC, you might be right, you might be wrong but it was a viewpoint that you held. So sometime after that I went to see him and said, "Look, you know, the price you are asking me to pay for a seat in your cabinet, I just can't afford." And, well, that was that. A couple of weeks later he sacked me! Now that really did shock me, and I think, on reflection, he felt that he had done the wrong thing which is why he brought me back a month later. But the whole encounter did sort of change the way I related to him.

Subsequently we had a meeting prior to the 1997 ANC national conference. Again he was trying, I think, to move the pieces on the chess board, trying to configure the leadership structures and he says to me, "There's one thing I like about you. You're not a yes-man. That's a good thing in a person, not to be a yes-man. But, you know, sometimes you've got to rein in your horses, put yourself outside of being such a stickler for certain things. Just be careful about that." I don't know why he was saying those things then, having been so rough with me, but my suspicion is that he was nervous about the succession and that was reinforced by what he said at a conference after Thabo Mbeki was elected. Among other things he said was that a wise president doesn't surround himself with people who agree with him.

AHMED KATHRADA:

I've always said you can't talk of Mandela without Sisulu. They complemented each other. Madiba wouldn't take a single step without consulting him. When he was president, often he would talk to Walter about issues. Walter was politically very astute despite having very little education beyond standard five or so. He was a leader but in a different way. People on the island with small or large problems would go either to Madiba or to Walter. Madiba would have a special type of person going to him because they always had legal problems – losing their house, families getting into trouble with the law, and so on. But everyone, no matter what organization, regarded Walter as the father. He was the most lovable man, a very humble person, very courageous.

Walter was very generous. He didn't know the meaning of private property and he didn't have much, but prisoners from the communal cells would smuggle themselves into our section and go straight to him. "We're short of everything," they'd say, so he'd empty his cell and then he'd walk into any of our cells, whether we were there or not, and he'd give away everything there too! Nobody would get annoyed. We all knew what Walter was like.

One can't talk of Sisulu, on the other hand, without Ma Sisulu. There was a chap called Sammy, who was being released after five years, and he managed to smuggle himself into our section to say goodbye. People said, "Look, when you get out, go to our houses, greet them, and say everyone's all right." So he went to Sisulu's house, passes on the message – and stays. Not only does he stay, but after a year or two he became part of the family to such an extent that he applied formally to change his name to Sisulu. People would come and go all the time in the Sisulu house. Ma Sisulu is that kind of person, a very caring person who would take people under her wing. And Walter was the same.

RUSTY BERNSTEIN:

Nelson Mandela, Oliver Tambo, and Walter Sisulu . . . together formed a remarkable triumvirate. . . . Their contrasting personalities complemented each other so fully that their combined influence . . . was far greater than the sum of their individual parts. . . . If great men ever mould a nation's history, the interconnection of these three great men shaped ours through the decades of struggle which led to the new South Africa.

Memory Against Forgetting

Above: Mandela and Sisulu embrace at the launch of Long Walk to Freedom *in 1994.*

Left, above: Mandela and an ailing Sisulu in 1994 at the launch of the biography Walter and Albertina Sisulu *by Elinor Sisulu.*

Left, below: Mandela and Oliver Tambo.

GILLIAN SLOVO:

Mandela is incredibly loyal. He has a very strong sense of: "Now your parents are dead, I am your father." He does act like a good father to many of the families of his old comrades, and he has a strong feeling for family in the wider sense of the ANC, a feeling that people are important. It has a slight religious edge, but it doesn't feel religious at all.

He also has that loyalty politically in a very strong way. When negotiations were about to start, de Klerk said he was not prepared to sit around a table with Joe Slovo, because he was a communist. Mandela's answer was, without hesitation: the Communist Party sustained us throughout those dark years and you will not tell me which of my friends I choose. He wouldn't waver on questions of principle.

Politically, Mandela has so much confidence. He does not feel threatened by other people's points of view or people's competencies. Joe said Mandela genuinely chose as his first cabinet those people he thought could do the job, not those he thought could shore up his position. We often think of politicians as people man-euvering to keep themselves in power but Mandela just hasn't been like that.

It's very easy to romanticize Mandela, but behind his incredible warmth and friend-liness is a man who was determined to make a revolution and turn that country around. The whole impetus of the Truth and Reconciliation Commission wasn't the pursuit of some abstract Christian goal, it was based on a very clear-sighted political goal. If the ANC had not conceded that the old apartheid government and its armed forces and police would not have to stand trial in the future for the things they had done, there would never have been an election. He is a consummate politician.

His ability to forgive was both genuine and politically very important. In his inaugural speech, he said that never again will South Africans have to "suffer the indignity of being the skunks of the world." Ordinary white South Africans felt a complete sense of relief. Many didn't actively support apartheid but they benefited from it, and now he was giving them a sense that they could have pride in their country. "You don't have to feel you have lost a battle. Welcome to the human race, blacks and whites together. We have done something magnificent." The use of the word "we" was incredibly important.

The fact that they won so completely and that Mandela went from being a prisoner to being a president made forgiveness easier. My father used to say that the fact that the people who killed my mother would never be punished was made easier because they were going to be forced to do something which was perhaps even more difficult than having to go to prison: to live in a society they had fought so hard against.

In the days before my father's death from bone-marrow cancer he spoke very little and toward the end slipped into a coma. Mandela came to visit him on the day which turned out to be his last. He sat by Joe's bed talking softly while Joe lay silent. About to leave, Mandela got up and resting his cheek against Joe's forehead, he said, "Goodbye, Joe," and Joe suddenly spoke: "Cheers." Later that night after Joe had died we stood in the living room, drinking a toast. We raised our glasses and repeated that one word, "Cheers."

Mandela came back at four the next morning to sit with us. The whole of South Africa seemed to arrive at the door over the following days to pay their respects, but Mandela had both a friendship with Joe and a tremendous respect for him and he had been a member of his government and so to us it seemed perfectly natural that Mandela would come around as soon as he heard – even if it was four o'clock in the morning. He started the conversation as he often does with a description of his travel arrangements, how having heard Joe was dead he had wanted to come immediately but there was no driver available. After a moment's silence he looked across at us and told us how one day he had gone to hug his grown-up daughter but she had flinched away from him and burst out, "You are the father to all our people but you have never had time to be a father to me."

Left: Mandela and Joe Slovo – Communist Party chief – had been close friends since their days together at Wits.

We all knew Joe was going to die but Mandela was obviously still very upset by it. Nonetheless, he took the time to speak to us, the three daughters of Joe, and acknowledge the difficulties that the choices made by his and Joe's generation had imposed on their children. There was a sort of joining together of his children's experience with ours. What he said was core Mandela: it was really a wonderful validation of us. It both acknowledged the heroism of their generation at the same time as the difficulties it had caused their children.

Before he died, Joe was awarded the ANC's highest medal, Isithwalandwe. Because they wanted to give it to him while he was still alive and they didn't have one ready, they first symbolically presented him with somebody else's. By the time his own was ready, he was dead, so Mandela decided to give it to us in a public ceremony. We decided May Day would be a symbolic moment, so we went with Mandela, who was in his first year as president, to the troubled KwaZulu-Natal. We all arrived at this stadium where there was a huge crowd. Mandela, who was surrounded by bodyguards, gave quite an angry speech about Buthelezi, who was causing a lot of problems at the time. Suddenly shots rang out and the bodyguards all surrounded Mandela and people began trying to move him out. But the people in the audience started shouting, "You're going to leave, you'll be safe. But after you're gone we're going to be slaughtered." So he instructed his bodyguards to keep back and he told everybody to file out while he stood there and waited until they had all gone. He wasn't in that much danger because he had these huge Rambo-like guards and there were Saracen tanks, but it was a very interesting symbolic way of saying I'm not going to leave you here to be slaughtered.

BETTY BOOTHROYD:

As Speaker of the House you are always invited to the state banquets at Buckingham Palace when heads of state are visiting which is where I met Nelson Mandela for the first time. These occasions are very grand – we girls all get our best evening dresses out and borrow diamonds and sparklers from our aunts and friends and the menfolk are in white ties. The next morning Mandela was coming to address both houses of Parliament in Westminster Hall. Usually heads of state address both houses in the Royal Gallery, but it wasn't large enough for Mandela because everybody wanted to come, so we had to have Westminster Hall. I was very scared because I had to take him down those treacherous steps in West Hall which have been worn down over hundreds of years. I knew that he had bad knees and he was quite frail and I was very concerned about him coming down those steps (and myself too for that matter!) with eight hundred people there and millions more throughout the world watching on television. So I said to him, "I just want to warn you about this. Take your time." And he said, "Yes, I will."

The next morning was lovely and sunny and there were thousands of people around St. Stephen's all cheering him and he said, "Isn't this wonderful? I never expected to have this sort of reception." They were just ordinary people who had come from their offices to see him. I said, "Now I reminded you last night. You take the lead and I will just follow on at your pace." I was in gold robes and I was very happy for him to go slowly because it's not very easy for me, but he turned to me and said, "Don't worry, Madam Speaker. After your warning I came at six o'clock this morning and had a look at the steps." That was typical of the man. His attention to detail!

With that, the state trumpeters started up and he took my hand at the bottom of St. Stephen's entrance and we walked up the steps and I helped him into his chair. It was the hands of history! The first woman Speaker in the history of our country and the first free president of South Africa! The West Hall is usually only used for grand occasions like the Queen's Jubilee and it's always a very splendid occasion, but this was electric. The lord chancellor made the speech of welcome and then I made a little speech and I think it was the best speech I ever gave. It was also probably the easiest, because it came from the heart. Clerks and civil servants never usually comment on anything you say in speeches, but after this one the head of my department, Sir Nicholas Bevin, said, "We are very proud of you." I shall never forget it. I almost cried.

Mandela made a long speech without a shred of bitterness. Here he was addressing what was the colonial power with Baroness Thatcher who, although it would not be correct to say she was sympathetic to apartheid, let's say she didn't put her head above the parapet, sitting on the front benches. And it was a very forgiving speech because we hadn't done very much as a country: there was no national boycott and Mrs. Thatcher had called Mandela a terrorist publicly. (The only question I ever put to a prime minister was to Mrs. Thatcher and I asked: "Does the Right Honorable Lady believe in one person one vote in South Africa?" And her response was, "That is completely the wrong question!" There was complete uproar.) But when he got up from his seat in West Hall and went down the steps, he went over to her and shook her hand.

I had the impression that Mandela really holds our parliamentary system in very high regard, and I think he was absolutely thrilled to be in that old hall which had witnessed so much history as the first free president of South Africa. He was also thrilled with his reception in London. I had said at the end of my speech, "On Friday, you will walk across to Trafalgar Square and into South Africa House as the first free president of your country to a house where you were once vilified." He couldn't believe the reception he got in the street. Wherever he went people came out to cheer and he was just overjoyed by this.

The most important events in my lifetime include the freedom of India, the fall of the Berlin Wall, and the ending of apartheid and the release of Mandela. His release is one of those events like the assassination of Kennedy: you will always remember where you were when you heard it. When we heard the news on the television we opened a bottle of champagne. Everyone rejoiced with him. He represents somebody who is never going to give up in the face of adversity. He represents the best spirit of human kind.

STUART HALL:

Mandela's Brixton visit in 1996 was an incredibly impressive and moving occasion. When politicians meet the public these days they are usually such inauthentic, stage-managed events. The fact he chose to go there, the way he behaved toward the crowd, and the feeling the crowd had for him created a real sense of connection. You felt he was addressing the long South African struggle. He was acknowledging that many people in the crowd had been involved in it in one way or another. They had followed his fortunes from afar and this was an opportunity to meet them face to face and say thank you for their support.

What people feel from him is authenticity or integrity. You look at Mandela's eyes and you can see he is as he presents himself: humane and fun. He can make jokes. People feel he's being straight with them and this is not a value now associated with politicians. He's not telling you what you want to hear; he's not telling you what suits his interests; he's speaking a kind of truth. Whatever you think about Mandela's values you know he would have gone to the death for them. He *has* gone to the death for them.

Mandela's charisma has a great deal to do with the respect for his political career. He remained an active presence during his prison years, a figure that they couldn't deny. To have come out after such a long time with his political instincts still in place, and to negotiate the way to a democratic South Africa by talking with his erstwhile oppressors is an incredible political feat. Normal politics don't work like that. Although South Africans have to remember apartheid and account for it, they don't have to remember that it ended in a vicious racialized civil war. I'm not saying everything is wonderful or that everything he did was right, but South Africa does have a sort of freedom to move on. Mandela had, from the early stages, an experience of the struggle which did not fit the convenient racialized view of what was going on in South Africa. His vision was one in which power had to shift to the black majorities but in which room had to be made for people who were, on another level, as culturally South African as he was.

The fact that Mandela is black is incredibly significant. Although there are many important black and Asian leaders, there are very few who command that kind of universal respect and no one else who has that capacity not only to embody and speak on behalf of the interests of the rising nations of the south but to represent a kind of consciousness which "includes people other than my people."

SIDNEY POITIER:

When I went to South Africa in 1949 to make the film *Cry, The Beloved Country* it was an eye opener. The preoccupation in the American press at that time was with what was going on in America, so South Africa was not as well covered then as it would become. I was shocked. I was appalled. I wasn't prepared for it. But the situation for blacks there came at me full force from the moment I landed. I wasn't permitted to stay in certain hotels. I had to live on a farm twenty-six miles out of Johannesburg; it was the only place apart from Soweto I could stay in.

While I was in South Africa, I was driven by an Indian man called Dickie Naicker, a member of the Indian National Congress. On one occasion he asked if I would like to go

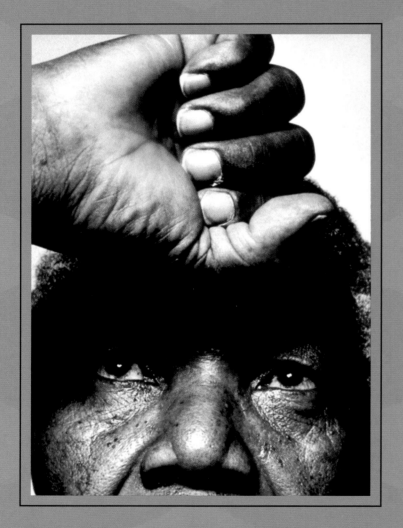

to a picnic somewhere in the forest. He wouldn't tell me much, only that there would be political people there. In the event I met various African National Congress members there and I've often wondered if Nelson Mandela was among them and whether our paths crossed then.

I came back to America having had the kind of exposure that left a real imprint. As the apartheid system continued, there was more coverage in the press. We read about Nelson Mandela, we knew what he was, we knew about the trial, we knew about the government in exile in Zambia. The way the American and British governments protected South Africa's apartheid government was really deplorable. People at the highest level in both governments behaved in ways which were just plain offensive in any human terms.

When Mandela came to the States for his first visit I was filming in California and the mayor of Los Angeles asked if I would be there. There were hundreds of people. Nelson was on his way to a balcony to greet the crowd outside and I was in the crowd alongside a carpeted walkway about ten rows back. He was looking at everyone and waving and then he saw me and said, "Sidney!" He stopped his procession and started toward me and I started toward him and when I got over to him he gave me a hug. It was quite moving, quite a moment. He must have recognized me either from films he'd seen or from magazines, but he saw me and picked me out in a crowd!

In 1997 I was asked to play Mandela in the film *Mandela and de Klerk* and Mandela invited me to Cape Town when I was filming. I went with my wife and daughter and her friend and it was a once-in-a-lifetime occasion. You only come close to great men very rarely in the course of an average life. We sat and had tea with him, listening to him. He was extremely gracious and we came away feeling completely justified in the feelings for him we had carried in our hearts.

We have met on a few occasions and have spoken about some of my films, probably ones like *In the Heat of the Night, To Sir, With Love, Guess Who's Coming to Dinner,* and *The Defiant Ones,* perhaps films in which he felt some kind of affinity with the roles. I was interested in hearing from his lips about his prize-fighting days. I was never prize-fighting material, but I did enjoy it. Our more in-depth conversations centered around my work. He knew he'd had my support all along and he was genuinely interested. I understood his interest because in a subtle way there were certain resemblances between his life and my own. I am not comparing myself with him at all, but fundamentally we were passionate people, passionate about our individual lives. At the point where he could make a living he became a lawyer, but if he were to be only what the country permitted him to be it would have been to function within a very small cage and he could not live with that. In my life I could not live with the strictures that were placed on African American actors in America especially in films and theater. I went into theater and film knowing that my chances were extremely slim, but I was determined that the industry would accept me on my terms rather than my having to exist on theirs. I couldn't do it. My chances were very slight, but I still couldn't do it. There is that kind of similarity. The industry in America was not an industry that welcomed African Americans in the manner it welcomes others. In South Africa we all know what the restrictions were.

When I read the script of *Mandela and de Klerk* I knew what I wanted to do with the character. By then I knew what he looked like, and how he sounded. I had seen how he had behaved over the years. I had to focus on the principles underpinning his morality, his integrity, that kind of view of the world that does not ordinarily come from men who have been incarcerated for twenty-seven years. There was something extraordinary – beyond our understanding – about the way he could endure all that and stand up and walk away. Obviously there was a powerful amount of courage native to the man that enabled him to endure what he endured, but courage doesn't come by itself, it is buttressed by other human qualities. There is a sense of decency about him that is stronger than courage, a sense of fairness. You could smell it, taste it, feel it – in the way he went about controlling his life under the most awful circumstances. Although he has a great sense of humor, he is a very serious man, and his laughter is part of his seriousness. He is not a frivolous person, but he has that breadth which can incorporate being light and humorous and making jokes from time to time. But these are flourishes around the gem.

Of course he has made a contribution to the status of black people, but I can't imagine there are too many people in the world for whom Mandela would not be a hero. Although we are characterized by differences of religion and culture, we are all one family and he has made a contribution unlike any other. When an individual astounds with his greatness, when he puts his life on the line, it serves to strengthen all of us. It leaves us with a little more courage, a little more insight, and a little more determination to exemplify that kind of integrity, fairness, and passion ourselves. He has been of such great service to us; it is our responsibility to carry forward that respect for what he has done.

PRINCE BANDAR:

Mandela is larger than life as a human being, and the more you know him the more he grows in your eyes. I have met with kings, prime ministers, leaders of communist parties, presidents and the aura around him is the most powerful I have ever seen. One of my favorite stories about him is when I introduce people to him he will always start by saying: "My name is Nelson Mandela!"

It is just typical of him to underplay his contribution to the resolution over Libya because what he had actually contributed was really the big effort. Colonel Qaddafi and his government decided they would like to have just one channel to deal with America and Britain over the issue of Lockerbie and preferably somebody who has a strong relationship with the West. And when they approached us we thought the best way would be to have a joint effort with another partner who also has credibility, so who better than South Africa and President Mandela? He thought it was a great idea and that it fit within his political outlook, sorting problems, helping the underdog as he perceived it, lessening tension between nations so people can co-exist and concentrate on more positive things. And I thought that between Saudi Arabia, which can take the conservative side of politics, and Mandela and South Africa, which can take the other side, we can cover both wings of the political arena and create this important middle ground.

Right: Mandela is led down the steps of his Pretoria residence by his former cellmate Ahmed Kathrada while Prince Bandar accompanies Graça Machel, on Mandela's eightieth birthday.

He immediately understood this and in fact right there and then he wanted a plan of action – what are we going to do tomorrow? Who should I contact? What do you need from me? Initially we just asked for his consent to approach the parties quietly and came to discuss it with Tony Blair and then with President Clinton. They were also looking for a way out and it was also important for them to have someone they trusted who could play a positive role. So once that was confirmed, we made a plan and the South Africans designated Professor Gerwel and the Crown Prince designated me and we then started moving to Washington, London, and then to Libya. Mandela came to Libya a couple of times, first to really give it a push with Qaddafi, and then the last visit was to seal the deal we announced a few weeks later.

Mandela is truly a wise man. This is an overused phrase for older leaders, but he has a simple powerful logic. He's a trained lawyer, but he has such a strong sense for justice. It's very powerful and it guides his political compass. He doesn't shy from calling a spade a spade, either to Qaddafi, Clinton, or Blair if he thinks their logic or their rationale is not fair. It's what I call standard "Advantage Mandela!"

In Africa, if you are a tribal head, you are supposed to be a father to everybody and part of your duties is to listen to all parties and bring people together. There's no doubt that the mentality of being the father of the tribe, not taking sides, has stuck with him. He just cannot stand injustice. For me, Mandela is regal. He has a sense of history, he's dignified, and I think he would have been a prince regardless of his background. Just like the movie *A Man for All Seasons,* this is a man for all generations, for all time. I think Mandela would have been a great human being whether it's in our century or the first century, or the sixteenth century, he's one of those people who comes once in a millennium.

DESMOND TUTU:

Mandela looks wonderful when he is very formal and wears a suit and tie, but he says he enjoys the freedom of his Madiba shirts after having been in prison where he was always being regimented and told what to do. He feels good that he can thumb his nose at all the rules, and now of course he has set a trend! It's all right when he teases me and says he can't understand a man who wears a dress in public being fussy about his own sartorial habits, but I still don't think too highly of his sartorial taste.

TONY BLAIR:

Meeting Mandela is like meeting no other politician or no other person. You feel you are meeting a legend. He has an extraordinary manner, at once very humble and ever so slightly unnerving because he's always making jokes. He's got a very naughty sense of humor and he was very funny around my little boy Leo. When he comes to Downing Street, he makes a point of shaking hands with everyone – the people who bring the tea, the people who are at the door, the police – and he always jokes with them. Actually I think he mocks his own position a bit: he's fundamentally a very rational human being and therefore takes it all with a pinch of salt.

Whenever Mandela and I speak on the phone he will always say to me, "You will send my very best wishes to the queen!" He has very much that sense of: "We'll keep to the proprieties and rules and everything" and it's genuine. And when he's here, we will often see the queen. He's someone who would have risen to the top in any political system anywhere. He is a very shrewd guy as well as being a great one.

In one of our early conversations I asked Mandela whether he did not feel hatred toward the people who imprisoned him during the most active and formative years of his life. I remember him saying, "What's the point? That's how the country was at that time, but now it's different." He was almost impatient to get on and talk about what was going to happen now. It is that absence of bitterness and the extraordinary desire to heal divisions that marks him out for people and why I think they feel they can invest so much affection and admiration in him. It's not just the fact that he spent so many years in prison – political martyrdom can happen, sadly, to a lot of people – but what marked him out was the magnanimity in the way he came through it. There are conservative politicians here who will talk of Mandela in awed tones, who, in the 1980s, if they were not actually accusing him of being a terrorist, were opposing sanctions. One of the things he did was allow people to forget their own involvement and because he didn't recriminate they feel they can be part of it too, whatever position they had at the time.

Mandela has certainly got the greatest moral stature of any political leader of our time, but he's also someone with a very shrewd appreciation of politics who showed tremendous political skill in maneuvering South Africa through the process of change. He didn't become a politician because he was imprisoned; he was imprisoned because he was a politician and he can relate to other leaders in a political way. I've never ever found him in a situation where he's been saying, "Well, look I'm a saintly person and you're just a politician." He's not like that at all. He's got a healthy respect for politics and political leaders because he knows decisions are difficult to take. He doesn't exploit his position to cause difficulties and that's why his relations with other political leaders are good. It's not just "Mandela magic"; he's not going to grandstand at your expense.

When he was involved in trying to get a different state of relations between ourselves, America, and Libya, he was very savvy about the political difficulties and creative about ways we dealt with that. The Libyan regime had been sponsoring terrorism and was responsible for the death of PC Yvonne Fletcher here and so it was obviously not an easy political call and it was not worth embarking on unless Qaddafi was serious – and what Mandela did was persuade me that he was.

It's probably true that if it had been anyone else I wouldn't have taken so much notice, but because it was Mandela you pay special attention. And his judgement about Qaddafi

turned out to be accurate, which is that Qaddafi had seen the world changing and didn't want Libya becoming a focus for extremism. On at least one occasion Mandela visited me straight after seeing Qaddafi, and once I could see a way through, then obviously I was discussing it with President Clinton and then with President George W. Bush. I think that showed both Mandela's vision but also his practical grasp.

Even when there have been areas where we have strongly disagreed, like Iraq, he's had a very good analysis of what the problems were from my perspective as a leader and has never been personally difficult about these things. On the contrary, he has offered good advice all the way through. In a funny way he reminded me of the pope in this. Pope John Paul II was also totally opposed to the war, but similarly had a very subtle and perceptive view of what it was like to be faced with these decisions. Even if they disagreed politically, they were going to be personally supportive and that makes a lot of difference. It is then a position from which they can influence the aftermath because you think, "These are not people who just want to make a political point. They're actually just trying to work their way through it and do the right thing."

Previous page: Mandela and Tony Blair in front of No. 10 Downing Street.

Left, above: Mandela with Blair and Cheryl Carolus, South Africa's High Commissioner in London.

Left, below: Tony Blair, with ex-presidents Mandela and Bill Clinton at a ceremony to celebrate the partnership between loveLife – an organization battling the HIV virus in Africa – and the Nelson Mandela Foundation.

Mandela has real qualities of judgement and empathy for decision-making. He once went into quite a long discussion of de Klerk and it was almost as if he was persuading me how difficult it had been for de Klerk! From a political leader's point of view it makes him stand out because you know he is not simply sitting saying the world should be perfect. He's not that sort of person at all. But I guess he is driven in the last instance by peacemaking. He's not someone who would be comfortable with the use of force. I think he's seen and done enough of that in his own life.

Mandela's strength of leadership on the whole question of Africa has been very important. He's passionate about Africa but also its responsibility to change itself. He is one of the toughest on the need for strong measures against corruption and has really no time for any wallowing in the past or any attempt to justify repression or bad government on the basis of colonialism. He has strongly supported the Commission for Africa. Because his standing is so high he's able to say things that other people would find quite hard: he can say how there is much about Britain he admires whereas other African political leaders, even if they thought it, would be a bit hesitant about saying it. But the great thing about him is he's able to say it and everyone says, "Oh, fair enough," because it's him. I think he does it in quite a naughty way actually.

Mandela will remain a great icon. The fact that a black man is the most respected figure in the world is also part of what he has brought about. The fall of apartheid was not only important for South Africa and for the world, but it also symbolized the last bastion of all that terrible bullshit you used to get about genetics. When apartheid fell, it was as if racism all around the world was suddenly put in the past. It's not that racism doesn't exist today, but it isn't countenanced as part of respectable society. I think he will be seen as a symbol of equality between the races in a multiracial world where people are respected irrespective of the color of their skin.

ANTJIE KROG:

When I was seventeen, Dr. Verwoerd was stabbed in Parliament and the teacher called me and said they wanted to bring out a special edition of the Kroonstad High School annual and wanted to open it with a poem on his death. Would I write it?

I went home and tried. Well, I didn't actually really know who Verwoerd was. However, three years later I wrote a poem about the possibility of living a life, an unrestricted life, with black and white being peaceful. The last stanza was, "where black and white hand in hand / can bring peace and love / in my beautiful land."

It was published in the school annual and parents protested, saying this is undermining the whole policy [of apartheid]. It was like a small-town gossip campaign. A stringer, an independent journalist living there, picked it up, and she spoke to several people and they all confessed to her, "*Ja*, I think it's very wrong," and someone else said, "It's such a good family. I don't know where she comes with these ideas," and someone said, "There must be something wrong with the school or at the house." That's how it manifested itself in the newspapers.

I had a completely free life in many ways. I read whatever I wanted. Writers and artists were friends of my parents and came to the farm. Thinking back, although it was never political, it was radical in lots of ways, but then it was also very restrictive. You respect the authors. You respect the politicians. We didn't necessarily realize it was a contradiction until this happened. And then my parents clamped down, because my father was called by the *Broederbond* to explain how I had ideas like that.

It was only twenty years later at the release of the first political prisoners that I learned that the poem was read on Robben Island by Ahmed Kathrada who copied it into his notebook. At the rally he said that the discussion around it was that if young Afrikaner girls were writing these kinds of things then they would be free in their lifetime. So one can assume Mandela was one of the readers.

I was asked by the comrades in the small town where I grew up to perform at a "Free Nelson Mandela" rally in the early eighties. It felt as if you knew everything about him but you realized you really knew nothing. And that's when I became aware that he must be physically somewhere and he must have a mouth, and a nose, and hair and hands. He must be a human being; he's not a symbol. I wrote a poem about Mandela being in the town: that he is sitting in the taxis, that he is sitting with us on the benches, that he is walking in the dust; that he is smelling the thorn trees; he looks out over the river; he lifts his fist in the jails; and he will come and free us there in Kroonstad. I decided to do it in Afrikaans, and the other poet then shouted it in Sesotho. There was a huge crowd and it was quite a steep learning curve in performance poetry . . . it was participation poetry. At one stage in the poem you would say, "This is Man-del-a. The face is Man-del-a," and then they would shout it back as a refrain after every stanza and it became a different entity altogether.

I saw him physically for the first time at a big rally held in Bloemfontein after he was released. You know, of all the physical appearances that exist in the world, the most fitting was given to Mandela. His physical appearance fitted the image, and the dreams that people had of him. We waited for hours in the sun and when at last he stood in that gate and he had a biscuit-colored suit on and a thin red tie it was like the most exquisite thing you've seen in your life. He was tall, he looked young, he looked strong, he looked so proud. There was a sort of boldness around him. God, we went crazy; it was like seeing an angel. And you know, the indigenous poetry, the praise songs about Mandela, always describe his physical body. There's his lip. And the mole on his upper lip. And in one of the poems they say his upper lip is "like being cored by a star," like you do with an apple, you take out the core.

The first time I was physically introduced to Mandela, not under my married name and not as part of a press corps, was when I was asked to be one of the translators for *Long Walk to Freedom*. When he heard "Krog" he stormed out to Zelda and said, "Do you know who's sitting inside?" And he comes back, and says, "I didn't know you were so young. I want to marry you!"

After that I was invited with my whole family to have dinner with him one evening here in Cape Town. He sat down and asked every child what their name was, what they were doing. And then he started by talking about Afrikaners and the first time he had contact with them on Robben Island. He then raised his glass and said to my children, "I invited you tonight. I want you to know that you should be very proud of your mother." Just for one moment it seemed that everything made sense to them, a moment of clarity for my children. Mandela tries constantly to say that he brings to

Mandela meets Betsie Verwoerd, widow of apartheid's architect, in 1995 as part of his efforts at nation-building.

political leadership an African world view point, but we don't want to hear that. We want to see him as an exception, so that we all can claim him. If he is part of a group then we must claim the group and claim what he says the group stands for. I think at times it exasperates him that we insist on taking him seriously, but not what he stands for.

All his actions are rooted in the notion that he can only become his fullest potential if his community becomes their fullest potential. By the end of the twentieth century black people had put on the table a fundamentally different but important alternative on how to deal with a past of injustice and racism. And yet the world persists in regarding Mandela as an icon rather than a great leader. They want to hold his hand . . . his face . . . take his photograph, but never, never to understand what he is trying to convey. There is a universal refusal to accept his soul.

NADINE GORDIMER:

The amazing thing about Mandela was that all the years that he was locked up on the island he was somehow with us, very much in the world. Indeed the impact of his personality predates his imprisonment and his release. It is interesting to look back at him on film footage and in various writings and see the way his independence of mind emerged. It is not usually characteristic of people who become great leaders because they tend to take a line and follow it absolutely rigidly, but Mandela even now takes an independent stance – on AIDS for instance, where he is sometimes very much at odds with the government. Of course, he is in the wonderful position now where he is virtually untouchable, unlike others who don't do what is politically correct for the time.

There is this sense of universal wonder about Mandela, and yet he's got this playful side, and he uses it quite skillfully. Once I had a problem in getting to see him about something very important and then finally he invited me to breakfast. If he really wants to talk to somebody he'll invite you to a very substantial breakfast – he eats salad plus all the other things that all of us might nibble and it's good to see him nourishing himself properly. I said to him, you know really, it was difficult to get to see you, whereas you are always perfectly available for instance if I had been a Spice Girl or somebody. And, of course, he laughed like anything. So there are these funny little things with him, and he'll always tease you a little bit, which is so nice. And he's got natural warmth. As soon as you appear, this memory image seems to flash back to him. His memory is absolutely phenomenal.

It's customary now for him to say whenever he's interviewed, "Well, I'm really getting very old now, but there are still things I have to do." But he has such belief in life and the love of life that he has gone on somehow living fully. He believes that you don't just give up: if you have the ability you must use it, if you have the spirit you must exhibit it. Of course, he will leave us a material legacy, for instance with the Children's Fund, but like some wonderful grandfather, he leaves us another in this incredible reality of a man who has suffered absolutely everything personally as well as politically: personal loss and disappointments as well as years and years of imprisonment.

It's difficult to assess the impact Mandela has had on writing in South Africa, because unless you are going to write a biography, you are not concentrating directly on your heroes. But I suppose the very fact that you are living at the same time as this remarkable person, does have an effect. In my novel *Burger's Daughter,* one of the characters remarks about living through the apartheid years: there was this terrible time, but wasn't it wonderful to be born in a time when there were heroes and heroines? So I think something to do with our idea of the times we've lived through colors our work. There's a little flame burning there and that flame was of course Madiba, and some of the others lit up around him.

I kept thinking over the millennium, as we changed from the twentieth century to the twenty-first, that out of those lists of people who had "made" that terrible century – one of the most violent ever recorded – two stood out like Mount Everests above the others. One was Mahatma Gandhi, and the other was Nelson Mandela. Gandhi's whole life was that long march to freedom, and Mandela's too has been the same – and I think he has not stopped marching. He does not turn away from the huge problems. Gandhi and Mandela, the two indisputably magnificent great people of the last millennium, are unique in their credible moral and humanistic stand. And we've still got Madiba with us.

ALI BACHER:

South Africa was readmitted to the International Cricket Council in London in June 1991 and the World Cup was coming up in February of 1992, but there was no discussion at all about our playing in it. In August of 1991 I brought out Clive Lloyd, the famous West Indian cricketer, to help promote cricket in the townships, and he was terrific. He wanted to meet Mandela so we went to Shell House and there was a huge contingent of Swedish media there. And the door was open and I saw him for the first time. "Cricket chaps, come in," he says, and we all go in and the Swedish media follow. He complimented us on the cricket development program in the townships. After about two minutes someone said to him,

"What about South Africa playing in the world cup?" And he said, "They've got to play," and that was it. Lobbying began within twenty-four hours and we played in the world cup. It was as simple as that. That was his muscle.

He's an extraordinary person, in his capacity to forgive, not forget. When it came to the Rugby World Cup, Mandela went out publicly to support the Springbok emblem. It was the main item on the news and I was asked what I thought. I said, "Look, we have enormous respect for Mandela, but . . . we're not going to support it." Mandela phones me next morning and invites me to lunch and for forty minutes he explained in simple terms that he knew how important the Springbok emblem in rugby was to the Afrikaner and he wanted to thank them for supporting him in democracy. How can you argue with that?

At the final of the Rugby World Cup when he walked onto the field, the crowd was ninety-nine percent white, mainly Afrikaners. And they were chanting, "Nelson! Nelson!" Mind-boggling. Before our team went onto the field he went into

Mandela holds the World Cup trophy after Sepp Blatter announced South Africa's successful bid to host the 2010 Soccer World Cup.

the changing room with his Springbok jersey. And Steve Tshwete tells me that on that morning Madiba had phoned him and said, "I want a No. 6 Springbok rugby jersey." Steve said he phoned somebody and got a No. 6 jersey, and they gave it to him. And then unannounced he walked onto the field wearing it. There was no way they weren't going to play for him.

And just to convey how his touch with kings, prime ministers, with the man in the street never changed: when we used to bring him to the cricket matches the first thing he'd do was go to the catering area. We're lined up – administrators white and black – but we've got to wait. And when we would introduce everyone one by one, he would use a stock phrase, "You might not remember me." You might not remember me! He phoned me just before the World Cup in January 2003. He said, "Ali, I just want to wish your team every success." I said, "Thank you very much, Mr. Mandela." He said, "My name is Madiba, Ali." I said, "Mr. Mandela, where I come from, if you respect somebody enormously you call him Mr." In a second he came back with, "Ali, where I come from if you don't call me Madiba you're not regarded as a true friend of mine." So he's just got this common touch.

In February 1992, I invited him and Walter Sisulu to a triangular one-day competition between South Africa, Pakistan, and the West Indies. At teatime there was a request that he come to the change room and meet the teams – you can't believe the emotion when these chaps were shaking hands with him. There were two ways back to the Long Room and Mr. Mandela chose to go onto the field and a chap who must have been five yards away threw an orange at him, like a missile. It missed him and I caught it. Mandela just carried on as though nothing happened. Just before he left, about five o'clock, I said to his main security bloke, "Did he see that?" He said, "Of course he did." I said, "Why did he stay so calm?" He said, "He wasn't going to show that person he was ruffled."

He's the greatest fund-raiser of all time. Whenever the phone rings and it's Mr. Mandela, the corporates say, "What's it going to cost us this time?" Once he asked to see me and he said, "Ali, you would agree that I've helped you chaps with cricket?" I said, "Of course, Mr. Mandela." He said, "Look, I've got this school in the Northern Province. I'm going to need a million rand to upgrade it." He said, "I think it would be nice if cricket gave a million rand." So I brought this up at the next board meeting and someone said, "We're not a charity organization. We have to administer cricket." So I said, "If you don't want to give it, you've got to tell him so yourselves." So Ray White, the chairman, said, "All those who are opposed put up their right hands." And of course, nobody did. Can you imagine if they had refused? It would have been around the country in a second. Nobody could say no.

SEPP BLATTER:

On May 15, 2004, Nelson Mandela triumphantly raised the FIFA World Cup trophy into the air to mark the historic occasion of the announcement of South Africa as host of the 2010 FIFA World Cup, the first ever to be held on African soil. As the crowd cheered and cameras flashed, our eyes met and I could see how important this moment was to him for he knew that this victory belonged not just to his country but to all Africans. In 2010, football will bring the world to Africa and bring Africa to the world. Long an enthusiast of the beautiful game, Mandela shares with me the belief in sport's incredible power to unify people in peace and friendship as well as its ability to promote important social and educational values as a "school of life." Thus, on behalf of the one billion people in the international football (soccer) community, we pay tribute to Mandela – the statesman, hero, and icon who has had such a profound impact on the world. He is a man with spirit which no walls can contain, with vision that no darkness can extinguish, and with a heart that knows no limit to the love it can give. I thank you Nelson, my friend.

SHAUN JOHNSON:

In 2003 and early 2004 extensive discussions were held by Mr. Mandela with his advisers and his family about his schedule of public appearances because it was absolutely unsustainable. It is not hyperbole to say that he remains the most desired and beloved human being on this planet, so something had to be done to give him a more reasonable schedule, without by any means removing him from the public eye, because he wouldn't want that. He doesn't want to go behind walls. He spent quite long enough behind walls. So, he first explained why he had to pull back and be more selective about what he wouldn't do. And for those of us who worked for him, for the first time in his life the question became, "Would he enjoy it?" rather than, "Must he do it?"

However, if he was going to make an announcement that there was to be a severe scaling back of public appearances – what we now jokingly refer to as "the retirement from retirement" – we felt, all of us collectively, that he had to say what happens with the Mandela legacy. So then came the announcement of how the three legacy organizations that bear his name – the Children's Fund, the Nelson Mandela Foundation (NMF), and the Mandela Rhodes Foundation – would work together. Part of Mandela's legacy is about children, families, and family values, and the Children's Fund is a mature organization that has been going for ten years. It has an endowment; it has its programs on the ground. The Nelson Mandela Foundation in Johannesburg is unique among the three, firstly because it controls his diary and his life, which is a very time-consuming business, but also because its programs express his legacy in terms of reconciliation and dialogue. It came into being in 1999 essentially in his postpresidential phase to give him some kind of infrastructure. The Mandela Rhodes Foundation is very new and my brief is to develop programs to build exceptional leadership capacity among Africans. It's modeled on the Rhodes Scholarships, but these scholarships aim to keep talented young Africans in Africa, at African institutions.

Mandela made this announcement on June 1 and said, in so many words, "Don't call me, I'll call you," and then, "these organizations are now the organizations that will express my legacy."

I've had the sense, often, while observing him in a private moment, of the loneliness of true greatness. And the greater the person, the lonelier his position is. His position is so elevated that he has to pay a heavy price for the normal human pleasures that keep us going: family relationships, just interacting normally with people, or having them interact normally with you. And I say that notwithstanding his utterly unbelievable ability to electrify a room. I'll never forget the night at Westminster Hall when the Mandela Rhodes Foundation was launched. There was a very charged atmosphere in the hall, and when Mandela came in about ten minutes late – quite unbelievable, you can't choreograph this – the great and the good of London just basically lost it. They were almost ululating.

Jakes Gerwel often says that Nelson Mandela had a sense of his own destiny and he really did from his chiefly days in the Transkei. So, while you could say that his amazing charisma is a gift, it's also one he is aware of. He's evolved into the kindly old uncle that just smiles at people but there's so much more to it beneath. If you look at him in 1990 you have a celebrity prisoner of a small, in economic terms, country at the southernmost extremity of the world's poorest continent. An amazing media story, but at that stage you

don't have the world's greatest icon. But when he came out and because of the decisions he took and the way he led his movement, he began to grow hugely in terms of world stature. Mr. Mandela understood that you then enter life's accidents, and he seized the opportunity. From the 1990s onward, the world grows more and more dangerous, more divided in every way. There are fewer and fewer major world statesmen from one of the superpowers or one of the G8s who have unqualified respect. It's almost as though the world needs a Nelson Mandela.

People still ask why he stepped down after only one term. And of course, part of the answer is – and it's highly admirable – because he wanted to show that not every African leader is a president for life. But secondly, in my view, he outgrew being president of South Africa at that point. I think he understood that perfectly: the icon that outgrew his country.

In the later years his political interventions have become fewer and fewer. But they are pointed and timely. It has reached the point now where the Mandela phenomenon has become such that he has merely to be somewhere to have his effect. He actually doesn't have to say anything any more. Often, he completely changes the atmosphere just by being there. I think South Africans should be immensely grateful that by a total accident of world history, he's ours.

NTHATO MOTLANA:

Madiba is quite something. He is such a peacemaker, and he doesn't often lose his temper. He's under such control. During the first elections in 1994, I visited him just to make sure he didn't get too excited. I remember sitting with him on the afternoon of April 28 when he heard that in parts of KwaZulu-Natal the ballot papers had not reached the polling stations and that the ANC and the other parties had agreed that the elections would be extended to the following day. He was so angry with some of the incompetent officials all over the country. When he came out of prison, one of the conditions he had was cardiomyopathy, which means enlargement of the heart, so I wanted to check his blood pressure. We were sitting in the lounge and I said, "Madiba, shall we retire to your bedroom so I can check your blood pressure?" He says, "What bedroom?" and he takes off his shirt and I check his blood pressure. And at this exciting, awful, stressful moment it was 120 over 80. I've never forgotten that – Madiba's blood pressure was like a sixteen-year-old's!

Another time, we were in Ireland and Madiba had gone from one meeting to another. It was 3 P.M. and he had had nothing to eat or drink and he was due to go to address a stadium full of young people. And Winnie was mad. She said, "Are you trying to kill my husband?" And so we all sat there arguing about whether Madiba was going to have lunch – by now it's almost four o' clock – and saying he must get dressed, all making a noise, and Madiba is snoozing! And after a few minutes he turns and says, "Let's go to the stadium. We are going to meet the youth of Ireland." He is under control at all times. Apart from that moment during the televised debate with de Klerk, I have never seen him lose his cool.

Madiba's memory is also something else. He's a wonderful raconteur. He can tell you what happened in the Youth League in 1944. My sister-in-law Helen Gama acted in *King Kong,* and sang a song called "Strange Things Happen in the Dark." Mandela was at the first night back in 1959 and he heard this little girl sing this song. When he saw her after his release from Robben Island, he remembered! Helen almost collapsed – that kind of memory is unbelievable.

I was Madiba's personal physician until 1998. I was very privileged because it allowed me to travel the world. But I was also privileged, you know, to be called out in the middle of the night. One time he phoned me at two-thirty in the morning because his grandson wouldn't sleep, kept on scratching his nose. And I said, "He's only scratching his nose. Please let me come and see him in the morning." But I could never say no to Madiba, and so I got up to go and see this little boy, and when I got there, he was fast asleep!

ZELDA LA GRANGE:

I first started working in the president's office in 1994. I was twenty-four at the time, and all I knew about Mr. Mandela was that he had been in jail for a very long time. I had thought of him as being a terrorist, because that was what I was taught to believe when I was much younger. I was just doing secretarial tasks there and did not really have any contact with him to start with, but about two weeks after I began, I ran into him as he was going out of the office. He started chatting to me in Afrikaans and made me feel at ease immediately.

It was a great honor to be working for the president. I found the work very interesting and challenging and, in terms of my general views on the world, I changed enormously through studying Madiba. After you see someone like him behave in a particular way for a few times you come to a conclusion that this is actually the way it should be done and it enriches you in a way no formal education could.

All the decisions Madiba took throughout his presidency were taken with reconciliation in mind. The smallest things, from deciding who to shake hands with first when he arrived at a meeting to who he would pose for a photo with first. These were all part of his vision for the country. He had obviously made a very well thought through decision before he was released that violence was not going to be the solution to South Africa's problems. He had the insight and the foresight to realize that bitterness was not going to change anything in history either and that rather he should look forward.

Mandela and Zelda la Grange at a Tri-Nations rugby game.

I think that anyone given my job would see it as a challenge and give two hundred percent of their energy and effort. I don't see it as something that people should envy – it's got its pros and cons like any other position. And in terms of its highlights, it's not necessarily moments like meeting a particular president that stand out for me, it's the smaller things. For instance, Madiba would notice a poor man that he used to know years ago, and he would ask us to do something for him and we would arrange donations of clothes, food, and so on. To see that man's life enriched, to know that it's within your power to do something for someone is really the sort of thing that makes the job.

Madiba is not a difficult person at all. There's a beautiful Afrikaans word for it: *gematigt*. "Moderate" probably doesn't describe it as it is described in Afrikaans, but it is close. He is moderate; he is not impulsive. If you have been working with him for a long time you know exactly how he's going to react to something. For instance, he hates it when people don't pay attention to punctuality, and he's very, very strict on discipline. But he's a human being, and deep inside he's a grandfather. He will sometimes surprise us by requesting to meet very simple people who other people wouldn't pay attention to. In the early days, he would go through the newspaper and notice people who had achieved something and ask us to arrange a meeting so he could congratulate them. And then after a while we could open the paper and predict who he would want to speak to. He leaves more of this to other people now, but he still surprises us by asking to phone someone he has read about.

If I could I would like to share the opportunity I have had to work with Madiba with as many people as possible so that their lives could be affected the way mine has been. If I had to explain that, I would start by talking about the sacrifices he has made because you cannot move him from the history or the role he has played. But I would also put that in context, because although we should give him all the credit for his leadership, as he is always the first to admit, it was a collective effort. I don't have any special abilities or anything; it's Madiba once again trusting and believing in the abilities of a normal human being and giving me that opportunity.

RICHARD ATTENBOROUGH:

I first became involved with Mandela at a great distance over making the film *Cry Freedom,* based on the life of Steve Biko, and also dealing with Donald Woods, the white editor of a South African newspaper. Before embarking on it I wanted to know whether Madiba would approve of a story which did not laud the black activist but lauded a partnership, a duo of conviction – a black man and a white man. Through Oliver Tambo and Thabo Mbeki I got messages back from him in prison saying everybody including Madiba was in favor. His answer was that if we couldn't manage a partnership between white and black, there was no future for South Africa. I was very touched about that.

Sheila and I first met Madiba in London at the home of Adelaide Tambo. He knew about my devotion to Gandhi, so immediately we had a rapport. He was extremely effusive about how important it was for South Africa to recognize those outside Africa who had been advocates of anti-apartheid and said something which is the only lie I've ever heard Madiba utter, which was that the impact of *Cry Freedom* on white South Africa in relation to ending apartheid was more valuable than any speech he'd made! There never was a more monstrous exaggeration but it was typical of Mandela.

Madiba always said to me, "You are not to come to South Africa without letting me know." So when my wife and I were in Johannesburg we rang his office, but learned that he had gone to the Middle East for an operation. We were packing to go to the airport on Saturday morning when the phone rang and they said, "The President has just landed and he wondered if you could call by the house on the way to the airport." So we went there and eventually down the stairs came Madiba in his dressing gown and pajamas. Obviously he's just had a shower after landing. "Hello, hello. How are you both?" he said. "Sheila, you must be one of the first white married women who found me in my pajamas." Wonderful!

He demonstrated his concern again after Sheila and I lost our daughter and granddaughter in the Boxing Day tsunami. He was in England shortly afterward for the Make Poverty History campaign and I got a phone call: "Could I go and see him?" I wasn't in London, I was at Sussex University where I am vice chancellor, and I was disappointed. But two days later the phone rings and on came Madiba from South Africa. "Oh, my dear Richard, I so wanted to see you because I know what the loss is. And I wanted to hug you. I want to hug you. I want to hold you in my arms. And I am so disappointed. But I will hug you with my voice and the next time we meet each other, I will hold you in my arms because I feel so sad and so sorry for you." It is absolutely typical of him. He didn't say, "I want to offer you my condolences." He said, "Richard, I want to hug you. I want to hold you in my arms."

There was only one other person I would have wanted to meet as much as Mandela and that was Gandhi. What I admire about both is they are such remarkable humanitarians. Every person who breathes has a resonance as far as Madiba is concerned. His bewildering ability to express forgiveness is comparable to Gandhi's. Unequivocally I feel really privileged just to have shaken his hand. But to have been embraced by him and to have him suggest that something I have done is worthwhile means as much to me as anything in my life.

KEN LIVINGSTONE:

During my time as leader of the Greater London Council, companies like Barclays were making a fortune out of the exploitation of South Africa by the apartheid regime. The city of London had its snout firmly in the trough. I felt therefore that we should use the GLC to mobilize opinion. We commissioned the bust of Mandela which stands outside the Royal Festival Hall, and I remember saying at the unveiling that it was an absolute tragedy that South Africa had been denied the chance to be led by this man. I don't think we got the statue quite right, looking at it now, but it was the best we could do given that we were working off pictures twenty years old. It never occurred to me that he'd get out alive. I assumed the only way apartheid could be changed was by armed struggle and a catastrophic loss of life. I don't think anyone conceived that someone who had been in prison for so long would have the sheer force of personality to go through this huge process of reconciliation. I don't have the capacity in myself to be that forgiving.

I am desperate to make sure the new statue of Mandela gets built in Trafalgar Square. Not one person in ten thousand knows who the statues standing there now are of, but in a hundred years people will still know who Nelson Mandela was and what he represented. When he was born, he was a citizen of the British Empire, so Nelson on his column and Nelson Mandela on his pedestal would in a sense encapsulate the beginning and the end of the British Empire. There's a real story for people to tell as they take parties and families around.

Right: Mandela dances to the music of a local band during a township visit.

Mandela represents the very best of what it is possible to get out of a political leader. No one else has that scale of imagination and compassion for the people who oppressed him. Of all societies, the idea that people in South Africa after all that apartheid represented could come to live together was the most unlikely. Not only have the whites not lashed out in fear, but the vast multitude of impoverished black people has been prepared to wait and trust. I find that quite remarkable.

Perhaps what Nelson Mandela has is just a richer and more sophisticated understanding of human nature than most politicians are blessed with. The very painful process in Northern Ireland and the Middle East desperately needs someone of his stature to carry both communities, but there's something abut the route you have to follow in politics that almost weighs against someone like Nelson Mandela coming in. Even in societies where violence isn't the norm, politics is about calculation and marginal advantage more than appealing to people's rationality and humanity. There's a total lack of integrity in modern political life. That's why we want the statue in Trafalgar Square. There is no other politician you can say this about: Mandela embodies integrity.

RICHARD BRANSON:

We were approached to fund the memorial to Steve Biko – a statue in East London in South Africa – and the day Peter Gabriel and I went there was the most incredible experience of our lives. It was 1997 and we were on a platform in front of about one hundred thousand people along with Madiba and Buthelezi and all the leaders of the various African movements, many of whom were Mandela's political enemies.

Mandela stood up and just ad libbed. The speech he gave was fantastic, turning to each person on the stage and then asking the crowd: "Shouldn't we be working together as one?" And the crowd was shouting "Yes!" The other leaders were squirming in their shoes! Most people see him only as a grand statesman doing good things, but it was interesting to see what a wily politician he could be. Then I suggested to Madiba that Peter should play his wonderful song "Biko." There was no band or equivalent, but he took the mike and those one hundred thousand people just sang along. Then the crowd started surging and the platform started collapsing and we only just got off in time before it did. It was an incredible day.

Mandela devotes himself to extracting money from people for his various causes. Once in London he brought along Graça and his children to lunch and I was expecting the worst. We got through the first course. We got through the second. We got through dessert. We were on to coffee and I began to think I'd gotten away with it. Then Madiba turns to me and says, "I had lunch with Bill Gates last week and he gave me fifty million dollars!" It was a very expensive lunch! Another time I dealt with him was the 46664 concert. His prison number had a lot of emotion attached to it and will be remembered long after Madiba has gone. We thought that a concert would raise awareness about AIDS. Mandela is ready to do all those concerts I think because he realizes what an important part musicians played in the effort to get him released. It is lovely seeing him dancing – he used to dance beautifully. That certainly gets the crowd going.

Like a lot of other people I did not think war was the way to deal with Saddam Hussein and Madiba, too, has spoken out strongly against it. When it became obvious that England and America were bent on war, I thought the only way of stopping it would be to give Saddam Hussein a graceful way out. Like an animal trapped in a corner, you had to give him a way out. The only person in the world who had a chance of persuading him to step down with his head held high was Madiba, and I contacted him. He said in principle he would be willing to do it if he had Kofi Annan's and Thabo Mbeki's blessing. Kofi agreed and we got a plane to stand by in Johannesburg, but by the time Mbeki came through the bombing had started. Who is to know if Mandela would actually have managed it? But there was a reasonable chance.

During the 46664 concert, Peter Gabriel and I were wondering what might have happened if Madiba had gone to Iraq and what we could set up that might have a lasting effect in the future. In an African village when there is conflict, people turn to the elders, so we set up an organization called "The Elders" and asked Madiba to be the founding elder. Certain people across the world command enormous respect and the idea is to bring them together to resolve problems. It's going to be very, very difficult to replace Mandela, but we wanted to get something going in his name which at least has his blessing.

GORDON BROWN:

What came to mind the first time I met Mandela, was a quote: "like a prince entering the room." It was partly because of his height, but equally because his demeanor is so striking and so friendly. Here is this enormously warm, friendly personality who also carries authority and stature. When you have read, seen, and talked about him over so many years, to meet the man who was the symbol of the anti-apartheid cause is not only awe-inspiring but humbling. I felt in awe of him.

Mandela is a source of personal inspiration. He was prepared to die for his beliefs at a time when the system wanted him to beg. He refused to do so and that is an illustration of the courage that he has shown throughout his life. It's the courage of someone faced with terrible odds who says quite honestly, "It was not that I was not afraid, it was that there was something more important that made me triumph over fear." Because the values he represents were so important to him, anything became possible. And that sheer courage is an inspiration to millions. But it was the lack of bitterness that accompanied the creation of the new South Africa that is absolutely critical to his success.

In 2005 Mandela was in London at the time of the G7 meeting of finance ministers. When he was in Lancaster House, he talked as equally to the waitresses serving the tea as he did to the heads of government. It would be easy to understand if he felt he didn't have time to talk to everyone, but I saw firsthand how he treated people equally, neither condescending nor arrogant. It's his innate sense of equality that lies behind his humanity.

In his personality Mandela reflects an African view of community which I think is going to become more important in the development of the continent. Graça Machel put it very well when she said, "In Africa, we are better at caring than you are" – which is almost certainly true in terms of how communities support individuals. In his autobiography Mandela writes that when he went on his travels he wanted to rediscover the roots of African culture because he'd been brought up in a British missionary school. He had to rediscover the strong sense of community and the idea of caring about people that is central in African culture – there's an African word for it: *ubuntu*. Mandela is community minded; his very personality expresses the importance of altruism, the sense of some-thing bigger than yourself, the sense of feeling the pain of others.

My young son was born in 2003, and our first child had died, and he phoned me the day my son was born. Suddenly I had this call from Nelson Mandela, out of the blue! It was as he always is with people, as if he had all the time in the world and yet it meant so much to us. He is so busy doing so many other things and he could be justified in having a retirement. His humanity shines through at every point. He has such a love of children and it was a great privilege having my eighteen-month-old son with me the last time we met.

Mandela has been such a huge force for change. It is amazing that this man who was born in 1918, the same year as my late mother, who spans this whole century, can still be an icon for young people, still inspire people by his courage and his lack of bitterness. He's leading the world again in making people understand what we must do about HIV and AIDS. When we were in South Africa it was the day after his son's funeral and he was as warm and friendly as ever, but you knew the tragedies which he as an individual has had to withstand are more than one person or many families should have to bear. He said,

"When I was in prison I had tuberculosis and people treated it like an illness. People must learn that AIDS is an illness and should be treated as an illness like TB."

In Tanzania I met a young AIDS sufferer in a hut in these awful surroundings and he said, "I know people despise me here because I've got AIDS, but are we not all brothers?" Mandela is playing a part in removing this stigma. It is a huge tribute to someone his age who could never have imagined such a disease twenty or thirty years ago, but has understood that it must be treated as an illness like any other.

Both he and Graça are wonderful people. Together they exude friendship and warmth. Graça has also been a wonderful influence in his later years. She has helped him achieve some of his political objectives while at the same time being such a friend. Their partnership has enhanced his ability to make a difference to so many causes: UNICEF, child poverty, HIV/AIDS, the millennium goals, the conflicts in Africa. Before the G8 Summit in July 2005, he sent a letter to the G7 ministers. Here he is at eighty-six sending a letter asking us all to remember what he had said before and to consider how much more we could do to alleviate poverty.

Of all the seminal events in the last one hundred years, the struggle for freedom in South Africa, Mandela's release and his building a multiracial nation will never be forgotten. Mandela will be remembered as someone who showed us that people are essentially good. Mandela says in his book that the good in people is a flame that can be hidden but never extinguished. He himself reflects that: he's totally modest and humble. His status and authority come from his personality, not from any position he has held. Even people who have never met him and perhaps know nothing about his life, understand almost just from seeing him that this is a man of stature, authority and great compassion.

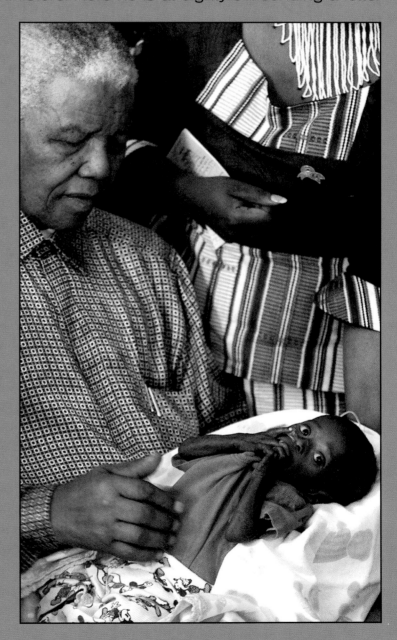

During a visit to a children's home in Cape Town, Mandela holds a six-month-old baby infected with HIV/AIDS.

BONO:

One of the first times I met Madiba was when my friend Naomi Campbell put together a concert in Barcelona for one of his charities. It was called Frock and Roll, can you believe it?! A lot of top names in fashion and a lot of people in music had agreed to do it but it was beset with all kinds of problems and the event had gone sour in Barcelona's local press. There had been rumors the concert was off, then it was on again. When we arrived the organizers explained that there hadn't really been that many tickets sold. And I said, "Like how many?" "A thousand." A thousand! In a stadium for twenty thousand! I said, "Don't worry. There'll be a big walk up. That happens sometimes in Spain."

So we went to the concert and Madiba was to walk on with myself and Naomi at 7:30, but there were only one thousand people there. So we waited till 8:30: two thousand. At nine, there were about five thousand, which in a stadium for twenty thousand was not a pretty sight. So there was much wailing and gnashing of teeth backstage. Who was going to tell the great man? Nobody seemed to want to, so they just turned the lights off and hoped he wouldn't notice! So we walk out on the stage and I'm just staring at my shoes. So's Naomi. Madiba comes to the microphone and says, "It is a dangerous thing to have high expectations. And I want you people to know in Barcelona that I had high expectations of this event." I'm staring harder at my shoes! "What can I tell you? You people have given me a reception I could never deserve. Thank you. Thank you from the bottom of my heart for turning up and turning out for the Nelson Mandela Children's Fund." And I

Mandela and Bono at the 46664 AIDS benefit concert in 2003.

look out. Same amount of people, but I swear it looked full. It was one of those moments. It was a real lesson for me because it's the way he sees the world. It wasn't an act, he genuinely was thrilled that so many people had turned up. If you've spent all those years in prison, the glass doesn't look half empty. I'm one of these people who have to constantly remind myself of such things, but he turned the event completely around. With your words you make things true sometimes. And I guess he's been doing that all his life: speaking the words, describing South Africa before it existed, bringing it into existence by speaking about it as if it was.

If rock and roll has anything at the core, if it's about anything at all, it's surely about liberation. Whether it's sexual liberation or spiritual liberation, just getting free of yourself and your limitations seems to be part of the theme of rock and roll. So it's natural that people in that music would be in awe of him. And he's cooler than any rock star or any hip-hop star you are ever going to meet. Cool is not something I generally look up to, but he actually has it.

And I think he finds these occasions very funny. There's playfulness and mischief – there's mischief in the eyes too. I think he likes to be around carnival a little bit. It lifts his spirits. He'll be there holding Naomi's hand and smiling and laughing and he's just living all the life he missed. I think that's it, he enjoys the carnival.

I look to Madiba for inspiration in many ways. When I go to meet him it's quite clear who is the rock star – and yet he's consistently trying to shrink himself. "Why would you come to see an old man like me!" He's always turning everything on its head. He's so very playful. I've always thought that laughter is the evidence of freedom and there's comedy in those eyes. They're evidence of life and liberty and I'm sure they were when they were behind bars.

I heard recently he had an operation on his eyes to fix his tear ducts. The sun bouncing off the quarry had damaged his eyes and apparently the salt had got into his tear ducts and he had not been able to cry properly and I just thought: there it is, right there. I thought about all those years Madiba wasn't able to cry. There's such poetry in that physical condition. When did he weep? And on what occasions did he weep for his country? I would be surprised if he hadn't. The man who couldn't cry.

For sure Mandela has a lot of bravery – but also strategy! I knew someone who actively opposed the anti-apartheid movement and I would try to avoid him. Then one day I was in a restaurant in New York and bumped into a very good friend of mine, an African American, sitting with this person. He introduced me and I sat down and we talked. Afterwards I pulled my friend aside and said, "What's going on here? You of all people must know what this person has been up to!" And my friend said, "Come on! Madiba was only out of prison six weeks before he called this guy. Now he's one of the biggest contributors to the ANC." I felt like one of those Japanese soldiers who came out of the jungle in 1957 still fighting the Second World War. Mandela is extraordinary, to use the force that was coming at you to defend yourself. You could call it judo.

He told me himself that when Margaret Thatcher, who had not supported the anti-apartheid movement, came to visit him, he asked for money, as he always does. With a big smile. Tourism is very expensive around Madiba. No sooner was Mrs. Thatcher in the door he asked her for some cash, and to her credit she wrote there and then a check for £100,000. That's an enormous amount of money if you have spent your life in politics. And he was very moved she should do that. Anyway, he took the check and somebody said, "How can you take this, Madiba, from this woman who fought against our movement?" He said, "If we sit and we break bread with de Klerk who squashed our people like flies, I can take the money from Margaret Thatcher." That's strategy, making unexpected alliances. I've tried to follow in those footsteps, always reaching out for people who you least expect to be your friend. Don't look in the obvious places. Always believe that people can surprise you and themselves with a change of heart. I don't know if he has faith in God, but he certainly has more faith in mankind than anyone else.

Madiba has the kind of nobility that just cannot be denied. The only way one race or people can keep another down is if deep down we believe the other race is not equal to us, not as capable as us. With Mandela it was very clear that he wasn't equal: he was way above everyone else. He completely turned it around again, like judo, using the language of the colonizing force better than they could, taking the words out of their mouths and arranging them in such a way that it was inconceivable that black and white should be kept apart, that it was always a ridiculous notion.

Franz Fanon talks about the crushing of the human spirit which comes with colonization. One of the things he describes is emasculation, how some countries have found it very hard to find their own identity and how myth becomes really important to people coming out from under the jackboot of colonization. Think of the way Ireland's writers, poets, and playwrights created a mythology for the Irish. The Irish came out believing that we were noble, that we had this rich past with mythic figures in it. Nobility is usually the first thing that you lose in oppression and men, particularly. usually then exaggerate their masculinity to make up for it. You get a lot of brutality to women, for instance. You see it in African American culture – guns and very male things. That's what is so bewildering about Mandela: he hung on to that nobility even seeing degradation all around. He's a gentleman and the white South Africans – of British and Dutch origin – could just not deny his gentility.

The power of words and the way Madiba puts them together cannot be under-estimated, and as it turned out, language was the ANC's most lethal weapon. The world discovered the potential of South Africa through the poetry of Madiba's speeches and his communiqués. His speech at the Rivonia Trial in which he said "I have fought against white domination, and I have fought against black domination" even then implied a future. He'd already jumped ahead in his own mind and was saying "in the new nation we will do things differently." It's imagination: it's not seen to be believed, it's believe it to be seen.

Even in his twilight, Madiba is still as adept, as quick on his feet to know how hard to push and when not to. Zaki Ahmed was someone who was HIV-positive who refused antiviral drugs until it was clear everyone would have the same right. He took the South African government to court and it led to a huge spat with the SA government, but Madiba went to see him and stood by him. That's him. As diplomatic as ever, doesn't want to interfere but knowing he had a moral obligation. He's still there.

GEORGE BIZOS:

Mandela jokes a lot about his age. He says, "You know, I can see why you don't greet me any more, because I'm eighty-six." But he hasn't given up. A mixture of traditional animism, Christianity, and the monotheistic religions all makes him believe there is a life after death. He always jokes that he's going to join the nearest branch of the ANC in heaven . . . it's said as a joke but it does betray something. I once quoted to him what Socrates said to Crito when Socrates was about to die. "Crito, I don't fear death. There may be a life after death. But that won't be such a bad thing. Can you imagine! I'll meet Homer, and Aeschylus, and Sophocles! And sit there and have a timeless discussion about things that we've been talking about here." And Mandela said, "But assume that there is no such thing. Have you ever had a night's sleep when you were not disturbed at all – no dreams, no fears – you just slept throughout the night? Didn't you feel very much happier? Can you imagine if there is this eternal sleep it's also all right? So what's there to be afraid of?"

CYRIL RAMAPHOSA:

What makes Madiba happy is to see our people happy; to see our people leading a better life. Everything that he did in power was not for self glory; it was out of a genuinely felt concern that the people of our country should have better lives. Madiba himself has led a very simple life: his house and nearly everything he has is simple, like a cloth that is cut according to his needs. He could have been the wealthiest man in this country, but he has led a simple life and he has wanted other people to have a similar life and that has been his main objective. That's what makes him happy – that and his grandchildren. His has been a life well lived.

SHAUN JOHNSON:

When he says, "Please don't overemphasize Mandela, I come from the masses," he really, really means it. He has a great knowledge of his predecessors in the ANC. He feels himself as part of a process. It would be lovely for someone to talk more to him about it. I think he takes it extremely seriously, while at the same time understanding that he's a superstar. His only question is, am I putting it to good use?

One of the reasons I think there's sometimes sensitivity among new generations of ANC leaders and others – and I sympathize with them – is that they almost get the feeling that the rest of the world (and by that they mean the European white world) treats Mandela, and also to an extent Tutu, as freaks. Somehow treat him as an exception – un-Africanize him. So what he tries all the time is to emphasize, "Uh-uh, I'm as African as you will ever find."

MAC MAHARAJ:

When Madiba says that the struggle is his life, he puts his finger on something very important. From the early 1940s when he dedicated his life to the freedom struggle, it began to shape his personality and produce the steadfastness that you see with regard to his vision of freedom. Many people find that commitment difficult to accept: to sit in prison for more than twenty-seven years and still come out so purely committed. To face the death sentence without wavering and say that he is prepared to die. The best quality of the man comes out when he made that statement from the dock at the Rivonia Trial, and the judge gave his verdict of guilty. The next day the court would, after hearing a plea in mitigation, pass sentence and the question was: what would each of the accused say if they were sentenced to death? In the notes made by Madiba on what he was going to say if the death sentence was imposed he says "I meant everything I said" – that he stood by everything in his statement from the dock. He went on to make the point that in the freedom struggle lots of people had lost their lives and then his last point was that if I have to die, I will die like a man. That brings out the character of a leader in a freedom struggle – a character of vision, steadfastness of purpose, and at the worst of moments a refusal to back down from that vision at whatever cost.

All of us are shaped in one way or another by the lives we lead, and it is the struggle that has made Madiba what he is. Today he is perceived as an icon by almost every racial community in South Africa across all classes, he is seen as an icon in Africa, in the developing world and also in the developed world. He has truly become humankind's hope for the future at a time when politics has become a dirty word, stripped of all morality and Machiavellian to its roots. Generations of young people around the world look to Madiba because they see him as the one person who symbolizes the possibility of bringing morality to the arena of politics. And that's why he remains the hope of this world.

THABO MBEKI:

When I first arrived in Johannesburg in 1960, I used to have regular consultations with Nelson Mandela. He had not yet gone underground, but by this time the ANC had been banned in the aftermath of Sharpeville and he himself was the subject of a banning order, so he or Winnie would phone occasionally to ask me over for a meal and we would discuss various things such as how we should conduct ourselves, what campaigns we should engage in, what we should do about youth organization, so to that extent there was a direct link between those of us who were involved in youth work and the senior leadership and he was interested to hear what my views were.

There was a lot of impatience among the youth who felt that the illegality imposed on the ANC made it inevitable that we would have to use different forms of struggle, particularly armed struggle, and this was certainly brought to the attention of the senior leadership. Nelson Mandela came to represent a response to these challenges. He was the principal speaker at the Pietermaritzburg All In Conference in 1961. Few among the delegates and the public were aware that some of his banning orders had expired the day before. The fact that he addressed an open meeting like that conveyed a strong message that we could not accept the immobilization of the movement. And again, by becoming MK commander he gave an answer to the question of the adoption of the armed struggle by the movement. These were early days but the atmosphere at the time was very optimistic in the sense that we were all convinced it wouldn't take too long for the liberation movement to defeat the apartheid regime.

Long before I and others in the ANC youth movement went into exile in 1962 there was an organizational relationship established between the senior leadership and junior cadres of the youth movement, and I believe our generation was very fortunate. We were brought up in the culture, tradition, and history of the ANC, and our understanding of the ANC's strategies and tactics was further deepened by the direct interaction we had with Madiba and other leaders both inside and outside the country and therefore issues, for example, of common understanding over a negotiated settlement, were not a problem. So when Oliver Tambo told me that Madiba was talking to the regime in South Africa, it did not come as a surprise or anything to be concerned about.

When we attained our liberation in 1994 my relationship with President Mandela in government was a continuation of a political relationship that went back a number of decades and the objectives we were pursuing were no different. But in 1994 the government was emerging from centuries of conflict – even as we took power many people were being killed. Furthermore, a substantial number of the white population was fearful of change, and the other national minorities, the Indians and the coloreds, were themselves somewhat uncertain of the future which was why they gave as much support to the new National Party as they did. We were dealing with issues of national reconciliation, but at the same time the rest of the world wanted to welcome Nelson Mandela and celebrate his release. We needed to respond to that and say to the international community that they had been right to support our struggle, right to support the ANC, while domestically we were having to deal with the question of the so-called "black on black" violence that we knew was being orchestrated and inspired by agents of the regime. So in a sense a natural division arose between Madiba and myself because he needed to be out there pulling together a nation, and also to be interacting with the rest of the world. If Madiba had to be addressing all those matters, he couldn't be expected to see to the day-to-day running and functioning of the government so this naturally fell into the hands of the deputy president. Also, Madiba was quite clear from early on that he did not want to serve more than one term because of his age and he was quite determined to use his first five years of democratic government to make sure that whoever succeeded him would take over conditions favorable to good governance of the country.

In terms of Mandela's leadership and negotiating style, as with all his generation of leaders, he is steeped in a set of values and principles he and others had formulated within the ANC. He'd always drive a hard bargain in the negotiation process to make sure those positions were sustained. Nevertheless, he also understood that sometimes you have to make compromises which may look as though they are compromising those values.

To understand where Nelson Mandela derives his strength from, one has to understand that he is in a sense a child of the ANC. He endured those many years in jail to bring about an outcome visualized by the ANC and his strength derived from the knowledge that the position of the ANC represented the popular will. You could see that he was very worried during the course of the negotiations at the instances of violence such as the Boipatong massacre, when negotiations got suspended. He thought we were losing the mass of the people, that we were moving too far ahead in negotiations with people who were responsible for the massacres. So we decided to stop the engagement with the "enemy" as it were, so we could engage with our people and sustain their support.

Many people around the world have said to me that when you look at the world today, the one country that gives hope to all humanity is South Africa. Others have said that in dealing with the many questions that we are dealing with here – the issues of building a nonracial society, a nonsexist society, of defeating poverty, of dealing with the gap between the developed and developing worlds – South Africa is a pilot project for all humanity and Mandela symbolizes that. When we talk about Mandela as an international icon, he is not only an individual, he is an individual with fundamental perspectives who represents a movement, a country, a process which is dealing with some of the most basic challenges facing humanity. To come out of jail, to come out of all these troubles that we faced as a country, and rather than conflict and confrontation, to choose consultation, I think that is really what is represented by the iconic status of Nelson Mandela.

Madiba and I have worked together for so many years. I hope that people like Madiba and others of that senior leadership see in the younger people like us that they have succeeded in a way in replicating themselves. I hope that he sees that the broad leadership of the ANC movement is committed to the perspective for which we all fought, committed to the perspective for which so many of our people sacrificed their lives. Madiba follows events, he reads papers, he listens, and each time we meet he will make the point that he is confident that a leadership steeped in the history, tradition, and culture of the ANC is quite capable of solving the problems and the challenges it faces. It has been a privilege for my generation to have among its teachers people like Nelson Mandela, Walter Sisulu, Govan Mbeki, Moses Kotane, J. B. Marks, Michael Harmel, Yusuf Dadoo, and Oliver Tambo. To have interacted with these people over many decades has, I think, helped the formation of this leadership in the tradition established by Mandela and his comrades and those who came before them.

This conversation took place at Nelson Mandela's home in Houghton, Johannesburg between Mr. Mandela, Tim Couzens, Verne Harris, Project Manager for the Nelson Mandela Centre for Memory at the Nelson Mandela Foundation, and Mac Maharaj.

When we arrived we were embraced by a wonderfully warm young woman called Meme Kgagara, and shown into a comfortable sitting room. Mr.Mandela came in soon afterwards and even before shaking hands (he, of course, knew Mac and Verne, but not me) he laughingly said, "I didn't know I was meeting such a formidable group!" and when I was introduced to him as a professor of literary history he said, "Does that mean you are clever?" which set the tone for the next hour.

What followed was more an amiable chat than a formal interview. Other than showing him the note he wrote on the day he was contemplating the death sentence in 1964 and an early photograph of himself, which was the main purpose of our visit, we had no agenda and decided to let the discussion drift wherever the warm spring morning and Madiba's mood took us. Our hope was to give as much as to get. After all that he has given his people and the world, he deserves not to be grilled for the umpteenth time about his prison life. He sat as he always does now, with his legs up and his stockinged feet resting on a soft stool. Except for a couple of moments which evoked dark or painful memories it was an hour filled with quiet irony, warm humor, and much open laughter. His mind and his responses were alert and vigorous and he made each of us feel, not only that we were welcome, but that we were of interest to him. His graciousness bespeaks the manners and speech of an age which, like many of his friends and colleagues, has gone. (For instance, "Oh, no" often means "Oh, yes!")

It was a rare privilege – to glimpse the private individual behind the public face. The two are compatible and not so very different. I dare say there is an even more private world but in the time I had, I wanted to meet the human being rather than the icon or saint. I did. The conversation started lightly, intending to lead toward the introduction of the document and photograph.

TC: Mr. Mandela, some people have heard of you in the world; a few people seem to have heard your name.

NM: A few people? [Laughing]

TC: And some of these even seem to be quite fond of you, and I think one of the reasons why so many people are fond of you is because they love your smile – the famous Mandela smile – and they love your sense of humor, so I'd like to start by asking you, has that smile always been with you and did that sense of humor start with you as a child?

NM: Well, it's better for others to answer that question, not me. Because when you are answering questions which make many people proud of you, you can actually exaggerate your qualities and I'd leave exaggeration to people like Mac. [All laugh]

MM: You haven't noticed, Madiba, you said "many people" but Tim was saying "a few people." [Madiba laughs]

VH: That's a trick answer. [All laugh, recalling that at the outset Madiba expressed the

TC: It seems to me your sense of humor must have started when you were quite young. Would you say that your childhood was a happy childhood? When you think back to your childhood do you smile about it?

NM: Well, some of these questions are very embarrassing and one would like to avoid them. But as you probably know, my father was a chief in that position and you, of course, occupied a position where many people wanted to talk to you, especially now when you are a little older and many people were insisting that I go back and take my father's position, but that came later when I was exposed to the ANC. And to leave the ANC and go and take a chieftancy I found that quite unacceptable.

MM: Madiba, Chief Jongintaba, whatever has been written about him, was quite a firm man, quite clear what he wanted. Did he have a sense of humor?

NM: Well, you know, kings and acting kings have to maintain a certain dignity. And they don't have, they didn't have, a sense of humor as far as I could assess. And certainly Jongintaba [Regent of the Thembu and also head of the Madiba clan] didn't have a sense of humor, as some of us. We have a sense of humor because we feel it is our duty to make people forget about their problems and to think of things which help them to understand the feelings of the people and their experiences.

MM: You've also talked about your mother and your relationship and you've written about it, that when you parted with her, when she took you to Chief Jongintaba's royal place, she just told you, *"Uqinisufokotho, Kwedini,"* there was no hugging, kissing, showing of strong emotion, but in your childhood when you were with her, was she a person who laughed?

NM: Oh, yes. Who "loved," or "laughed"?

MM: Laughed.

NM: Oh, I see. . . . Oh, no, no, no. In that society the tradition was not to laugh too much. You had to be serious. Part of leadership was to be a serious person. Not to engage in laughter. That was the tradition in those days.

MM: So what you are telling us is you always remained a mischievous boy.

NM: [Madiba laughs] Not really. But it was important for you to maintain a certain dignity. Laughing didn't help you to maintain that dignity. You had to be serious.

TC: But you're well known for your sense of humor. Even in serious situations you've often made jokes. Where does that come from? Why do you do that?

NM: Well it's very difficult for me to say this comes from this. But I like, you know, people being relaxed because even when you are discussing a serious matter relaxation is very important because it encourages your thinking, so I like to make jokes even when examining serious situations. Because when people are relaxed they can think properly.

TC: It seems to me, as well, in a way you've taken your childhood through to your adulthood and manhood, and that humor is part of it. You're well known for loving children but also what is interesting is the way young people, young adults, or teenagers, also respond to you. It seems to me that your sense of humor is one of the ways you get through to young people.

NM: People want to forget about the painful experiences which they've had and when they meet somebody who helps them to forget about their past, at least for the moment when you are talking to them, they like people like that. Yes. So we have learned from the countryside to make people happy by making jokes and making them forget about their painful experiences. It's very important.

TC: You've always seemed to have said that the youth are the most important people in your life. Verne has told me that you once said to him that the young people should be critical, that they should always keep politicians and leaders on their toes.

VH: Well, I was remembering an occasion when you spoke to relatively young people – John Matshikiza and James Sanders – and you said, "Yes, you young people, you must keep troubling us." That was the incident I was referring to.

NM: Well, it is good for you to be amongst people who don't take things for granted just because it is yourself. You sharpen your ideas by reducing yourself to the level of the people you are with and a sense of humor and a complete relaxation even when you're discussing serious things does help to mobilize friends around you. And I love that.

MM: That's not my experience with you, Madiba!

NM: Yes? [Laughing]

MM: My experience with you is when you were working on your autobiography. We used to go out in the yard [on Robben Island]. There was one brick, a concrete one, that would stand upright and you would sit on that, tall as you are. There was a rock that was low that I would sit on. And for two weeks we cancelled your autobiography work and discussion because I used to rush out and sit on your brick and you said, "No, that one is mine." And I used to say to you, "But I can't keep talking to you looking upwards." Now where's the story that you like young people to challenge you? [Grinning]

NM: No, you may have certain experiences depending on with whom you are at the moment but you have your own ideas as to how to promote society. It depends on the level of the people, the level of education. If you go to people who are traditional, most of whom have never been to school, you can't speak as if you are speaking to you. You have to talk about things among which they grew up. You can't talk like a PhD to people who have never gone to school. You talk about things around them which they understand.

MM: Madiba, you went to prison when the word "nonsexism" hardly existed. You came out of prison twenty-seven years later a very vigorous champion of women's rights. You championed in Thembuland the idea of the appointment of the widow of a chief to occupy the chieftancy. You took the matter up with the elders but when you ran into trouble you ran away from there and sent Walter Sisulu to explain the problem. How is it that after twenty-seven years, you caught up with the world and with nonsexism so fast?

NM: Well, I must say firstly, Mandela was the son of a Pondo princess. And then the mother of Mandela the princess ruled the southern part of Thembuland where the Matanzimas are now. We have women, we've had women, in Thembuland taking leading positions, ruling the country and the mother of Mandela was such a person. And there is an area where the Matanzimas are, when they see you they remember the stories about your grandfather Mandela.

MM: But in 1962 you were a bit of a male chauvinist. In 1990 you became a nonsexist.

NM: Well, you know, sitting down in jail and reading you discover things which you have never known outside, and that is the one advantage of being in prison, to read literature that opens your mind and makes you realize that some of your ideas in the past were completely wrong.

TC: When you first came to Johannesburg were you a bit scared?

NM: No, of course, it was a new experience and I did not know what I was going to find. But I was going along with Justice [Dalindyebo], the son of the regent, who was quite used to various groups including whites. When we left home – of course, we ran away – in Queenstown we hired a car. Then the friend of the owner of the car, a lawyer, said, "All right, my mother is going to Johannesburg. You can be in the same car but I want £15 from you." Which we gave him, because we had sold some cattle of the regent's, so we had a lot of money. The old lady was sitting next to the driver in front and Justice was behind her. Now Justice never feared whites – he was talking loudly. So the old lady, because she had never met a fellow like this who doesn't fear whites, along the journey she said, "No, this boy must sit there and let this quiet one sit behind me." [Much laughter] So we changed but she was unhappy about Justice and kept a hawkish eye on him for the rest of the journey although occasionally unbending to his witticisms.

TC: A few years ago you said to Pallo Jordan that when you went to Johannesburg either you or Justice had a gun in your suitcase.

NM: Oh, yes. Yes, quite. It was in my suitcase. [Smiling]

TC: [Laughing] Why did you have a gun?

NM: I was coming to Johannesburg for the first time and I'd heard terrible stories about what they can do to you.

VH: Madiba, is it true that it was your father's gun?

NM: Yes.

VH: So it had come to you from your father?

NM: Yes, quite. And it was licensed but [laughing] not to me.

VH: Madiba, we'd like to show you a document now. Mac, do you want to introduce it?

MM: Madiba, during your trial, the Rivonia Trial, besides your speech – "I am prepared to die" – you had to face the problem, several weeks later when the judge found you guilty, the prospect of the death sentence. The notes that you made – which seem like preparation for what you were going to say – were found in the archives. Anthony Sampson has reproduced it [in his biography]. It's a five-point note, but he says you and he could not decipher your own handwriting, which is not unusual.

You know the story of Madiba on Robben Island joining the team, handwriting the news given to the main section. Madiba insisted on joining the team and sharing the work but the main section responded, "Whoever wrote that, please can you remove him from the team because it is impossible to read it." So we started a new team. [Much laughter]

However, Tim phoned me one night to say he thinks he has found a way to understand what you had written in that sentence, the sentence you could not work out with Anthony Sampson. [See page 128.]

NM: I see.

MM: There are five points here [showing Madiba a copy of the note]. One, two, three, and five are very clear. It's point four that was not clear. Now, Sampson says you could not work out what you had written there. But Tim, myself, Kathy [Ahmed Kathrada], during discussions on this question, think we now know what you were saying. I want Tim to put it to you and then I'm going to show you what Joel Joffe says. He says the day you were found guilty the lawyers visited you all in prison to discuss what would happen the next day. So all this helps us to understand what you said in number four.

I want to put to you what we think you were saying. We want to see whether you think that is right because, for me, this note is even more important than your speech, "I am prepared to die."

I think you can see the first one: *Statement from the dock.*

NM: Yes.

MM: *I meant everything I said.*

NM: Yes.

MM: *The blood of many patriots in this country have been shed for demanding treatment in conformity with civilized standards.*

NM: Yes.

MM: And this one, *That* something . . .

NM: That army . . . that army . . .

MM: Yes.

NM: Um . . . is being and grown, heh?

MM: Is that a "t"?

NM: Is it not "and"?

TC: We thought it might be one or two things. Either "that army is beginning to grow o 'that army is busy and growing."

NM: [Pause] This looks to be "and."

MM: Good. "And." But you're saying that looks like "army"?

NM: Well, to me, it looks like "army."

TC: Yes. Everybody we've showed it to can never read that word. And that's what we eventually discovered.

NM: You see, this is "a" and "r" and "my."

TC: Yes, good, that's what we thought.

MM: You see, Madiba, you should never have had Anthony Sampson as your biographer [Madiba laughs wholeheartedly] because he couldn't work it out. But Tim and Verne and come here and you tell us it's "army". This is the thing we've spent hours working out – i s "army."

TC: I interviewed Arthur Chaskalson and we talked about that and he said he'd never been able to decipher it either. And Sampson said you couldn't decipher it so it seemed to me a challenge that I had to take up. The key is the word "army."

NM: Ah, the "army."

MM: This is clear. It is "grow" but whether it is "growing" . . .

NM: No. "That army is being grown." Is it possible?

MM: Could be. The meaning is the same. Either you say, it is beginning to grow, is coming into being and growing. But you are saying, "What I said in the dock I stand by, this thing s growing, these people who have shed blood, will continue, the army is growing, and if must die I want everyone to know, for all the world to know that I will meet my fate like a man."

NM: Yes, quite. I remember that very well.

TC: I think, Mr. Mandela, that this is probably the most important and moving document n the whole of African history. For me it's just fantastic.

MM: This is not the "I am prepared to die" speech. This is, you were preparing to speak i they imposed a death sentence on 12 June. It was seven weeks after you'd made the " am prepared to die" speech. And what makes this thing for me one of the most profound statements on our continent is that in seven weeks you had time to think of the consequences of your "I am prepared to die" speech. You had time to say, "Do I want to pull back a bit? To save my life?" Not just for yourself. To save your life for the struggle. To save your life for your family, for your children. After all that thought you say here, "I'm not backing off. I stand by everything and if I'm going to die I will meet my fate like a man." So your look was straight, only on the future, and it was not about you, it was entirely abou the struggle.

NM: That's true.

MM: It was one of the most moving speeches in Africa. A speech you didn't get a chance to make because you were not sentenced to death.

Now I want to tell you what Joffe says about you. You were found guilty on 11 June. Your speech was made on 23 April. He says on the way home they stopped at the jail to talk to the accused. "The accused were calm, living now in the shadow of death. The strain and detention was becoming almost unbearable. Yet the only matter that the accused wanted to discuss was how they should behave in court if the death sentence was passed. We told them that the judge would ask the first accused, Nelson Mandela, 'Have you any reason to advance why the death sentence should not be passed?'"

And when the lawyers told you that this is what would happen, he says, "Nelson decided that he would have a lot to say. He would tell the court that if they thought by sentencing him to death they would oust the liberation movement they were wrong. He was prepared to die for his beliefs, and he knew that his death would be an inspiration to his people in their struggle. As he had said before, in a document which was an exhibit in the case, 'There is no easy walk to freedom. We have to pass through the shadow of death again and again before we reach the mountain-tops (of our desire).'"

So, coming back to this sentence, the meaning of it, even if we can't get every word correct, is that you were saying, that that army of freedom is coming into being and is growing. That is the meaning we were going to put to you and what pleases us is that before we could put it to you you discovered it.

It's the first time, in my knowledge, that you have been able to read your own handwriting. [Madiba laughs]

NM: Yes, now, I'm getting used to it now. [Uproarious laughter]

MM: [To TC] Are you happy with that?

TC: Absolutely.

MM: We were afraid that you were going to say, "No, chaps, I don't remember. It's not important. Does it matter what I said?"

VH: Time is running out for us now. Can we show you a photograph?

NM: OK.

VH: It's a famous photograph [shows photograph]. [See page 23 for a reproduction.]

NM: [Recognizing it and chuckling] Oh yes.

VH: The question is, is that your first suit? Or did you have an earlier one?

NM: No, I think it is my first suit, if I'm not mistaken. The first suit and the shoes were given to me as I was going to Clarkebury Institution. I went to my class early in the morning and there were two ladies sitting in the corner and now, these boots, I was wearing boots for the first time, and what made things worse was the floor of the classroom was, uh, was planks so I walked like a horse on spurs! And one of the ladies who was sitting there said, it's clear I'm wearing boots for the first time! It did not help me because it was true and I advanced toward her but she then screamed and I realized, oh, but this is a woman and I retreated!

MM: Now, Madiba, on this story, in your book you mentioned one of these young ladies and you give her name as Mathomi.

NM: Mathona.

MM: Mathona. But there is also a report that one of the women was Phyllis Ntantala, Pallo's mother [Pallo Jordan].

NM: No, no. That's not true. Phyllis was far ahead of me. Far ahead.

MM: But you do say you became very good friends with Mathona.

NM: Yes, quite. Oh yes.

MM: You overcame the fact that she told you you were uncivilized.

NM: Yes. [Laughs]

VH: Can I just ask where that photograph was taken?

NM: I see. No, this photograph was taken at Jongintaba's place.

VH: What age were you there?

NM: Then, I think I was about fourteen or fifteen.

VH: Thank you, so much.

MM: Madiba, can I ask you the last question? You said in answering the question on nonsexism, prison gave you the chance to reflect, think, and develop ideas. Your record in prison among your comrades was that you never feared to encourage them to think. Back to this question of nonsexism. Is there anything that stands out in what you read or in discussion in prison that led you to revise your thinking of women and the importance of their enjoying . . .

NM: Well, in prison we had the privilege of reading, and expanding our thinking. Women throughout the world have led their countries. Strangely enough, I had never thought so much about my own family as I did when I now discovered that there were many women in the world in leading positions. Because the mother of Mandela, when the English came to our area, she decided to fight them. She came from the Pondo house of Sigcau and so the English when they defeated her deported her back to Pondoland. But at least she had the distinction of mobilizing the Thembu to fight against the whites. And that's why they deported her back to her home where she came from.

MM: It shows how you've changed, Madiba. In prison you told us about your father's rebellion. In prison you told us about your father's defying the magistrate.

NM: Oh yes, he did.

MM: But you never told us about . . .

NM: Yah, no, you were backward you know. You didn't want us to praise women! [Much laughter]

And so a meeting that began with a smile ended with a laugh. And that laugh is unforgettable to anyone who has heard it.

Houghton, August 13, 2005

CONTRIBUTOR BIOGRAPHIES
BIBLIOGRAPHY
ACKNOWLEDGEMENTS
NOTES AND INDEX

CONTRIBUTOR BIOGRAPHIES

DR. NEVILLE ALEXANDER: Author, academic, and cofounder of the National Liberation Front, Dr. Neville Alexander was convicted of sabotage in 1964 and sentenced to ten years on Robben Island. In 1981, he was appointed director of the South African Committee for Higher Education.

MUHAMMAD ALI: Three times world heavyweight boxing champion, Muhammad Ali has been a powerful advocate of equal rights all his life. A member of the Nation of Islam, his refusal to serve in the military resulted in a five-year prison sentence and the stripping of his heavyweight title. He works tirelessly for countless charities and causes, despite battling against the onset of Parkinson's disease.

KOFI ANNAN: Kofi Annan was appointed Secretary-General of the United Nations in 1997, and elected for a second term in 2001. His efforts to invigorate the UN were recognized in 2001 when he and the UN itself were jointly awarded the Nobel Peace Prize.

LORD RICHARD ATTENBOROUGH: Among actor, director, and filmmaker Lord Attenborough's most acclaimed works are the films *Gandhi* and *Cry Freedom*. A lifelong campaigner against apartheid, Lord Attenborough and his wife, actress Sheila Simms, lost their daughter Jane and granddaughter Lucy in the tsunami on December 26, 2004.

DR. ALI BACHER: Former test cricket captain of South Africa, Dr. Ali Bacher presided over the administration of South African cricket during its re-entry into the world arena in the post-apartheid era, and as managing director of the United Cricket Board of South Africa ensured that equal opportunities were provided for cricketers of all races. In 2003 he masterminded the ICC Cricket World Cup hosted by South Africa.

JUDGE FIKILE BAM: Fikile Bam became an underground activist while studying law at Cape Town University. He spent ten years on Robben Island with Nelson Mandela before being released in 1974. Judge Bam was appointed judge-president of the Land Claims Court in 1995.

HIS ROYAL HIGHNESS PRINCE BANDAR BIN SULTAN BIN ABDULAZIZ: International statesman and diplomat Prince Bandar was ambassador of the Kingdom of Saudi Arabia to the United States 1983–2005.

HILDA BERNSTEIN: Anti-apartheid activist Hilda Bernstein was a communist, active member of the ANC Women's League, and was one of the instigators of the Federation of South African Women. She and her husband Rusty were subjected to various banning orders from 1953 onward and in 1960 she was detained without charge following the Sharpeville shootings. In 1964, following the Rivonia Trial, the Bernstein family escaped from South Africa into exile in London.

GEORGE BIZOS: Human rights advocate George Bizos was part of the team that defended Nelson Mandela and his comrades at the Rivonia Trial. As Mandela's lifelong lawyer and confidant, he was a constant visitor throughout his prison years and defended Winnie Mandela several times in court. In the 1990s George Bizos played a key role in the establishment of constitutional law in South Africa and was prominent in the investigation of apartheid-era crimes in the Truth and Reconciliation Commission.

THE RIGHT HONORABLE TONY BLAIR MP: Prime minister of Britain since 1997, Tony Blair is the Labor Party's longest-serving prime minister and the only person to have led the party to victory in three consecutive general elections. Educated at Oxford University, he has been an MP since 1983.

JOSEPH BLATTER: International sports administrator Joseph (Sepp) Blatter has played a key role in football's (soccer) international governing body FIFA since 1975. In 1998 he was elected president, and he was re-elected to that position in 2002.

BONO: Internationally acclaimed rock musician and member of U2, Bono is a committed campaigner on debt relief for Africa, first with Jubilee 2000, and more recently with DATA and Make Poverty History.

BARONESS BOOTHROYD OF SANDWELL: Baroness Boothroyd has had a lifelong commitment to the anti-apartheid cause. A member of the British parliament since 1973, she was Speaker of the House 1992–2000, the first woman ever to hold this position. In 1994 she was appointed chancellor of the Open University.

CHRISTO BRAND: Christo Brand worked as a prison guard on Robben Island and later at Pollsmoor Prison.

SIR RICHARD BRANSON: British entrepreneur Sir Richard Branson is best known for his global brand Virgin, which encompasses businesses from the entertainment industries through to the airline Virgin Atlantic and the Virgin train networks. Sir Richard is a trustee of several charities including the Virgin Healthcare Foundation which promotes research into current healthcare issues.

ANDRE BRINK: Novelist, playwright, translator, critic, and academic, Andre Brink is one of South Africa's most distinguished literary figures. He is the author of sixteen novels, now translated into some twenty-six languages, and has been awarded many prizes both in South Africa and internationally.

THE RIGHT HONORABLE GORDON BROWN MP: Gordon Brown was appointed Britain's Chancellor of the Exchequer in 1997. Educated at Edinburgh University, he has been an MP since 1983 and was Shadow Chancellor from 1992.

AMINA CACHALIA: A prominent member of the Indian Youth Congress, and later an ANC member and founding member of the Federation of South African Women, Amina Cachalia was subjected to banning orders for a total of over fifteen years. Her anti-apartheid activities brought her close to Nelson Mandela who became a friend and mentor.

JUDGE ARTHUR CHASKALSON: Judge Chaskalson acted as defense counsel in a number of important political trials during the apartheid era including the Rivonia Trial and played a key role in the drafting of South Africa's interim constitution in 1993. In 1994 he became the first president of the new Constitutional Court, and he served as Chief Justice of South Africa 2001–2005.

PRESIDENT BILL CLINTON: International statesman and president of the United States 1993–2001, President Clinton has been a lifelong advocate for civil rights and racial equality. Through the Clinton Foundation, he has been at the forefront in the fight against HIV/AIDS in Africa.

EDDIE DANIELS: A member of the Liberal Party and the African Resistance Movement, Eddie Daniels was sentenced to fifteen years' imprisonment on Robben Island for sabotage. He entered prison with an eighth-grade education and left with two university degrees.

BASIL DAVIDSON: An honorary fellow of the London School of Oriental and African Studies, Basil Davidson is the author or editor of some twenty-seven books on Africa. His support of the ANC saw him banned in South Africa.

EBRAHIM EBRAHIM: A member of Umkhonto we Sizwe from 1961, Ebrahim Ebrahim was arrested in 1963 and sentenced to fifteen years on Robben Island for sabotage. He was released in 1979 and went into exile in 1980, but was kidnapped in Swaziland by the South African security forces in 1986 and sentenced to twenty years on Robben Island for high treason. On his release in 1991 he was elected to the national executive committee of the ANC. He was elected an MP in the national assembly in 1994 and in 1997 became chair of the Foreign Affairs Committee.

DENNIS GOLDBERG: A leading member of the Congress of Democrats and a political activist, Dennis Goldberg was sentenced to life imprisonment alongside Nelson Mandela in the Rivonia Trial, the only white man among those of the accused to be found guilty. He served sixteen years in Pretoria Local Prison before his release.

NADINE GORDIMER: Acclaimed novelist, essayist, short story, and screenplay writer Nadine Gordimer is the winner of eleven literary awards including the 1974 Booker Prize for Fiction and the 1991 Nobel Prize for Literature.

PROFESSOR STUART HALL: Leading academic, broadcaster, and cultural theorist Professor Stuart Hall was appointed director of the Centre for Contemporary Cultural Studies at Birmingham University in 1968. He was appointed professor of sociology at the Open University 1979–97 and is currently professor emeritus there and visiting professor at Goldsmith's College, University of London.

LORD DENIS HEALEY: Lord Healey served the British government as Secretary of State for Defense 1964–70 and as Chancellor of the Exchequer 1974–79. He retired as an MP in 1992 and received a life peerage.

LORD ROBERT HUGHES: A Labor MP and former chair of the anti-apartheid movement in Britain, in 2004 Lord Hughes was awarded the Order of the Companions of O. R. Tambo by the South African government for his contribution to the anti-apartheid cause.

LORD JOEL JOFFE: International human rights lawyer Lord Joffe was part of the defense team at the Rivonia Trial. On his move to Britain, he became one of the founders of Allied Dunbar and served until 2000 as chair of the board of trustees for Oxfam UK. He was awarded a peerage in 2000.

SHAUN JOHNSON: Former newspaper editor and media executive, Shaun Johnson is chief executive of the Mandela Rhodes Foundation.

ZWELEDINGA PALLO JORDAN: Pallo Jordan has served on the national executive committee of the ANC since 1985 and was the party's main media spokesman before and during the 1994 elections. He has held a number of parliamentary posts since then and is currently South Africa's Minister of Arts and Culture.

FERGAL KEANE: Author and journalist Fergal Keane covered southern Africa for the BBC throughout the 1980s and was BBC correspondent in South Africa from 1990 onward.

SIR SYDNEY KENTRIDGE: Sir Sydney Kentridge played a leading role as an advocate in the anti-apartheid movement, representing Nelson Mandela and others accused at the infamous Treason Trial in 1956 and the family of Steve Biko at the 1977 inquest hearing into the activist's death. Now living in Great Britain, Sir Sydney was knighted in 1999 for his services to international human rights.

GLENYS KINNOCK: Glenys Kinnock worked for many years for the anti-apartheid cause. She is currently a member of the European Parliament, and president of the African, Caribbean, and Pacific States ACP-EU Joint Assembly.

LORD NEIL KINNOCK: Leader of the British Labor Party 1983–92, Lord Kinnock was active in the anti-apartheid movement in Britain from the early 1960s. He served as a member of the European Commission 1995–2004 and is now head of the British Council.

ANTJIE KROG: Acclaimed poet, novelist, and journalist Antjie Krog has written extensively of South Africa's transition from apartheid to democracy.

ZELDA LA GRANGE: Executive personal assistant and spokesperson to Nelson Mandela, Zelda la Grange joined the office of the president in August 1994 initially as a senior ministerial typist before being promoted. In 1999 when President Mandela retired he asked her to continue working with him following his departure from government.

KEN LIVINGSTONE: Leader of the Greater London Council from 1981 until it was abolished by Margaret Thatcher in 1986, Ken Livingstone served as a Labor MP 1987–91 and was elected mayor of London in 2000 and again in 2004.

ESME MATSHIKIZA: Widow of the jazz musician, journalist, and composer of the celebrated musical *King Kong,* Todd Matshikiza, Esme Matshikiza left South Africa with her family in 1960, subsequently moving to live in exile in Zambia before returning to South Africa after democracy.

PRESIDENT THABO MBEKI: Thabo Mbeki served as a youth organizer for the ANC before being briefly imprisoned and then leaving South Africa to live and campaign overseas. In 1989 he was head of the ANC delegation in talks with the South African government that led to the unbanning of the ANC and the release of prisoners including Nelson Mandela. In 1994 Mbeki became deputy president of South Africa in the first democratic elections and in 1999 he succeeded Mandela as president of South Africa.

DR. FATIMA MEER: Writer, academic, and author Dr. Fatima Meer was a prominent anti-apartheid activist. Constantly subjected to banning orders, she was also detained in prison. A close friend of the Mandela family, whom she supported for many years, she is the author of the first authorized biography of Nelson Mandela, *Higher Than Hope*.

IQBAL MEER: Iqbal Meer is an English solicitor and is also admitted to practice in South Africa and Zambia. He has been Nelson Mandela's personal lawyer for many years. He is a trustee of the Nelson Mandela Children's Fund (UK) and is also a trustee of the Nelson Mandela Statue Fund.

THE REVEREND DOCTOR STANLEY MOGOBA: Stanley Mogoba served as president of the South African Institute of Race Relations 1987–89 and as presiding bishop of the Methodist Church of South Africa 1988–94. He was elected president of the Pan African Congress in 1997 and has also served as vice-chairman of the National Peace Committee.

RUTH MOMPATI: A member of the ANC's national executive committee 1966–73, Ruth Mompati served as its chief representative in the UK 1981–82 and was part of the delegation that opened talks with the South African government in 1990. In 1994 she was elected as an MP and was appointed ambassador to Switzerland 1996–2000.

DR. NTHATO MOTLANA: Political activist, businessman, and community leader Dr. Nthato Motlana remained in close contact with Mandela throughout his imprisonment. He is a member of the Nelson Mandela Foundation executive committee.

BILLY NAIR: Trade unionist, member of the South African Communist Party, and anti-apartheid activist Billy Nair was sentenced in 1963 to twenty years on Robben Island for sabotage. After his release he became active in the United Democratic Front and was again detained several times. From 1986–90 he went into hiding. He was charged with nine others in the "Vula" trial in 1990, despite having been granted indemnity. In 1994 he was elected an MP in the first national assembly.

LORD DAVID OWEN: British foreign secretary in the Labor government 1977–79, Lord Owen was joint author with Cyrus Vance of the failed Owen-Vance Peace Plan to end conflict in Bosnia.

SIR SIDNEY POITIER: Actor, writer, director, and diplomat, Sir Sidney Poitier is internationally recognized as a cultural icon. He was the first African American to win an Oscar for Best Actor. Over fifty years after his performance in the 1951 film *Cry, The Beloved Country*, he returned to South Africa to play Nelson Mandela in the 1997 docudrama *Mandela and de Klerk*.

PETER PRESTON: Peter Preston was editor of the *Guardian* newspaper in Britain 1975–95, and continues to write a weekly column for the paper.

CYRIL RAMAPHOSA: Political activist and trade unionist Cyril Ramaphosa was twice detained without trial for his political beliefs during the apartheid era. He went on to play a crucial role in the negotiations leading to South Africa's first democratic elections and was elected chair of the new constitutional assembly in 1994. He is currently Secretary-General of the ANC.

LORD ROBIN RENWICK: Lord Renwick was British ambassador to South Africa 1987–91 and subsequently British ambassador to the United States 1991–95.

JUDGE ALBIE SACHS: Appointed by Nelson Mandela as a member of the South African Constitutional Court in 1994, Judge Sachs was a leader in the struggle for human rights in South Africa and a member of the ANC. In 1966 he went into exile, first in England and then in Mozambique where in 1988 he was seriously injured by a car bomb placed by South African security agents, losing an arm and the sight of one eye. In 1990 he returned to South Africa to take part in the negotiations that led to democracy.

GILLIAN SLOVO: Novelist Gillian Slovo is the daughter of two of South Africa's foremost anti-apartheid activists. Both her parents were members of the South African Communist Party. Her father, Joe Slovo, was the first white member of the ANC and a minister in Mandela's first cabinet. Her mother, the journalist Ruth First, was murdered by the South African secret police in Mozambique.

GEORGE SOROS: International financier and philanthropist George Soros set up the Open Society Foundation, which operates in several countries funding projects fostering democracy and open societies.

ALLISTER SPARKS: One of the most distinguished journalists and commentators in South Africa, Allister Sparks edited the *Rand Daily Mail* 1977–81 but was dismissed by its board after their controversial decision to make the paper appeal more to the affluent white community. Sparks played a major part in the reform of the media after Mandela came to power. He founded a journalism training institute in South Africa and has been a visiting professor in Europe and the United States.

RICHARD STENGEL: Author and journalist Richard Stengel collaborated with Nelson Mandela on his autobiography, *Long Walk to Freedom*. He is now chief executive of the National Constitution Center in Philadelphia, Penn.

HELEN SUZMAN: First entering the South African Parliament as a member of the United Party in 1953, in 1959 Helen Suzman founded the Progressive Party, remaining its only representative in Parliament for fifteen years. As an MP, Suzman campaigned tirelessly for the improvement of prisoners' living conditions, although she refused to support Mandela and the other political prisoners in their demands to be released unless they renounced violence. In 1989 Suzman retired as an MP, but still remains active in South African politics.

ARCHBISHOP DESMOND TUTU, ARCHBISHOP EMERITUS: Cleric and activist Archbishop Desmond Tutu rose to worldwide fame during the 1980s as an opponent of apartheid. Tutu was the first black Anglican archbishop of Cape Town and primate of the Church of the Province of Southern Africa. He was awarded the Nobel Peace Prize in 1984. In 1995 he was appointed to chair South Africa's Truth and Reconciliation Commission which reported on apartheid-era crimes and atrocities.

SELECT BIBLIOGRAPHY

Archives:
The Apartheid Museum, Johannesburg
The Nelson Mandela Centre of Memory, The Nelson Mandela Foundation
Mayibuye Centre, University of the Western Cape

Books:
Alexander, Neville, *Robben Island Prison Dossier 1964–1974*, UCT Press, Cape Town, 1994
Benson, Mary, *Nelson Mandela – The Man and the Movement*, Penguin Books, London, 1994
Bernstein, Rusty, *Memory Against Forgetting – Memoirs of a Life in South African Politics 1938–1964*, Viking, London, 1999
Callinicos, Luli, *The World that made Mandela – A Heritage Trail: 70 Sites of Significance*, STE Publishers, 2000
Clarke, Steve (ed.), *Nelson Mandela Speaks – Forging Democratic Nonracial South Africa*, David Philip Publishers, Cape Town, 1993
Couzens, Tim, and Patel, Essop (eds.), *The Return of the Amasi Bird – Black South African Poetry 1891–1981*, Ravan Press, Johannesburg, 1982
Kathrada, Ahmed, *Memoirs*, Zebra Press, Cape Town, 2004
Krog, Antjie, *Country of My Skull*, Random House, Johannesburg, 1998
     A Change of Tongue, Random House, Johannesburg, 2003
Maharaj, Mac (ed.) *Reflections in Prison*, Zebra Press and Robben Island Museum, Cape Town, 2001
Mandela, Nelson, *Long Walk to Freedom*, Little, Brown and Company, London, 1994
Mandela, Winnie, and Benson, Mary (ed.), *Part of My Soul*, Penguin Books, London, 1985
Meer, Fatima, *Higher Than Hope*, Skotaville Publishers, Johannesburg, 1988
Ministry of Education, *Every Step of the Way – The Journey to Freedom in South Africa*, HSRC Press, Cape Town, 2004
Modisane, Bloke, *Blame Me on History*, Dutton, New York, 1963
Paton, Alan, *Cry, the Beloved Country*, Jonathan Cape, London, 1948
Sachs, Albie, *The Jail Diary of Albie Sachs*, Grafton Books, London, 1990
Sampson, Anthony, *Drum – The Making of a Magazine*, Collins Publishers, London, 1956. Republished by Jonathan Ball Publishers, Cape Town, 2005
     Mandela – The Authorized Biography, HarperCollins Publishers, London, 2000
Sisulu, Elinor, *Walter & Albertina Sisulu – In Our Lifetime*, David Philip Publishers, Cape Town, 2002
Smith, Charlene, *Mandela – In Celebration of a Great Life*, Struik Publishers, Cape Town, 2003
Suzman, Helen, *In No Uncertain Terms*, Jonathan Ball Publishers, Johannesburg, 1994
Truth and Reconciliation Commission, *Truth and Reconciliation Commission Report*, Juta Publishers, Cape Town, 1998
Tutu, Desmond, *No Future without Forgiveness*, Random House, New York, 1999

Public Records:
Department of Correctional Services, Pretoria
Department of Justice, Pretoria

Web sites:
http://www.anc.org.za   http://www.nelsonmandela.org   http://www.truth.org.za
http://www.pbs.org/wgbh/pages/frontline/shows/mandela/   http://www.sahistory.org.sa

NOTES TO THE NARRATIVE BIOGRAPHY

PART ONE
The Call of Freedom, 1918–1964

1 Nelson Mandela, *Long Walk to Freedom*, 15;   2 Ibid. 32;   3 Ibid. 34;   4 Ibid. 43;   5 Ibid. 54;   6 Ibid. 98;   7 Ibid. 100;   8 Anthony Sampson,
Mandela – The Authorized Biography, 61;   9 *Long Walk to Freedom*, 136;   10 Ibid. 226;   11 Ibid. 145;   12 Ibid. 172;   13 Ibid. 177;   14 Ibid. 186;
15 Ibid. 183;   16 Ibid. 189;   17 Ibid. 186;   18 Ibid. 207;   19 *Drum*, January 1957;   20 *Long Walk to Freedom*, 242;   21 Ibid. 304;   22 Ibid. 320;
23 Ibid. 327;   24 Fatima Meer, *Higher Than Hope*, 149;   25 *Long Walk to Freedom*, 416;   26 Ibid. 422

PART TWO
Out of the Darkness, 1964–1990

1 *Long Walk to Freedom*, 456;   2 Ibid. 475;   3 Ibid. 477;   4 *Mandela – The Authorized Biography*, 218;   5 *Long Walk to Freedom*, 501;   6 Ibid. 506;
7 Ibid. 529;   8 Ibid. 531;   9 *Mandela – The Authorized Biography*, 252;   10 *Long Walk to Freedom*, 549;   11 Ibid. 583;   12 *Higher Than Hope*, 233;
13 *Long Walk to Freedom*, 589;   14 Ibid. 608;   15 *Higher Than Hope*, 247;   16 *Long Walk to Freedom*, 616;   17 *Mandela – The Authorized Biography*, 349;
18 *Long Walk to Freedom*, 633;   19 Ibid. 656;   20 Ibid. 673

PART THREE
Free at Last, 1990–present

1 *Long Walk to Freedom*, 673;   2 Mandela's address in Cape Town on his release, 11 February 1990;   3 Mandela's address, 11 February 1990;
4 *Long Walk to Freedom*, 682;   5 *Mandela – The Authorized Biography*, 446;   6 Ibid. 447;   7 Ibid. 448;   8 Ibid. 411;   9 *Long Walk to Freedom*, 690;
10 Ibid. 695;   11 Ibid. 697;   12 *Mandela – The Authorized Biography*, 449;   13 Ibid. 441;   14 *Long Walk to Freedom*, 711;   15 Ibid. 719;
16 Mary Benson, *Nelson Mandela – The Man and the Movement*, 244;   17 13 April 1993;   18 *Long Walk to Freedom*, 731;
19 *Mandela – The Authorized Biography*, 485;   20 *Long Walk to Freedom*, 741;   21 Ibid. 12;   22 Ibid. 742;   23 *Cape Times*, 3 May 1994;
24 *Long Walk to Freedom*, 748;   25 Ibid. 747;   26 Mzwakhe Mbuli, SABC-TV broadcast, 10 May 1994;   27 *Mail & Guardian*, 13 May 1994;
28 *Mandela – The Authorized Biography*, 499;   29 Ibid. 477;   30 Charlene Smith, *Mandela – In Celebration of a Great Life*, 51;   31 Ibid. 162

INDEX

Page numbers in **bold** indicate illustrations; page numbers in *italic* indicate interviews. As there are so many photographs of Nelson Mandela, most have not been indexed.

PHOTOGRAPHIC SOURCES AND PERMISSIONS

Every effort has been made to trace the copyright holders of the images reproduced in this book and the publisher apologizes for any unintentional omission. We would be pleased to hear from any not acknowledged here and undertake to make all reasonable efforts to include the appropriate acknowledgement in any subsequent editions.

Corbis: 4 and 304 Hans Gedda; 153, 247 (above and below) and 280 (below) David Turnley; 260 and 264 Patrick Robert/Sygma; 270 and 272 Peter Turnley; 279, 299, 323 and 325 Louise Gubb

Getty Images: 6 Alexander Joe/AFP; 106 (top left) Mary Benson/The *Observer*; 111 and 145 Cloete Breytenbach/Hulton Archive; 231 Anna Zieminski/AFP; 244 Bill Foley/Time Life Pictures; 245 Don Emmert/AFP; 256 William F Campbell/Time Life Pictures; 267 Keith Schamotta/AFP; 268 Gerard Julien/AFP; 270 (above) and 300 Walter Dhladhla/AFP

Duggan-Cronin Collection, McGregor Museum, Kimberley: 12, 14, 15 and 17

Nelson Mandela Foundation: 19, 97, 159, 161–3, 169, 171, 176, 179 and 214; 72, 123 and 130 courtesy Palace of Justice, Pretoria; 315 and 319 Matthew Willman

Methodist Church Collection, Cory Library, Rhodes University: 20

Howard Pim Library, University of Fort Hare: 23

Robben Island Museum Mayibuye Archive: 25 (above and below), 35, 37, 53, 75, 80, 86–7, 90, 102, 112 and 157 Eli Weinberg; 28 and 33 Leon Levson; 68 Laurie Bloomfield; 99 (all) and 143 (Cloete Breytenbach) courtesy RIM/Mayibuye Archive; 104 (above and below) and 139; 106 (all except top left) Mary Benson/IDAF Collection; 216 IDAF Collection

Museum Africa: 26 (above), 30 (above) and 76

Bailey's African History Archive: 26 (below), 39, 43 (above), 61 (bottom left), 63 (above), 66–7, 83 and 101; 44 (all), 56 and 61 (bottom right) Bob Gosani; 78 Peter Magubane; 93 Ralph Ndawo; 116 Alf Kumalo; 184 Mike Mzeleni

Elinor Sisulu/Sisulu family: 30

Jurgen Schadeberg: 38, 43 (below), 46–7, 49–51, 54, 55, 59, 61 (top four), 63 (below), 65 (all), 79, 89, 258 and 295

***Guardian* (South Africa), ANC archive, courtesy RIM/Mayibuye Archive**: 41

Sportsfile: 45 Ray McManus

Johannesburg Public Library: 84 courtesy JPL

Alf Kumalo: 94, 98, 100

JonCom Publications: 110

Rivonia Papers, courtesy Historical Papers, University of the Witwatersrand Library: 114 (all), 118–19, 128 and 340

South African National Archives: 124–5 and 129; 177, 182–3, 188–9, 191, 193, 205, 210 and 219 courtesy Nelson Mandela Foundation

Robben Island Museum: 134, 137 and 151 Matthew Willman

The Bigger Picture: 154 and 333 David Goldblatt/South; 196 (middle), 225, 227, 236 (above), 266 (top two) and 274 (below) Graeme Williams/South; 212 (top) Gill de Vlieg/South; 212 (middle), 274 (above), 281 (below) and 282 Paul Weinberg/South; 212 (bottom) and 213 (top left and middle left) Guy Tillim/South; 213 (top right, middle right and bottom two) Gideon Mendel/South; 233 Chris Ledochowski/South; 235 and 236 (below) Gisele Wulfsohn/South; 251 Rick T Wilking/Reuters; 255 (top left and two bottom) Greg Marinovich/South; 266 (bottom) John Robinson/South; 266 (bottom) Kevin Carter/Reuters; 271 Philippe Woljazer/Reuters; 280 (above), 287 and 321 Juda Ngwenya/Reuters; 289 Reuters; 309 Michael Crabtree/Reuters; 310 (above) Jonathan Evans/Reuters; 310 (below) Chris Young/Reuters; 316 Andreas Meier/Reuters

iAfrika Photos: 155 Jeremy Jowell; 200 Eric Miller; 253 (top and bottom) Rodger Bosch

Nandha and Beverley Naidoo: 164

Sipa Press/Snapper Media: 186 Johann Kuus

Raghubir Singh: 192

South African History Archives, courtesy Historical Papers, University of the Witwatersrand Library: 194, 196 (left and right), 197, 204, 215 and 220

photographer unknown: 199

Trace Images: 203, 298 (below) and 307 Adil Bradlow; 234, 238, 243 (above and below), 253 (middle), 269, 298 (above) Louise Gubb; 276 Denis Farrell; 290 Benny Gool; 327 Obed Zilwa; 329 Karin Retief/Cape Argus

Morris Zwi: 208

The Clinton Presidential Library: 248

Picturenet Africa: 255 (top right, middle left and right) Ken Oosterbroek; 285 Paul Velasco; 313 Henner Frankenfeld

Guy Stubbs: 281 (above)

Additional photography: Matthew Willman, Kevin Rudham and Tristan McLaren, AM Digital

Additional archive research: Ruth Muller and Alice Kentridge

ACKNOWLEDGEMENTS

We would like to thank all those who have contributed to *Mandela – The Authorized Portrait* and along with the people and organizations mentioned in this section we would particularly like to thank the following for their help in compiling the book: Mr Mandela's attorney Iqbal Meer; Verne Harris, Anthea Josias and Mayra Roffe Gutman of The Nelson Mandela Foundation, and the South African National Archives.

The publisher is grateful for literary permissions to reproduce those items below subject to copyright. Every effort has been made to trace the copyright holders and the publisher apologizes for any unintentional omission. We would be pleased to hear from any not acknowledged here and undertake to make all reasonable efforts to include the appropriate acknowledgement in any subsequent editions. (See page 348 for further bibliographic information and references.)

p. 3: President Bill Clinton, excerpt from a speech at a reception for Nelson Mandela at the White House on 22 September 1998.

p. 13 and throughout book: Quoted material from *Long Walk to Freedom* reprinted by kind permission of Nelson R. Mandela.

p. 15: Chief Meligqili's speech to Mandela and his fellow initiates at their circumcision ceremony, taken from *Long Walk to Freedom*.

p. 32: *Shanty Town*, taken from *The Return of the Amasi Bird – Black South African Poetry 1891–1981* by Tim Couzens and Essop Patel (eds.). Reprinted by permission of Pan Macmillan South Africa.

p. 41 and throughout book (including p. 167): Quoted material from *Mandela – The Authorized Biography* reprinted by permission of HarperCollins Publishers Ltd © Anthony Sampson 2000.

p. 74: Quoted material from *Drum* magazine, courtesy Bailey's African History Archive.

p. 103: Ahmed Kathrada, excerpt from the *Independent* (South Africa), 11 July 1998, reprinted by permission of Ahmed Kathrada.

pp. 105, 178 and 195: Quoted material from *Higher Than Hope* reprinted by permission of Dr. Fatima Meer.

p. 113 and throughout book: Excerpts from Nelson Mandela's speeches and writings (unless otherwise specified) reprinted by kind permission of Nelson R. Mandela.

p. 175: Fikile Bam, quoted in the documentary "The Long Walk of Nelson Mandela", May 1999, courtesy Ochre Media and Story Street Productions.

p. 188: Eric van Ees, quoted in the documentary 'The Long Walk of Nelson Mandela', May 1999, courtesy Ochre Media and Story Street Productions.

p. 203: Extract from *Memoirs* by Ahmed Kathrada reprinted by permission of Zebra Press and Ahmed Kathrada.

p. 212: Chris van Wyk, *Injustice*, taken from *The Return of the Amasi Bird – Black South African Poetry 1891–1981* by Tim Couzens and Essop Patel (eds.). Reprinted by permission of Pan Macmillan South Africa.

p. 254: Extract from *Reporting South Africa* by Rich Mkhondo (1993): James Currey Publishers, Oxford. Reprinted by permission of James Currey Publishers.

p. 288: Extract from letter from Graça Machel to Nelson Mandela taken from *Samora Machel: A Biography* (Panaf Great Lives), Iain Christie, Zed Books, London, 1990. Reprinted by permission of Zed Books.

p. 291: Obituary tribute by Nelson Mandela to Walter Sisulu, taken from the *Independent* (South Africa).

p. 299: Extract from *Memory Against Forgetting* by Rusty Bernstein, reprinted by permission of Mrs. Hilda Bernstein.

EDITORIAL CONTRIBUTORS

Mac Maharaj – Editorial consultant
Sentenced to twelve years on Robben Island in 1964, Mac Maharaj has played a key role in the anti-apartheid struggle both inside and outside South Africa. On his release from prison he escaped into exile and was appointed to maintain the underground ANC within South Africa. In 1988 he returned in secret as the overall commander of Operation Vula and was arrested, despite having been granted immunity, in 1990. After his release in 1991 he became joint secretary of the negotiating process. He was appointed minister of transport in the first democratic government and retired from Parliament in 1999. He is a member of the board of the Nelson Mandela Foundation.

Ahmed Kathrada – Editorial consultant
As a leading member of the ANC and a dedicated political activist, Ahmed Kathrada was among the accused in both the Treason Trial and the Rivonia Trial, where he was sentenced to life imprisonment. He spent eighteen years on Robben Island before moving, with Nelson Mandela and Walter Sisulu among others, to Pollsmoor Prison for a another seven years. He was released in 1989 and elected an MP in the first democratic government, serving as parliamentary counselor in the office of the president. In 1997 he was elected chair of the Robben Island Council. He is also a member of the Nelson Mandela Foundation Executive Committee.

Mike Nicol – Author of the narrative biography
Educated at the University of South Africa, Mike Nicol has had a distinguished career both in South Africa and the UK as an author, journalist, and poet. Among the many newspapers to which he has contributed are the *Sunday Times*, *Mail & Guardian*, the *Guardian*, the *Sunday Independent*, the *Cape Times* and *Business Day*. He has also written for magazines including the *New Statesman*, *London Magazine*, *Discovery*, and *GQ*. Mike Nicol is the author of four critically acclaimed novels published in South Africa, the U.S., the UK, France and Germany. His best-known nonfiction work is his book on *Drum* magazine, *A Good-Looking Corpse* (Secker & Warburg, 1991), widely regarded as one of the most compelling accounts of the vibrant culture in the black townships of the 1950s. Mike spent 1997 in Germany on a Berlin writer-in-residence grant and was a writer in residence at the University of Essen in 2002. He has held a similar position at the University of Cape Town.

Professor Tim Couzens – South African interviewer
Tim Couzens is currently an honorary professor in the School of Arts at the University of the Witwatersrand. He is the author of three full biographies: *The New African – A Study of the Life and Work of H I E Dhlomo* (Ravan Press, 1985), *Tramp Royal – The True Story of Trader Horn* (University of the Witwatersrand, 1991) and *Murder at Morija* (Random House, 2003). His most recent book is *Battles of South Africa* (David Philip Publishers, 2004). He is also a freelance travel writer.

Dr. Rosalind Coward – UK and international interviewer
Author, academic, journalist and broadcaster, Ros Coward was educated at Cambridge University and has taught at Goldsmiths College, University of London, and the University of Reading. She is a regular contributor of features and political comment to the *Guardian* and *Observer* newspapers, and has also written for the *Sunday Times*, *Daily Telegraph*, the *New Statesman*, *She* and *Cosmopolitan*. The author of a number of academic books on women and the media, her book *Diana – The Portrait*, Authorized by the late princess's estate, was published in 2004 to critical acclaim, in over twenty-one countries. Ros Coward appears regularly on television as an arts and media commentator and is also an accomplished radio presenter.

Amina Frense – South African interviewer
Born and brought up in Cape Town, Amina Frense has been a practicing journalist both abroad and in South Africa from the apartheid years through the country's transition to democracy. She has been involved in the transformation of the media since democracy and has held several positions at the South African Broadcasting Corporation, including executive producer, commissioning editor for the first (1994) and subsequent democratic elections, political editor, and parliamentary bureau chief. Amina Frense is on the board of the Institute for the Advancement of Journalism, which provides training for mid-career journalists, and is also one of the executives of the South African National Editor's Forum and the Media Institute of Southern Africa. She has worked as a producer on several documentaries on and about Nelson Mandela including the 1997 Oscar®-nominated documentary *Mandela, Son of Africa*. Amina's close relationship with the Mandela family goes back a long way and she has accompanied Mr. Mandela on several official occasions.

Kate Parkin – Editor
After many years as a senior publishing executive, Kate Parkin now runs a publishing and management consultancy based in London.

Gail Behrmann – Picture researcher
Johannesburg-based Gail Behrmann has been doing archive research for museums, documentaries, and feature films for fourteen years. Her credits include the Emmy®-nominated documentary *The Long Walk of Nelson Mandela* and Joe Sargent's docudrama *Mandela and de Klerk*. This is her eighth assignment on Nelson Mandela and her first book.

This edition published in 2006 by Andrews McMeel Publishing, LLC,
an Andrews McMeel Universal company, 4520 Main Street, Kansas City,
Missouri, 64111, United States.

First published in 2006 by PQ Blackwell Limited,
116 Symonds Street, Auckland, New Zealand.

Cover design: Cameron Gibb
Cover image: Henry Grossman – Time Life Pictures/Getty Images
Back flap, top image: Reuters/The Bigger Picture; bottom image: Sahm Venter

Printed by Midas Printing International Limited, China

ISBN-13: 978-0-7407-5572-9
ISBN-10: 0-7407-5572-2
Library of Congress Cataloging-in-Publication Data: On file

www.andrewsmcmeel.com

www.pqblackwell.com

PQ BLACKWELL

Publisher: Geoff Blackwell
Editorial Director: Ruth-Anna Hobday
Managing Editor: Caroline Bowron
Design: Paul Dashwood
Production Manager: Jenny Moore
Studio Production: Annatjie Matthee
Print Coordination: Alison Jacobs
Research Assistant: Pearl Wilson
Proofreader: Susan Brierley
Index: Diane Lowther

**Andrews McMeel
Publishing, LLC**
Kansas City